A.S.A. MONOGRAPHS

General Editor: MALCOLM RUEL

11

Rethinking
Kinship and Marriage

RETHINKING

KINSHIP AND MARRIAGE

Edited by Rodney Needham

TAVISTOCK PUBLICATIONS

London · New York · Sydney · Toronto · Wellington

*First published in 1971
by Tavistock Publications Limited
11 New Fetter Lane, London EC4
This book has been set in Modern Series 7
and was printed by T. & A. Constable Limited,
Edinburgh*
© *Association of Social Anthropologists of the Commonwealth
1971*

SBN 422 73690 2

This volume derives in the main from material presented at a conference on 'Kinship and Marriage', sponsored by the Association of Social Anthropologists of the Commonwealth, held at the University of Bristol, 1-4 April 1970

*Distributed in the USA by
Barnes & Noble, Inc.*

Dedication

The contributors, with one protesting exception,
join in dedicating this volume to

EDMUND LEACH

in grateful recognition of the quality of his
empirical analyses, the provocative originality of
his theoretical excursions, and the moral example
set by the verve and the unpretentious radicality
with which he has advanced the study of kinship
and marriage

Contents

Contents

Contents

Contents

Prefatory Note

It is the normal practice of the Association for each of its annual conferences to ask one of its members to organize the conference on a selected topic, and he is free to do so as he wishes. The convener of the conference acts as editor to the ensuing ASA Monograph and contributes his own Introduction to it. In this, as in other volumes, the views expressed by the editor and the contributors are those of the individual writers and should not be taken as representing the views of the Association as an organized body.

INTRODUCTION

Rodney Needham

'Menard used to declare that censure and praise were
sentimental operations which had nothing to do with
criticism.'

JORGE LUIS BORGES

I

BACKGROUND

At the annual general meeting of the Association of Social
Anthropologists, held at the University of Sussex in April 1969,
the chairman, Dr Edmund Leach, suggested that the next
conference ought to get back to 'firm anthropological ground'.
The members present decided that this meant kinship and
marriage, and they asked me to act as convener. This was
ironic, for Leach had prominently argued that marriage was not
an isolable institution, nor subject to any universal definition
(1961, ch. 4), and I had contended that kinship was a thoroughly
misleading term and a false criterion for the comparison of
social facts (1966: 31-2).

Nevertheless, our colleagues were definite that these were
the topics they wanted discussed, so with an unfeigned reluct-
ance I agreed to organize a conference on kinship and marriage.
Leach, whose participation I naturally judged to be essential,
at once consented to prepare a paper for it, but thereafter the
organization admitted various possibilities, each with its own
difficulties. One course was to select a theme and to invite contributors to address themselves to this; another was to concentrate on theoretical issues, or alternatively on empirical problems; a further possibility was to circumscribe an ethnographical
province and to work comparatively within that; and so on.
But this range of procedures implied a degree of liberty which
I soon had to realize I did not possess; for it appeared to me
that the real and fundamental difficulty, and one that attached
to any kind of arrangement for the conference, was simply to
find a squad of social anthropologists who were sufficiently
interested in the topics, technically competent, and willing to
prepare essays for public debate. I mention these considerations
because for me they were the first lesson of the conference, in

driving home more forcefully the condition of the profession in these respects and the theoretical state of affairs with regard to the topics in question. Also, readers are entitled to a report on the circumstances in which the conference took shape and on some of the reasons for the ultimate constitution of this volume.

As it was, I invited in the first place people whose work I respected, no matter what their field of interest and without any restriction or guidance as to choice of subject. All I asked was that they should talk about something that interested them. An exception was Mr McKnight: I knew he had visited the Wikmunkan, so I asked him specifically whether he would like to address the association on his findings in that society. Some whose collaboration I particularly desired could not be free for the occasion or, understandably, did not want to take part in an academic gathering when term was over and they could otherwise get some work done; some others were too far away, in places such as Australia and Brazil, to come to England for the purpose. In the end, however, as I trust readers will agree, matters worked out very well: we had enough speakers, and their papers proved to complement one another very nicely. Then there were posterior benefits which materially improved the monograph: Mr Forge, who had delivered an authoritative commentary on Mrs Korn's analysis of the Iatmul system, very kindly consented to compose his notes into a formal assessment for publication; Dr Beidelman, who had agreed to take part but found himself unable to attend, afterwards sent an essay on the Kaguru; Mr Wilder, who had made a vigorous contribution to the discussions at Bristol, offered an examination of Purum descent groups which I had a special pleasure in including; and Dr Fox, who had not been able to participate in the conference, later submitted (after the volume had been prepared for publication, and thus not in time for appropriate mention in this introduction) an expanded version of the paper that he had intended to deliver.

Apart from the additional papers, the essays which make up this volume present a full record of the main proceedings of the conference. Some of them have been slightly rewritten at certain points (all the authors had the opportunity to do so), but for the most part the arguments remain as they were delivered.

Introduction

The papers speak clearly enough for themselves, and there would be no point in an editorial recapitulation of their major themes; but there are some aspects of them which call for further emphasis, and the discussions at the conference raised other matters which deserve comment. It may serve to interconnect the individual contributions, and make for a more rounded presentation of the outcome of the proceedings, if I offer here some observations on certain recurrent or otherwise prominent themes. For some readers, also, it may be helpful if I briefly supply background information on some issues which have to do with much of the present theory and practice of social anthropologists in the field of kinship and marriage.

II

PHILOSOPHY

Perhaps the chief point of theoretical division among the participants was the abstract nature of some of the papers (Needham, Southwold, Rivière) and the adduction of explicitly philosophical issues and authorities. Wittgenstein is the inspiration of my own 'Remarks', and even a parenthetical observation on academic debate finds its most cogent expression in Hume; Southwold refers to Frege, Tarski, Carnap, Hempel, Quine, Scriven, and Robinson; Rivière turns to Plato and to Bambrough for illustrations, and adopts two crucial analytical points from Wittgenstein. The philosophical tenor of these three papers encountered, it seemed, quite considerable opposition in a number of the members present. One senior critic wittily put their case in the form of an anecdote about the consternation that afflicted the United States government when 'Sputnik I' went up. The officials were concerned to find out why the Russians were so far ahead of the Americans in space technology, and arrived at the answer: 'Their Germans are better than ours'. Just so, contended the anthropological sceptic, the contributors in question had shifted the argument about kinship and marriage on to a plane where confrontation might have to be resolved by conceding that 'Their philosophers are better than ours'. What we ought to be doing instead, he maintained, was really to take our stand on firm

Rodney Needham

anthropological ground and to concentrate on the solution
of specific problems in empirical data: stick to these, he
urged, and the analytical categories would take care of themselves.

The response to this objection, though, is that problems do
not present themselves phenomenally: they have to be conceived, and this means the formulation of propositions in terms
of categories. If our category words are employed uncritically
they may lead to misconceptions and to the inappropriate
statement of problems. A well-known example of a crudely
formulated problem is Gluckman's hypothesis that 'divorce is
rare and difficult in those [African tribes] organized on a system
of marked father-right and easy to obtain in other types' (1950:
190). Gluckman hoped that even if the hypothesis was wrong it
might still be useful, and this indeed was the ground on which
it was defended by one or two of those present at the conference.
But there was never any need for it to be as ill phrased as it was,
and in the end it proved to be not simply wrong but too confused to be of any use. It certainly led to renewed debate about
marriage stability, and it elicited from ethnographers valuable
accounts of the institutions of other societies in Africa and
elsewhere; but as a theoretical venture it wasted a deal of time
and effort. Leach has convincingly exposed some of its defects,
and has made an empirical refutation (1957: 1961, ch. 5), but
the chief point of present relevance is that a critical appraisal
of the categories in question would not easily have permitted
the formulation of such a clumsy and simplistic hypothesis.
Gluckman himself made this point, in effect, when he mentioned
'difficulties' arising from 'the vague and embracing use of
categories and concepts (of which I too am guilty) such as
patrilineal, lineage, marriage, divorce, etc.' (p. 202); but he did
so only towards the end of his paper, after the exposition of the
argument, and in the form merely of a saving clause. If, however,
these category words were in fact seen to entail conceptual difficulties, then the obvious thing to do was to resolve these
difficulties first and to rectify the formulation of the hypothesis
before embarking on the argument. 'Il faut réfléchir pour
mesurer, et non pas mesurer pour réfléchir' (Bachelard 1938:
213). This amelioration could well have been accomplished by
a close examination of precisely those concepts of descent and

xvi

marriage which some members of the conference found inappropriately philosophical.

One reason that this kind of conceptual criticism is misprised by numbers of anthropologists (particularly, perhaps, British ones) is doubtless the lingering sway of the scientism which is most prominently signalled by the name of Radcliffe-Brown, but it is nevertheless curious that even the most pragmatical of functionalists should find it hard to accept that the disciplined scrutiny of the forms of thought (i.e. philosophy) should have something to teach them in the formulation of hypotheses and the translation of exotic categories. It is all the odder when one recalls that for Radcliffe-Brown himself the primary task of social anthropology, as a putative natural science of society, was classification. Yet in 1957 Leach had to be very forceful in trying to persuade certain of his colleagues to re-examine their basic premises and to realize that 'English language patterns of thought are not a necessary model for the whole of human society' (1961: 27); and in 1970, at the Bristol conference, it was still objected by some that this philosophical kind of criticism was beside the real point of social anthropology.

It is to be hoped, anyway, that the three critical papers in question may induce a few anthropologists of that inclination to subject their categories of anthropological thought to a radical revision. I do not suggest something so dramatic as a conversion, but any such shift of view apparently has to implicate deep-rooted conceptual commitments. It is far harder than talking in substantive terms about lineages and marriage, or propounding naïve two-factor correlations. This is why Leach has spoken with such vigour about rethinking and starting all over again. A strenuous inner effort is called for, and an austere self-criticism that not all can be expected to find congenial. Some merely slight alteration of view, such as might then be expanded into a more comprehensive improvement, is unlikely to serve, for 'it is difficult to deviate from an old line of thought *just a little*' (Wittgenstein 1967, sec. 349). What is needed is a completely new start: 'ethnographic facts will be much easier to understand if we approach them free of *all* . . . a priori assumptions' (Leach 1961: 27). To attain this desirable condition is essentially a philosophical undertaking, and it can be achieved only by each anthropologist rigorously searching his own mind for linguistic addictions and other habits of thought which deflect and distort his apprehension of social reality. I have no idea what chance there is that the conference papers will have a positive effect, for I am afraid that what really divides social anthropologists into two main theoretical camps is not so much a matter of public argument or a conflict of theories as it is what Dumont has well designated a 'conflict of mentalities' (1961: 77). This division is integral with the philosophical opposition of idealists and realists (cf. Needham 1967: 49-50), and it is not very likely that the temperamental adherents to one doctrine will ever be persuaded to the other by means of essays on kinship and marriage. Still, it is possible to school ourselves, by reflection and introspection, to a stance of systematic self-doubt, and to commit ourselves in our analyses to 'the quiet and patient undermining of categories over the whole field of [anthropological] thought' (Waismann 1968: 21), and these philosophical exercises really can bring a greater insight into the way we think. Of course, this does call for an unrelenting moral application, and probably not many of us will long be capable of such a demanding regimen, but I cannot see that the disciplined interpretation of the forms of human experience (by which I mean 'social anthropology') calls for anything less than an attempt at this intellectual ambition.

Thankfully, not everything about it is so stern. The romantic appeal of some of the exotic usages that we try to comprehend is one assuaging influence, and not all philosophical excursions are exigently abstract. On this latter score, perhaps I may recommend a philosophical parable which brings out, and exaggerates to the point of derangement, the concern with valid classification that inspires these observations. It is 'Funes, The Memorious', a story by Borges (1967: 35-43). Funes had been an ordinary man, but one day he fell from his horse and lost consciousness. When he recovered, his perception and his memory had become infallible, and his apprehensions were so rich and bright as to be almost intolerable. In the seventeenth century, Borges reminds us, Locke postulated (and rejected) an impossible idiom in which each individual object, each stone, each bird and branch had an individual name. Funes, in his new condition, once projected an analogous idiom, 'but he had renounced it as being too general, too ambiguous':

'He was . . . almost incapable of general, platonic ideas. It was not only difficult for him to understand that the generic term *dog* embraced so many unlike specimens of differing sizes and different forms; he was disturbed by the fact that a dog at three-fourteen (seen in profile) should have the same name as the dog at three-fifteen (seen from the front).'

Funes conceived, then, a world in which there were nothing but details, almost contiguous details – like, it may be, the notebooks of an unusually perceptive and diligent ethnographer newly arrived in the field, or a scholar before he can draw together the minutiae of his cryptic texts into some order (cf. Needham 1963d: vii-viii). We could not for long retain our professional sanity in such a condition, for we think about these details, and 'to think is to forget a difference, to generalize, to abstract' (Borges, p. 43). Nor, on the other hand, should we impose any alien classification on to the particulars, provided merely that it was coherent, for we are obliged to justify the correspondences between categories and phenomena. In the blunt realism of Radcliffe-Brown, for whom the structure of a society was as patent as the form of a sea shell, there was scarcely room for any such issue; and among his latter-day congeners the unqualified employment of notions such as 'father-right', 'divorce', and so on betrays a similarly unreflective attitude to the tasks of observation and conceptual translation. But Borges, by happy contrast, lightly forces us to ask ourselves again where to draw the lines of discrimination, and to consider more narrowly what justification we think we have for doing so. In the same intention, Leach suggests below that 'we should go right back to the beginning and think again about just what it is that we are talking about when we discuss "a kinship terminology" ' (p. 75). If we deliberately deprive ourselves of the conventional typological guidelines, and approximate to the multifarious wonderment of Funes, the first consequence is that we shall rely more directly on the indigenous categories and be able more readily to think in terms of these. We can thus learn, as Hocart and Leach have urged, to take each case as it comes, and to apprehend it as it presents itself.

Berkeley, writing about the epistemological difficulties in which eighteenth-century philosophers found themselves, was inclined to think that most of the obstructions to knowledge were entirely due to the philosophers themselves: 'we have first raised a dust, and then complain we cannot see' (*Principles,* sec. III). The burden of the three critical papers in this volume is that we anthropologists have indeed raised a conceptual dust which prevents us seeing aright, and that it is time for someone to start complaining about an unnecessary obscurity and cloudy refraction in the study of kinship and marriage. For my part, at any rate, and as far as this branch of inquiry is concerned, I should certainly wish to echo Berkeley in his suspicion (sec. IV) that

> 'those lets and difficulties which stay and embarrass the mind in its search after truth, do not spring from any darkness and intricacy in the objects, or natural defects in the understanding, so much as from false principles which have been insisted on, and might have been avoided.'

Some of the false principles (and false categories) in social anthropology have been isolated in the papers referred to, and some means of reformation have been suggested; but it may be thought that more explicit recommendations, perhaps of a technical kind, ought also to have been provided. Dr Rivière and I have proposed a conceptual therapy in certain particulars, in the hope of conducing to a reassessment of premises, but we have not taken it as our task to stipulate any more specific procedures. Dr Southwold resorts to a logical notation, and thus presents a technique which could be applied in other cases, but his main concern too is to expose a category mistake and to bring about a reassessment of what is at issue in the study of kinship. We have thought these general considerations to be of fundamental importance, which is why we chose to write about them for the conference, but there remains admittedly a question about what precisely ought to be done in the analysis of kinship and marriage.

III

FORMALISM

One quite fashionable technical recourse is the rigorous practice of formal analysis, and it is perhaps regrettable that this volume contains no paper on that topic. As a matter of fact, I had planned to invite such a critique, specifically on the subject of transformational analysis, but I could not think of a member of the ASA (in Britain or otherwise conveniently placed to attend the conference) who was both well enough informed on the matter and sufficiently interested to undertake a basic re-examination of the formal methods which have become prominent in American anthropological literature.

In the end perhaps this was as well, for at the conference there seemed to be a general lack of interest in such methods: none of the papers employed techniques of the kind, and some participants were pretty negative or dismissive when they alluded to them. Thus Leach declared his view (below, p. 75) that 'the austerely mathematical contributions of Hammel and Lounsbury' (in Hammel 1965) were 'self-destructive' procedures:

'In their pursuit of elegance and formal rigour the more ingenious practitioners of the art of componential analysis habitually move so far away from the original ethnography that the whole exercise becomes worthless.'

Less directly, Southwold touched on transformational analysis when, in discussing a certain wide application of 'congeniate terms' in Buganda, he concluded that 'an analysis which would explain this usage on the basis of the telescoping of parentate relations is misconceived'. At the discussions which followed, these statements, and other more casual observations to parallel effect, passed entirely without contest or even comment. Nevertheless, a few remarks on some aspects of formal analysis, with a glance at the underlying reasons for such a marked lack of interest, may be in place here.

The formal analysis of kinship has a long history: it has repeatedly been taken up, then dropped for years, and then revived, only to fall out of sight yet again. The current impetus from the direction of linguistics is merely the latest surge in a long-running undulation of professional interest of the kind.

This recurrent inspiration can readily be appreciated, and it needs no justification. What counts, rather, is the theoretical benefit that might be expected to accrue, and the several advantages which the successive proposals have been intended to secure. These questions can best be considered by way of a rapid historical survey of some of the more noteworthy attempts. I shall make this in a very brief form, dwelling at any length on the less familiar cases only and on points of special interest.

The approaches in question differ one from another in the type of operations suggested, but they have in common the ambition to achieve an exactitude in the listing and analysis of terms of relationship which the common English words for relatives do not permit. As Francis Galton expressed the issue, with characteristic clarity (1883: 61):

> 'We were apt to underrate the difficulty of expressing relationship owing to the imperfect nomenclature to which habit has accustomed us, but as soon as we found it necessary to define a relationship accurately, the imperfection of our language and the vagueness of our ordinary conceptions became apparent.'

These defects in turn made it hard to compare various jural systems, including the law of marriage, inheritance of property, and so on. The impulse to reform was thus quite strong in the last century, and especially in the lawyers and scientists who were so influential in the development of social anthropology.

An early and eminently respectable landmark was Mac-Farlane's paper on the analysis of consanguinity and affinity (1883), an investigation undertaken at the suggestion of Tylor. This has latterly been entirely ignored (cf., e.g., Hammel 1965; Buchler & Selby 1968), so far as my knowledge of the literature goes, but it contains much that is fundamental, and it far forestalls certain more recent exercises which have been unduly regarded for their theoretical or methodical novelty. MacFarlane's intention is to develop a systematic notation which will 'bear a relation to the ordinary system of terms, the same as that which the notation of chemistry bears to the arbitrarily chosen names of substances'. Like the chemist, he says, we must first analyse as much as is possible, then choose symbols for the elements resulting from the analysis, and express the compound ideas in terms of

xxii

these fundamental symbols. His system is based on the parent–child relationship, which is a combination of the 'two fundamental relationships of the highest generality, namely *child* and *parent*, the one relationship being the reciprocal of the other' (47). These can be combined so as to express any of the complex relationships; examples are provided for the first five orders, an 'order' being determined by the number of persons through which the connexion is traced. A simple alphabetical notation permits the statement of relationships of varying distances, and these can also be expressed by means of a graphic notation employing opposite diagonals for ascending and descending relationships, and symbols (+ and ○) for male and female. The alphabetical expressions of 'genus relationships' are distinguished according to whether or not they are reducible; a simple criterion for the recognition of reducibility is provided, and the method of 'reduction' is demonstrated.

This is all clear and impressive enough in MacFarlane's exposition, but a more decided interest is to be found when he goes on to characterize the various 'classes' of relationships thus distinguished. This he does by means of what would now be called 'componential analysis' by the criteria of step-, lineal, collateral, affinal, ascending, and descending relationship, and degree. The combinations of these criteria, which can be further qualified by features of the formulas by which the class membership is expressed, define ('generate' would be the cant term nowadays) the relationships in question. The formalization continues with an 'index' for each relationship, giving a reduced numerical expression to the preceding definitions by class, etc.; then a 'sign' (composed of + and − symbols) giving an elementary indication of ancestry, descent, collaterality, and affinity; and finally a 'grade', read off from the alphabetical notation, which assigns each status to a genealogical level. Thereafter, MacFarlane develops his analysis with more general observations on the analysis of kinship, particularly by reference to the views of McLennan, Morgan, and Maine, and demonstrates the application of his technique to the English laws of marriage and to the question of the validity of the scheme on which Morgan's tables were based.

This summary account by no means elicits all the points of interest in MacFarlane's ingenious and radical paper, but I hope I have reported enough of it to permit a new estimation of latter-day undertakings (not always, alas, of such simplicity or thoroughness) of the same kind. From this basis we can proceed more rapidly over ground that is more familiar.

The next landmark is Kroeber's justly renowned paper on classificatory systems of relationship (1909). This has been repeatedly acknowledged in recent years as the theoretical source of modern componential analysis, and has thus received its due, if very belatedly; but I would stress that it followed MacFarlane's paper at a very long interval and had itself to wait even longer for useful recognition.

Over the next twenty years, as it was to appear, Radcliffe-Brown had (he reported) been 'constantly' employing a certain system of notation for expressing relationships, and this he published in 1930. He did so, he said, on the ground that he himself had found it of great use in fieldwork, not only in that it saved much time but also that it helped towards 'greater accuracy' (Radcliffe-Brown 1930). 'All relationships', he states, 'can be shown as reducible to a single assymetrical [sic] relation, that between parent and child.' The graphic notation proposed employs opposite diagonals for ascending and descending relationships, and symbols (+ and ○) for male and female, with the addition of two further signs (< and >) for older and younger respectively. These signs can be combined to express relationships of increasing distance. 'It is convenient to distinguish what I am accustomed to call "orders" of relationship' (122), and Radcliffe-Brown presents examples of formulas up to the fifth order. He supplies no reference to any other formal notation, or to any other author, and indeed he conveys the firm impression that the notation described is his own invention. Nevertheless, one cannot fail to be struck by the very close similarity, in vocabulary, graphic devices, and exposition, that his short paper bears to the prior work of MacFarlane, published forty-seven years earlier. Radcliffe-Brown adopts the same relationship as the basis of his system; he employs the identical diagonal lines for ascent and descent, and the identical symbols (certainly not conventional in his day) for male and female; he assorts relationships by their degree of distance into 'orders', confining his examples similarly to those of up to the fifth order; and after these interesting parallels it may even appear significant that he echoes (as it might seem) MacFarlane's term that all relationships are 'reducible' to that of parent-child. The notational similarity can be well appreciated by a comparison of their respective diagrams for the depiction of the relationship of two men connected through their father (*Figure 1*). Apart from the superficiality of Radcliffe-Brown's

FIGURE 1   *Coincidence of notations*

(*a*) MacFarlane 1883   (*b*) Radcliffe-Brown 1930

approach, and his failure to demonstrate the application of the notation to any social facts, the only difference is that, whereas MacFarlane links up his graphic elements to form plane figures, Radcliffe-Brown places them separately on the line, so that juxtaposition serves the same purpose as lineal connexion (this explains the slight difference of form between the diagrams in *Figure 1*). All the same, he does also suggest the other method: 'While it is generally sufficient to write the notation along one line it may sometimes be useful to use it in such a way as to show the generations' (122), i.e. in a plane figure in which vertical intervals stand for genealogical levels. As an example, he displays a relationship of 'the fifth order', namely MMBDD, in a continuous representation just like MacFarlane's.

Radcliffe-Brown's venture into formal analysis, rudimentary and unproved though it is, can thus be regarded in its turn as a landmark of a kind. The least that can be said – and the most, perhaps, in this place – is that the degree of precise correspondence between his notation and that of MacFarlane merits a close scrutiny and calls for some reflection. Whatever the outcome of each reader's own assessment, it is certainly a case of such historical interest as to demand a place in any account of the elaboration of formal techniques for the analysis of kinship and marriage.

Thereafter, the direction of anthropological effort in this field is more straightforward and better known. A few years later, Davis and Warner published their 'Structural Analysis of

Kinship' (1937), in which they attempted to formulate 'the principles upon which kinship rests and upon which any intrinsic classification of concrete systems must accordingly be based' (291-2), and proposed a novel notation. In the next decade this was followed by Greenberg's 'Logical Analysis of Kinship' (1949); and in the decade after that there appeared Goodenough's 'Componential Analysis and the Study of Meaning' (1956), a paper in which methods of componential analysis, as developed for the study of linguistic forms, were applied to the Truk terminology of relationship. This last paper opened a period in which anthropologists turned increasingly to linguistic techniques in the hope of methodical or theoretical advance, and since its appearance several papers of a similar kind have been published. The same year also saw the publication of another well-known paper, inspired by the same linguistic examples as Goodenough's, namely Lounsbury's analysis of Pawnee kinship (Lounsbury 1956). This too has had sequels and imitations which have attracted quite a wide interest. A substantial embodiment of this interest is to be seen in the collection of papers on formal semantic analysis which appeared as an *American Anthropologist* Special Publication (Hammel 1965).

The linguistic trend continues to be prominent, but it is not the only kind of formal approach that is purveyed today. A more substantive view is exhibited in Schmitz's work on basic forms of kinship (1964), in which various combinations of rules of descent, marriage practices, post-marital residence, and so on are exhibited as in a handbook; and in a more abstract vein there is Löffler's forthcoming monograph on the foundations of a social anthropology of kinship (1969), a non-diagrammatical disquisition in which the analysis is presented throughout in a notation analogous to that of symbolic logic.

Without the listing of any more titles, therefore, it can be seen that the formal analysis of kinship and marriage has indeed continually attracted anthropologists, and that in fact we are at present in a period of resurgent attention to methods of the kind. The current effervescence, on the part especially of certain anthropologists in the United States, could even lead to the idea that a turning-point had been passed and that the analysis of kinship and marriage was henceforth to assume a far more exact and scientific character. There are, however, a number of considerations which must call so hopeful a view into question, and which can be thought to justify to some extent the scepticism that marked the Bristol conference. It is here that the short historical sketch that I have presented above, partial and unbalanced though it has had to be, can provide a clearer perspective.

The first thing that may strike a non-partisan observer is that the works in question are neither numerous nor extensive. In fact it is a little puzzling that componential analysis, transformational analysis, and so on should have attracted such attention in the profession as they have done. In recent years the same few modern titles have been cited over and over again, but when one considers how much actual work has been published, and how many empirical cases have been examined, it is hard to account for the stir that they have occasioned. The answer ought to be, one would surmise, that the papers in question, though few, were of such theoretical acuity and had led to such advances in research that their sparseness was irrelevant. After all, no one would think of disparaging the *Tractatus Logico-Philosophicus* merely on the ground that it ran to only 81 pages. But the latest exercises, particularly the linguistic ones, have not obviously exhibited a comparable merit. Though doubtless educative for their authors, in coming to terms with their materials, they have not been demonstrated to possess any more general power of instruction: they have neither rectified nor reconstructed kinship theory, and they have not achieved any singular success in the description or analysis of individual systems. Even MacFarlane's outstanding pioneer paper did not do as much; and this example suggests one possible factor in the explanation of a continuing failure that has been registered by mathematical and linguistic modes of formal analysis.

MacFarlane was a mathematician; Radcliffe-Brown was avowedly emulating what he took to be the methods of natural scientists; Greenberg is a linguist, Goodenough was trained as a linguist, and Lounsbury is a practising linguist. Hammel, in fact, lays special stress on this, pointing out that Goodenough's and Lounsbury's 1956 papers 'were published as papers *in linguistics*' (Hammel 1965: 4; original emphasis). In a significant number of instances, therefore, the proponents of certain kinds of formal analysis have not, as it would seem, been responding to problems intrinsic to the understanding of social life, problems posed empirically and for which a contextual comprehension has proved to be insufficient. It appears plausible, rather, that certain formal approaches have been devised because of reasons extraneous to the essential concerns of social anthropology. It would not be easy to justify such a surmise in each case, but it is a likelihood that cannot readily be dismissed. Nor, for that matter, is it in the least discreditable to any of the formalists. If a mathematician or a linguist thinks that he can see how to extend into the elucidation of social classification and corporate institutions certain methods which have proved revealing in his own subject, it is entirely to the good that he should try his hand at it and show the anthropologists what his method is. The decisive point, though, is whether the formal analyses really do provide students of society with advantageous methods of understanding what they are trying to understand. So far it seems that no such advantage has been demonstrated. Matters may improve in future, of course, as techniques are made more subtle or are better accommodated to the subject-matter, but the future must make its own case. The past, at any rate, offers no encouragement, for there is a ready explanation of the sporadic appearance of formal undertakings in the study of kinship, and of the long gaps of inattention between them. It is simply that they have not worked.

The first gauge of this ineffectiveness is the neglect of MacFarlane's fundamental paper: so far as I can discover, it led at the time to no further work of the sort, it was not adduced in the analysis of kinship systems, and it did not guide ethnographical inquiries. Although well received by anthropologists at the meeting to which it was read, it then fell completely out of sight and it seems to have languished in that condition until the present notice. Radcliffe-Brown, it is true, claimed that he had found his MacFarlane-type notation to be 'of great use in fieldwork', presumably in Australia, but he does not mention this use in his ethnographic reports; nor, incidentally, do these suggest that his investigations had been sufficiently extensive or detailed to permit the useful application of the technique. After its publication, moreover, no one else seems to have tried to make anything of it; and even Fortes's recent eulogistic

Introduction

account of Radcliffe-Brown's achievements in the field of kinship (1969) does not so much as mention the title. A similar neglect was suffered by Davis and Warner's paper, and in this too there is the curiosity that although Warner had been a pupil of Radcliffe-Brown the paper does not cite the latter's earlier publication. Greenberg's paper, next, also dropped out of view, and it was not until a few years after Goodenough's and Lounsbury's early papers that there was any professional response. We are still in the middle of this, however, and it remains to be seen whether linguistic techniques will prove any more effective than their forerunners. For the most part, therefore, it can be seen that the various and successive attempts at formal analysis since 1883 have fallen by the wayside, and the obvious explanation is that they were not found to be useful.

As for the indifference of many social anthropologists, including very experienced ethnographers, in the face of current linguistic formalism, the preponderant reason would appear to be the same; and even the fact that Goodenough and some other practitioners of componential analysis have done fieldwork does not provide a decisive encouragement to adopt their methods. This might, however, be a consequence of the sheer intricacy, and the taxing character, of the techniques. Thus Hammel has declared, with reference to the collection of densely argued papers that he edited, that 'it is difficult to perform these kinds of analyses' (1965: v):

> 'It is not that there is any mystery about them but just that they demand continual attention to detail, repeated scrapping of hypotheses, a concern with symmetry and analytic closure, and most of all, time. . . . Our colleagues will find that these analyses are difficult to read, for the same reasons that they are difficult to write. . . .'

It could be, therefore, by this account, that the more commonsensical British anthropologists, and particularly those not much drawn to the logical manipulation of abstractions, have found themselves ill fitted to cope with such difficulties and hence have shunned techniques from which they might profit.

I must say that I should not myself find this a convincing explanation, though I understand that it expresses a view that is held by some proponents of formalism. The essential objection,

it seems to me, is that the analyses in question are not in fact
all that difficult. On the contrary, although the techniques are
given the elaborate externals of algebraic rigour and scientific
exactitude, they are basically quite simple and even conventional. It is partly because of this, perhaps, that some social
anthropologists find certain formal techniques not only gratuit-
ously complex but also rather pretentious. This judgement is
not that of British functionalists alone, for an exceedingly
acute American critic, the late Dr Allan Coult, has very forcefully expressed the same view. In demonstrating that Lounsbury's intricate analysis of Crow- and Omaha-type terminologies (1964) achieves no more than Tax did in 1937, and indeed
not even as much, he draws a very pointed contrast between
the 'obfuscation' of Lounsbury's exposition and the simplicity
of Tax's (Coult 1967: 28). Löffler, himself an accomplished for-
malist, similarly finds that Lounsbury's system of symbols is
'not only rather intricate, but from a purely logical point of view
is open to further reduction' (1969: 3). In other words, the
notation is more complex than it need be, and the mode of
analysis is made to appear more difficult than it is. In any case,
I do not suppose many of my colleagues would accept that
other types of analysis are any less taxing than the extremely
formal kind. Dr Korn's analysis of Iatmul society, for instance,
very patently demanded 'continual attention to detail, repeated
scrapping of hypotheses, a concern with symmetry and analytic
closure, and . . . time'; the same is obviously true of Leach's
paper on the language of Kachin kinship (1967), for instance;
and I should certainly claim as much, to cite further cases of
present relevance, of my own analyses of the Purum and Wikmunkan systems (1958; 1962b). More than all this, the mere
factor of difficulty – supposing this to exist – is surely not likely
to deter anthropologists of any persuasion from the adoption of
even the most alien or intricate techniques. Ethnographers in
particular are deeply committed to the comprehension of their
own findings, which sometimes they have acquired at real cost
to themselves, and it would not be reasonable or plausible to
suggest that they would knowingly neglect any method whatever that might help them to do so.

In the end, therefore, although I cannot pretend to speak on
behalf of the critics of recent formal analysis, I tend to think

the following is a fair account of the situation. The majority of
the sceptics know of the techniques in question, have read some
at least of the analyses in which these are employed, and are in a
respectable position to assess whether they really advance
understanding. In the main, they seem to have concluded that
there is nothing to be learned from them, and that there is
nothing to gain by adopting such methods in their own work.

Naturally, the formalists are not going to be quite content
with this kind of conclusion. They will not be persuaded, probably, that to set them in an historical context spanning some
ninety years indicates that their concerns are essentially conventional if not old-fashioned; nor, more certainly, are they
likely to agree that their own exercises will become merely
historical examples of a perennial quest for exactitude. They
have a right to demand that their methods be subjected to as
intensive an examination as they themselves devote to terminologies, and I am only sorry that the conference reported here did
not provide them with it. On the other hand, it is they who are
required to make their case in the face of scepticism, and to
demonstrate that their techniques effect or facilitate an improvement in the understanding of social life and collective
representations. With the best will in the world, and with due
recognition of the intelligence and serious purpose of the formalists, it cannot be conceded that they have yet done so.

These observations have been concerned with linguistic
paradigms, but similar considerations attach to mathematical
analyses as well. These involve specific technical difficulties of
a purely mathematical kind, and it could indeed be said that
social anthropologists have abjured them because they cannot
understand them. Nevertheless, the mathematical analysis of
kinship is a type of formal argument which should not remain
unmentioned in a volume such as this. Without embarking on a
survey of the position, perhaps I may usefully mention a couple
of cases.

Lévi-Strauss, discoursing on the future of kinship studies, has
referred approvingly to computer analyses of kinship and
marriage (1966), but the one precise result that he reports is
not in any way encouraging. He got a mathematician to cal-
culate the number of 'marriage types' for societies with Crow-
Omaha systems and different totals of component clans, two

of which clans (the mother's and the father's) were to be prohibited as sources of spouses (1966: 20). One result was that in a society consisting of thirty clans (modest enough in fact; the Nyoro, for instance, have about 100) the number of marriage types is 297,423,855. There is no telling what this is supposed to show, and Lévi-Strauss himself does nothing with this extraordinary total; but a figure of nearly *three hundred million* marriage types, in a society of a scale likely to be associated with the type of terminology in question, clearly has no direct connexion with the categories, ideas, and values in accordance with which men marry women. The obvious inference is that the mathematician was supplied with inappropriate premises, these being the products of a defective understanding of the system, and that the proponent of so extreme a mathematical conclusion has an insufficiently realistic appreciation of social facts (cf. Needham 1969: 165 n. 1).

A more revealing and decisive case is that of the Tarau, a society which has acquired a remarkable prominence in recent publications on the mathematical analysis of kinship and marriage. Professional attention began with *Les Structures élémentaires de la parenté* (1949), where Lévi-Strauss presented an account of the Tarau system. This, although it was partial and superficial, happened to be adopted by mathematical analysts as a paradigm case for the demonstration of the use of permutation models in social anthropology. From the early fifties until 1968, a series of writers (Bush; Kemeny, Snell, & Thompson; Boudon; Pin-Hsiung Liu) took up this case in order to press for the introduction of mathematics into the study of kinship and marriage. Dr Korn and I then felt that we had to do something about an increasing accumulation of theoretical pronouncements which had less and less to do with social reality or responsible analysis. We therefore made an intensive examination of this case (Korn & Needham 1970). The argument concludes that the mathematical techniques are inappropriate to the study of even such simple and closed forms of society as prescriptive systems, and that permutation models are neither more convenient nor more precise than non-mathematical means of comprehension. Moreover, the ethnographical reports on the Tarau – who were in any case practically extinct – prove to be exiguous, dubitable, contradictory, and incapable of a reliable interpretation. In this instance, too, the conclusion is that 'the [mathematical] techniques have not been brought to bear in response to anthropological problems: instead, they have appealed, as techniques, to non-anthropologists who have then looked for some occasion to apply them to social reality' (417). Of course, our argument is itself an analysis and subject to critical scrutiny, but pending any degree of refutation I cite it because it permits, for once, a conclusive assessment of the value of certain mathematical models in the analysis of a particular type of society. The results, although entirely negative as far as mathematical analysis is concerned, seem to me to be very instructive in more fundamental respects.

I should not like it to be thought, however, that these reservations betoken any general hostility in principle to the practice of formal analysis. In the present volume, Korn's rigorous examination of the Iatmul terminology is an excellent example to the contrary; and my own work elsewhere (e.g. 1962b; 1969) contains repeated refutation of such an inference. The question is simply one of method. To be disappointed by the failure of certain techniques imported from linguistics does not imply that one rejects linguistic analogues or stimuli in principle. Leach's paper below, based as it is on Jakobson's researches, makes that point. Similarly, to object, as I should do, that the so-called transformational analyses of relationship terminologies are misnamed and misleading, on the initial ground that they do not effect transformations, does not mean that one denies the possibility of theoretical inspiration by linguistic parallels. Only it may be that to attempt a simple transposition of techniques is not the most useful thing to do. For my part, at any rate, I certainly share Chomsky's opinion that in the study of kinship systems *'nothing has been discovered that is even roughly comparable to language'* (1968: 65; italics supplied). This authoritative finding tends at once to confirm that the linguistic anthropologists (Lounsbury *et al.*) really are on the wrong track, and also to explain why it is that the linguistic models have failed to produce useful or interesting results.

The real value of a linguistic example, rather, may lie in abstract analogies between the study of language and the study of social facts that are expressed in language. For instance, there is a significant parallel, it seems to me, between the ideas of Kroeber and Lowie about the combinations of rules and principles in the constitution of forms of social classification, an approach which I try to develop in my 'Remarks' (secs. V & VII), and Chomsky's conclusion (1968: 75-6):

> 'It is reasonable to suppose that a generative grammar is a system of many hundreds of rules of several different types, organized in accordance with certain fixed principles of ordering and applicability and containing a certain fixed substructure, which, along with the general principles of organization, is common to all languages.'

Similarly, we may think of certain fixed principles of ordering in forms of social classification, but obviously it is the prior work done in anthropological analysis that permits us to see that there is an analogy at all. Linguistics therefore does not reveal a novel mode of interpretation to us, or at least not in this instance, but it can proffer a respectable inducement to continue in social anthropology with the attempt to determine the logical constraints on systems of kinship and marriage and thus to isolate 'the possibilities of phenomena' (cf. below, p. 32).

IV

ANALYSIS

One of the most challenging statements in this collection of papers is Leach's conclusion that 'the utility of the study of kin term systems as sets ... is pretty well worked out' (pp. 76-7). He goes on to say that he does not wish to imply that 'analysis of the formal logic of kin terms is a wholly valueless activity', which is encouraging, but he still firmly maintains that in our present state of knowledge 'the marginal rewards which come from investigations of this kind are becoming very small'.

Clearly these contentions are meant to stir a response. My own inclination would be to declare that they are quite wrong, but Edmund Leach's statements are sometimes marked by an engaging touch of hyperbole, and it might therefore be rather stolid to take these utterances as meaning precisely all that they would appear to mean. Nevertheless, the provocative vigour of Leach's contentions always has a point that is well worth taking seriously, and he certainly intends to be taken so in this case. There is an initial difficulty, though, in that it is not clear what his targets are; for there are different kinds of formal analysis, which have been employed for a variety of purposes, and the practitioners he lists run all the way from Morgan to myself, leaving it to be surmised what it is that we are supposed to have in common. Still, let us try to make the most of the argument that seems to be implicit in the statements.

If to study a relationship terminology as a set means that the set is arbitrarily circumscribed, by the deliberate exclusion of certain meanings which happen not to fit the analyst's purpose, technique, or presuppositions, then it may be agreed that such an approach seems likely to bring only marginal rewards. Thus when Lounsbury assumes that 'the *primary* function of kinship terminologies is to delineate the relation of ego to the members of his personal bilateral kindred . . .' (1964: 382, original emphasis), that other social denotations are 'extensions' from basic terminological features which are the 'causal matrices' (352), and that non-social denotations such as sun, moon, heavenly beings, etc., are to be left out of account as 'varieties of . . . metaphorical extension' (382), this is convenient to his technique and obviously expresses his presuppositions, but it quite segments and disorganizes the comprehensive system of meanings that attaches to the terminology. This appears to be one kind of analysis that Leach has in view, and indeed it is unpromising. For that matter, I do not think it has yielded even marginal rewards, and the procedure seems in fact (to the minor extent that it has been publicly demonstrated) to be intrinsically unproductive. But this does not entail that investigations of the kind are 'worked out'. There is no universal legislation for the circumscription of phenomena, and it is for each anthropologist to decide what to include in the set that he isolates. The real ground for criticism is whether or not the procedure leads to novel or otherwise interesting results. This is a matter for assessment in each particular instance, and cannot be decided by any wholesale judgement.

Leach's criticism of the investigation of what he calls the 'formal logic' of terminologies assumes, further, that the analyst comes to a halt in his study once he has isolated certain abstract principles of order. It is true that some recent analyses have done so, and these sterile exercises give substance to Chomsky's reservations about the use of structural linguistics as a model, e.g. that 'the structure of a phonological system is of very little interest as a formal object; there is nothing of significance to be said, from a formal point of view, about a set of forty-odd elements cross-classified in terms of eight or ten features' (1968: 65). Similarly, there is very little interest in a generative analysis of a terminology if the investigator stops there, and Leach has a sounder case when he says that such procedures are 'self-destructive'. Indeed, as far as the 'pursuit of elegance and formal rigour' is concerned, he could well have adduced a telling parallel from Dumont's observations on the study of caste: 'Sociology can after all only reflect the social experience of mankind', he writes, but the translation of types of experience cannot be done without painstaking effort and research, nor, as he caustically puts it, 'by incompetent persons manipulating sophisticated paradigms or computers' (Dumont 1966: 24). In the study of kinship and marriage as well there seems to exist a growing danger that formal studies, however rigorous they may be, will rightly incur the same kind of derogation, and for essentially the same reason, namely the neglect of the task of translating human experience in favour of the quasi-mathematical satisfactions (e.g. the achievement of 'elegance') that are afforded by mere techniques. Here also, as Wilder has occasion to underline below when discussing the Ackerman matrix, 'c'est sa *méthode de mesure* plutôt que l'*objet de sa mesure* que le savant décrit' (Bachelard 1938: 213).

But the practice of formal analysis, of whatever kind, does not at all entail that it shall be taken as an end in itself. The real interest begins, and the real value emerges, when the formal features thus discerned are used as keys for the interpretation, in each individual instance, of the form of social experience that is to be understood. The practical effect of formal analysis is ultimately to detect an order in social phenomena and collective ideation, though this order may prove to diverge considerably from the formal features, and in this regard it is very far indeed from being 'worked out'. On the contrary, my own view is that it has scarcely been recognized yet in the practice of perhaps the majority of social anthropologists. It would be

negative and invidious to single out pieces of work, ethnographical and theoretical, which are flawed by the lack of formal
analysis, but the case for beginning at the formal level is well
made in this volume by Korn's analysis. The questions she
raises are fundamental, both theoretically and in the interpretation of Iatmul social life, but they could not have been formulated without a rigorous scrutiny of the terminology. (It
may be stressed, too, that she nowhere finds it necessary or
profitable to resort to 'sophisticated paradigms', algorithms,
contrived notations, or any other of the intricate apparatus
that is fashionable in some quarters). On a minor scale, also,
my modest formal analysis of the Gurage terminology (1969)
has admittedly a technical focus of interest, in that it concentrates on the unusual form of that system of classification, but
its ultimate justification is that it leads to the formulation of
more exact, and apparently revealing, sociological questions.
In this case also it would easily have been possible to trick out
the analysis with an elaborate notation and 'rewrite rules' (and,
incidentally, to make it far longer and perhaps more impressive
in consequence), but there was no prospect that a mock-
algebraic display of this sort would in any way have helped to
an understanding of Gurage social affairs. In the much simpler
style that I adopted, however, this case nevertheless demonstrates once more that formal analysis is not only technically
instructive, and indispensable to comparative research into
modes of classification, but that it can also be a uniquely useful
preliminary to empirical inquiries into the meanings and con-
sociations of a form of social experience. There are demonstrated advantages in these respects, and indeed it is hard to
see how the interpretation of social facts can well be carried out
except by recourse to some kind of abstract analysis. The only
question, then, is again how this shall best be carried out. This
is a matter for decision by the test of practice and results, and
so far the chief general lesson is that we should look for the
simple way of doing things. Francis Galton set an excellent
example a long time ago when he was trying to understand the
famous Kamilaroi version of the four-section system. He wanted
to find, namely, 'an easy clue to this strange custom, feeling
assured that no aboriginal Australian brain could acquire the
accurate and almost instinctive knowledge they all have of it

without one' (Galton 1889: 71). It needs only a glance at the tangles into which modern formalists have worked themselves, especially in the construction of models of this very simple system of prescriptive alliance, to appreciate what a splendidly sensible precept this is. Its cogency derives in the first place from the realization that the social categories in question are guides for real people in the conduct of their social lives, and that what the anthropologist has therefore to grasp are the principles of interpretation and application that the people themselves employ. They do not use rewrite rules and skewing rules and the rest, so why should we? The real clues are likely to be quite easy, but they may also be quite singular – perhaps, as Leach has demonstrated in his examination of the language of Kachin kinship (1967), the properties of individual languages. This was what Hocart was talking about, too, when he maintained that 'the student of Fijian customs can never even understand what the people are talking about until he puts behind him all the sociological classifications of the schools' (1952: 25). The point of formal analysis, after all, should be to understand what the people are talking about.

The main force in Leach's criticism, then, is the implied injunction to presume no arbitrary boundaries to the significance of social categories, but to trace semantic connexions as far as they will go. He has himself provided an illuminating example of this procedure in the paper that I have just referred to, an investigation that I regard as one of the very finest ethnographical analyses of kinship ever published. This paper makes a point, incidentally, about the relevance of philosophy (above, sec. II), for in it Leach opens with a consideration of Aristotelian natural kinds and 'the atomism . . . dominant in English philosophy for at least a century' (129), criticizes Firth for his 'empiricist-nominalist position', and acknowledges the 'existentialist-phenomenologist' assumptions behind his own argument (130). More particularly, the present relevance of the paper is that, instead of treating kinship terms as 'a self-defined closed set of words', Leach examines 'their context of use in a variety of different dimensions' (131). In doing so he succeeds in conveying Kachin modes of classification with a very convincing impact, and shows that in order to grasp the meanings of a terminology of asymmetric prescriptive alliance it is necessary to examine the extensive non-jural connotations of the terms as well. In doing so, he takes the words in question in their full extension (in a philosophical sense), without introducing any arbitrary discriminations between, for example, those usages that deal with 'kinship' and those that are 'metaphorical'. All of this is an extremely clear and well-argued demonstration, but there are two qualifications to make.

The first is that the Kachin words in question, in their jural application to persons and groups, form a systematically coherent vocabulary; and in order to grasp this as a practical classification it is necessary to conceive it in some more or less abstract frame, i.e. formally. Thus Leach, in another place, first considers graphic conventions and 'type marriages' before he assesses the various ways of conceiving asymmetric alliance and their applicability to the Kachin evidence (1961, ch. 3). The way in which such a terminology is conceived and then represented can affect the comprehension of social reality, as Leach has shown, and to assess the aptness of the various alternatives calls for a degree of comparative formal analysis. Leach himself chooses a specific representation (1954: 305, Table II), a form which has analytical implications (cf. Needham 1960: 105), and although this representation is not reproduced in 'The Language of Kachin Kinship' the order that it describes is nevertheless presumed in the argument of his paper. Thus in his own work Leach relies in part on formal considerations in order to discern meaning.

The second qualification is that, although Leach's critical point is of the first importance, it has not gone quite unrecognized before by other anthropologists. He asserts that 'in anthropological discussions of kinship classifications it has always been assumed that we are interested in the classification of individuals according to their social roles' (below, p. 82), as though the concern were always narrowly sociological and neglectful of other realms of meaning. Doubtless this is true in many cases, but it is not 'always' so. Since the mid-thirties, students of asymmetric prescriptive alliance at any rate have repeatedly and explicitly analysed societies of the kind as systems of total classification, and they have examined the terms in question not only as jural categories of descent and alliance but also in their symbolic and metaphorical connotations (Vergouwen 1933; van Ossenbruggen 1935; van Wouden 1935; Onvlee 1949). Perhaps I may mention also that in a series of analyses since 1958 I have consistently adopted this synoptic approach and have treated terminologies, so far as the literature allowed, without any deleterious prior division into what was kinship and what was something else. Korn's analysis constitutes an effective example of the same approach, in which formal parallels and semantic resonances are traced without prejudice throughout the full range and contextual variety of the ethnographic evidence. A similarly comprehensive attention to the connotational scope of institutions is seen also in Rivière's relation of marriage to the 'cosmic order', and in Forge's conclusion that the explanation of a type of marriage among the Iatmul is to be sought in 'the area of cosmology'.

When, however, Leach goes on to investigate the possibility that 'contrasts in meaning are likely to correspond to contrasts in sound pattern' (1967: 127), that close relationships may be signalled by 'easy' sounds and awkward relationships by difficult ones (below, pp. 78-9), he is urging a means of interpretation which is genuinely innovatory and which touches a fundamental aspect of the linguistic representation of experience. His suggestions encountered more dubiety than enthusiasm at the conference, if I read the mood correctly, but there could not have been many who did not at once respond, as readers of this volume surely will, to the intriguing character of the problems raised.

V

WIKMUNKAN

A contribution to this collection that awakens a special interest is McKnight's re-analysis of the Wikmunkan system. In the first place it deals with an Australian aboriginal society, and Australia has been the source of much of the most interesting work on kinship and marriage. No symposium on these topics would seem complete without an Australian case, and it was an unexpected stroke of fortune that McKnight was in a position to provide one. Secondly, McKnight's investigation presented a most unusual opportunity to test in the field the conclusions

xl

of an analysis of the ethnographic literature. I had published four articles on Wikmunkan society in which I examined all of the sources and worked out a 'total structural analysis' (Needham 1962b; 1963a; 1963b; 1965). In doing so I arrived at a novel representation of the system, and one which was at great formal variance from that of Ursula McConnel (the ethnographer who had published most on this society), but which was open to exact empirical test. It must be exceedingly seldom that a literary analysis such as mine can be speedily checked by direct and independent inquiry among the people in question, and much was therefore to be looked for from McKnight's stay among the Wikmunkan. Also, if I may mention a more personal aspect that will be appreciated by any comparativist, I regarded my first and basic paper on the Wikmunkan (1962b), long and demanding though it was, as technically the most proficient analysis of a prescriptive system that I had published, so in this regard too I awaited McKnight's original findings with a heightened expectation.

It will be helpful to readers who are unfamiliar with a quite extensive and certainly confusing ethnographical literature, and who have not mastered the points of interpretation and debate already published, if I quickly set out the theoretical status of the main questions that McKnight deals with (p. 146). It should then be easier to estimate the novelty and value of his conclusions, and to assess the theoretical implications of this noteworthy case for the study of kinship and marriage.

1. 'How valid is McConnel's analysis and presentation of the Wik-mungkan system of kinship and marriage?' (McKnight). My own conclusion was that the analysis was not valid (1962b: 239-42). The chief defects, I argued, were that McConnel was misled by a prohibition on marriage with the genealogical FZD into thinking that the system was based on matrilateral cross-cousin marriage; that the obligation to marry the daughter of the MyB (to the exclusion of MeBD), combined with a general distinction of older and younger categories of persons, led her to think of a man as marrying 'down'; and that her evident failure to distinguish between absolute and relative status led her to conceive a series of marriages in an 'age spiral'. McConnel constructed her diagrams in accordance with these suppositions,

and I gave reasons to infer that her interpretation of the system was based largely on features of her diagrams rather than on Wikmunkan statements and in accordance with Wikmunkan ideology. 'Such notions as "line," "direction," "up," "down," and "spiral" are, I suspect, features of the diagram itself rather than renderings or explications of Wikmunkan social ideas' (1962b: 239). In particular, I suggested the procedure which she had followed in drawing up her kinship chart, and how her decisive emphasis on the genealogical prohibition of FZD led her to separate FZD and MBD as distinct (quasi-categorical) statuses, one on each side of Ego. The central and continuing cause of McConnel's misunderstanding was, I pressed, her failure to distinguish genealogy and category, a genealogical definition of a category from a classificatory status.

In most of these critical contentions, I am happy to see, McKnight's perusal of the literature that I had examined permits him to agree with my conclusions: 'like Needham, I would argue that all this is not so, and I think I have shown the weakness of McConnel's analysis . . .' (p. 154). It is true that he slightly rephrases the issues, and that he emphasizes some different points in the ethnography (a matter to which we shall return), but it will be easily appreciated that his analytical conclusions are gratifyingly identical with my own. This much may be taken therefore as a detailed confirmation of my analysis of the published evidence, and McKnight's answer to his first question claims a proportional importance.

McKnight, however, is able to go further, and to be more definite in these conclusions, by adducing reports of his conversations with Wikmunkan. These clearly support McConnel in her crucial statements that the father's sister's daughter cannot be married. However, it does not appear explicitly from McKnight's observations that the father's sister's daughter is actually called 'cousin-mother' or that her husband is called *pinya* (FeB). The useful precision of his report that the father's sister's daughter's child is called *nengka* (S, D), which perfectly accords with her own status as cross-cousin, makes it advisable to seek further assurance on the point. Since the categories are of prime analytical interest, it is of particular significance to learn definitely whether or not this relative is called *kattha*, 'mother', as certain of McKnight's allusions appear to imply.

2. 'How many descent lines do they have?' My argument was that McConnel was mistaken in concluding that there were six, and Lévi-Strauss in proposing that there were three, and that in fact the Wikmunkan terminology is constituted by only two lines (1962b: 243, 244-5). McKnight agrees with me: '. . . I think it is reasonable to argue that among the Wik-mungkan there are two lines of descent, and not six as claimed by McConnel or three as is said to be the case by Lévi-Strauss' (p. 157).

This confirmation, however encouraging, leaves unanswered, however, a question which in my analysis I thought had a fundamental interest. I wanted to know, namely, what McConnel could have meant by 'lines', and how she had arrived at the view that there were six of them. I thought I had worked out how she arrived at the total, in the construction of her diagrams, but the status of the concept of 'line' remained unclear: 'The statements of the informants do not establish that this is the way in which the Wikmunkan themselves conceive their society, and I think it can be shown that the lines are purely analytical constructs' (1962b: 240). It would have been of the first importance therefore to discover from the Wikmunkan themselves whether they have any word or idea corresponding to McConnel's 'line'.

3. 'What are the kinship terms?' The terms are reported in a number of places in the literature by McConnel and by Thomson, with an abundance of genealogical specifications. There are slight orthographic variations, but no terminological disparities of any systematic analytical importance. The one point of query is whether the term for DS and DD is *naityiyu* or *naitia*. Both forms are reported by McConnel, who unambiguously says that *naitia* also means MF, FM, etc. Since Thomson reported *ngätjiyang* for DS and DD, I adopted McConnel's *naityiyu*, which appeared superficially to be the orthographic counterpart to Thomson's term (1962b: 230).

McKnight found that the suffix *-yiyu* indicates seniority, and that the suffix *-yang* is applied to terms in the grandchild generation, which would seem to settle the matter. (Though Sayers, incidentally, renders the term for mother's father, in the Coen dialect, as *ngatjiyitutu*[1964: 53].) There are two further points that it may be helpful to add. The first is that to accept *naitia* (*naitya*) as the term for DS and DD helps to restore the ethnography to the relative simplicity of McConnel's main account of 1934, i.e. before she was struck by the idea of the 'downward age spiral' and the rest of the intricacies which she later ascribed to Wikmunkan society. The second is that, although the clarification exposes again the analytical uncertainty that is inseparable from an ignorance of the language in which a terminology is expressed, my 'wrong choice' between the published alternatives was of no categorical importance as far as the two-line scheme of classification was concerned. The only really wrong choice, from a structural point of view, would have been to assign the term *poliya* to the '*naityiyu*' positions. A particle is one thing, but this would have been a consequential mistake.

4. 'What type of marriage system do they have?' In dealing with the question of moieties, I suggested that the Wikmunkan might distinguish moieties only peripherally, where they were in contact with tribes (such as the Kandyu) which certainly have named exogamous moieties (1962b: 249). McKnight confirms that the moiety designations Kuyan and Katpi are inland terms, 'possibly *Kandyu*'. He himself thinks it possible that there are 'unnamed patrilineal moieties' among the Wikmunkan. His inquiries, however, apparently did not take into account my demonstration that all of the reported alliances were consistent with exogamous moieties, or my proposal that the Wikmunkan might distinguish moieties 'not by proper names but by general designations or descriptive circumlocutions' (1962b: 249-50). On the first score, the technique that I employed is very simple, and only two corresponding questions needed to be put to the Wikmunkan, namely whether the wife-givers of wife-givers could themselves be wife-givers, and whether the wife-givers of wife-givers could also be wife-takers. On the second score, McConnel repeatedly reports a ceremonial partition into 'brother' clans and affinal clans, and she speaks of the 'rivalry' and 'opposition' between groupings of this kind; so one would expect that close questioning might reveal some form of designations for these moiety-like contrasts, for it does not seem likely that so trenchant a division should have no general description.

McKnight candidly admits that he neglected to ask whether wife-takers could also be wife-givers to the same clan, i.e. whether direct exchange was practised, and this omission is indeed rather a pity since it is so central to the analysis of the system. But the published ethnography nevertheless makes it appear fairly clear that direct exchange is the rule and is in fact practised. At a number of places McConnel is quite definite on this point, not only by way of her own comment but also in the words of informants. We have moreover the testimony of the alliances which can be traced in the literature and which I brought together in my analysis. These provide the following instances of direct exchange between clans: 2↔12, 4↔5 (Needham 1962b: 245), 10↔11, 11↔13 (cf. Needham 1963b: 143). It is true, as I have demonstrated in various places since 1957, that a distinction must always be looked for between descent group and alliance group, so that relationships among the former cannot automatically be regarded as constituting the alliances as contracted and distinguished by the people themselves. McKnight is prudent therefore in adopting this point, and in subscribing the view that intermarriage may be direct or indirect according to the institutional level at which the analysis is carried out; but there are numerous indications in the Wikmunkan literature that, although individual families arrange marriages, it is entire clans (defined by territory and totem centre) which are thus brought into alliance, and that the appropriate relationship terms are applied reciprocally and uniformly among intermarrying clans. To distinguish wife-givers from wife-takers, as McKnight reports the Wikmunkan to do, is not at all inconsistent with this state of affairs. Hocart has made this clear in his reports on marriage in Fiji, where a two-line terminology is also employed (Hocart 1954: 94), and I have elsewhere stressed the analytical significance of the fact (Needham 1963c: 278).

As for Lévi-Strauss, of course he is quite mistaken in his assertion that the Wikmunkan system exhibits a transition from generalized to restricted exchange, just as he is in characterizing it by 'matrilateral' marriage and three central lines (Needham 1962b: 242-3). His conclusion that there are two marriage possibilities, 'either in a direct cycle of generalized exchange, or in an indirect cycle of restricted exchange' (1969:

211) – which I had first taken to be self-contradictory by
definition (1962b: 262 n. 7), only to be told by Lévi-Strauss
that it was intended to be read as it stood (Needham 1963b:
146 n. 3) – makes no apparent sense.

McKnight's finding that marriage should be within Ego's
genealogical level is a welcome confirmation of the explicit
statements to this effect in McConnel and is consistent with the
betrothal procedure described by Thomson. Since it has for
some years been 'difficult for a man to find a wife without breaking marriage laws' (McConnel 1957: 167), it is particularly interesting to learn that marriage with a classificatory DD (*naitya*),
though 'wrong', causes the least opposition. Perhaps I may add
that I did not in fact 'dismiss' McConnel's inconsistent statement that a woman in this position might be married, but only
pointed out that there was 'no ethnographic evidence that this
was the case' (1962b: 232). It is now confirmed by McKnight
that such a woman ought in fact not to be married.

5. 'Does the ethnography support Homans and Schneider's
interpretation and their theory of marriage?' I have demonstrated that it does not, and specifically that my dissentient
colleagues 'assert not only what is not in the sources but even
the very opposite of what is in them' (1962b: 261; 1963b: 149-
150). It is not actually the case, either, that Homans and
Schneider 'have continued to adhere' to the belief that the
Wikmunkan ethnographic data support their theory, for since
my more detailed refutation (1963b; cf. 1962b: 259-61) they
have offered no public observation on the issue. There does not
seem to be any real question here.

6. 'Are the kinship attitudes in accordance with Lévi-Strauss's
Law of the Atom of Kinship?' At this point McKnight departs
to some extent from the published ethnography, and from my
commentaries, and registers a considerable factual advance.
The exposition, however, is not free of uncertainties. For instance, Thomson does not say, *simpliciter*, that 'some restraint
is required with actual or blood relations'. After describing a
number of types of joking relationship, he concludes: 'With
the actual relations in each case, some restraint is required'
(1935: 484). This is a qualification which attaches, as he writes,

to each case; but only in the case of the *muka* (MeB) does he specifically add that 'some decorum must be observed'. It is this express attitude, with this individual relative, that was rendered in my scheme of Wikmunkan sentiments with (in comparison with the attitude to the father) a negative sign. I cannot, incidentally, very well 'persist' in characterizing any Wikmunkan relationship in any way: I can only point out what the ethnographers wrote. In this instance, I assume merely that Thomson meant what he wrote. Naturally, if this report is wrong as a matter of fact, because the relationship with the mother's brother is actually 'friendly, easy, and indulgent', then the sign has to be changed; but McKnight's finding to this effect was not unfortunately in the report by Thomson that I was analysing.

There does not seem however to be any such ethnographical basis, let alone a 'logical' one, for summing up the attitude to a man's own father with a minus sign, as McKnight thinks should follow from my reading of the evidence. Thomson is perfectly definite in his detailed reports that 'love and freedom' characterize the relationship with all those to whom the term *pipa* (F, FyB) is applied, that father and son 'play up', and that 'the greatest indulgence is shown by a father to his children' (1936: 385; cf. Needham 1963b: 147). There is no hint of a negative qualification here. Moreover, the restraint with 'actual relations' to which McKnight alludes does not (so far as the published ethnography goes) attach to all categories of relatives. Thomson was writing about joking relationships, which hold between certain classificatory relatives, and the restraint attaches only to the immediate members of the categories in question. The father is not a joking relative, and the contextual restraint reported has nothing to do with the relationship between father and child.

McKnight appears to be quite correct in drawing an affective distinction between MeB (*muka*) and MyB (*kala*). As Thomson clearly says, while some 'decorum' must be observed towards the *muka*, 'extreme deference' must be shown to the *kala* (1935: 483; cf. Needham 1963b: 144, 146-7). Admittedly the relationships are different, but for the purpose of Lévi-Strauss's formula (1963, ch. 2) they nevertheless both call for a minus sign. The sign does not imply, after all, that the two relationships thus marked have the identical quality, but only that there is a distinctive contrast between each and another relationship, in this case F/S. Lévi-Strauss makes this quite clear by his assimilation of this kind of research to phonology, and there is no occasion to misunderstand him on the point.

The three additional schemes of sentiments that McKnight reports are very welcome additions to the literature, but they do not in themselves bear out his contentions. He argues, namely, that 'there is no justification for believing that the component [Wikmunkan] attitudes have, or have not, been correctly determined, on the basis of whether or not they are in accordance with Lévi-Strauss's formula or law', and also that the Walbiri scheme 'disproves the universality of Lévi-Strauss's Law of the Atom of Kinship'. These conclusions are too unqualified. The first contrary consideration is that when I worked out the Wikmunkan scheme, in early 1963, there was indeed apparent confirmation of Lévi-Strauss's formula. In addition to the six schemes isolated by Lévi-Strauss, I had elicited from Oxford colleagues five more schemes (Dinka, Kaguru, Limba, Nyoro, Toro) which, in spite of their variations, fitted Lévi-Strauss's formula. Certain other checks, in the literature, also seemed to confirm it; so when I published a scheme for the Wikmunkan (1963b: 148) there was reasonable justification to think that its correspondence with the formula indicated that the component attitudes had each been correctly determined. This degree of confidence was not to be dissipated by the first contradiction that the formula was to encounter. For example, De Heusch had already published in 1958 two schemes which did not fit, and I knew well enough that the Penan did not fit either; but in each case it seemed that we might be trying to match sentiments from types of society for which the formula had not been designed (cf. Needham 1962a: 34-5). This seemed an explanation, too, of the contradictory evidence which Turnbull, who had deliberately set out to test the formula in the field, was to bring back from the Bambuti (Turnbull 1965: 283-4). Also, the formula was of such interest, and Lévi-Strauss had made such fundamental theoretical claims for it, that there was no question of simply abandoning it in the face of initial adversity. In other cases, moreover, ethnographers of first-rate calibre, e.g. Rigby among the Gogo (1967: 653; cf. 1969: 291-3), have latterly found it to be both exact and revealing. Clearly, therefore, even the various schemes now (1970) reported for the Wikmunkan, or the scheme discoverable in the Walbiri ethnography, are not so unexpected or consequential as McKnight appears to suppose. In any event, the 'universality' of Lévi-Strauss's formula was not an issue: anybody who had tested it at all knew that it was not universal. The really interesting thing was that in a significant number of cases it seemed to work. What had to be found out, then, was why it worked in some cases and (as was readily apparent, and established by De Heusch, myself, and others) did not work in other cases. The latest Wikmunkan findings, and the Walbiri scheme, contribute two additional negative instances, but that is all. They cannot in themselves, i.e. as unanalysed schemes from only two societies, constitute an effective criticism of Lévi-Strauss's intriguing idea.

There is only one way to do this, and that is by an intensive analysis of Lévi-Strauss's premises and his interpretation of the evidence, and then a comparative survey of as large a number of schemes as can be had. As McKnight courteously mentions, I have in fact undertaken such a study (referred to in Needham 1967: 51 n. 27), based so far on 115 schemes, and I shall publish it in the near future. For the present, in its relevance to the Wikmunkan case, I feel I have done enough work to declare that Lévi-Strauss's argument and his formula are very much mistaken. Nevertheless, the inquiry has yielded results of a marked theoretical interest. One finding, for example, is that a certain scheme of sentiments which Lévi-Strauss regards as 'basic' has in fact a clear statistical preponderance. There is certainly something in the idea, therefore, and a set of correlations well worth looking into.

Finally, on McKnight's re-examination of the Wikmunkan case, perhaps I may venture to extend my appreciation of his argument with a critical comment or two.

It may certainly be reckoned an encouragement of a sort that his reading of the ethnography so closely supports my own, and that his conclusions so neatly parallel those that I had previously published (cf. his n. 8), for it is a common defect in anthropological writing that altogether too much tends to be taken for granted. But it may occur to some readers that it would have made for a more economical direction of effort if McKnight had instead begun by merely registering his agreement with my analysis, so that he could then have advanced directly to the question of attitudes and other points to which his own field inquiries were especially relevant. The mission records, too, may not prove everything that they are reported to convey, but I myself would certainly have foregone the pleasure of the validation of my work in favour of some indication of the alliance patterns which should be discoverable in those facts which the missionaries have so patiently accumulated and with such generosity handed to a visiting anthropologist.

This brings me to a closing observation, but one that has a moral importance as well as analytical consequence. McKnight thinks that Ursula McConnel's interpretation of the Wikmunkan system 'seems to rest on a weak foundation, viz. what a non-Wik-mungkan told her to be the case among the Wik-mungkan'. 'Apparently,' he continues, 'she never verified what she was told at first hand' (pp. 146-7). Out of a sense of respect for the late Miss McConnel's ethnography, I think a note of firm dissent is in place here. McConnel spent the best part of two years in 1927-9 camped among the Wikmunkan, and she re-visited them in 1934. Her *Myths of the Mungkan* (1957) is special evidence of her closeness to the people, her attachment to them, and her assiduous investigations and recording. Nothing in her publications suggests that she was the sort of observer who would rely on one outsider for crucial information on a system of kinship and marriage and then neglect to check what she was told. As a matter of published fact, there are (as the reader deserves to be told) numerous indications in her articles that she made extensive and careful inquiries on these topics among the Wikmunkan themselves. Two particularly prominent instances are the long verbatim passages in which she records the marriage laws as given by a Kendall-Holyroyd man and by an Archer River man (1940: 438-9). What McKnight must have in mind is merely the solitary circumstance in which McConnel, after leaving the Wikmunkan, was told by a woman of a northern tribe (apparently Kandyu) about a 'cousin—mother' among the Kandyu. This woman, who mixed with the Wikmunkan and 'seemed to know all about the Wikmunkan

1

system', told McConnel about a similar institution among the Wikmunkan. This information brought home to McConnel the 'significance', as she tellingly writes, of the 'downward age spiral and of intermarriage between different generations in *older* and *younger* lines in the Wikmunkan genealogies' (1940: 444; her italics). In other words, although McConnel came to think that the 'cousin–mother' and her husband were the crux of the situation, she already conceived and had recorded the Wikmunkan system in terms of downward marriage, the age spiral, and older and younger lines; and these views were not based on the unverified statement of a single non-Wikmunkan woman. Moreover, McConnel herself later wrote explicitly that her final analysis was based on the statement of a Wikmunkan man about marriage with a *naityiyu*, and that she doubted whether the Wikmunkan age spiral worked in the same way as the Kandyu informant's assertions had led her to think (1950: 109). On such grounds I think McConnel's reputation is secure against McKnight's allegation. All of this has the analytical consequence, also, that the 'cousin–mother' feature has not the importance that he ascribes to it. (Further on this issue, incidentally, see Jackes [1969: 129], who examines the institution to interesting effect.) McConnel had a systematic conception of Wikmunkan society, composed of a number of inter-connected abstractions; the 'cousin–mother' report was consistent with this prior conception, and it occasioned McConnel's eventual representation of Wikmunkan society, but it alone is not the key to her analyses and it is certainly not her evidence in favour of that interpretation.

The positive outcome of a comparison of McKnight's conclusions and procedures with my own should not, however, lead to the assurance that a definite analysis of the Wikmunkan system, in these respects, has been achieved. On this score let an ethnographer have the last word. Donald Thomson, whose death while this volume was in preparation was a grievous loss to Australian ethnography and to the cause of the aborigines, once lent me an unpublished typescript on kinship and social organization in Cape York Peninsula (Thomson n.d.). It bore no particulars of composition and I do not know when it was written; it was sent to me. I think, in response to my analysis

Rodney Needham

(1963a) of a paper by Thomson on the avoidance of first-cousin marriage among the Wikmunkan, i.e. in 1963 or later. Those who share some of the interest that McKnight and I have found in the study of this fascinating society will doubtless wish to learn some of Thomson's conclusions.

'There are . . . no named moieties in the large and once powerful Wik Mongkan tribe of the Archer River, although these occur again in the Wik Alkan and Wik Ngätarra tribes, immediately to the south' (p.2); among the Wikmunkan 'there are no named moieties' (p. 81). 'Marriage in the Wik Mongkan is with a second cross-cousin, usually with the father's mother's sister's daughter's daughter' (p. 82). There are two ways of acquiring wives: (1) from the *pin kentj* who is the daughter of the *ngätjawaiyo mällän*, (2) by the exchange of sisters (p. 84). And most importantly (p. 85):

'There is no prohibition of marriage with the daughter of a man who stands in the relation of mother's *elder* brother, as stated in the preliminary account by Miss McConnel. . . . It happens frequently that a man applies the term *"mukk'amp* . . ."* to his actual father-in-law, *mukk'* being the term for mother's *elder* brother. And since marriage of sisters is permitted, it follows that only one of the men concerned can marry the daughter of a *kal'* and that the other must necessarily marry from a *mukk'*. Under these conditions however the single term of *moi'* is used reciprocally between these people before marriage. The prohibition therefore is not on marrying the daughter of the *mukka* (mother's elder brother, own or classificatory), but on marriage with a *first* cross-cousin.'

Very clearly, as Jackes writes, 'the subject of Wikmunkan society has not been exhausted' (1969: 128).

VI

AFFECT

The discussion above about affective attitudes stresses the topic of affect, which is touched upon in a number of the papers. Leach writes that anthropological studies of kinship termino-

lii

logies have usually been concerned with the problem of how discriminations in the terminology distinguish social roles and the allocation to social groups. 'Most such analyses assume that the emotional loading of the different terms is neutral. It seems to me that this neutrality is not only open to doubt but rather improbable' (p. 97).

Most likely it is true that anthropologists do neglect the emotional aspect of relationship terms, but it should be conceded that not all have done so. Malinowski was one famous exception, and Nadel was another. Radcliffe-Brown quite probably had his interest in collective sentiments (remarked by Leach) prompted by reading Malinowski on the family among the Australian aborigines, and also, in the wider context of norms and ritual, by the works of the *Année sociologique* school. Durkheim and Mauss, in their turn, were stimulated in this interest by the psychological researches of Ribot – and I suspect, incidentally, that it was the title of one of Ribot's books which gave Radcliffe-Brown his phrase (nowhere, alas, explicated or given substance by him) about 'the logic of sentiments' (1950:70). Latterly, of course, we have had the development of this line of inquiry by Lévi-Strauss, and an increasing number of reports by ethnographers such as Falkenberg, Turnbull, Faron, Rigby, Shack, and Rivière. So, whatever the general failings of the profession, there is certainly a respectable tradition of theoretical interest in socialized emotions. (Fortes, by the way, is pointedly derogatory about Lévi-Strauss's ingenious contributions to this topic, the only worth in which he attributes to the example of Radcliffe-Brown [Fortes 1969: 48]. He is wrong on this score, if only because Radcliffe-Brown's argument is so defective [cf. Needham 1962a: 32-40], and his own observations contain, as will be seen below, no argument which Lévi-Strauss would need to take seriously.) For students of human experience these sentiments are of ultimate importance, and the long and increasing attention to them on the part of sociologists and anthropologists shows a readiness to recognize this fact. So far, however, the interpretative position has not much improved since the seventeenth century (for that matter, I should say that it has rather deteriorated), and the question now, posed especially by this volume, is what social anthropologists in particular ought to do next.

Leach's suggestion, that relationship terms may be phonetically capable of signalling different degrees of affect, is a stimulating extension of the line of research to which I have alluded. It remains for linguistic critics, and further checking by ethnographers, to decide what substance there is in the hypothesis. I am afraid my own contribution to the conference discussion on this issue was not promising. I had to point out, namely, that the Penan words for 'father' and 'mother' were *tamen* and *tinen,* which scarcely made the required contrast; and that the term of address for the father (in the Eastern Penan dialect) was *mam,* whereas the terms for the mother were the glottalized or otherwise 'hard' sounds *e'e, i'i,* or *ide,* so that the phonetic contrast went contrary to the hypothesis. Having nothing positive to offer in this respect, therefore, I should like to revert for a moment to a simpler method and to cite Bateson's admirable monograph, *Naven* (1936), analysed below by Francis Korn. Readers of Bateson's work, one of the most intelligent, modest, and engrossing ever written by a social anthropologist, will recall that Bateson contends that 'Culture standardises the emotional reactions of individuals, and modifies the organization of their sentiments' (115), and that accordingly he devotes special attention to the manifestations of the 'emotional content' of Iatmul institutions. Dr Korn economically decided not to expand her analysis by an account of Iatmul collective sentiments, which had no patent or direct bearing on the formal and jural features that she was examining, but it may be found particularly relevant to the present theme of affect if I report here, as a footnote to her paper, my own reading of the evidence.

The attitude towards the mother's brother (*wau*) is warm, protective, and thoroughly positive, as is attested throughout the monograph. There is a 'close and friendly relationship between brother and sister' (Bateson 1932: 288). Between father and son there is 'restraint', each 'respects' the other, and both are 'rather quiet and stiff' when talking together (1936: 41-2). As for spouses, finally, the repeated impression, made specific when novices who are 'mercilessly bullied' are spoken of as the 'wives' of their tormentors (131), is that the affective attitude between husband and wife is negative. The Iatmul scheme of sentiments thus appears to be:

$$MB/ZS : B/Z :: F/S : H/W$$
$$+ \qquad + \qquad - \qquad -$$

This not only happens to fit Lévi-Strauss's formula, but in the light of my own comparative survey of the social organization of the emotions (the structure of sentiment, as it might have been called) the Iatmul pattern can even be recognized as, in the terms appropriate to that investigation, a standard patrilineal scheme. The formula thus makes a contribution to the discernment among the Iatmul of the standardization of the *ethos* on which Bateson lays such stress.

Fortes is very definite, however, in his assertion that such findings 'explain nothing' (1969: 48 n. 8), and all due weight should be accorded to the authority of this contention. The first difficulty, however, is that the force of the assertion depends on just what is meant by to 'explain'. In the common acceptation of this word I should find it very hard to concede that a social anthropologist had ever explained anything. I should prefer, rather, to follow Wittgenstein (continuing the quotation that Rivière [n. 9] adduces) in saying that we wrongly expect an explanation, 'whereas the solution of the difficulty is a description' (1967, sec. 314). Very appositely, one would have thought, for an anthropologist: 'What is needed for the explanation? One might say: a culture' (1967, sec. 164). In the Iatmul case, then, we might say that Lévi-Strauss's formula has helped us to isolate another instance of collective order in that culture, and in a sense this is explanation enough. Quite likely it is the only kind of explanation that social anthropology will ever be capable of. This would not satisfy Fortes, though. He declares that the real problem is to throw light on 'the structural mechanisms responsible for the differential assignment of authority and indulgence by status in the constellation' (48). He does not make clear what such mechanisms might be, or how precisely light might be thrown on them, and he does not show by example that any social anthropologist (himself, perhaps) has ever done as much in any sphere of investigation. Pending that mechanical revelation, it looks as though we shall have to make do with Wittgenstein.

In any case, Fortes's definition of 'the real problem' is doubly mistaken in its premises. He assumes, namely, that a 'differential assignment' of authority and indulgence underlies the configuration of sentiments, but this is a needless misapprehension. Firstly, Lévi-Strauss has demonstrated, originally in 1945, that there is no necessary connexion between rule of descent (including allocation of authority) and the conventional ascription of sentiments; a variety of schemes of sentiments can be associated with a given rule of descent, and the same scheme can be associated with different rules of descent. (For a simple representation of Lévi-Strauss's findings, see Needham [1962a: 34, Table 1].) Secondly, I have shown, from the Wikmunkan evidence in fact, that 'jural authority does not necessarily preclude or inhibit a warm and intimate relationship' and that conversely the 'lack of effective jural authority does not entail that the relationship with the person in question shall be intimate . . .' (1963b: 148). In other words, as has been known now for a fair number of years, (1) there is no simple connexion between authority and sentiment, and (2) there is no necessary disjunction of authority and indulgence such as would justify the assumption of 'differential assignment'. It is not therefore the case that, as Fortes firmly concludes, 'It is *only* by considering the problem in terms of the *locus of jural authority* that the structural principles underlying all forms of the so-called avunculate can be elicited' (1969: 48 n. 8; my italics).

A better approach, in that to begin with it makes a direct resort to social facts, is exemplified by Dr Beidelman's paper in this volume. It opens with the valuable and salutary observation that 'we know relatively little regarding the attitudes towards incest in other societies'. Nonetheless, most students of anthropology will recall Murdock's striking phrase about 'the sense of grisly horror with which most peoples invest the very idea of incest' (1949: 288). It does not emerge from his work on social structure how he knows that most peoples are moved by this horrid sentiment, though it has often enough been assumed by writers in the nineteenth century and since, and Beidelman clearly has a case when he says that in fact we really do not know much about what people actually feel. Yet in the sphere of sexual prohibitions we might well expect some affective element, considering the highly charged activity that they are concerned with, and as Beidelman well urges we ought to start finding out. His own approach is by way of Kaguru folklore, in the study of which he has become a noted resuscitator of an anthropological interest which was once exhibited by great figures such as Andrew Lang and van Gennep but has since succumbed to functionalist and other modernities of academic fashion. Since he makes his own argument by means of his folktales, perhaps I may offer a few comments on a more immediate way of discovering what people feel about the regulation of sexual conduct, namely by talking to them about it.

My own experience has not at all accorded with Murdock's generalization, and it may be worth while if I briefly report some of my observations in the hope of encouraging other ethnographers to publish what they have discovered among other peoples. For my part, I remember particularly clearly my surprise at the calm amusement with which the Penan of the interior of Borneo used to answer my textbook questions about incest. (Incidentally, in connexion with sec. VI of my 'Remarks', the Penan do not commonly employ a distinct word for 'incest': they speak rather of *sala' ngan do*, [to do] wrong with a woman. Certain Western Penan use the word *suvang*, which is obviously cognate with the Malay *sumbang*, but I cannot tell for sure whether that is its derivation; perhaps the fact that a *suvang* is a drinking-vessel indicates that it is.) The Penan laughed at the idea of sleeping with your mother, and asked with amusement whether that was the sort of thing the English did. The conduct itself was absolutely forbidden, all the same, and no one could recall that it had ever happened. Understandably, there was no fixed secular punishment: they expected that such an offender would be killed by God, and conjectured that he would also be expelled in the meantime from his group. The extreme retribution proposed expressed the rigour of the law, but there was never a hint of horror or of any special emotional response to the idea of incest. On the other hand, the Penan were vehemently outraged by the suggestion that a Penan might decline to share whatever food he had brought back to camp; and they were horrified by the idea that they might (as I told them other peoples did) abandon to their death the aged and very sick.

Among the Kodi, in western Sumba, I listed all the sexual relationships that were forbidden (a perfectly straightforward legal matter, no horror); and I then recorded, when it was seen that I had a curious interest in the topic, at least one case, with names and details, of the known infraction of every one of the prohibitions. Everybody knew about them, it seemed, and nobody cared. The Kodi attitude was much like that of Mrs Campbell, that she did not care what people did so long as they did not do it in the street and frighten the horses. It is true that I also recorded one famous case in which an aristocrat had been expelled from his village for an incestuous affair, which he refused to break off, with a classificatory sister in his own patrilineage; but then there were other factors at work (politics, property, the perpetual contentiousness of that class), and I was given to understand that the incest was merely a good excuse to get him out.

In central Malaya, next, Siwang men equably discussed with me the possibility of breaking their sexual prohibitions, and again with none of that 'peculiar intensity and emotional quality' that Murdock avers (288). Nevertheless, the hypothetical consequences of incest, inflicted by God, were dreadful: a breech-birth, followed by the death of the woman and her child, or else the crushing of the man beneath a falling tree (Needham 1956: 63).

Elsewhere in Malaya, finally, I did encounter expressions of rather shocked reserve, among educated Malays, when I broached the topic; but they have an exquisite sense of propriety and they could no more speak easily with a foreign visitor about sleeping with their mothers and sisters than could the bourgeois residents of North Oxford, the Seizième, or Beacon Hill.

Presumably there do exist people who are obsessed by the horror of incest, as perhaps (significantly) were the play-goers of fifth-century Athens, but clearly we cannot now assume anything on this score. Perhaps one reason that the horror has been so readily assumed is that usually the punishments for incest are indeed horrifying; the inference therefore presents itself that it is a sense of horror at the act which inspires such extreme and even atrocious forms of retribution. But this inference rests on psychological premises which are at least disputable in principle and happen to be contradicted by ethnographical evidence. Anyway, the matter is plain, as Beidelman helps us to realize, that even with the topic of incest and its emotional concomitants, where there has been so much agreement, we have to begin again and start looking and asking for what really happens.

More generally, Beidelman's paper has the useful effect, in its concluding observation on the function of 'tension and self-consciousness' in a critical sphere of Kaguru life, of drawing the attention of social anthropologists back to a more Durkheimian view of the organization and maintenance of social sentiments. In spite of the examples of Malinowski and Bateson, anthropological work on the emotions has been only sporadic, incidental, and slight. It is to be hoped that Beidelman's paper will be a further inducement to his colleagues to concentrate on what is of such radical and pervasive importance in human experience.

VII

PRESCRIPTIVE ALLIANCE

Throughout this monograph there recurs, in one way or another, a topic which has stirred considerable controversy, and which can even be said to occupy the forefront in current disquisitions on kinship and marriage, namely prescriptive alliance. My own remarks naturally make some mention of it, and Rivière expectably alludes to it in his consideration of marriage. The chief societies called upon by Leach are both prescriptive systems: the Sinhalese, symmetric; the Kachin, asymmetric. Korn's analysis deals explicitly with the question of preference and prescription; and Forge's commentary therefore also examines that categorical form of Iatmul marriage which in itself would constitute a prescriptive system. McKnight's contribution, on the Wikmunkan, is about a symmetric system; and Wilder's, on the Purum, is about an asymmetric system of prescriptive alliance. This central topic has, however, become obfuscated by tendentious animadversions on 'alliance theory' *vs* 'descent theory' and by contrived muddles, and its relevance to the study of kinship and the social order has encountered ill-informed and unreasoned suspicion. The impression has even been propagated that prescriptive alliance is no more than a modern polemical fabrication, having neither prior justification in scholarship nor empirical counterpart in social life. I think, therefore, that I ought to provide an historical perspective. This will have to be brief, but it should help to frame many of the issues taken up elsewhere in the volume.

From the middle of the nineteenth century, reports began to be published about the marriage arrangements of the Australian aborigines. In the seventies there was a burgeoning of ethnographical investigation in that continent, and the reports that ensued gave rise to an anthropological debate which not only has flourished ever since but has come to have a prime importance in the attempts to formulate theories of kinship and marriage. A characteristic feature of nearly all of the aboriginal societies under discussion was that men got their wives by exchange; this was called sister-exchange and, later, direct or restricted exchange, and has latterly been referred to as symmetric alliance. One means of regulating this type of exchange was the four-section system. This was discovered by 1846 and was thereafter found to be distributed over practically the entire continent; it became a prime focus of research and was generally taken as characterizing Australian aboriginal societies, the exceptions being regarded as special mutations (e.g. the Aranda and other eight-section systems) or as peripheral relics of such a system (e.g. Kurnai). The sections were unalterably related in such a way that if a man from section A married a woman from section B, then a man from section B married in return a woman from section A. This interrelation, by section-membership, was explicitly recognized by the aborigines, and was often expressed in terms of exchange; in some cases marriage was effected by an actual exchange between the groups, sometimes even the individual men, who were parties to the alliance. But the sections were not the only means of regulating such exchanges. There were also the relationship terminologies, closed systems of social classification which had in effect an unlimited range of application. These terminologies were so ordered that there was only one marriageable category; this absolute determination of the spouse expressed a positive rule of marriage which was phrased as an obligation on any man, whatever his section, to take as a wife a woman from that single category alone. This form of terminology, and the accompanying marriage prescription, were repeatedly confirmed to exist among tribes throughout the Australian continent, tribes which were often culturally very dissimilar and some of which had neither sections nor exogamous moieties. The observers chose different ways of describing this type of system, but anthropologists eventually agreed in seeing it as based on bilateral cross-cousin marriage. There were many incidental sources of complication, as was to be expected, but fundamentally what counted was the prescribed (obligatory, enjoined, pre-ordained) relationship of direct exchange between categories of persons.

Now the point I want to make especially is that although these symmetric systems of prescriptive alliance were thought to be singular and intriguing by observers and theorists – some of whom indeed found them admirably ingenious – they were not thought to be improbable or, in principle, perplexing. For that matter, at the end of the nineteenth century and in the early part of the twentieth they had become a topic of educated discourse among people who had little or no professional connexion with Australia or with a nascent anthropology. Just as a century earlier the dowagers and socialites of Königsberg had made earnest conversation about the *Kritik der reinen Vernunft,* so at this time the lawyers, merchants, and gentlemen of means who composed such gatherings as the London Ethnological Society, not to mention a man like Andrew Lang (who had a hyper-intelligent interest in practically anything of humane concern), were quite familiar with the marriage rules of the Kamilaroi and the arrangement of their sections. Similarly, the reports of near-identical classifications in the 'Dravidian' systems of South India, accompanied also by a positive rule of marriage with the bilateral cross-cousin, occasioned no dubiety about the feasibility or reality of prescriptive systems of this kind. Just as easy a reception was given to reports of the same type of society in Melanesia and South America. These symmetric systems were seen to be extremely simple, they were understood to be governed by an absolute determination of the category of spouse (though variously expressed by reference to sections, moieties, descent groups, categories, or

relationship), and as such they have become firmly and quite
uncontentiously established in anthropological literature and
in elementary academic instruction.

There was a parallel development, though at first far slower
and less well known, in the study of a contrasted form of prescriptive alliance. This had to do with a type of system defined
by asymmetry. In this type there was similarly a positive rule
of marriage, categorically formulated, but with the matrilateral
cross-cousin to the exclusion of the patrilateral. This unilateral
and absolute rule had the consequence that instead of direct
exchange between pairs of alliance groups or partners there was
a chain of non-reciprocal affinal alliances linking groups or
persons in what came to be denoted variously as 'circulating
connubium', 'unilateral connubium', 'marriage in a circle', 'tri-
clan system', 'simple structure of generalized exchange',
'indirect exchange', and 'asymmetric prescriptive alliance'.
(Korn's analysis of the Iatmul system shows that the matrilateral cross-cousin type of prescriptive system is not the only
'asymmetric' form, but in the present context this unqualified
designation will serve.) The system was discovered in widely
separated parts of mainland and island Asia, and its main
features were established practically contemporaneously in the
last two decades of the nineteenth century.

In 1885-7 Neumann capped a number of indications, dating
back to the eighteenth century and even before, that the Batak
of Sumatra practised asymmetric alliance (see, e.g., Neumann
1886), and further substantiation followed in subsequent
ethnographies. In 1887 MacGregor reported a similar system,
in which marriage with a classificatory 'mother's brother's
daughter' was obligatory, among the Kachin of upper Burma;
in 1889 Needham contributed decisively to the record of Kachin
relationship terms; and in 1904 Wehrli brought together these
and other sources, dating back to 1849, to compose a solidary
and systematic account of matrilateral 'connubium' in this
society. In particular, Wehrli showed that there was a systematic
correspondence among (*a*) the unilateral alliances contracted
between patrilineal descent groups, (*b*) the obligatory rule of
MBD marriage, complemented by a prohibition on the FZD,
and (*c*) certain equivalences in the terminology, compounding
cognatic and affinal specifications, such as MB = WF and

Introduction

ZS = DH (Wehrli 1904: 26-8, 32). In 1892 Sternberg discovered a structurally identical system among the Gilyak of Sakhalin, in eastern Siberia. His report, which was read to an anthropological meeting and thereafter relayed in the Moscow press, has indeed a special place in the history of European thought, for it was at once seized on by Engels, who in the same year published a German translation of this 'recently discovered case of group marriage' (Engels 1892). The ethnographical report appeared in a learned periodical in 1904 (Sternberg 1904) and was followed by a series of very extensive further accounts of Gilyak society. These were summarized in 1914 by Czaplicka, who clearly set out the cyclic feature of the system, alliances being contracted unilaterally in the closed sequence $A \rightarrow B \rightarrow C \rightarrow (A)$ (Czaplicka 1914: 99).

In 1925 Hodson published a formulary characterization of the Kachin scheme, in order to establish its absolute and unilateral character. In isolating this type of system, he drew a distinction between an 'absolute insistence' on marriage with the classificatory MBD, such as the Kachin exemplified, and a 'preference' for such a marriage. There was a scale from 'permission and preference' to an 'absolute prescription' such as produced the Kachin system. This prescription, he maintained, constituted 'a distinct mode of social structure' which had to be distinguished from 'those cases of symmetrical structure which depend on or are derived from a dual structure – such as the Australian groups. . . .' Citing Czaplicka, he pointed out that a Kachin-type scheme of marriage arrangements existed also among the Gilyak (Hodson 1925: 165, 167, 168, 174). In 1933 a consolidated edition of Sternberg's findings on the Gilyak was published in Khabarovsk. In the same year Fortune published a radically important theoretical paper, of a formal kind, in which he demonstrated, among other points, the structural contrast between a system based on matrilateral cross-cousin marriage and a system based on marriage with the patrilateral cross-cousin (1933); in the former there was a regular transmission of women in one direction between lines, whereas in the (hypothetical) patrilateral system there was a constant alternation of direction.

In the Indonesian field, meanwhile, matters were developing very quickly. In 1932 Ypes, in a study of land law, published a long and very detailed account of the lineage system of the Toba and Dairi Batak, together with valuable incidental information on affinal relations (Ypes 1932); and a year later Vergouwen brought out a study of social organization and customary law among the Toba Batak (1933) which was a milestone in the progressive understanding of asymmetric alliance (cf. Needham 1966b). These two works together put a comprehensive construction upon, and in part superseded, the huge prior literature on Batak society. They also stimulated, moreover, a most remarkable concurrence of academic effort, under the leadership of the late J. P. B. de Josselin de Jong, in the synthetic and theoretical examination of asymmetric prescriptive alliance. In 1935, all in the same year, there appeared in the Netherlands a set of works which definitively established the distinctive features of asymmetric systems in Indonesia, their distribution, variations, and symbolic aspects. These publications were in the main the work of Leiden anthropologists: De Josselin de Jong (1935), van Ossenbruggen (1935), and van Wouden (1935). They were paralleled by a survey of affinity in Indonesia made by Fischer of Utrecht (1935), and the theoretical impetus carried Held, another Leiden scholar, further afield in his analysis of the social organization underlying the *Mahābhārata* (1935).

It might well have been thought, then, that a most respectable anthropological tradition had been founded. Asymmetric prescriptive alliance had been isolated, in a structural contrast with symmetric alliance on the one hand and with the postulated patrilateral form of alliance on the other; there were good ethnographical accounts of asymmetric systems in Siberia, Burma, and Indonesia; the characteristic institutions of this type of society had been established; and there was a body of theoretical literature on the type.

Yet this substantial and accelerating progress was not to be sustained. First there was the second world war, which of course put out of the question the study of asymmetric prescriptive systems in precisely those places where they had been most thoroughly attested (though Leach, with his Kachin irregulars, was arduously implicated in one); but it was not the war, and the disruption of scholarship, that was essentially responsible for the checks and disturbances that future work on the subject was to suffer. It was, ironically, the publication of a long theoretical work on both symmetric and asymmetric systems: Lévi-Strauss's *Les Structures élémentaires de la parenté* (1949).

I do not want to say much about it, for it is not only a complex book but obscure and confusing as well, and it has occasioned so much controversy that no brief observations here could be decisive. (As far as the present collection is concerned, Korn's paper makes precisely the kind of scholarly and analytical case that I myself think is essential for an estimation of the value of Lévi-Strauss's work.) The chief points that I wish to make are historical matters of patent fact which are not open to dispute. Firstly, Lévi-Strauss introduced the topic of asymmetric alliance to a far wider body of scholars than had known of it before. Most of the works by the Dutch ethnographers and scholars which I have cited above were printed in Dutch, and this had limited the circulation of their findings; Sternberg's books were mostly in Russian; and Leach had yet to collate in English the numerous scattered ethnographical reports on upper Burma (Leach 1954). Simply by writing in French, therefore, Lévi-Strauss gave asymmetric alliance a new prominence. This medium in turn, however, still restricted the exact dissemination of his views among anthropologists; Lévi-Strauss has complained that some critics of his book have not fully understood him because of their lack of familiarity with the French language (1969: xxviii), and it is an open professional secret that one prominent critic at least is not able to read French. Nevertheless, asymmetric alliance was impressively resuscitated, and in an explicitly theoretical context of wide generality and illustrious ancestry. But my second factual point much reduces the significance of this turn of events. Lévi-Strauss, it turned out, had not only ignored (or, at any rate, not cited) Fortune's crucial paper of 1933 on his chosen topic, and most specifically the alternating character of the patrilateral construct, but he had altogether failed to exploit the vast ethnographical resources on alliance systems in Sumatra and eastern Indonesia, and he had failed to consult the works by the Dutch scholars (except Held, who had written in English) such as van Wouden on the theory of 'circulating connubium'. He did, however, present an account of the Gilyak system; this he knew of from an English translation (to which he was directed, reportedly, by Roman Jakobson) which had been deposited in New York. Sternberg's researches were thus rescued, to such degree, from oblivion, and the existence of asymmetric alliance in Siberia was again (i.e. after Czaplicka) reported in a European language. Lévi-Strauss also used some of the sources on the Kachin, and presented an integral interpretation of them; in this case he did turn to an authority who had already carried out such a work of synthesis, namely to Wehrli (1904), and also to Gilhodes, who had published extensively on Kachin kinship and marriage, including a detailed account of the relationship terminology and its principles (1913). This resuscitation also had its value. A more novel enterprise, though, and one of direct relevance to current academic debate and to Wilder's paper in this volume, was the chapter in which he skimmed over the literature on some of the Kuki-Chin tribes of the Indo-Burma border in connexion with the 'simple formula of generalized exchange' which they exemplified (1949, ch. XVII). One of these societies, mentioned briefly in passing (333; 1969: 273), was the Purum.

VIII

THE PURUM CASE

The Purum, as Wilder says, are now part of the established anthropological order. They thus join such famous cases as the Dieri in the nineteenth century and the Murngin in this. In order to see how they have arrived at this position, and also to grasp more firmly the burden and the relevance of Wilder's paper on Purum descent groups, it will be helpful to sketch in the background. Though much compressed, this account will still have to be rather long, but the facts and events in question need to be responsibly set out if the reader is to be able to form a confident judgement. The story will be found instructive, also, in respects having nothing to do directly with the Indo-Burma border or prescriptive alliance.

From this point, I am afraid, my own name becomes rather prominent, but I had in fact something to do with the subsequent state of theoretical affairs, and my initial concern is after all to provide an historical view. Perhaps I may begin by saying,

therefore, that in 1950 I had worked at the University of
Leiden under Professor J. P. B. de Josselin de Jong, who had
introduced me to van Wouden's book (see English ed., 1967: xi),
and that in 1955 I made an ethnographical reconnaissance in
Mamboru, on the island of Sumba in eastern Indonesia, where
asymmetric prescriptive alliance is practised. In 1956, while
searching for further comparative leads to the understanding
of what I had found on Sumba, I wrote an analysis of the Purum
ethnography. My only personal connexion with the Purum was
that as an infantryman I had marched through their country
in the war (to the south-west, as it gives me pleasure to think,
of Edmund Leach and his Kachin), so that I relied entirely on
the published sources. These had been available to Lévi-Strauss
also, though he had not in fact taken advantage of them, and
they have since remained accessible in immutable print to a
series of later commentators and critics. In the years since the
publication of that analysis (Needham 1958) the Purum system
has been the subject of many independent scrutinies and points
of debate, but it would not be easy to claim that the repeated
attentions to this society have displayed a consistently encouraging level of professional competence or dispassionate
analytical concern.

The beginning of the professional stir about the Purum was
my monograph *Structure and Sentiment* (1962a). This was
about 'the possibility of explaining social institutions by reference to individual sentiments' (page 1, lines 1 and 2). In it I
took as my test case Homans and Schneider's attempted
refutation of Lévi-Strauss's *Les Structures élémentaires de la
parenté*. My intention in doing so was 'to contrast two radically
different means of understanding social life' (2). Fortes, dis-
regarding what the author himself thus declared to be the
purpose of the book, permits himself to characterize *Structure
and Sentiment* – in a phrase in which judiciousness of expression
matches scholarly objectivity – as 'a furious attack on Homans
and Schneider for their temerity in disputing Lévi-Strauss's
theory of kinship and marriage' (1969: 83). But the true issue
was that unilateral cross-cousin marriage provided a crucial
test of theory (Homans & Schneider 1955: 3) and that it was
possible in this confrontation of theories to show, for once, that
one view was essentially right and the other demonstrably

lxvii

wrong (Needham 1962a: vii). In demonstrating accordingly that Homans and Schneider had published a bad argument, I took as an empirical instance a matrilateral system that was of the type Lévi-Strauss dealt with but which he himself had not analysed, namely the Purum. The analysis I presented (1962a, ch. 4) was an abbreviated version, explicitly leaving out of account certain discrepancies and ethnographic minutiae, of the 1958 paper. The Purum system, I contended, could not be understood or explained by Homans and Schneider's argument, but it could be systematically comprehended by means of certain notions which had been fashioned by the *Année sociologique* school and applied to the study of prescriptive alliance by Lévi-Strauss. That was all. But very soon, in this special context, my interpretation of Purum society attracted vigorous assessments such as otherwise it might well never have received. I shall not mention every reference, but only those which have manufactured the present situation and which bring out the lessons that I shall argue can be extracted from the example of the Purum case.

White, in a technical treatise on the mathematical analysis of kinship, devoted fifteen pages to the Purum (1963: 130-45) and concluded that 'neither the recorded marriages nor the kinship terminology' were consistent with a system of matrilateral prescriptive marriage (145) — as defined, that is, by his own axioms (34-5). But, as Leach pointed out, the first two axioms alone were inconsistent with known types of social organization which I called prescriptive (Leach 1964), and so in fact was the third. Certainly the axiomatic did not correspond with the facts of Purum social life (cf. Korn and Needham 1970: 395-6). White concluded his monograph, all the same, with the statement that prescriptive marriage was an 'ideal type': 'One should not ask whether a tribe has a prescriptive as opposed to a preferential marriage system, but rather to what extent the tribe conforms to one or to some mixture of prescribed marriage systems . . .' (148). To which Leach responded: 'The Sinhalese and the Kachins, to take two examples, both have a prescriptive marriage system in the sense employed by Dr Needham. The prescriptive marriage is not merely "ideal type" but actual' (1964). A factor of some conceivable relevance, also, was that White's anthropological adviser, whose comments he said had much influenced his thinking, had been Schneider (White 1963, Preface).

The theoretical turbulence really set in with Ackerman's paper on the Purum case in the following year (1964). By a statistical analysis he arrived at the conclusion that 'No tendency to avoid the direct exchange of women exists in the distribution of actual marriages' and that therefore 'Purum marriage choices are not ordered by a matrilateral connubium' (64). Now I had in fact selected the Purum as an illustration in *Structure and Sentiment*, rather than the Batak or the Sumbanese, precisely because the published numerical data made this society 'the most useful for testing Homans and Schneider's argument' (1962a: 74), so if Ackerman's statistical conclusions were right I had signally failed to supply empirical evidence for my case. Moreover, he argued that I had got the terminology wrong as well, and that in 'the sibling and cousin terminology' there was no systematic characterization of women as 'prohibited woman' and 'potential wife'. Since I recognized a prescriptive system by its relationship terminology, this criticism too was extremely serious in its implications for my argument as a whole. I was a little taken by the reported fact that Ackerman was a pupil of Homans, and was at the time employed as his assistant, but this intriguing circumstance did nothing to obviate the apparent force of his demolition of that example by which, as I had claimed, I had refuted Homans and Schneider's theory about the causal effect of individual sentiment on the formation of institutions.

Naturally, I replied with a detailed rejoinder (1964a), but I was to discover that quite independently five other anthropologists, four Americans and one German, had also written to protest that Ackerman had got things quite wrong. They had been provoked to do so, not because they were particularly interested in the Purum or in the prescriptive alliance, but because they objected to Ackerman's misuse of statistics. Their conclusions were very definite indeed, and because of what was later to be published about the Purum case, and because of their present relevance also to Wilder's paper, I want to quote some of them in detail. Lest this seem wearisome, let me say that it is essential to do so if anything is to be made of the

Purum case, and if one is to learn from this anything of more general importance about the quality of anthropological works on the subject of kinship and marriage.

Cowgill: 'The data given by Ackerman, taken at face value, do not mean what he says they mean. Specifically, it is easy to show that they overwhelmingly support two of Needham's assertions which Ackerman rejects' (1964: 1358). 'Ackerman has failed to find evidence for a tendency to avoid direct exchange of women in Purum society because he has used a method which is terribly insensitive on just this point' (1360). 'In terms of the same data used by Ackerman, I find that the notion that the Purum *tend* to avoid direct exchange of women is very strongly supported indeed' (1363). 'The data used by Ackerman in fact show overwhelming evidence both that the Purums do tend to avoid direct exchange of women between lineages and that they do tend to follow their marriage norms in practice. . . . Needham is right on both these points and Ackerman is wrong' (1364).

Geoghegan and Kay: 'The particular statistical tests that Ackerman employs seem to us ill-adapted to the hypothesis he wishes to verify. In fact, Ackerman's data support the hypothesis he rejects rather than the one he advances'; 'contrary to Ackerman's conclusions, there is evidence in his own data both for the avoidance of direct exchange and for the existence of asymmetric alliance'; 'the data confirm Needham's claim for asymmetric alliance and require the rejection of Ackerman's assertion to the contrary' (1964: 1351). 'Ackerman actually counts alliances rather than marriages, and thus eliminates from consideration the asymmetry in the distribution of actual marriages' (1353). 'Even if we count alliances rather than marriages . . . the data confirm the asymmetry hypothesis' (1354). 'If we look at the distribution of marriages we see the same [asymmetric] effect even more dramatically' (1355); 'the actual distribution of marriages conforms to what we should reasonably expect from a system of asymmetric alliance' (1356). 'The data Ackerman presents, when analyzed appropriately, support Needham's conclusions rather than Ackerman's' (1356).

Introduction

Müller: 'Ackerman's procedure is in more than one way unfit for the purpose and on many points his statistics are incorrect' (1964: 1371). 'Instead of the marriages, he counts the cells of his matrix' (1373). 'If we understand the term MBD in Needham's sense, we observe a clear statistical significant preference of unilateral CC [cross-cousin]-marriage in the behavior of the Purum' (1374). 'The result is . . . striking evidence of the unilateral form of the Purum CC marriage'; 'his [Ackerman's] results corroborate Needham's theory . . .' (1375). 'Ackerman's treatment of kinship-terminology is very peculiar'and introduces differences from the ethnographic source which are 'unintelligible' (1375-6).

Wilder: 'The evidence Ackerman produces [about the incongruence of the terminology with asymmetric alliance] is a series of misrepresentations of Purum categories' (1964: 1366). 'In numerous . . . equations the terminology supports most convincingly the hypothesis of matrilateral prescription' (1367). 'There are many cycles relating Purum descent groups and Purum themselves have a theory of cycles of exchange. Nothing in Ackerman's "tests" explains this correspondence. In fact, explanation is, for all intents and purposes, ruled out by the way Ackerman treats the "actual marriages" of the Purum' (1368). 'Ackerman assumes that the named lineages are fixed alliance groups, whereas Needham and Leach have both shown that in practice alliance groups are constantly forming through lineage segmentation and "deviant" marriages' (1369). 'Ackerman is remarkably ignorant of how a society such as the Purum really works'; his argument is 'unconvincing . . . misleading, and even wrong, because its procedures and conclusions are based on isolated, uncharacteristic or misinterpreted facts' (1370).

After this barrage of precise criticism Ackerman was obliged to make some response, but in more than half of the space of his rejoinder (1965) he proffered observations in which, as he conceded, 'I have ignored my critics' (87). When he did turn to them, briefly, he bypassed their numerous and specific arguments and concentrated instead on the question of prescription and preference. This he did by asserting what he had previously

denied. Whereas he had clearly written that there was *no*
tendency to 'avoid direct exchange', he now wrote that everyone was agreed that 'there is a marked asymmetry revealed in
Purum marrying activity'. Whereas he had positively declared
that 'Purum marriages are not ordered by a matrilateral
connubium', he now wrote that the 'matrilaterality of the
Purum norm has never . . . been questioned by any analyst'
(87) – as though the marked matrilateral asymmetry in the
actual marriages had nothing to do with the explicitly matrilateral norm. He did not explain in what sense this congruence
of norm and practice failed to qualify as matrilateral connubium, nor did he seem to grasp the contradictions between these
conclusions and his previous assertions. Instead, he wrote that
'Geoghegan, Kay, Cowgill and Müller have not shown that the
norm is prescriptive, have not shown that the norm is not
preferential; they have demonstrated only that the norm is
asymmetric and that the Purums adhere to it' (87). This remarkable reversal of opinion thus conceded in effect, though the
expression was clearly designed not to say as much, precisely
what I had said existed in Purum society, viz. a matrilateral
norm and a marked asymmetric contraction of affinal alliances.
In response to myself Ackerman confined his rejoinder to a few
lines on two relationship terms. To the many technical objections, particularly those made by expert critics about his use of
statistics, he returned no defence.

The exchanges then drew to a close with a final set of weary
comments of my own (1966b). These were intended to show,
point by point and with precise published ethnographical support in each instance, that Ackerman had misread the ethnography and had got certain important facts wrong, in a way
which proved that he could not have understood the principles
of Purum social classification. On the question of figures, although I had left the statistical issues to colleagues who were far
better fitted than I to deal with them, I did stress the telling
fact – which quite contradicted Ackerman's unrevoked assertion that there was no statistical tendency to avoid direct
exchange of women – that 92·3 per cent of Purum marriages
had been contracted asymmetrically (1966b: 175). I stress this
point here also because of what was to follow when the Purum
case was taken up in a far wider academic context.

Introduction

Now I hope no anthropological reader will have found this a tedious relation, for to me it seems the very stuff of anthropological debate: the reasoned and public assessment, in a theoretical frame, of variant interpretations of ethnographical reports. In these respects, the Purum case is what social anthropology as a discipline is all about. The point then at issue, it seems to me, is this. Wilder opens his paper on Purum descent groups by writing that the Purum are 'one of the most thoroughly analyzed peoples in the literature', and I am sure he is right. More than this, the exceptional concentration of professional attention decisively proved the correctness of my analysis of Purum society. Even though my early (1958) paper was an apprentice effort, and my first attempt at a 'total structural analysis' (1964a: 1377), my conclusions about the alliance system were upheld, in quite unqualified terms, in a set of independent and penetrating scrutinies by colleagues who were by no means dogmatically or polemically committed to my views on prescriptive alliance. I am sure, indeed, that any social anthropologist would be delighted to see his work so repeatedly, expertly, and convincingly validated. More generally, also, the debate had the effect of establishing yet another system of asymmetric prescriptive alliance, thus extending the catalogue of known instances from Burma, Siberia, and Indonesia, and further justifying the discrimination of a distinct mode of social classification and marital organization

But this was not the way matters were seen by other commentators, anthropologists who had not themselves collaborated in the Purum debate or otherwise done any of the work that was essential to the formation of a practised judgement. The first such was Schneider, writing in a paper published in *ASA 1* and since circulated in the academic world with all of the outward authority that such a medium should procure for it. This disquisition, 'Some Muddles in the Models', appeared in 1965, and thus before the conclusion to the Purum debate but, *nota bene*, after the conjoined criticism that I have just reported. 'A closer look at the Purum', Schneider declared, 'makes it appear to fit only very loosely into Needham's type' (1965: 69). He did not actually direct any such look at the evidence, or report in detail what anybody else had reliably determined about the degree of fit in question. In particular, he notably failed to make any mention, even in a footnote added in proof, of the striking justifications registered by Cowgill and the others in 1964. Instead, he cited White (1963), whose investigation he himself had guided, and an unpublished master's thesis by a student in his department. He did not say what was the argument of this latter authority. He did not consider, either, that the type of society I had in mind was in fact derived from the empirical study of forms of social life. In the case of the Purum, my own concern had been simply to put the clearest and most comprehensive abstract construction on the reported social phenomena, and the analysis contains no grounds for asserting that a factitious order has been 'imposed', as Schneider alleged, on the evidence. As for the notion of asymmetric prescriptive alliance being my own 'type', as he maintained, I can only say that I should be proud to have made such an interesting discovery – but, as I have shown in sec. VII, I had been forestalled over seventy years before by a number of gifted ethnographers and scholars. No one who was familiar with that long tradition could have ascribed the construct to my invention in 1958; and, if I may say so, no one who was ignorant of it could be in a position to express any respectable judgement of the validity of the type. Nevertheless, after this glancing allusion to the Purum, Schneider returned more expressly to this case, at the very end of his paper, with a forthright castigation of 'Needham's *gross manipulations* of the Purum data . . .' (79; italics added). Since he somehow overlooked the necessity to document this hard and injurious charge against the scholarship of a colleague, I published a short and moderate response (1966b) in an attempt to discover where the gravamen lay. I reported (as I should like to put on record here) that Tarak Chandra Das, the ethnographer of the Purum, had been familiar with my work, that we had corresponded about the Purum over a period of five years, and that we had met; and that 'in no way did he dissent from the results of my analysis or protest at my handling of his evidence' (175). It is a matter of public record that he never published any indication of disagreement or disavowal. (As a matter of fact, I think I may add that in person and in writing he never expressed anything but gratification at the attention I had paid to his ethnography, together with modest regret that he was unable to answer certain questions, e.g. about the equation MBD = yZ, that I put to him.) It was hard, therefore, to see the grounds for a charge of 'gross manipulations' when the ethnographer himself made no complaint. I drew to Schneider's notice, anyway, that four independent analyses, by Cowgill *et al.*, had confirmed my interpretation, and pointed out that he himself had provided no contrary argument in the eight years in which he could have tried to do so. Now, four years later, I can only remark that he has had more than twelve years in which to undertake and to publish a more correct analysis of Purum society than my own, and to expose in factual detail the extent and consequences of my 'gross manipulations' of the Purum data. That gross charge continues to circulate, but Schneider has still not made an argument. On this score I shall only say that there is more to scholarly responsibility than a discourteous phrase.

If this were only an isolated case of academic dereliction it would be deplorable enough, but it would not in itself frame a professional lesson (as I have intended) bearing on the question of scholarship in social anthropology, nor would it justify the space devoted here to the Purum case. But it is not isolated, and worse, if possible, was to come. In a textbook on anthropological theory, published in 1968, Harris brought up the Purum case again in connexion with the vindication of Lévi-Strauss. 'But no reasonably alert graduate student', he surmised, 'could avoid the tidal wave of disbelief which Needham's presentation of Purum ethnography set in motion' (1968: 507). Under the bold heading, 'Purum do not abide by their Matrilateral Prescription', Harris then referred to the examination of the facts; but the 'tidal wave of disbelief' turned out to be no more than Ackerman's controverted criticisms of 1964. The alert student was nevertheless assured that Ackerman had isolated a proportion of 30 per cent of Purum affinal relationships *violating the fundamental condition of general exchange* (Harris's italics), that 48 per cent of marriages were with women outside the prescribed category, and that there was 'no tendency to avoid the direct exchange of women'. The theoretical burden of this account was that prescription was thereby shown statistically to be 'a degree of preference rather than a sharply different structural matter' and that Lévi-Strauss's basic distinction between restricted and generalized exchange was thus a 'logical exercise' (508-9). The truly remarkable feature of all this was that Harris, who advanced no analysis or argument of his own, neglected entirely to take into account the detailed and unrebutted demonstrations, by myself and a number of others, that the figures in question were quite mistaken and the conclusions therefore erroneous. The student was told nothing at all about the set of rejoinders which, in the same volume of the *American Anthropologist* as Ackerman's paper, had conclusively proved the falsity of the very points on which Harris insisted. All the same, his version of the issue remains in print and has even entered the 'history' of the subject.

Another textbook, of a technical kind this time, perpetuated the same travesty of the printed record, but in an even more instructive manner. Buchler and Selby, namely, were concerned to expose my 'positivistic error' in thinking that asymmetric systems of prescriptive alliance really existed. What I had actually managed to demonstrate was, they contended, the precise opposite of my thesis 'that . . . matrilateral systems of alliance systems [sic] exist *in puris naturalibus* in the world (they don't) . . .' (1968: 124). The distinction between prescription and preference was a 'conceptual misapprehension' upon which had foundered analysis after analysis (presumably my own) of 'asymmetric alliance' (125), and I was quite wrong therefore in looking for 'an empirical replica' (126). 'It seems clear that prescriptive marriage cannot exist empirically. . . . Ethnographic evidence and computer simulations are against it, and not a single case appears to be extant' (126). It was only because I 'insisted on ignoring the weight of the evidence', ethnographical, statistical, and mathematical (125), that I persisted in my erroneous positivism. These contentions remained as mere assertions except in the section headed 'The Ethnographer's Objection' (125-7). The 'ethnographer' turned out to be Schneider, of all people, and his objection was presented in the following stark passage (125):

'As Schneider (1965) has pointed out so clearly, Needham has tortured the ethnography repeatedly to make the facts fit his model of asymmetrical systems.'

Introduction

The kind of error 'perpetrated by Needham', Buchler and
Selby continued, 'can be examined by the examination of
specific cases and attempting to demonstrate the physical
reality of the movement of women . . .' (126). This was indeed
most encouraging, for at least it proposed a recourse to empirical
test. The specific case that they chose for this crucial test was
the Purum system, and they conscientiously listed most of the
relevant literature: Ackerman 1964, 1966; Cowgill 1964;
Geoghegan and Kay 1964; Müller 1934; Needham 1966b (but
not, unfortunately, the major rejoinder of 1964); Wilder 1964.
Their reading of these sources, however, could not possibly
have been foreseen by anyone who was acquainted with what
these really said: 'given the ethnographic facts and demographic parameters,' Buchler and Selby reported, *it seems
clear that the Purum cannot and do not conform to Needham's
model*' (126: my astounded italics). The present reader will now
appreciate to the full why it was necessary to quote the critical
authorities in question in that much detail as I said was advisable. I should like to suggest that anyone who cares for exact
argument, if not much about the Purum or prescriptive alliance,
should read those quotations again and compare them with
Buchler and Selby's conclusion.

I am confident that by this point many readers will be dis-
mayed, horrified, or otherwise perturbed by this increasingly
disreputable course of events. But I am afraid it is not quite
the end. Just before the Bristol conference there appeared yet
another work in the same vein. Fortes, in a general work on
'kinship', wishes to make the point that 'the "models" put
forward by alliance theorists are apt to be so formal and abstract
that it is frequently impossible to connect them unequivocally
with the data they purport to represent' (1969: 82). The example he selects in order to illustrate this impossibility is the
Purum system, and his justification is my statement that
whereas a simple model of asymmetric alliance is constituted
by a single cycle, the factual situation is, 'as we should expect',
very much more complex (Needham 1962a: 81). Fortes comments merely that 'Subsidiary qualifications therefore become
necessary to enable us to read back from the model to reality'
(82). Well, of course. Any such model is an abstraction, i.e. it
leaves things out, so that rules of implementation have to be

lxxvii

provided in order to show its correspondence with the phenomena. (This is called synthesis.) But Fortes does not in any case
demonstrate wherein it is 'impossible' to connect the formal and
abstract nature of the asymmetric model with the Purum data.
Instead, he adds a footnote in which he cites Ackerman as
authority that 'Needham's "model" is irreconcilably at variance
with the actuality of Purum marriage' (82 n. 35), and then
continues: 'The same numerical data are claimed by others,
using different statistical methods, to support Needham's
thesis (cf. the discussion of Ackerman's article)'. He gives a
precise reference to Ackerman's paper and duly includes it in
his bibliography; but he does not say who the 'others' are and
does not specify their publications. He thus succeeds in leaving
the unwary reader with the decided impression that Ackerman
is right, and that all there is to the contrary interpretations is
a choice of statistical methods, not (as is the truth) that different
methods have all equally and concordantly (cf. Cowgill 1964:
1364 n. 1) proved Ackerman's analysis to be fallacious. Fortes
does not venture to express any judgement of his own, but he
puts a peculiar slant on the issue with his concluding observation: 'Needham's own defense of his position in this discussion
points the moral. It is that ethnographic and numerical data
as defective as those on which his Purum "model" is based
can be manipulated to satisfy quite contradictory "models" of
the formal and hypothetical type that is the stock-in-trade of
"alliance" theorists.' Once again, he does not supply any reference or list in his bibliography any publication where I might
have offered such a defence. In fact, and as I now formally
assert, I have nowhere said that 'the data . . . can be manipulated to satisfy quite contradictory "models" ' of the Purum
system, or anything of the kind. Nor should I ever have done
so, for it is not correct – and no one who had paid responsible
attention to the evidence could have thought it was. Fortes
nonetheless purveys this crooked view of the Purum case under
the guise of a scholarly assessment, and purportedly as an
empirical test of 'the theoretical concepts and method of
analysis characteristic of "alliance" theory'. One sees better
thereafter what led Dumont once to refer to Fortes's 'magis-
terial polemical skill' (Dumont 1966: 77 n. 1), but it would be
going too far to extend such a courtesy here.

Introduction

As far as the Purum are concerned, the situation rests in this rather mangled state. I can only hope that the dismaying account that I have had to render may tend to restore to the issue a care for exactitude and a sense even of probity such as used to characterize work on prescriptive alliance before this regrettable modern decline. There are, moreover, certain lessons that I should like to bring out. I have presented a straightforward historical narrative of the inception and development of a certain branch of study in social anthropology, that of prescriptive alliance, and I have done so simply by means of a chronological series of factual statements and quotations which can easily be checked (sec. VII). The story, I think, speaks for itself. What it says, though, with particular regard to the later discussions of the Purum case, is not very inspiring for a professional anthropologist today. The social systems in question were discovered and recorded in the last century by men who were not for the most part anthropologists, and the first theoretical benefits were secured, chiefly by Dutch scholars, decades ago; but the state of knowledge rapidly became distorted and dissipated when prescriptive alliance was made a topic of more general debate in social anthropology. The ignorance and misrepresentation which have been evident in recent statements about the Purum case, with their insidious talk about manipulations and their patent fabrications, have presented a sorry and deteriorating exhibition from a subject that is supposed to be a learned discipline. Still, this is what has happened, and I suppose it is as well that it should be known. If anyone wants to learn something of what can really go on in social anthropology, in the supposedly crucial area of kinship and marriage, the topic of prescriptive alliance and the latter concentration on the Purum system can provide a luridly illustrated primer.

There is a curiosity about it, too, which I have hinted at early in this section and which is itself matter for anthropological attention. It is strange, namely, to compare the easy acceptance of prescriptive systems fifty and more years ago with the opposition that is nowadays provoked, and even in prominent academics, by the very suggestion of them. Fison, Howitt, Ridley, Mathews, Thomas, and many others perfectly easily accepted the presence of symmetric instances in Australia; and Sternberg, Gilhodes, Wehrli, Neumann, Wilken, Vergouwen and the rest (including, incidentally, Granet on China) accepted just as calmly that asymmetric systems existed in Asia. But in recent years there has grown up a quite vehement opposition to their reality. I am not saying that the critics are wrong to be reasonably sceptical, but it seems to me that sometimes (as instanced above) they very much overdo it. 'Doubt must go no further than vigilance; otherwise it can become dangerous' (Lichtenberg 1958: 270). Moreover, an intelligent doubt calls for a command of the evidence in question, and it is surely not reasonable for a critic to be contentiously opposed to students of prescriptive alliance when, like Schneider, he admits that he has 'not tried to fit their models to the ethnographic facts' (Schneider 1965: 73), or for others to be adamant that prescriptive systems do not and cannot exist when, like Buchler and Selby, they give no evidence of knowing either the history of the subject or the ethnographical literature. In some such cases, it seems, an exaggerated doubt has reached a pitch that, to judge by style and polemical gambits, really looks more like hostility. Fortes, for instance, persists in placing 'alliance' between quotation marks as though to convey that there is something questionable about the very word – though Radcliffe-Brown had no qualms on this score, for in listing 'the four modes of alliance' the first example he gave was alliance 'through intermarriage' (1940a: 208). Signs of the kind are abundant in the works that I have just cited, and it is indeed curious to observe an 'intensity and emotional quality', in critical comments, such as Murdock would have us associate with incest. I should like to imagine, however, that this might yet be reduced if only Schneider, Harris, Fortes, and so on would seriously apply themselves to the comprehension of the ethnographic evidence – work before talk.

Before I close on this point, there is another curious aspect that is worth referring to. This is the contrast between the reception of symmetric and of asymmetric alliance. There is a fairly wide readiness to accept that the Australian aborigines, South Indians, Sinhalese, Caribs, etc., really do have, or may well have, positive marriage rules, and that in these societies the spouse is categorically prescribed. But recently a special objection has been lodged against the idea that societies also exist in which the category of spouse is unilaterally prescribed.

I do not know why this should be, though the fact is plain. Sometimes one can glimpse the probable motives of individual critics of the notion, but once more I can only desire that continued demonstrations and repeated pleas to examine the evidence (cf. sec. VII) may yet bring about some mollification of this attitude. I wish far more that I could understand it, and render it intelligible to students of social anthropology as a collective undertaking, for clearly there are factors at work which (irrational and unconscious though they may be) have a fundamental importance in the direction of thought and the formation of judgements.

For the present, I trust that the above account of the background, compressed and incomplete though my exposition has had to be, will have supplied the reader with an extended basis for the appreciation of a recurrent theme in this volume and for an assessment of Wilder's paper on the Purum.

About this latter contribution I need only say that it is the kind of inquiry that in my opinion most needs to be conducted. Wilder takes a specific factual question – how many alliance groups do the Purum have? – and looks minutely into the literature to see how it may best be answered. He has an excellent case when he states that 'discussions [of the Purum system] grow more distant from the original sources', and his own concentration on the recorded facts ought to do something to counter that deleterious trend.

IX

COMPETENCE AND AUTHORITY

At places in the preceding sections of this introduction I have alluded to standards of professional competence and have called into some question the authority of certain professionals. These stands of principle have to do with grounds of evaluation which underly the entire branch of study that is called kinship and marriage. Something should therefore be said about these grounds, and here I venture to submit that some rather plain speaking is called for. From this point, too, I shall not be addressing my more jaded and circumspect colleagues, teachers who have formed their own seasoned judgements on matters that they know as well as I do. I shall have in mind those readers, especially university students of social anthropology, who are taking a fresher and more exploratory look at one aspect of the progress of the understanding of man in society.

The university student is in a very uncertain position when he takes up the subjects of this volume. He is persuaded that they are important, and he sees that many anthropologists have accordingly written about them, but he has not the knowledge or the standards of assessment to choose among the many publications or to confide in one authority rather than another. The situation is made more difficult, also, by the fact (as I take it to be) that it is not those who do the most, and perhaps the best, work on kinship who make the most noise about it. In the writing of textbooks and the prosecution of debate it is rather, as Hume said of the metaphysics of the eighteenth century (*Treatise*, Introduction), that:

> 'The victory is not gained by the men at arms, who manage the pike and the sword; but by the trumpeters, drummers, and musicians of the army.'

For the most part, those who do the hard and detailed scholarly work that advances the subject do not write textbooks and introductions and didactic pieces. They tend to stick to problems and to devote themselves to the elucidation of these. Yet there is a demand for general textbooks and surveys (whether there is any serious intellectual need for them is another matter of which I am not persuaded), and these, unfortunately perhaps, have to contain chapters on kinship and marriage. On this score I shall merely assert that usually they are by no means good enough, and that sometimes they are deplorable. Some initial reasons for this state of affairs are easy to see: the history of the topics is quite long, the literature is large and in parts recondite, and the average anthropologist cannot be expected to have mastered all this as well as everything else that he will be required to put into his textbook. But none of these reasons, understandable though they are, is any help to the student. He wants to know what the issues are, he wants to be taught how to analyse and how to judge, and he wants to be told by an expert. He cannot do by himself the work on kinship and marriage that even the textbook writer is not capable of, so

perforce he reads what is conveniently published; and he tends
to read what is boldly trumpeted to be authoritative, what is
easily assimilable rather than complexly analytical, and what
makes memorable and resounding claims rather than scholarly
proofs. Thus for every student who has read the early papers of
such masters as Kroeber and Lowie there are perhaps a thousand
who will read Buchler and Selby; for every reflective reader of
Wake there are probably more yet who are swayed by
Schneider's abrupt asseverations; and for each admirer of
Hocart there will be a greater number who think they have
to read Fortes. A medley of practical occasions therefore lures
and urges the student into a trap of necessarily ignorant
assent.

One way out of these confines is to offer the student good
reason not to take at face value, by the standards of textbook
and syllabus, what is merely supposed or said to be competent
and authoritative. There are certain criteria for a moderately
sceptical criticism which do not depend on great knowledge or
technical capacity, and these can be inculcated by demonstration, as I shall try to do in a moment. Even more importantly,
it seems to me, the student needs and wants to be told plainly,
in print, what his teachers really think. He finds out soon enough
that there can be a great disparity between the official mask of
social anthropology and the palpable features underneath.
The name of an authority on kinship may be in every work of
elementary instruction and every examination, yet the grounds
for this prominence may be hard to discover, and the student
may find that the authority in question is actually disregarded
by teachers who ought to be in a position to know. The impression may even be formed in him that the status of an authority has gone to someone who is more like 'The Idea-Man' in
van Gennep's story (1967, ch. 10), the megaphonic 'spirit of
synthesis', and not to someone who in social anthropology has
paralleled the demonstrated excellences of science and scholarship in other branches of academic inquiry. Now I am not
framing an oblique case against a single character when I
mention these matters, nor am I formulating a wholesale judgement on a class of academics (textbook writers, formalists, or
anyone else). I am reporting some of the doubt and dejection
that is often found among serious students who try to come to

grips with kinship and marriage but are confused and uneasy about the proper assessment of competence and authority.

Without wishing in the least to make myself awkward, I am convinced therefore that it is essential to specify the sort of case that I have been talking about and to supply, by means of a clear and even dramatic example, some factual grounds for a reasonable scepticism about conventional evaluations in the field of kinship and marriage. An obvious and almost unavoidable instance is the fame of A. R. Radcliffe-Brown. I realize that to take this particular case may involve the risk of giving affront in certain influential quarters, but my purpose is to present an effective demonstration which will have consequences in the minds of students, and there is no reason (apart from the ignoble considerations of academic politics) why I should not examine a personage of importance and say what I really think about some of his claims to intellectual renown.

Radcliffe-Brown's name has a marked and apparently almost indispensable prominence in works on kinship, his writings are set texts in the curricula, and his views are adduced in virtually every examination paper on the subject. In introductory works and surveys his position seems to be safely pre-eminent and even unassailable. What did he really do? Beattie, claiming Radcliffe-Brown as one of the 'founding fathers of social science', says that he 'introduced clarity and order into what had hitherto been something of a jumble of ethnographic *minutiae*' (1969: 185). This judgement seems actually to be lifted from Lévi-Strauss, who some years earlier had written that Radcliffe-Brown 'introduced some kind of order where there was only chaos' (1963: 303), but this derivation only makes the claim more weighty. If Radcliffe-Brown did that much, then his fame is well merited. Now in fact Lévi-Strauss was not talking about kinship in general but specifically about the study of Australian systems, and in this context the tribute is definitely undeserved. The allusion is to Radcliffe-Brown's *Social Organization of Australian Tribes* (1931), but this had been long forestalled by Thomas's *Kinship Organisations and Group Marriage in Australia* (1906), a comparative work which also surpassed Radcliffe-Brown's in historical perspective, exploitation of sources, clarity of exposition, and soundness of analysis. If there had been Thomas alone before him, it would be indefen-

sible enough to assert that Radcliffe-Brown introduced order
into a 'jumble' or a 'chaos'; but in fact there were men of the
calibre of Fison, Howitt, and Mathews in Australia, not to
mention Daisy Bates, and acute and scholarly synthesizers
such as Durkheim and Lang in Europe, who in the preceding
fifty years had indeed achieved an admirable order in the study
of the multifarious data on Australian social organization.

Lévi-Strauss had more especially in mind the formulation of
analytical notions in this field of study, and he attributed to
Radcliffe-Brown the definition of 'the basic operational terms,
such as "cycle", "pair", and "couple" ' (303); but this too is
historically inaccurate, as any close student of Australian
anthropology knows. Elkin has documented the fact that it was
R. H. Mathews, who began his researches in 1870 and published
his results between 1894 and 1907, who devised precisely these
notions and these very terms (Elkin 1956: 249). Radcliffe-Brown
took them from Mathews's writings, as he took a great deal
else, only without saying so. As Elkin moderately puts it,
'references confirming and acknowledging Mathews' findings
would have been appropriate' (250). Not only that, but they
would have prevented the ascription to one man, in definite
academic pronouncements, of advances actually made by
another. There is nothing argumentative in this conclusion,
either, but only a matter of simple historical facts. All that is
necessary to an estimation of Radcliffe-Brown's achievements
in these respects is a knowledge of those facts. An obvious
implication, if I may be so blunt as to draw it, is that anyone
who does not have that knowledge would do well to say nothing
about them.

A more general ground for praising Radcliffe-Brown, and at
least a debatable one, is the claim: 'his great merit was that he
discerned very clearly the essential elements in the welter of
kinship material'. This he accomplished, it is maintained, by
means of such notions as 'the unity of the sibling group' and
'the unity of the lineage' (Beattie 1939: 185). Most recently,
indeed, Fortes has declared that the principle of the unity of
the sibling group is

'one of the few generalizations in kinship theory that, in my
opinion, enshrines [sic] a discovery worthy to be placed side

by side with Morgan's discovery of classificatory kinship; and, like Morgan's, it has been repeatedly validated and has opened up lines of inquiry not previously foreseen.'

This, I am afraid, is a very defective assessment and disputable on every count. To begin with, as a matter of intrinsic historical interest, Morgan did not (*pace* Rivers) discover classificatory kinship. Lafitau, in 1724, has a far better claim to that credit (he is not in Fortes's bibliography); but even in his case it is not at all sure that he was the discoverer of this type of social classification. The principle of the unity of the sibling group has not been repeatedly validated; it is not even clear what would count as a validation, and Fortes at any rate neither validates the principle nor supplies any reference to others who have (repeatedly) done so. It has not opened up any lines of inquiry, and once again there is a difficulty in conceiving (in default of a demonstration) what these might be; Fortes does not specify any, nor does he himself follow such a line in any empirical analysis. In fact, although his assertions are decided enough in their tone, it is exceedingly hard to give them a substantive meaning.

Even so, other claims are made for Radcliffe-Brown's principles. According to Fortes, they 'enabled inferences to be made from terminologies about the categorization and grouping of kinsfolk and suggested predictions of the institutional forms these might take' (1969: 51). None of this, unfortunately, is correct. Let us leave aside the fact that once more no empirical substantiation of these assertions is made. Logically, no inference about categorization can be made from a terminology; the terminology is itself a 'categorization' and the supposed inference would be no more than a tautology. Empirically, it is not feasible to make correct inferences from a terminology about grouping; as Dumont has abundantly demonstrated, 'kinship terminologies have not as their function to register groups' and 'the type of terminology, although part and parcel of the social order, is not necessarily linked with one particular kind of group organization' (1964: 78; 1957; cf. my 'Remarks', sec. V). This is an elementary point, though historically a hard-argued issue, and there is no serious question about its validity; so on this score too Radcliffe-Brown's principles could not have the interpretative capacity that is claimed for them. Fortes need only to have tried to prove this mode of inference, as he signally does not do, in order to find that it is not possible. Even more certainly, if I interpret his rather vague phrasing exactly, the principles do not permit predictions about 'institutional forms'; an extended demonstration can be found, with reference to empirical cases which are the more conclusive because of their very simplicity, in the set of analyses presented in my 'Terminology and Alliance' (1966d: 1967). Moreover, it is a simple philosophical point also that in principle nothing can be inferred from the form of a classification about any objective properties in what is classified; in this regard a kinship terminology is no different from any other kind of classification, and on this ground as well Radcliffe-Brown's principles could not have the uses that Fortes asserts.

All the same, it is further maintained that the principles are not only useful but supremely so:

> '. . . The supreme merit of Radcliffe-Brown's set of "principles" by contrast with its competitors, lay and lies in its applicability to the observed facts. It provides a key, which no other theory can match, to the basic rules followed in the construction of classificatory terminologies. Applied to a particular system, the "principles" give us the elementary features on which its structural logic is built up. They also demonstrate a form of genotypical analysis that can be expanded to disclose variations of and additions to the original "principles".'

At this point, unaccountably, the disquisition on these purported advantages comes to an abrupt end; no empirical examples are provided in order to display the applicability of the principles to social facts. This is not all that surprising, in a way, since Radcliffe-Brown himself never did as much with his own principles, i.e. he did not prove that they provided a matchless key to the construction of terminologies. Fortes's own phrase about 'structural logic' is rather grand, but a scientific case is better made by empirical demonstration. This would involve taking a variety of terminologies and analysing each one in detail. Until this much of a demonstration is effected there is no reason to accept Fortes's declamations at even their face value. A curiosity here, incidentally, is that the principles should ever be thought to require such forceful advertisement. After all, they were enunciated quite a long time ago, and every anthropological student knows of them. If they really had the supreme usefulness that is claimed for them, they would surely have become integrated into the ordinary practice of social anthropologists and thus would not need such special pleading. The results achieved would make all the case they needed. It is the more telling, by contrast, that Fortes does not (and in my view could not) provide technical proof of this kind.

There is no need to go any further, in this place, into the worth of Radcliffe-Brown's principles. My own judgement on this score (as will be borne out elsewhere in an extended critique which I hope will deliver a final quietus to such embarrassments) agrees completely with Murdock's admirably phrased conclusion that 'the alleged principles are mere verbalizations reified into causal forces' (1949: 121).

The question of assessment by analytical results, however, leads to one matter which may well be found awkward but which ought to be brought up, namely the work on which Radcliffe-Brown's reputation as an expert on kinship is based. In one place, in a fairly late and comprehensive paper on the study of kinship systems, he makes an impressive allusion: 'If you will take the time to study two or three hundred kinship systems from all parts of the world . . .' (1940b: 17). The implication is that he himself had done at least as much, and I imagine that this degree of familiarity with the subject-matter might indeed be expected of an expert.

It really is about time, then, that someone pointed out that Radcliffe-Brown never published a single scholarly, technically exact, and comprehensive analysis of any 'kinship system'.

There is no art or tendentious burden in these terms of assessment. By scholarly I mean in the first place simply going to all reasonable lengths to master, and then take publicly into responsible account, all available evidence; by technically exact I refer to a systematically coherent and accurate interpretation, with comparative reference; and by comprehensive I mean taking a terminology as a classificatory whole, without any prejudicial circumscription, and then relating it as fully as possible to the social facts. On the first count, it is a matter of very easy demonstration that Radcliffe-Brown nowhere, not even in his monograph on the social organization of Australian tribes, took due scholarly advantage of the fund of evidence that should have been exploited; indications of this failing in his Australian work have been published by Elkin (1956), and more generally Evans-Pritchard has flatly recorded his un-qualified judgement that Radcliffe-Brown was not a scholar (1970: ix). As for getting things right, the difficulty is that Radcliffe-Brown published very few testable interpretations; when he did not take over the views and findings of his pre-decessors, he usually confined himself to methodological in-junctions. But in one instance, recently examined by one of the contributors to this volume, he did make an analytical inter-vention that is open to technical evaluation. This was in an article of 1914 in which he offered a reconsideration of certain obscurities and possible errors in Howitt's account of the Dieri system. (This was a society to which he returned in print in 1951, making a general assessment of the type of system found in it; the early analysis was not revised then.) In this paper he maintained that the identification of two crucial terms, as made by the ethnographer, was in error; so he redrew the Dieri rela-tionship table, assigned the terms in question to other positions, and proposed an interpretation which was designed to show that with these modifications the system was 'wonderfully simple and logical' (Radcliffe-Brown 1914: 34). I need only refer to Francis Korn's conclusive demonstration that the as-signments he made were themselves erroneous and actually impaired the systematic coherence of the evidence (Korn 1971). We have to go quite a long way back, therefore, to find a test-able analysis by Radcliffe-Brown, and on that occasion he simply got it wrong. As for the final score, viz. the interpretation of the full connotations of a relationship terminology, it calls for no demonstration that Radcliffe-Brown nowhere published such an investigation.

In the light of the circumstances, which are clear enough in spite of the summary presentation, it is a puzzle to account for Radcliffe-Brown's fame as a kinship expert. It is like a chemist who climbed to the highest status in his subject without making analyses, or a physicist who carried out no experiments giving public proof of his capacity. Radcliffe-Brown certainly wrote, of course, in an assured and didactic manner which made it appear that his researches had earned him that status, and perhaps that had something to do with it. In a more general context, Leslie White's solution is that 'Radcliffe-Brown's importance lay in the fact that he was prominent and influential in a *social organization of scholars* rather than in his contributions to *scientific fact or theory*' (1966: 51; original italics). By this account, then, his advancement was political rather than the due recognition of intellectual achievement. There were professional circumstances which make it historically more understandable that it should ever have been possible to gain academic stature in that way, but they do not much reduce the dejecting effect of having to take seriously so unpalatable a conclusion in this case.

At this point, knowing the turns that anthropological debate can take (cf. sec. VIII above), I have to defend myself against any charge of animus against Radcliffe-Brown. This is made particularly necessary by a recent allusion of the kind. Fortes takes a very carefully qualified and tentative point of argument that I have advanced (Needham 1962a: 36) and finds it 'staggering' that I should adopt such a position (though 'apologetically', as he has it) 'solely out of zeal to confute Radcliffe-Brown' (Fortes 1969: 33 n. 2). This is not only a piece of literary bad manners, in that it impertinently alleges a personal motive (and even concocts a fictitious apology for it) where there is no evidence, but it asserts what in fact is not in the least true. At the place in question an argument by Radcliffe-Brown appeared open to refutation on certain grounds; and if my critical point was mistaken, the scholarly response would have been to prove as much by showing that the facts were unreliable or that my inference from them was invalid. If we really have to accept that the proper conduct of an argument is itself a matter for debate, as would appear, then I take my position with Kant: 'Let your opponent . . . speak only with the voice of reason, and combat him with nothing other than the weapons of reason' (1787: 772). My eminent colleague chose not to defend Radcliffe-Brown by argument, but to put on the issue a personal and discreditable cast which removed it from the sphere of rational debate. I do not know, then, what more I should say in explication of the critical observations that I have had to make about Radcliffe-Brown's supposed achievements, except to declare explicitly that my concern has been solely with matters of fact and logic. If I am inspired by any zeal, it is only to get things straight. If I am wrong, there are rational means of demonstrating as much.

For the present, my case rests. It seemed potentially instructive to make a reassessment of Radcliffe-Brown's theoretical contributions to the study of kinship and marriage, and I am afraid my conclusion is that I really do not know of any specific contributions that he did make.

So long as this finding goes unrefuted, however, there are still some positive consequences to be expected from this rather disheartening inquiry. The student whom I had first in mind now has more reason to be responsibly sceptical about anthropological authority and the grounds on which it may be attributed. He has better cause, also, to demand that any anthropologist who claims authority in a certain field shall actually do what he talks about; and he may demand that what is represented as excellent shall have withstood the test of published and scholarly scrutiny. These may seem modest enough conditions in an academic subject, but they are fundamental. In this kind of professional or technical assessment we can admit no limitation, within the bounds of courtesy, on the freedom of criticism: 'Nothing is so important . . . that it may be exempted from this searching examination, which knows no respect for persons' (Kant 1787: 766). Let us by all means praise famous men, but let us not praise men just because they happen to have become famous.

This injunction brings us appositely to another person for whom great claims have been made. If Radcliffe-Brown was a dominant figure in the field of kinship before the second world war, Lévi-Strauss is certainly the most renowned authority after it. His fame rests primarily on his work about the elementary structures of kinship (1949; 1969), and I am certainly not going to attempt an assessment of that here. It must be said, however, that in many respects it is an exceedingly defective work: as I have claimed elsewhere, it suffers from serious lacks as regards sources (cf. sec. VII above), it contains numerous ethnographical errors and misinterpretations of the facts, and in spite of the quality of Lévi-Strauss's insights 'it cannot be said that he has employed them to their proper effect in the analysis of any single system' (Needham 1962a: 3). In repeating these points I do not for a moment wish to deny the sheer intellectual excitement that Lévi-Strauss's classical monograph has to offer, or the theoretical stimulation that can be had from it by anyone who seriously tries to master its argument. My concern at the moment is to consider briefly what are the real grounds for the immense reputation that has accrued to Lévi-Strauss, on the basis of this book, as an expert on kinship.

Since Leach and I were together, for a number of years, the foremost exegetes and the most assiduous propagators of Lévi-Strauss's views in the English-speaking world, perhaps I can let Leach take over here and make the case for me. I quote from chapter 6 ('The Elementary Structures of Kinship') of his book on Lévi-Strauss (Leach 1970), a sympathetic and most uncontentious introduction which on the whole achieves a notably balanced exposition; some indeed think that Leach has been altogether too charitable and accommodating in the face of failings which they think call for a sharper treatment. At any rate, Leach's estimation of the great book is assuredly not hostile. A few extracts will serve. 'Logical arguments are *illustrated* by means of allegedly appropriate ethnographic evidence, but no attention whatever is paid to the negative instances which seem to abound' (103; original italics); the argument rests on the 'rudimentary' error of equating rules of exogamy with 'the converse of the incest taboo' (103); Lévi-Strauss's 'discussion of marriage rules . . . was distorted by his erroneous belief that the great majority of primitive societies have systems of unilineal descent' (105); 'the final end product is largely fallacious' (111). A specially telling criticism, made only incidentally but attaching to the whole undertaking, is that 'as time goes on, it becomes increasingly difficult to understand just what Lévi-Strauss really means by "elementary structures" ' (105).

These points are expressed in a very moderate fashion, but it will be seen that they add up to a serious indictment. My own inclination would have been to go considerably further and to be yet more explicit in exposing the book's scholarly and analytical inadequacies. In this place I shall only stress that something must be very wrong indeed with a monograph on kinship when even Leach finds it *increasingly* difficult to understand what it is really about; and when another social anthropologist, and an ardent admirer at that, can be told by the author that he is guilty of a 'fundamental misunderstanding' of the very title and subject-matter of the book (Lévi-Strauss 1969: xxxiii; cf. xix), in other words that he just does not understand what it is all about. So long as it could be taken to deal, even if not consistently, with what the very opening lines of the first edition expressly said it was about – viz. 'systems which prescribe marriage with a certain type of relative' (1949: ix, lines 4 and 5) – a great deal of interest could be found in it; but if it is not about prescriptive systems, after all, then it is indeed hard to accord it the same importance as it would seem literally to claim. Cut off from the long scholarly tradition to which it would otherwise naturally be assigned (cf. sec. VII above), it makes an idiosyncratic and baffling impression which in the end may defy a coherent interpretation. In that case I, for my part, must indeed bow to authority and admit that I no longer think I know what Lévi-Strauss can actually mean by 'elementary structures'. I have to concede that Lévi-Strauss is quite right: I really have no idea what *Les Structures élément-aires de la parenté* is about. On this score I can make no clearer or more definite an admission; but something of a question then remains. If neither Leach nor I can understand Lévi-Strauss's argument, whose fault is that?

These fundamental difficulties do not however prevent the detection, in more particular respects, of the many defects in Lévi-Strauss's monograph; indeed, these become more and more glaring as one investigates more closely, in case after case, the detail of its argument and its exploitation of the ethnographic evidence. Outright mistakes (Leach 1969) and contradictions abound, the individual analyses are sometimes completely wrong (Korn 1971; Needham 1962b) and usually unsatisfactory, and the extraordinarily quaquaversal nature of Lévi-Strauss's exposition of his views makes it impossible for even the most informed, engaged, and sympathetic reader ever to be sure that he understands what the author intends finally to convey. It is true that, in marked contrast with Radcliffe-Brown, Lévi-Strauss did an immense amount of real work on kinship and marriage, but there remains after all the crucial question whether he actually got things right.

Francis Korn has in fact written a monographic enquiry into the scientific value of Lévi-Strauss's theory of kinship (Korn n.d.), and I trust that it will not be too long before its publication presents the academic world – and the literary critics who, rather unaccountably, have been much impressed by Lévi-Strauss's notions on elementary structures – with the first scholarly and technically competent critique of *Les Structures élémentaires de la parenté*. (In the interim, see in the present volume Korn's Iatmul analysis, secs. I, XV-XVIII; cf. Korn 1969.) In this connexion, perhaps I may report here that Dr Korn's critique tends to confirm my own more cursory assessment that Lévi-Strauss makes no decisive advance on the classical Australian material or on the related work by the Dutch, and that it is an arguable matter whether there is a single theoretical proposition in it which is both novel and valid. Here too, I am afraid, we have an authority on kinship who not only has feet of clay but seems on closer inspection to be largely friable. It is hard to imagine what will be made of this figurehead of our times when social anthropologists in the future (if there still are any then) pick up the pieces and try to read off something intelligible from them. My own guess is that, echoing a genial aphorism from the eighteenth century (Lichtenberg 1958: 357), they may well conclude: 'This whole theory is good for nothing except to dispute about'.

It is scarcely necessary for me to say that it is with no disrespect that I arrive at this disappointing estimation of Lévi-Strauss's substantive contributions to the study of kinship and marriage; nor do I have any doubt that *Les Structures élémentaires* will deservedly retain an absolutely secure place in the history of social anthropology. It is the work, after all, of a brilliant and speculative intelligence, if also a most intricate and contradictory one, and it is an expression of imaginative and literary qualities which in other of his endeavours have brought Lévi-Strauss a wide acclaim. Some of this public excitement is superficial and purely fashionable, of course, and when even academics on their own ground are baffled and uncertain it is not probable that the literary claque quite understands what it so vigorously applauds. But by no means all of the response is of this kind, and there are some of us who must remain deeply grateful for the appearance of Lévi-Strauss on an anthropological scene which was otherwise scarcely inspiring. In the end, though, the inexorable factors of rational argument and empirical demonstration must alone decide the issue, in the branch of study with which this volume is concerned, and under these pressures there is no substitute, however profound or stimulating, for getting things right. As Revel neatly says of philosophy, 'un système philosophique n'est pas fait pour être compris: il est fait pour faire comprendre' (1957: 25), and this is what we have to demand of an anthropological doctrine as well.

It will be seen, therefore, that I think that there is a means of getting things demonstrably right in the study of kinship and marriage, and also that it is possible to specify why even the most prominent figures may get things wrong. These are matters, I should stress, which are by no means to be taken for granted, for it could be that the interpretation and comparison of systems of descent and alliance was no more susceptible to objective analysis and technical resolution than are works of art or theological dogmas. I suggest, in fact, that they are far more like these other products of imaginative intelligence, in the ordering of human experience, than they are like the legal codes, natural organisms, and functioning mechanisms to which they are often assimilated. As it is, however, there is at least the appearance of the possibility of systematic understanding of thought and conduct in this field, and it may be that some kind of theoretical progress is not out of the question.

One lesson, in this regard, which the otherwise incommensurable examples of Radcliffe-Brown and Lévi-Strauss have in common to convey, is the danger of trying prematurely to construct a grand theory. In Radcliffe-Brown's case the model was a very simplistic and faulty conception of natural science, whereas in Lévi-Strauss's the inspiration was that of a materialist social philosophy, but the scope of their explanatory ambitions was very much the same. It does not however seem likely that to attempt to think on such a scale is yet the right way to account for systems of kinship and marriage. 'La tare la plus grave que la philosophie a transmise à la sociologie', observes Revel in connexion with *Les Structures élémentaires*, 'est . . .

Rodney Needham

l'obsession de vouloir constituer d'emblée des explications
intégrales' (1957: 155). Both Radcliffe-Brown and Lévi-Strauss,
in their different ways, made this attempt and in the event
they disastrously (or perhaps, in Lévi-Strauss's case, 'splendidly', as Leach has put it) failed.

So, too, on another plane, has Fortes in his long and ambitious
work on kinship and the social order (1969), and essentially for
the same reason. In his case the acknowledged inspiration was
second-hand, namely a view of social anthropology as a kind of
natural science of society which he had from Radcliffe-Brown.
When he was elected to the chair at Cambridge, after some
fifteen years already as a social anthropologist, he emphasized
in his inaugural lecture that 'human society exhibits regularities
consistent with those found in *the rest of* nature' (italics supplied); this was thought sufficiently validated by 'the discovery
and elucidation of classificatory kinship systems'. Thence he
contended explicitly that 'the main aim of social anthropology
is to investigate the general tendencies, or laws, manifested in
them [i.e. the regularities]' (Fortes 1953: 35). I shall not dwell
on the questionable equation of laws with general tendencies,
particularly as this might be dismissed as a merely philosophical
question, but wish only to underline the ultimate ambition of
this contention. It is significant also in its implications as a
programmatic statement of the main aim of social anthropology
on the part of a speaker who was assuming a leading position
in it. Such declarations, of course, have been common enough;
what alone counted in this instance, and what were to be expected, were results. Another fifteen years later, with presumably the added advantage of departmental researches that had
been guided by the inaugural statement of intent, there duly
appeared *Kinship and the Social Order*, a weighty and supremely
confident summation of long-matured views on the subject.
The nearest thing to a 'law' that it was found to contain,
announced as an issue in 'structural theory', was the Axiom of
Amity (ch. XII): 'Where kinship is demonstrable or assumed
. . . there amity must prevail' (234).

This 'prescriptive altruism', or 'ethic of generosity', is not
confined to the descent group. 'Its roots are in the familial
domain and it embraces the bilateral kinship linkages of this
domain. Kin by complementary filiation are also embraced

xcvi

within the orbit of kinship amity.' The essential idea is that descent relations are assimilated to familial relationships, and that the actor 'projects' on to the former 'the ethic of the familial domain' (234). It will at once be recognized that this is Radcliffe-Brown's idea of the extension of sentiment from the elementary family, only that here what is allegedly extended is not a specific attitude, contrasted with any other within the family, but a vague and not very discriminating sentiment of 'amity'. It is thus open to similar logical and empirical objections, but it is not these that I wish to take up here. What is relevant at this point is firstly the very marked contrast there is between the high expectations aroused by the search for laws of society and the commonplace generalization actually formulated, between the impressively formal term 'axiom' and the accumulation of imprecise descriptions which illustrate but do not exactly define its scope. All that the axiom appears to mean, in fact, is that kinship implies co-operation and that one is obliged to be on good terms with those with whom one co-operates. This interpretation is supported by the converse of the axiom, viz.: 'where amity is the rule in the relations of clans or tribes or communities, there kinship . . . is invoked' (234). Once more, I am not interested in exposing the intrinsic defects of this proposition, but I have to emphasize the extent to which any genuinely theoretical expectation is frustrated by this vague phrase. In the end, it seems to me, both the axiom and its converse are empty tautologies, expressing no more than a particular presupposition of what 'kinship' really is (cf. my 'Remarks', sec. II).

Now I do not wish to sound at all derisive in drawing out this flat conclusion, but only to exemplify with a recent and prominent case the kind of theoretical failure to which a grandiose conception of anthropological inquiry tends to lead.

Perhaps, also, in making this assessment, I may quickly suggest a simple but salutary test of such an axiom, or any other general proposition of an expressly theoretical kind. It is a procedure which immediately draws attention away from the rather distracting question of what a particular critic thinks and why he thinks so, with the attendant circumstance of an academic confrontation, and places the issue quite impersonally under the very best professional judgement. The setting is to imagine the presence of some acknowledged and accomplished authority in the relatively distant past, someone who undeniably helped to shape the tradition to which the proposition in question pertains. My own historical figures would include, e.g. Hocart, Kroeber, Rivers, Durkheim, and Lang. The test then is to conjecture what the ghostly critic would respond if the proposition were put to him as a significant discovery or intellectual achievement. In this instance, any of my panel would serve as far as I am concerned, but if necessary some other mutually acknowledged authority could doubtless be agreed upon instead. Let us therefore conjure up Durkheim, who would certainly accept Fortes's premise that there are regularities in human society, and have the proposition put to him. With myself thus safely out of it, I am content to leave it to the reader to imagine what would be Durkheim's assessment of the theoretical worth of the 'axiom of amity'.

The several conclusions to the assessments of competence and authority that I have just ventured prove thus to be rather negative, but I trust the demonstrations will not be negative in their effect. The first expectable response is the question: If these are not sound authorities, who is? There is little difficulty in compiling a list of respectable names in the past; e.g. Wake, Lang, Durkheim, Rivers, Kroeber, and Lowie. In the present, my own judgement is that the true masters in the study of kinship and marriage are Dumont and Leach. All these researchers have one thing significantly in common: they do not characteristically propound grand theories about kinship in general, but instead concentrate on the resolution of particular problems and the analysis of individual systems. It is this lesson, in the first place, that I should like the present volume to convey. Korn's impressive paper (which for me is the centrepiece of the collection) exemplifies the difficulties and the theoretical benefits of such intensive analysis, and Forge's epilogue about metaphysical ideas and values confirms the final importance of indigenous philosophy; the formal impact of Southwold's taxing analysis depends on his intimate understanding of the meanings of Ganda terms; McKnight's queries about the Wikmunkan, and my own critical commentary, demonstrate the degree of particularity that is called for; and the supreme importance of cultural detail, interpreted in its local context, is brought out also by Wilder's investigation cf Purum descent groups and by the course of the debate about the Purum case.

Methodologically, therefore, the inference is clear: we should pay first attention to the analysis of particular cases, and extract the theoretical lessons progressively from these. Not until we have a sufficiency of competent analyses of this kind should we try to put into effect any grander ambitions. A corollary of this injunction is that we shall do better to demand of putative authorities repeated and public demonstrations, carried out in case after case after case, of their actual competence in the empirical analysis of systems of kinship and marriage. The greater the variety of systems (whatever typology is had in mind) that the anthropologist successfully explicates, the better founded, naturally, will be his reputation for analytical ability, and the more reasonable will it be to expect that his more general ideas on kinship and marriage will be worth taking seriously. In the exact sciences, after all, it is taken for granted that a great deal of painstaking routine investigation of this sort is unavoidable, e.g. in determining molecular structure or making spectrum analyses of stellar sources of light; but in social anthropology the dominant tendency has been to leap from the study of one society (Melanesian, Brazilian, West African) directly to the most ambitious generalities about all kinship. This approach was never likely to work, given the great jural and moral variety of descent systems, and the assessments made above indicate that in fact it does not work. It might be more feasible to generalize, or to formulate more abstract theoretical propositions, if only we possessed in social anthropology a usefully large range of well-attested analyses of systems of different types; but in my view we have not this secure knowledge about relationship terminologies and their social concomitants, and indeed I should say that we are only just beginning to discern the constituent elements of such systems (cf. Needham 1968: 327-8).

A related advantage of the truly analytical approach that I have been advocating is that the quality of technical argument, in the terms appropriate to each case, can be made more exact and testable. I do not wish to suggest too much, though, by using this word 'technical', for the systems themselves are generally very simple in principle (as Galton leads us to realize) and the means of accounting for them are also simple in practice. For the most part, indeed, I should maintain that little more is required in their analysis than the precautions that are conventional in any branch of scholarship and the 'classical rules' of which have been given lapidary expression by Dumézil (1948: 12-13). Let me take two current examples to demonstrate the means of proof that I have referred to.

Buchler and Selby's textbook (1968), which is presented as an introduction to theory and method and as a general stock-taking of developments in the study of kinship and social organization, looks exceedingly impressive and technical with its preponderantly formal exposition and its quasi-mathematical notations, tables, diagrams, and formulas. But when the authors get down to cases the outcome is disproportionately modest in effect and uncertain in results. The first case that I have in mind refers to the 'Dravidian' type of system, a type which occupies a prominent and extensive place in the textbook (see the index). This is only expectable, for Dravidian systems have an historical and theoretical importance which guarantees them a strong representation in any general account of kinship systems. Today, moreover, there is the special factor that Dumont's studies of such systems in South India can be considered the very finest examples of the scholarly and technical analysis of kinship and marriage in anthropological literature. With such advantages, Buchler and Selby's expository task would appear to be absolutely straightforward. Here, if anywhere, is a 'textbook case'. But this is how they introduce 'The Dravidian Case' (135):

> 'Dravidian systems on the surface appear to be simplicity itself. They are patrilineal systems associated with matrilateral cross-cousin marriage.'

They could scarcely have got things more wrong. Dravidian terminologies contain no formal indications (such as lineal or alternating identifications) of any particular rule of descent; they are lineal terminologies, i.e. they are constituted by descent lines, but that is all that can be said on this score. As for jural rules of descent, it is a crucial and thoroughly attested point that a Dravidian terminology can equally well accommodate a patrilineal or a matrilineal rule of descent; in fact, Dumont's examples (1957) are almost all matrilineal. Not only this, but it may not be feasible to say that such a system is either patrilineal or matrilineal; the Sinhalese of Pul Eliya, who employ a classically simple terminology of the kind (see Leach's paper below), cannot be said to have a definite rule of descent, and the same is true of comparable systems such as the Trio in Surinam. If by 'patrilineal' Buchler and Selby further have in mind the existence of patrilineal descent groups, then just as certainly the response is that the Dravidian terminology does not entail any kind of descent group at all (Needham 1964b: 237-8). The mode of marriage, finally, is quite variable and cannot be inferred from the structure of the terminology that gives the type of system its name. There is no general association with matrilateral cross-cousin marriage; patrilateral marriage can as well be found (Dumont 1957), or bilateral, and sometimes oblique, marriage with the sister's daughter as well. Buchler and Selby actually list in their bibliography some of the titles where these very points are made, but it does not appear that they could possibly have read them. The Dravidian form of social classification (alternatively, a two-line prescriptive terminology) is indeed 'simplicity itself', and it needs no intricate technical apparatus to discover the simple facts about the social systems which employ it. But if even this famous, elementary, and basic type of organization is misrepresented, in every single definitive respect, it is hard to see to what end Buchler and Selby need to parade their calculi.

The second case is more particular but just as telling as a commentary on method. It is relevant here, too, because it arises in connexion with Buchler and Selby's examination of the Purum system. They take up my doubtful observations about the equivalence MBD = yZ in the Purum terminology, and they assert that it is not in fact a 'disquieting anomaly' in an asymmetric prescriptive system, on the ground that in both the Chawte and the Lamet terminologies 'we encounter the equation MBD = Z in the context of asymmetric alliance' (271). As authority for this statement they cite my analysis of the literature on the Chawte (1960b), but they totally ignore my findings. It is true, to begin with, that one ethnographer (Roy) does report MBDy = yZ, but a fair part of my paper is devoted to an intensive demonstration that this record of the terminology is in general incoherent, inconsistent with other evidence, and in parts incomprehensible (see also Needham 1962a: 77 n. 5). As for the rule of marriage, it may be, as earlier accounts slightly indicate, that the Chawte used to practise asymmetric prescriptive alliance, but we do not know that they did so. Later publications point on the contrary to a symmetric system. In either event, it is a matter of some consequence that the people whom Shakespear described as 'Chawte', in the basic account of that people, may well not have been Chawte at all, but Purum (Needham 1960b: 243-4). The further one goes into the assessment of local ethnographical details, the less feasible is it seen to be to draw any reliable inferences as to the type of system the Chawte had. In fact, the express conclusion to my paper is that the ethnography is 'too confused and contradictory to be of any secure use in comparative studies or theoretical analysis' (251). The reader of Buchler and Selby's textbook, with its unqualified citation of the Chawte case, cannot be expected to know any of this; but the authors of a work of instruction surely ought to do better.

With the Lamet, on whom no authority is cited, the situation is even less understandable. The Lamet do indeed practise asymmetric alliance, but in this instance the equation 'MBD = Z' simply does not exist: MBD is *haem*, yZ is *yū* (eZ, *al*) (Needham 1960a). Neither of Buchler and Selby's references, therefore, makes their point of argument, and they could not have thought they had evidential support in these instances if they had merely read the sources.

Incidentally, the Lamet case provides a further comment on Schneider's derogation of my treatment of ethnographic evidence, and on Buchler and Selby's subsequent gloss that I have repeatedly 'tortured' the ethnography. Schneider writes: 'A closer look at the Lamet does not yield so neat a picture as one might have expected from Needham's [1960a] paper' (1965: 69). He does not actually direct a closer look at the ethnography, or report anyone else who has done so, or specify wherein my interpretation is excessively neat; but the impression that is nevertheless conveyed by this unsubstantiated observation is that I have, as he says, 'imposed' on the data an 'elegance and order' which are not to be found in them. Another gross manipulation, it might be thought. This seems a suitable place to record, therefore, that the ethnographer of the Lamet, Professor K. G. Izikowitz, whose work (1951) I gratefully analysed, has nowhere indicated the slightest disagreement with my handling of his evidence. I think I may say also that he has personally signified only his approval of my analysis. The extent of his approval is testified to by the fact that he has requested, and I have readily agreed, that my paper shall be included as an appendix in the forthcoming French edition of his book.

It will be seen, therefore, that each of these matters of analytical debate can easily be resolved and that, as I said above, the quality of technical argument can be made more exact and testable by giving first place in our endeavours to the examination of particular cases. It is obvious also, in these instances at any rate, that no grand theory or intricate apparatus is called for. Here the systems and the issues are simple indeed, and a moderate care for the ordinary prudencies of scholarship could have obviated any difficulty in their explication. This much may well be acceded to, but what will probably not have been so fully appreciated, without the identified exposures that are made here and in sec. VIII above, is the extent to which even the most arresting, weighty, and formalized disquisitions on kinship can be undermined by a neglect of such fundamental considerations of rational inquiry.

Presumably there are many reasons why individual anthropologists should have lapsed in these regards, but we can guess at one quite deterrent factor which may have had its effect. The painstaking and minute analysis of one empirical case after another is hard, unglamorous, and modest work. To analyse the literature on just a single society may involve the mastery of a large literature in four or five languages, a knowledge of the history of the area, an acquaintance with the grammar of the vernacular, a visualization of the society in terms of people on the ground (which may entail the capacity to translate a map into a landscape, weather records into environmental changes), and much else in the unwearying pursuit of any relevant detail. Eventually, with patience and synthetic application, the particulars may be composed by an imaginative apprehension into a mental facsimile of the mode of life under study. Then the theoretical analysis can begin, with all the external considerations that this will further necessitate.

No wonder that there are people, even in a learned profession, to whom this serious and fundamental style of investigation is not attractive; but as Heraclitus said, 'Men who love wisdom should acquaint themselves with a great many particulars' (Wheelwright 1959: 19, fr. 3), and if any are not prepared to exert themselves so far, perhaps they should ask themselves whether they really ought to be trying to explain phenomena of such ultimate complexity as the collective modes of human experience.

It is certainly much less arduous, by contrast, and to a certain type of character evidently more tempting, to join the 'trumpeters, drummers, and musicians' of the anthropological army, creating a clamorous and resounding stir among the populace with grand talk of theories, laws, axioms, mechanisms, structural logic, and the rest of such high-sounding devices of advertisement but obscure import. Yet the better course, as it has been the intention of this section to demonstrate, is to enlist under Hume and to 'manage the pike and the sword' in the unlauded encounter with problems. To concentrate thus on the progressive explication of series of particular cases does not, moreover, rule out more explicitly theoretical advances, even if these are so far likely to be quite modest. Let me indicate just a few examples.

Dumont's researches in South India have much increased our understanding of 'Dravidian' systems, not by any technical short-cuts but by profound scholarship and by the patient demonstration of the cultural combinations of rules of descent, marriage preferences, and other variations on an underlying conceptual order. Scheffler's re-examination of the Ambrym case (1970) seems to have demolished the accepted idea that a six-section system existed there, and thus to have relieved anthropology of an incomprehensible arrangement which was impossible to relate to other section systems and tended increasingly to become a theoretical embarrassment. Rivière's delineation of a new type of prescriptive alliance (1966) creates a formal possibility which parallels Fortune's patrilateral construct, and similarly provides a model against which to comprehend, in South America and South India, the varying degrees to which institutions approximate oblique discontinuous exchange. Korn's analyses have given a new clarity to the comprehension of four-line symmetric systems (1971), five-line asymmetric systems (the Iatmul paper below), and the feature of alternation. More generally in the comparative study of prescriptive alliance, as I perhaps rather naturally tend to think, there has been a gradual progress in cumulative understanding, as differing systems of terminology and alliance have been successively analysed, and it is now possible to compile a quite respectable catalogue of empirical generalizations and technical formulations about this type of organization. Perhaps I may cite, too, my own investigation, starting from 'logically possible criteria of classification', into the factor of relative age in the social employment of relationship terminologies (1966a). This not only propounded a testable correlation which seems to be borne out, but it has provided ethnographers with a new method for analysing kinship systems; Rivière's study of the Trio system (1969), for example, could not have been undertaken to the same analytical effect without it. As concluding examples, of special importance are Leach's study of 'the structural implications of metaphysical belief' in connexion with descent and alliance (1961, ch. 1) and Moore's paper on the representation of brother and sister as a symbolically parental couple in descent ideologies (1964).

I am not suggesting of course that these problematical pieces of work represent the only sort of advance in understanding social life, specifically systems of kinship and marriage. Campbell's splendid study of the Sarakatsani (1964) is neither formal nor expressly theoretical, and it is not directed to any one issue, but his sympathetic account of the life of Greek shepherds nevertheless provides, in its convincing detail and the reliability of its generalizations, a comprehensive scheme of theoretical expectations by reference to which the features of other cognatic societies can be better determined. Similar lessons can be drawn from numbers of other ethnographical studies the authors of which had no special care to make theoretical advances. Still, the investigations that I have listed make it especially clear that progressive research into kinship and marriage, inspired by explicitly theoretical aims, does get done in social anthropology. The musicians, it is a relief to see, do not have the field to themselves; gradually the pike and the sword are gaining ground, even though they may never hope to win the day. 'We must not believe, when we make a few discoveries here and there, that this will just keep going on for ever. . . . Sooner or later, man everywhere encounters the incomprehensible' (Lichtenberg 1958: 285).

Three features characterize most such researches as I have taken to be promising or exemplary: they embody, and often they begin with, formal considerations of some kind; they are couched in, or at least derive directly from, a grasp of the myriad cultural details of individual societies; and they result in more or less abstract, sometimes testable, formulations which can guide inquiry in other cases and facilitate comparison. Of these features, it is the central one that provides the real key to theoretical advance, namely the *comprehension* of singular modes of social life. This humane kind of concern runs through practically the whole of the present volume also. Whatever the place of principles of classification, schemes of exchange, or phonetic contrasts, it is always the *meaning* rather than the form of social facts that occupies the contributors.

In the intensive and ultimately semantic kind of investigation that I have been urging as the means to real advance there are no techniques, and probably no theoretical premises either, which link one inquiry to another and thus constitute a method of analysis. Competence in the analysis of one system, or even one type of system, carries little or no guarantee of success in the analysis of another. To be recognized as an authority on one cultural realm of meaning does not confer authority elsewhere. If we really take each case as it comes, then each of our results should be taken as it comes.

It needs stressing, perhaps, that if it is indefensible to class together institutions and systems of very different kinds under the rubric of 'kinship' (Needham 1966a: 31-2; cf. 'Remarks', sec. II), it is yet less justifiable to think that the style of investigation appropriate to one case will be suitable for the understanding of another. Once past the initial stage of the formal analysis of terms of social classification, the analyst has scarcely any more technical or theoretical support than if he were analysing a purely metaphysical doctrine. A jural code governed by the 'kinship' terms may indeed be isolated, and this may at first seem systematically recognizable, but this also will rest on values, ideas, and premises for the determination of which there can be no technical preparation. Even in the analysis of the terminology, for that matter, there is a hidden factor which may disrupt the possibility of drawing even the simplest of inferences from the formal features. The principles of such a form of social classification are worked out from the structure of the terminology, but the specifications which define each term and chart its distribution may denote statuses of unequal, contrasting, or even incomparable significance. This can be appreciated by glancing at the Purum term *pu* and its specifications (Needham 1962a: 77), and then considering the variety of functions and meanings which are attached to the several statuses that are subsumed under the term.

The situation is rather like that described by Evans-Pritchard in connexion with the Nuer word *kwoth*, spirit. 'The great variety of meanings attached to the word *kwoth* in different contexts and the manner in which the Nuer pass, even in the same ceremony, from one to another may bewilder us.' The term *kwoth*, or a statement in which this word appears, cannot be understood immediately; the meaning of the word depends on a ritual and social context which may itself call for minute description and particular explication. Hence, 'It may help us to think of the particular spirits as figures or representations or refractions of God in relation to particular activities, events, persons, and groups' (Evans-Pritchard 1956: 106, 107). Similarly the meanings of the Purum term *pu* are refracted in several contexts of activities, events, persons, and groups. The significance of the context cannot be inferred from the structure of the terminology of which this word is a member, or from the distinctive distribution of the term, or from the genealogical specifications. So it is not only that we cannot make sociological inferences, about institutions, groups, and persons, from the structure of a terminology ('Remarks', sec. V), but we cannot even infer that the statuses denoted by any one term will have anything significant in common. Here the Wittgensteinian view of classification (cf. 'Remarks', secs. IV & VII) is again borne out. There may be serial likenesses between such senses of *pu* as, e.g. ancestor, grandfather, wife-giver, maternal uncle, and wife's brother's son, but we cannot assume that there is any one property that is common to all of them. Moreover,

even if we take one single denotation from within this series
of statuses, e.g. maternal uncle, it is still a matter of context
whether this person will be protector, father-in-law, overseer,
creditor, or ritual suppliant (cf. Needham 1962a: 87-96). Thus
the deeper the analyst goes, the more he is obliged to concentrate on singularities of cultural signification: this involves
trying to put a coherent construction both on an unpredictable
variety of meanings and functions that any individual term
may have and on the set of terms in combination.

It is the more evident, therefore, that techniques, axioms,
and other alien procedures and notions can in the end have
little application to the statuses, symbols, values, and so on
which together constitute the ideology of a 'system of kinship
and marriage'. This being so, it is the personal and even moral
qualities of the individual analyst that will really count:
intelligence, imagination, serious interest, and scholarly responsibility. Furthermore, comparison of usages from different
cultures can hence have only limited objective value if proper
account is to be taken of the meanings that are intrinsic to
each mode of life; and with this severe restriction the likelihood
of a general theory of kinship much decreases.

By this account, 'kinship' is certainly a thoroughly misleading
term and a false criterion in the comparison of social facts. It
does not denote a discriminable class of phenomena or a distinct
type of theory ('Remarks', sec. II), and it does not admit of
special canons of competence and authority. Accordingly, it
cannot be said that a social anthropologist is 'good at kinship';
what he is good at is analysis. What that means depends on
whatever he happens to be analysing.

X

ACKNOWLEDGEMENTS

Thanks are due in the first place to the participants in the
conference. There was a large attendance, the discussions were
well sustained, and the exchanges of views were usefully forthright while also amicably moderate in their expression.
The general conclusion afterwards appeared to be that in
these important respects things had gone rather well. It

Introduction

was not entirely easy, I am afraid, for those present to make a
successful conference, for there were last-minute changes
in the persons and order of the speakers, and it had not
proved feasible to circulate advance copies of all of the papers.
Since my own in particular had to be taken cold, and in two
sessions at that, I am especially grateful to my colleagues for
the good nature with which they accepted these defects of
organization.

Professor Fred Eggan, of the University of Chicago (and at
the time a visiting fellow of All Souls), and Professor Dr P. E.
de Josselin de Jong, of the University of Leiden, kindly accepted
invitations to attend the conference as distinguished guests of
the Association.

Our hosts were the University of Bristol, represented by
Professor Michael Banton in his capacity as head of the Department of Sociology. The local arrangements for the conduct of
the conference and the lodging and welfare of the participants
were most efficiently made by Dr Ian Hamnett, to whom I am
additionally obliged for the patience with which he accommodated himself to the final pressures and to the changes imposed
on the organization of the proceedings. Dr Peter Lloyd,
honorary secretary of the ASA, capably made the administrative preparations.

The debt to my fellow-speakers is patent, for without their
generosity in consenting to deliver papers there would have
been neither conference nor monograph. As convener of the
conference, I found them as excellent a company of collaborators
as one could well hope for; and as editor of the monograph,
especially in the composition of this introduction, I have
received the most varied intellectual stimuli in responding to
their thoughts.

Dr Edmund Leach was the professional and moral focus of the
meetings. His ideas were adduced at many points by the contributors and were constantly cited in the discussions, he himself
took a leading part in the proceedings, and in my view it was
his enthusiastic and knowledgeable participation which gave
direction and an air of lively interest to the conference. It was
an inspiration to sense his ebullient yet modest commitment to
the topics of argument, and a reassuring privilege to have in
him the presence of a master of the subject. At the final session

Rodney Needham

I had the great pleasure of delivering an address in his honour, expressing gratitude and respect for his contributions, both ideal and empirical, to social anthropology.

The royalties on the sales of this monograph go entirely into the Radcliffe-Brown Memorial Fund.

REFERENCES

ACKERMAN, CHARLES. 1964. Structure and Statistics: The Purum Case. *American Anthropologist* **66**: 53-65.
—— Structure and Process: The Purum Case. *American Anthropologist* **67**: 83-91.
BACHELARD, GASTON. 1938. *La Formation de l'esprit scientifique: contribution à une psychanalyse de la connaissance objective.* Paris: Vrin.
BATESON, GREGORY. 1932. Social Structure of the Iatmül People of the Sepik River. *Oceania* **2**: 245-89, 401-51.
—— 1936. *Naven.* Cambridge: Cambridge University Press.
BEATTIE, JOHN. 1969. A. R. Radcliffe-Brown (1881-1955). In: Timothy Raison, ed., *The Founding Fathers of Social Science* (pp. 178-87). Harmondsworth, Middlesex: Penguin Books.
BERKELEY, GEORGE. 1710. *Treatise concerning the Principles of Human Knowledge.* London.
BORGES, JORGE LUIS. 1967. *A Personal Anthology.* Edited and with a Foreword by Anthony Kerrigan. London: Cape.
BUCHLER, IRA R. & SELBY, HENRY A. 1968. *Kinship and Social Organization: An Introduction to Theory and Method.* New York: Macmillan.
CAMPBELL, J. K. 1964. *Honour, Family and Patronage: A Study of Institutions and Moral Values in a Greek Mountain Community.* Oxford: Clarendon Press.
CHOMSKY, NOAM. 1968. *Language and Mind.* New York: Harcourt, Brace & World.
COULT, ALLAN D. 1967. Lineage Solidarity, Transformational Analysis, and the Meaning of Kinship Terminologies. *Man* n.s. **2**: 26-47.
COWGILL, GEORGE L. 1964. Statistics and Sense. More on the Purum Case. *American Anthropologist* **66**: 1358-65.
CZAPLICKA, M. A. 1914. *Aboriginal Siberia: A Study in Social Anthropology.* Preface by R. R. Marett. Oxford: Clarendon Press.
DAVIS, KINGSLEY & WARNER, W. LLOYD. 1937. Structural Analysis of Kinship. *American Anthropologist* **39**: 291-313.

DUMÉZIL, GEORGES. 1948. *Mitra-Varuna: essai sur deux repré-sentations indo-européennes de la souveraineté.* 2d ed. Paris: Gallimard.

DUMONT, LOUIS. 1957. *Hierarchy and Marriage Alliance in South Indian Kinship.* Occasional Papers of the Royal Anthropolo-gical Institute, 12. London: Royal Anthropological Institute.

—— 1961. Marriage in India: The Present State of the Question. *Contributions to Indian Sociology* 5: 75-95.

—— 1964. Marriage in India: The Present State of the Question – Postscript to Part One. *Contributions to Indian Sociology* 7: 77-98.

—— 1966. A Fundamental Problem in the Sociology of Caste. *Contributions to Indian Sociology* 9: 17-32.

DURKHEIM, EMILE & MAUSS, MARCEL. 1963. *Primitive Classi-fication.* Translated from the French and edited with an Intro-duction by Rodney Needham. Chicago: University of Chicago Press.

ELKIN, A. P. 1956. A. R. Radcliffe-Brown, 1880-1955. *Oceania* 26: 239-51.

ENGELS, FRIEDRICH. 1892. [A Recently Discovered Case of Group Marriage.] *Die neue Zeit* 1: 373-5. Reprinted as an appendix to *The Origin of the Family* (pp. 205-9). London: Lawrence & Wishart, 1942.

EVANS-PRITCHARD, E. E. 1956. *Nuer Religion.* Oxford: Clarendon Press.

—— 1970. Foreword (pp. ix-xi) to Hocart 1970.

FISCHER, H. TH. 1935. De Aanverwantschap bij enige volken van de Nederlandsch-Indische Archipel. *Mens en Maatschappij* 11: 285-97, 365-79.

FORTES, MEYER. 1953. *Social Anthropology at Cambridge since 1900.* An Inaugural Lecture. Cambridge: Cambridge University Press.

—— 1969. *Kinship and the Social Order: The Legacy of Lewis Henry Morgan.* Chicago: Aldine.

FORTUNE, R. F. 1933. A Note on some Forms of Kinship Structure. *Oceania* 4: 1-9.

GALTON, FRANCIS. 1883. Discussion of MacFarlane 1883. *Journal of the Anthropological Institute* 12: 61-2.

—— 1889. Note on Australian Marriage Systems. *Journal of the Anthropological Institute* 18: 70-72.

GENNEP, ARNOLD VAN. 1967. *The Semi-Scholars.* Translated from the French and edited with an introduction by Rodney Need-ham. London: Routledge & Kegan Paul.

Rodney Needham

GEOGHEGAN, WILLIAM H. & KAY, PAUL. 1964. More Structure and Statistics: A Critique of C. Ackerman's Analysis of the Purum. *American Anthropologist* **66**: 1351-58.

GILHODES, C. 1913. Mariage et condition de la femme chez les Katchin, Birmanie. *Anthropos* **8**: 363-75.

GLUCKMAN, M. 1950. Kinship and Marriage among the Lozi of Northern Rhodesia and the Zulu of Natal. In: A. R. Radcliffe-Brown and Daryll Forde, eds., *African Systems of Kinship and Marriage* (pp. 166-206). London: Oxford University Press for the International African Institute.

GOODENOUGH, WARD H. 1956. Componential Analysis and the Study of Meaning. *Language* **32**: 195-216.

GREENBERG, J. H. 1949. Logical Analysis of Kinship. *Philosophy of Science* **16**: 58-64.

HAMMEL, E. A. (ed.). 1965. Formal Semantic Analysis. *American Anthropologist* (Special Publication) **67**, no. 5, pt. 2. Menasha, Wisconsin.

HARRIS, MARVIN. 1968. *The Rise of Anthropological Theory: A History of Theories of Culture*. London: Routledge and Kegan Paul.

HELD, GERRIT JAN. 1935. *TheMahābhārata: An Ethnological Study*. Amsterdam: Holland.

HOCART, A. M. 1952. *The Northern States of Fiji*. [Ed. Lord Raglan.] Occasional Publications of the Royal Anthropological Institute, 11. London: Royal Anthropological Institute.

—— 1954. *Social Origins*. [Edited with a foreword by Lord Raglan.] London: Watts.

—— 1970. *Kings and Councillors: An Essay in the Comparative Anatomy of Human Society*. Edited and with an Introduction by Rodney Needham. Foreword by E. E. Evans-Pritchard. Chicago: University of Chicago Press.

HODSON, T. C. 1925. Notes on the Marriage of Cousins in India. *Man in India* **5**: 163-75.

HOMANS, GEORGE C. & SCHNEIDER, DAVID M. 1955. *Marriage, Authority and Final Causes: A Study of Unilateral Cross-cousin Marriage*. Glencoe, Ill.: Free Press.

HUME, DAVID. 1739-40. *A Treatise of Human Nature*. 3 vols. London.

IZIKOWITZ, KARL GUSTAV. 1951. *Lamet: Hill Peasants in French Indo-China*. Etnologiska Studier, 17. Göteborg: Etnografiska Museet.

JACKES, MARY. 1969. Wikmunkan Joking Relationships. *Mankind* **7**: 128-31.

cxii

Introduction

JOSSELIN DE JONG, J. P. B. DE. 1935. *De Maleische Archipel als Ethnologisch Studieveld*. [Inaugural Lecture, University of Leiden.] Leiden: Ginsberg.

KANT, IMMANUEL. 1787. *Kritik der reinen Vernunft*. 2d ed. Riga.

KORN, FRANCIS. 1969. The Logic of Some Concepts in Lévi-Strauss. *American Anthropologist* **71**: 70-71.

—— 1971. Terminology and 'Structure': The Dieri Case. *Bijdragen tot de Taal-, Land- en Volkenkunde* **127**: 39-81.

– n.d. *Elementary Structures Reconsidered: Lévi-Strauss on Kinship*. [Submitted for publication.]

KORN, FRANCIS & NEEDHAM, RODNEY. 1970. Permutation Models and Prescriptive Systems: The Tarau Case. *Man* n.s. **5**: 393-420.

LEACH, E. R. 1954. *Political Systems of Highland Burma: A Study of Kachin Social Structure*. London: Bell.

—— 1957. Aspects of Bridewealth and Marriage Stability among the Kachin and Lakher. *Man* **57**: 50-55.

—— 1958. Concerning Trobriand Clans and the Kinship Category 'Tabu'. *Cambridge Papers in Social Anthropology* **1**: 120-45.

—— 1961. *Rethinking Anthropology*. London School of Economics Monographs on Social Anthropology, 22. London: Athlone Press.

—— 1964. Review of White 1963. *Man* **64**: 156.

—— 1967. The Language of Kachin Kinship. In: M. Freedman, ed., *Social Organization: Essays presented to Raymond Firth* (pp. 125-52). London: Cass.

—— 1969. 'Kachin' and 'Haka Chin': A Rejoinder to Lévi-Strauss. *Man* n.s. **4**: 277-85.

—— 1970. *Lévi-Strauss*. London: Collins.

LÉVI-STRAUSS, C. 1949. *Les Structures élémentaires de la parenté*. Paris: Presses Universitaires de France.

—— 1963. *Structural Anthropology*. Translated from the French by Claire Jacobson and Brooke Grundfest Schoepf. New York: Basic Books.

—— 1966. The Future of Kinship Studies. *Proceedings of the Royal Anthropological Institute* 1965: 13-22.

—— 1969. *The Elementary Structures of Kinship*. Edited by Rodney Needham; translated from the French by J. H. Bell, J. R. von Sturmer, and R. Needham. Boston: Beacon Press; London: Eyre & Spottiswoode.

LICHTENBERG, GEORG CHR. 1958. *Aphorismen*. Edited by Max Rychner. Zürich: Manesse.

LÖFFLER, LORENZ G. 1969. *Grundlegung einer formalen Ethnologie der Verwandtschaft.* (Unpublished mimeograph, 100 pp.) Heidelberg.

LOUNSBURY, FLOYD. 1956. A Semantic Analysis of the Pawnee Kinship Usage. *Language* **32**: 158-94.

—— 1964. A Formal Account of the Crow- and Omaha-type Kinship Terminologies. In: Ward H. Goodenough, ed., *Explorations in Cultural Anthropology* (pp. 351-93). New York: MacGraw-Hill.

—— 1965. Another view of the Trobriand Kinship Categories. In: Hammel 1965 (pp. 142-85).

MCCONNEL, URSULA H. 1940. Social Organization of the Tribes of Cape York Peninsula, North Queensland. *Oceania* **10**: 434-55.

—— 1950. Junior Marriage Systems: A Comparative Survey. *Oceania* **21**: 107-45.

—— 1957. *Myths of the Mungkan.* Melbourne: Melbourne University Press.

MACFARLANE, A. 1883. Analysis of Relationships of Consanguinity and Affinity. *Journal of the Anthropological Institute* **12**: 46-63.

MOORE, SALLY FALK. 1964. Descent and Symbolic Filiation. *American Anthropologist* **66**: 1308-20.

MÜLLER, ERNEST W. 1964. Structure and Statistics: Some Remarks on the Purum Case. *American Anthropologist* **66**: 1371-6.

MURDOCK, GEORGE PETER. 1949. *Social Structure.* New York: Macmillan.

NEEDHAM, RODNEY. 1956. Ethnographic Notes on the Siwang of Central Malaya. *Journal of the Malayan Branch, Royal Asiatic Society* **29**: 49-69.

—— 1958. A Structural Analysis of Purum Society. *American Anthropologist* **60**: 75-101.

—— 1960a. Alliance and Classification among the Lamet. *Sociologus* **10**: 97-118.

—— 1960b. Chawte Social Structure. *American Anthropologist* **62**: 236-53.

—— 1962a. *Structure and Sentiment.* (Fourth impression, with corrections, 1969.) Chicago: University of Chicago Press.

—— 1962b. Genealogy and Category in Wikmunkan Society. *Ethnology* **1**: 223-64.

—— 1963a. A Note on Wikmunkan Marriage. *Man* **63**: 44-5.

—— 1963b. The Wikmunkan Mother's Brother: Inference and Evidence. *Journal of the Polynesian Society* **72**: 139-51.

—— 1963c. Symmetry and Asymmetry in Prescriptive Alliance. *Bijdragen tot de Taal-, Land- en Volkenkunde* **119**: 267-83.

Introduction

—— 1963d. Introduction (pp. vii-xlviii) to Durkheim and Mauss 1963.

—— 1964a. Explanatory Notes on Prescriptive Alliance and the Purum. *American Anthropologist* **66**: 1377-86.

—— 1964b. Descent, Category, and Alliance in Sirionó Society. *Southwestern Journal of Anthropology* **20**: 229-40.

—— 1965. A Corrective Comment on Wikmunkan Marriage. *Man* **65**: 22.

—— 1966a. Age, Category, and Descent. *Bijdragen tot de Taal-, Land- en Volkenkunde* **122**: 1-33.

—— 1966b. Comments on the Analysis of Purum Society. *American Anthropologist* **68**: 171-7.

—— 1966c. Review of Vergouwen 1964. *American Anthropologist* **68**: 1265-8.

—— 1966d. Terminology and Alliance I. *Sociologus* **16**: 141-57.

—— 1967. Terminology and Alliance II. *Sociologus* **17**: 39-53.

—— 1968. Endeh: Terminology, Alliance, and Analysis. *Bijdragen tot de Taal-, Land- en Volkenkunde* **124**: 305-35.

—— 1969. Gurage Social Classification. *Africa* **39**: 153-66.

NEUMANN, J. B. 1886. Het Pane- en Bila-stroomgebied op het Eiland Sumatra (Studiën over Batahs en Batahlanden, III.) *Tijdschrift van het Koninklijk Nederlandsch Aardrijkskundig Genootschap*, 2e ser., **3**: 459-543.

ONVLEE, L. 1949. Naar Inleiding van de Stuwdam in Mangili. (Opmerkingen over de Sociale Structuur van Oost-Soemba.) *Bijdragen tot de Taal-, Land- en Volkenkunde van Nederlandsch-Indië* **105**: 445-59.

OSSENBRUGGEN, F. D. E. VAN. 1935. Het oeconomisch-magisch Element in Tobasche Verwantschapsverhoudingen. *Mededeelingen der Koninklijke Akademie van Wetenschappen*, Afd. Letterkunde, 80, ser. B, **3**: 63-125.

[RADCLIFFE-] BROWN, A. R. 1914. The Relationship System of the Dieri. *Man* **14**: 33-5.

—— 1930. A System of Notation for Relationships. *Man* **30**: 121-2.

—— 1940a. On Joking Relationships. *Africa* **13**: 195-210.

—— 1940b. The Study of Kinship Systems. *Journal of the Royal Anthropological Institute* **71**: 1-18.

—— 1950. Introduction to: A. R. Radcliffe-Brown and Daryll Forde, eds., *African Systems of Kinship and Marriage* (pp. 1-85). London: Oxford University Press for International African Institute.

REVEL, JEAN-FRANÇOIS. 1957. *Pourquoi des philosophes.* Paris: Pauvert.

RIGBY, PETER. 1967. Time and Structure in Gogo Kinship. *Cahiers d'Études africaines* **7**: 637-58.

—— 1969. *Cattle and Kinship among the Gogo: A Semi-pastoral Society of Central Tanzania.* Ithaca, N.Y.: Cornell University Press.

RIVIÈRE, P. G. 1966. Oblique Discontinuous Exchange: A New Formal Type of Prescriptive Alliance. *American Anthropologist* **68**: 738-40.

—— 1969. *Marriage among the Trio: A Principle of Social Organisation.* Oxford: Clarendon Press.

SAYERS, BARBARA. 1964. The Phonemes of Coen Wik-Munkan. In: W. & L. Oates *et al.*, *Gugu-Yalanji and Wik-Munkan Language Studies* (pp. 51-6). Occasional Papers in Aboriginal Studies, 2. Canberra: Australian Institute of Aboriginal Studies.

SCHEFFLER, H. W. 1970. Ambrym Revisited: A Preliminary Report. *Southwestern Journal of Anthropology* **26**: 52-66.

SCHMITZ, C. A. 1964. *Grundformen der Verwandtschaft.* Basler Beiträge zur Geographie und Ethnologie, Ethnologische Reihe, 1. Basel: Pharos-Verlag Hansrudolf Schwabe.

SCHNEIDER, DAVID M. 1965. Some Muddles in the Models: or, How the System Really Works. *The Relevance of Models for Social Anthropology* (ASA Monographs 1), pp. 25-88. London: Tavistock Publications.

STERNBERG, LEV. 1904. Giliaki. [The Gilyaks.] *Etnograficheskoe Obozrenie* **1**: 1-42; **2**: 19-55; **4**: 66-119.

THOMAS, NORTHCOTE W. 1906. *Kinship Organisations and Group Marriage in Australia.* Cambridge: Cambridge University Press.

THOMSON, DONALD F. 1935. The Joking Relationship and Organized Obscenity in North Queensland. *American Anthropologist* **37**: 460-90.

—— 1936. Fatherhood in the Wik Monkan Tribe. *American Anthropologist* **38**: 374-93.

—— n.d. Kinship and Behaviour in North Queensland: A Preliminary Account of Kinship and Social Organisation on Cape York Peninsula. (Unpublished typescript; 123 pp., diagrams.)

TURNBULL, COLIN M. 1965. *Wayward Servants: The Two Worlds of the African Pygmies.* Garden City, N.Y.: Natural History Press; London: Methuen, 1966.

VERGOUWEN, J. C. 1933. *Het Rechtsleven der Toba-Bataks.* The Hague: Nijhoff. [English edition, translated by Jeune Scott-Kemball: *The Social Organisation and Customary Law of the Toba-Batak of Northern Sumatra.* (Koninklijk Institut voor Taal-, Land- en Volkenkunde Translation Series, 7.) The Hague: Nijhoff, 1964.]

WAISMANN, F. 1968. *How I see Philosophy*. Edited by R. Harré. London: Macmillan.

WEHRLI, HANS J. 1904. Beitrag zur Ethnologie der Chingpaw (Kachin) von Ober-Burma. *Internationales Archiv für Ethnographie* **16** (Supplement).

WHEELWRIGHT, PHILIP. 1959. *Heraclitus*. Princeton: Princeton University Press.

WHITE, LESLIE A. 1966. *The Social Organization of Ethnological Theory*. Rice University Studies, vol. 52, no. 4. Houston: William Marsh Rice University.

WILDER, WILLIAM. 1964. Confusion versus Classification in the Study of Purum Society. *American Anthropologist* **66**: 1365-71.

WITTGENSTEIN, LUDWIG. 1967. *Zettel*. Edited by G. E. M. Anscombe and G. H. von Wright; translated by G. E. M. Anscombe. Oxford: Blackwell.

WOUDEN, F. A. E. VAN. 1935. *Sociale Structuurtypen in de Groote Oost*. Leiden: Ginsberg. [English edition, translated by Rodney Needham: *Types of Social Structure in Eastern Indonesia*. (Koninklijk Instituut voor Taal-, Land- en Volkenkunde Translation Series, 11.) The Hague: Nijhoff, 1967.]

YPES, W. K. H. 1932. *Bijdragen tot de Kennis van de Stamverwantschap, de inheemsche Rechtsgemeenschappen en het Grondenrecht der Toba- en Dairibataks*. Leiden: Adatrechtstichting.

1

Rodney Needham

Remarks on the Analysis of
Kinship and Marriage

'What is theory in musical composition? – Hindsight. It
doesn't exist. There are compositions from which it is
deduced.'

IGOR STRAVINSKY

I

INTRODUCTION

To consider the analysis of kinship and marriage leads at once
into a paradox.

'Kinship is to anthropology what logic is to philosophy or
the nude is to art,' declares Robin Fox; 'it is the basic discipline
of the subject' (1967: 10). Certainly it is a well-established part
of the subject: Lafitau began the comparative study of unilineal descent and classificatory terminologies as long ago as
1724, and Morgan inaugurated in 1871 what has since become a
recognized topic of academic investigation and theory. The
syllabuses of university instruction in anthropology now invariably include kinship; no textbook is thought adequate without
some treatment of it; and in all the variety of examinations in
anthropology it occupies a central and unavoidable position.
You cannot gain a certificate of competence as a social anthropologist without demonstrating a command of kinship theory,
and it is expected of most anthropologists that they will make
some contribution to it. Indeed, most of those who have made
great names in anthropology – e.g. Rivers, Kroeber, Radcliffe-
Brown, Lévi-Strauss – have gained their prominence largely
by their publications on kinship. If there is one topic, therefore,
which is indispensable to social anthropology, and which defines
what social anthropologists essentially do, it would appear to
be kinship. Here, if anywhere in the subject, we should expect
to find discipline, methodical rigour, and theoretical advance.

This much is, I suppose, a standard account of the matter;
but an inside look at what really goes on reveals a curious

1

situation. The majority of students of anthropology, and their teachers, are apprehensive and uncertain about kinship, and they have as little to do with it as they can get away with. Examination scripts seldom show much enthusiasm or sound knowledge, and the professionals often seem not to be particularly good at the practical analysis of kinship systems. There is a comparative paucity of published works on the topic, and progress in understanding kinship systems has been sporadic and slight. The current theoretical position is obscure and confused, and there is little clear indication of what future developments we can expect or should encourage.

In view of the constant professional attention extending over roughly a century, and a general improvement in ethnographic accounts, this is a remarkably unsatisfactory situation in what is supposed to be a basic discipline. Obviously, after so long a time, and so much field research, it is not just facts that we need. Something more fundamental seems to have gone wrong. What we have to look for, perhaps, is some radical flaw in analysis, some initial defect in the way we approach the phenomena. Edmund Leach has already explored this possibility, in his salutary address 'Rethinking Anthropology' (1961: 1-27), but there is little sign that even his verve, clarity, and ingenuity have yet had much effect on received ideas and ordinary practice. What I want to do here, then, is to resume Leach's iconoclasm and to look with him for a way out of our present uncertainties.

A possible diagnosis may be that the trouble lies not so much in the substantive study of institutions of kinship and marriage as in our conceptual premises, and most decisively in the way we conceive the classification of phenomena. The failings basically responsible for the present situation are, I shall argue, firstly what Wittgenstein has called 'a craving for generality' (1958: 17) and secondly the lingering delusion of a natural science of society, a conception which has led to a kind of analysis that has produced few useful results. You will already recognize in these contentions an echo of Leach's strictures on 'butterfly-collecting' and on biased premises. For that matter, what I too want to press for is precisely to 'take each case as it comes' (Leach 1961: 10). But I think there is a conceptual therapy by means of which we can prepare ourselves better to do so, and for this purpose I suggest that we should turn back to Lowie's *Culture and Ethnology* (1917) and to Wittgenstein's *Blue Book* (written in 1933-34, published 1958). You will see therefore that I cannot pretend to be telling you anything very new. But since it has taken me a long time to see the relevance and the useful effect of views published decades ago, I suppose there will be others to whom it will be helpful if I rehearse them on this occasion.

My argument is presented in the form of remarks on a series of topics, not as a progressive exposition, and without any large apparatus of scholarly and ethnographical references. I adopt this means for two chief reasons. The first is that I have already published enough work on kinship and marriage to excuse me presenting any detailed demonstration of what I think ought to be done by way of analysis. This permits me to make my points in a cursory style which may stick more readily in the memory. The second reason is that a fuller citation of pronouncements on kinship uttered by many of my colleagues would have to be rather dissentient, whereas my intention is to be positive. For the most part, then, I shall cite only those with whose opinions I agree, and not even many of these. The essential is not to tax you with facts or with academic controversy, but to concentrate on the concepts that we are professionally inclined to employ when we analyse institutions of kinship and marriage. I shall deal, rapidly, with the notions of kinship, marriage, descent, terminology, and incest.

II

KINSHIP

There has been a fair amount of discussion about what 'kinship' really is. My own view is that much of this debate is pretty scholastic and inconsequential, and I shall not recapitulate any of it or embark on yet another definitional exercise. Let me simply adopt the minimal premiss that kinship has to do with the allocation of rights and their transmission from one generation to the next. These rights are not of any specific kind but are exceedingly various: they include most prominently rights of group membership, succession to office, inheritance of property, locality of residence, type of occupation, and a great deal else. They are all, however, transmissible by modes which have nothing to do with the sex or genealogical status of transmitter or recipient. Certainly they have no intrinsic connexion with the facts, or the cultural idioms, of procreation. It is true that the possession and exercise of these rights is defined by reference to the sex of the persons thus related; but then so is the division of labour in the simpler societies, yet we do not for that reason think this method of distinguishing statuses so remarkable as to deserve a special designation and to call for a distinct type of theory.

These jural systems and their component statuses can be genealogically defined. Why this should be so is a fundamental question that has never been properly resolved, and I cannot take it up here. Let us merely admit the fact. It is certainly a very convenient fact, but the method of description does not entail any particular property in what is described. The circumstance that two societies can be described by the same means does not argue any significant similarity, either sociologically or semantically, between them. Still less does it mean that the relationships in question are genealogical or that they are so conceived by the actors.

What information is given, then, by the report that an institution has to do with 'kinship'? Nothing, really, about social facts. For the label designates no distinct type of phenomena; it provides no clue to comprehension; and it does not indicate the kind of analysis that will be appropriate. The use of the word 'kinship' is to be found, rather, in the multiple connotations of common usage, in the organization of ethnographical accounts, and in the conventions of academic discourse. When an ethnographer gives one chapter the heading 'Kinship', and another the heading 'Sacrifice', we have a rough preliminary idea of the different matters they will describe. It may well turn out, though, that there is a close connexion between them, just the same, and very likely neither will be comprehensible without the other. Similarly, if a colleague tells you that he is interested in kinship, his choice of phrase implies that he could have stated instead that he was keen on subsistence economies or primitive law, and the word he actually employs does indeed give you a vague idea of his theoretical bent, the books he has presumably read, and the kind of technical conversation he is likely to engage you in. In this case as well, however, it cannot be inferred that his interest in kinship will be unconnected with economics or law; and in fact, of course, it will probably turn out that he has to deal with these topics also and that they in turn demand a recourse to kinship.

I am not denying, therefore, that the word 'kinship' is useful; and still less should I wish to try to reform our professional vocabulary by narrowing the definition of the word or, on the other hand, by urging that it be abandoned altogether. What I am saying is that it does not denote a discriminable class of phenomena or a distinct type of theory. We are tempted to think that it must have this specificity, because it is a substantive and because it is an instrument of communication. But it has an immense variety of uses, in that all sorts of institutions and practices and ideas can be referred to by it. Segmentary organization, section systems, widow inheritance, polyandry, teknonymy, divorce rates, and so on – all these topics and very many more can be subsumed under the general rubric of kinship. In other words, the term 'kinship' is what Wittgenstein calls an 'odd-job' word (1958: 43-4), and we only get into trouble when we assume that it must have some specific function. In a way, it could be said that the trouble is not very serious, since when we actually investigate an institution, or compare ways of explaining it, we do not generally speak of kinship at all. Indeed, this common circumstance demonstrates that the word has in fact no analytical value. On the other hand, anthropologists do often get into trouble, of a timewasting and discouraging sort, when they argue about what kinship really is or when they try to propound some general theory based on the presumption that kinship has a distinct and concrete identity.

To put it very bluntly, then, there is no such thing as kinship, and it follows that there can be no such thing as kinship theory.

III

MARRIAGE

Very similar considerations apply to the concept of marriage and to the theoretical propositions of anthropologists about marriage. I need not say much about this topic because the case has been well made by Leach: 'marriage is . . . "a bundle of rights"; hence all universal definitions of marriage are vain' (1961: 105).

I think there is no refutation of this argument. What I should like to re-emphasize, simply, is Leach's conclusion that 'the nature of the marriage institution is partially correlated with principles of descent and rules of residence' (108). Perhaps it is not so much correlated, though, as it is defined in any particular instance by what we divisively call the 'other institutions' of the society. It is not only jural institutions, either, that we have to take into account, but moral and mystical ideas as well, and these in an unpredictable and uncontrollable variety. The comparison of marriage in different societies needs therefore to be contextual, and ultimately 'total' in a Maussian sense, if we are to be sure that we understand what we are trying to compare.

In this connexion, the designation of marriage has a special interest. Ethnographers do not on the whole report the indigenous terms for marriage, or investigate the connotations of such terms, yet we need not look far to see that these can be revealing. For instance, the modern German *Ehe* derives from MHG *ē, ēwe*, law, statute, and its recent narrower meaning merely singles out marriage as one of the most important jural institutions. The English 'marriage' and French *mariage*, however, come from the Latin *marītus*, husband, which is usually referred to IE **mer- *mor-*, represented by various words meaning 'young man, young woman'. It is at once evident that even two European traditions can embody, etymologically, two quite distinct kinds of ideas about marriage. More than this, there may not be any designation for marriage at all. In classical Greek, as Aristotle observed, 'the union of man and woman has no name' (*Politics*, I, 3, 2). Even though marriage was essential for the preservation of the 'houses' (οἶκοι), which were the constituent elements of the Athenian city-state, there was no single word which could be taken to stand for 'marriage' – nor, for that matter, were there words in classical Greek which stood for 'husband' and 'wife' (Harrison 1968: 1). And to take a contrasted enough civilization, whereas the Penan of Borneo do have words for husband (*banen*) and wife (*rēdu, do*), they too have no word for marriage. One wonders, therefore, how many other societies make no lexical recognition of that institution which has so commonly been regarded in anthropology as categorically essential and universal.

As soon, however, as we adopt some technical definition of marriage, whether or not it is held to be universal, we run the risk of leaving out of account precisely that feature (e.g. chastity, allegiance, life-giving) which in one or other of the societies compared is in fact central to the institution. This is of course a familiar quandary in comparative studies, but I think it is a question whether its lessons have everywhere sunk fully home. At any rate, large-scale correlations are still attempted, and these can be carried out only by means of fairly strict definitions which are nevertheless presumed to be widely applicable, but the stricter they are the less likely it is that they will cope adequately with social reality.

Once again, though, I am not denying that 'marriage' is a very useful word. On the contrary, it has all the resources of meaning which its long history has conferred upon it, and we should now find it hard to communicate without these. For that matter, it is a more indispensable word than 'kinship' is, and it directs us more precisely to an identifiable kind of relationship. If an ethnographer sets out to tell us about marriage, we have at least a preliminary indication that he is not going to focus directly on dam-building. But I choose this latter example, all the same, precisely because Onvlee has shown that in eastern Sumba, where marriage is prescribed with the matrilateral cross-cousin, you cannot understand the organization of dam-building unless you first understand the norms of marriage (Onvlee 1949). Conversely, you cannot understand the marriage institution without knowing the forms of co-operation which follow from it. There are also cosmological grounds to both aspects of Sumbanese social life. As Hocart says in another context, 'There is much more to the cross-cousin system than the classification of relatives; there is a whole theology . . .' (1952: 237). But nothing in the ordinary connotations of the English word 'marriage' prepares us to grasp a situation such as this, and nothing in anthropological usage gives the word any technical value either.

So 'marriage' too, is an odd-job word: very handy in all

sorts of descriptive sentences, but worse than misleading in comparison and of no real use at all in analysis.

IV

DESCENT

The classification of modes of descent is a specially effective example of conceptual difficulty, because the topic has been a constant anthropological concern since Bachofen and McLennan. In spite of this prolonged concern, however, there is still no general agreement on the matter.

Anthropologists habitually use terms such as 'patrilineal' or 'matrilineal', yet cannot easily claim that these are specific descriptions. Even when the ethnographic facts are not in dispute, it is sometimes possible to argue about the type of descent system to which a given society should be assigned. Or when it is agreed that a society is patrilineal, for example, it is possible to argue about whether it is a strong or a weak instance of the type. Such arguments might be all to the good if they led to cogent and agreed decisions, but for the most part this is just what they cannot do. What we are left with is not theoretical advance but a wordy conflict of rival definitions. I need not go on, or supply examples, for the situation is familiar to any anthropologist. What is important is to find a way out of this typological confusion.

Some anthropologists (e.g. Köbben, Lewis) have contended that we cannot assimilate different societies on the mere ground that they are 'patrilineal', but that this wide designation needs to be broken down into the component functions. It is the kinds of rights that are governed by the rule of descent which decide the respects in which societies are to be counted as patrilineal and thus as comparable. 'The functional implications of descent are often much more significant than whether descent is traced in the patri- or matri-line' (Lewis 1965: 109). This approach has a well-established ancestry – it was embarked on by Fison in 1879 and continued by Wake in 1889 – but it is not, I think, the answer. The difficulty remains that this substantive concentration on complexes of rights makes comparison as uncontrollable and as hard to carry out as the rights may be various.

Simply to specify more narrowly what 'patrilineal' means in a particular description does not make the rubric any more useful; in fact, it tends to show how inappropriate it really is. On the other hand, no one needs it in order to define a single jural system that is under study, for an exact survey can report the social facts without summing them up under any such general label. In any case, the proposed reconsideration is not fundamental enough. Lewis, for example, still takes it that 'descent' is traced in some line, only that this tracing is affected by 'other principles of organization' (1965: 106). Yet it is this very notion of 'descent' that needs investigation.

A more radical course is pointed by Leach's suggestion that such typifying devices as 'patrilineal' and 'matrilineal' may have no sociological significance whatever:

> 'It *may* be that to create a class labelled *matrilineal societies* is as irrelevant for our understanding of social structure as the creation of a class *blue butterflies* is irrelevant for the understanding of the anatomical structure of lepidoptera' (1961: 4).

This is a bracing notion, and in fact it is far from clear that there is any convincing defence of the class of matrilineal societies. My own inclination is to doubt whether there are any useful propositions about matrilineal systems which distinguish these, as a class, from societies with other rules of descent and thereby justify the typology. This may be thought a matter of debate, but at least there is enough reasonable doubt about the issue to call the conventional typology into renewed question.

Yet can we do without it? After all, Bachofen and McLennan created a stir because they had discovered something; and the jural differences between the Minangkabau and the Batak are real, not the result of an unfortunate typology. The troubles begin, however, when we try to characterize and compare the Minangkabau and the Sirionó, merely on the ground that they are both matrilineal; in other words, when we extend the characterization beyond those features which prompt the description 'matrilineal' and then talk as though this label applied to all the other institutions also. Here I think we have a double instance of the craving for generality: we classify societies together because by some definition they possess in common the feature of 'matrilineal descent', even though the rights so governed and the functions they serve may be quite disparate; and in each case we classify institutions together, as composing a 'matrilineal society', because various other usages, which may not be common properties of members of the class, happen to accord with that mode of transmitting the definitive rights.

Clearly the method is wrong, but all the same there is something to be wrong about. What is the solution? There is one way out, I think, namely to resort to purely formal criteria; i.e. to cease concentrating immediately on substantive and jural aggregates of many kinds, exercising different functions, and to think instead in terms of logical possibilities. I am not referring to the use of systematic models, but to a far more basic procedure. It may strike you as excessively simple, but I think it has advantages.

Given two sexes, and transmission of rights defined by these, we may distinguish six elementary modes of descent. Let us denote male by m, and female by f. The modes are then as follow:

1. $m \rightarrow m$
2. $f \rightarrow f$
3. $(m \rightarrow m) + (f \rightarrow f)$
4. $(m \rightarrow f) + (f \rightarrow m)$
5. $(m \rightarrow m) \parallel (f \rightarrow f)$
6. $m/f \rightarrow m/f$

These formal modes correspond severally to functional paradigms. Mode 1, male to male: patrilineal. Mode 2, female to female: matrilineal. Mode 3, a combination of modes 1 and 2 in the definition of any status: two conjoint rules of descent, i.e. bilineal. Mode 4, male to female, female to male: alternating. Mode 5, male to male, female to female, defining distinct sexual statuses: two disjunct rules of descent, i.e. parallel. Mode 6, male or female to male or female: cognatic.

Naturally, once alternation is admitted the number of additional possibilities (i.e. variations on mode 4) is increased, but these six modes are elementary.

The modes are not to be conceived as characterizing societies holistically. Indeed, modes 4 and 5 probably could not be employed socially as regular and exclusive principles of transmission and incorporation, though certain rare and uncertain approximations to them have been reported. My point, rather, is that in any society different rights may be transmitted according to different modes. The ethnographer's task is then to sort out the rights, according to the indigenous classification in the first place, and to establish the various rules by which they are governed. To cite an extremely simple case, Penan society could be partly analysed in this way:

descent name	mode 1
residence	mode 2
inheritance	mode 5
group membership	mode 6

The result is thus a complex of rights and rules not corresponding entirely to any single principle of descent. The jural complex thus arrived at is likely to be singular, not only in the kinds of rights culturally distinguished, but also in the association of these with different modes. Only in the extremely improbable event that a society were to transmit all rights uniformly by one single mode would it conform literally to any conventional type such as 'patrilineal' or 'matrilineal'.

It would of course be possible to construct a new and much extended typology of descent systems, composed of all the logically possible combinations of the elementary modes. This would give a total of 63 types. Whether this was worth doing would depend on the results, but since my present concern is to undermine such typologies it is not an undertaking that I should recommend. The intention is to preserve the specificity of the social facts, yet at the same time to make possible a comparison that is not based on merely contingent assemblages of institutions or 'functions'. This we can do by resorting to those simple logical possibilities which govern equally both the practical fabrication of social systems and our own abstract conceptions of the forms they can take. That is, our analysis will be guided by the same logical constraints as must have been effective in producing the systems that we study.

Of course, there is still ample room for the arbitrary or mistaken discrimination of kinds of rights or modes of transmission, as well as for speculative alternatives in the selection or classification of those rights or modes that an investigator is interested in. We can never obviate these sources of imprecision, and variations, but at least a purely formal approach gives us the chance of making a less biased start.

Let me admit at once, moreover, that this has been a cursory exposition, and that I have not distinguished exactly, as might ultimately be done, all of the jural variables involved. The main reason is that I am not trying to work out a technique, complete with instructions for use, but to bring about a change in the conception of descent systems. This change offers, it seems to me, a number of advantages.

1. To begin by listing logical possibilities, without regard to their social feasibility or known realization, actually accords better with social reality. The indigenous classification of rights can be directly adopted, and these can then be distributed without prejudice among the formal modes, not in accordance with some theoretical predisposition or academic fashion. The approach thus conduces to an accurate ethnographic description, a possible benefit which is surely of the very greatest importance.

2. It removes the temptation to characterize a descent system univocally as patrilineal or matrilineal, etc., and in doing so to make a biased choice of any one kind of right which is then taken to define 'the' rule of descent.

3. It renders less easy, consequently, a comparison of different systems by reference to the transmission of only one kind of right, e.g. membership in a descent group, and the overriding of jural and other differences which might qualify or invalidate the comparison.

4. A logical analysis presents a constant discouragement to the employment or elaboration of defective empirical typologies which have proved not to advance our understanding of the phenomena.

5. The formal approach allows anthropologists of any theoretical persuasion to collaborate, or to understand each other, without the customary obstacles of variant technical vocabularies or opposed connotations implicitly attached to conventional labels.

12

A consequence of conceiving descent systems in this way, and one that has a special analytical value, is that among a number of societies compared in any formal respect there will not be assumed to exist any empirical feature common to all. It will more readily be seen, in other words, that they may not compose a class in the conventional sense. Instead, they can exhibit what might be called serial likenesses. As a simple illustration, take three societies (A, B, C), each constituted by three features (p, ..., v):

A p, q, r
B r, s, t
C t, u, v

Let r and t be each a type of right transmitted in mode 1. There is then a resemblance, r, between A and B, and another, t, between B and C, but none between A and C. Yet in ordinary anthropological practice they could all be classed together as 'patrilineal'. A crucial misdirection can thus be given to our thought by the uncritical employment of the received idea as to what a class is; whereas to analyse and compare by reference to formal, rather than empirical, types can lead to a clearer view of the distinctive features by which similarities and dissimilarities are gauged.

In sum, I am suggesting that the present theoretical confusion about descent has its origin in two basic conceptual defects: (1) an addiction to empirical generalizations, and (2) a subscription to a conventional but unrealistic idea of how a class is formed. These are matters to which I shall revert below in the discussion of other topics. For the present, I must introduce a note of reserve. A direct consequence of the approach that I am advocating is that comparison becomes far more difficult, and on any large and detailed scale perhaps impracticable; for the distribution of rights among logical types increases the factors in question and does not make the rights thus discriminated any more comparable.

v

TERMINOLOGIES

In the study of relationship terminologies we ought to be on firmer ground, one might think, than when we are dealing with anthropological abstractions such as overall rules of descent, for in this field of inquiry we are dealing with the explicit linguistic categories by which other peoples classify their social experience. But even here certain familiar conceptual defects have led to a theoretical stultification. Here too a premature urge to construct empirical typologies has led to a battery of nominal types that we can do very little with because the phenomena have been mistakenly grouped.

A good example is the so-called 'Omaha' type of terminology, defined essentially by the equation MB = MBS. This famous type has a current and very prominent employment in ethnographical reports, in comparative studies, and in theoretical exercises. Yet I do not think it is going too far to say that nothing of any real elucidatory value has come out of all this attention. The reason is simply that a variety of terminologies all possess this supposedly definitive feature but differ from each other in practically everything else. Thus the Araucanians, Iatmül, Miwok, Nyoro, and Thado, to cite no more societies, have all been typed and classed together on the ground that they have Omaha terminologies, whereas the quickest survey shows that their forms of social classification (not to mention their institutions) are systematically disparate. Intensive analyses of individual 'Omaha terminologies' have repeatedly confirmed the invalidity of the type, and with increasing certainty as the structural range of terminologies studied is extended. The Ungarinyin terminology, for instance, exhibits the supposed Omaha equation yet differs extremely (in statuses distinguished, number of descent lines, and rule of marriage) from the Purum, which similarly exhibits the Omaha feature; and the Purum terminology in turn differs extremely from the Gurage, which also makes the equation in question but is structurally quite different again. When an integral comparison of these terminologies is carried out, it is at once obvious that there is no systematic resemblance among them.

This is an expectable result by now, and it gives rise more forcefully to the question of what the 'Omaha' label is supposed to tell us. The answer is that there exists no useful generalization about this factitious class of Omaha terminologies. It is true of course that the minimal equation is associated with patriliny (in a conventional acceptation), but no one could well

14

claim that this was a theoretical result arrived at by means of the type. It has been well known, at any rate, since the last century, when both Kohler and Durkheim made the point. And it is surely not surprising that the terminological identification of a man and his son is accompanied by a transmission of status through males. If, then, an ethnographer reports an Omaha terminology, he tells us nothing of any descriptive value; and in representing the terminology to himself under this label he tells himself nothing of any analytical value either. No systematic comprehension is thereby provided, nor does the assignment to the Omaha type offer any clue to the analysis of the society which employs the terminology. There really is no such thing as an Omaha terminology, except that of the Omaha themselves, and it leads only to confusion and wrong conclusions to suppose that there is.

A parallel case is that of the so-called 'Crow' terminologies, typically defined by the minimal equation FZ = FZD. There are many very different forms of terminology which possess this feature, and they do not compose a systematically definable class. A telling illustration is provided by Eggan's paper on historical changes in the Choctaw kinship system (1937). He begins by conceding that 'if we examine various Crow . . . kinship systems we find a series of variations . . . , so that there is some difficulty in deciding whether a given kinship system is a Crow type or something else' (35). The cases that he compares demonstrate this point. The Choctaw terminology varies from the Crow type in the curious features FZ ≠ FZD and FZS = FZSS. The Chickasaw classification differs in other particulars, the Creek from these, and the Cherokee yet again. Finally, the Yuchi terminology, which shows still further divergences from the Crow type, is thought to suggest a Crow system because of the inferred equation (FM) = FZ. But these terminologies, in spite of all their differences one from the other, can nevertheless be classed together as 'Crow' – and it is a question why anthropologists should wish to do so.

Eggan's own purpose is primarily historical: 'These kinship structures,' he writes, 'originally Crow in type, were progressively modified by varying degrees of the same acculturational process' (47). This argument is convincing, but it serves at the same time to impair the concept of a Crow terminology.

Even though these terminologies can apparently be traced back to forms of classification which more nearly resembled each other, in their reported condition they are really very different – yet they are still typed as 'Crow'. And even if they have undergone a similar kind of change, under similar pressures, the degrees of variation which they exhibit must reduce any theoretical effect in classing them all as Crow terminologies. For the point in discriminating a class of phenomena is to be able to formulate propositions which hold for all members of the class. But in these cases the terminological variations are argued to correspond to different degrees of social change. In other words, however similar these societies may previously have been, they are now disparate in certain institutional respects, and these differences are ignored when they are subsumed under the 'Crow' label. On the other hand, the label is neither essential nor helpful in the sociological analysis of each of the societies which are thus classed together.

I have cited Eggan's investigation precisely because the ethnic connexions and other similarities of circumstance make a comparative study especially feasible, but even in this case the conventional typology of terminologies has no comparative or analytical value. This conclusion becomes yet more clear when a comparison is extended to societies in other culture areas, e.g. to the Mota of the Banks Islands or the Ramkokamekra of Brazil; for the Crow designation then refers to nothing more than the common feature of matrilines, which is exactly the basis on which the class-designation is applied, and there is no further sociological property which can be ascribed to members of the class.

Similar conclusions could readily be reached if we were to scrutinize other conventional types of relationship terminology, e.g. 'Dakota', 'Sudanese', 'Eskimo', 'Hawaiian'. In each instance it is possible to demonstrate that the class has been invalidly constituted; and in each instance, so far as I can judge, no propositions of scientific value have been arrived at by means of the typology.

What I wish to propose therefore is quite seriously that this kind of typology, i.e. one in which the types are defined by isolated features of named societies arbitrarily selected as paradigm cases, should be entirely abandoned. It is methodically faulty, it misdirects research, and it has served no useful purpose.

I cannot even say, as though in recognition of a theoretical advance now accomplished, that the time has come to make this conceptual change, for what I recommend is no more than what Lowie pressed for in 1917. Our only advance since then, as far as this issue is concerned, has been in factual knowledge, such that we now possess superior ethnographic resources for the demonstration of his points. Lowie argued, in his neglected but masterly work *Culture and Ethnology*, that any given system is a complex historical growth that cannot be adequately defined as a whole by some such 'catchword' as classificatory, Hawaiian, or what not (1917: 116). 'It cannot be too strongly urged,' he emphasized, 'that a given nomenclature is molded by disparate principles' (122). 'There is no Hawaiian *system*, no Dakota *system*' (123).

How, then, should we analyse relationship terminologies? By abandoning types and concentrating on principles. 'We shall . . . do well to amend our phraseology and to speak rather of kinship categories, features, or principles of classification than of types of kinship systems' (105).

For my part, I have tried to make this point in a number of places, so perhaps I may simply refer you, for a recent demonstration, to my analysis of the Gurage terminology of social classification (1969). This terminology includes the features $MB = MBS$ and $FZC = ZC$, so that by these criteria it clearly belongs to the 'Omaha' type. But the really interesting thing about the Gurage terminology is that it is a quite singular form of classification, particularly in the lineal equations in the line of reference, and systematically unlike any other that I have been able to discover. I have tried to show in that paper that the distribution of the terms can well be elucidated by a sociological analysis of Gurage institutions; but at no point in the investigation is the Omaha label, or any other aspect of the typology to which this designation belongs, of the slightest use. Instead, the analysis proceeds by an attempt to understand Gurage social classification through the categories and principles proper to the terminology itself. The most prominent principle of this classification happens to be exhibited in the extensive lineal equations that are effected. But this feature

17

does not constitute a type, or assimilate the Gurage terminology to the Omaha or to any other type. It is simply one cultural exemplification of the fact that there are only two formal possibilities in the terminological identification of statuses in a descent system, viz. lateral and lineal. A terminology may recognize either dimension, exploit either possibility, in a variety of ways. All that the Gurage have done, by their lineal equations, is to make an unusual exploitation of an elementary principle of classification. What is interesting, then, is the specific configuration in which a terminology takes advantage of this possible dimension of categorical order. The reasons for which it distributes certain categories lineally can only be discovered, I have argued, by an intensive examination of the facts of the particular case. A recourse to principles and to formal possibilities enables this to be done; but to place a terminology under a substantive rubric such as 'Omaha', in the conventional typology, serves no such purpose. We must indeed take each case as it comes; only I would add that the way we take it can be guided by formal considerations which help us to recognize more clearly the intrinsic characteristics of the case.

This example introduces the stock question about the connexion between terminology and social forms. It will support the general burden of this paper to make just a few remarks on this topic.

There are presumably two main purposes in trying to establish correlations between categories and action. One is to permit such inferences that the analysis of a particular society shall be facilitated: given a certain distribution of categories, the investigator will then know what to expect in his study of institutions. The other is to permit sociological comparisons: given similar terminologies, it can then be assumed, for the sake of whatever theoretical issue is under investigation, that the institutions will be similar also.

The sad fact of the matter, though, is that neither of these conditions obtains. The outcome has been generally discouraging in these regards; but let us review the situation and see what lessons nevertheless emerge.

1. Relationship terminologies can be divided formally into (*a*) lineal and (*b*) non-lineal. By the former term (lineal) I refer to

classifications in which the typical feature, in the medial three genealogical levels at least, is the distinction of statuses according to whether relationship is traced through persons of the same sex or not. The consequence of this principle is to assort jural statuses into descent lines, such that, e.g. F = FB, FBS = MZS, S = BS, as contrasted with F ≠ MB, FBS ≠ MBS, S ≠ ZS. Examples are lineal descent systems such as the Kaguru, Mapuche, or Nyoro. Non-lineal terminologies have no such positive feature, but are characterized by the lack of this principle of distinction. Examples are cognatic societies such as the Penan, Sarakatsani, or Siwang.

This is such a simple and fundamental division of forms of classification that here, if anywhere, we might expect to find a good correlation with institutions. There are indeed certain common associations, but it is never safe to make sociological inferences from the presence or absence of the distinctive feature. A lineal terminology does not entail a lineal rule of descent, and still less does it entail the presence of lineal descent groups. Examples of societies with lineal terminologies but without fixed rules of unilineal descent or corresponding descent groups are the Sinhalese of Pul Eliya and the Trio of Surinam. On the other hand, a non-lineal terminology can be accompanied by a lineal transmission of certain rights, e.g. succession to office or inheritance of real property. Examples are Bali and rural Japan. These empirical conclusions accord with what I have suggested above (sec. IV) about descent.

2. Where we find lineal terminological equations, either direct (e.g. MB = MBS, as among the Gurage) or alternating (e.g. MB = MBSS, MBS = MBSSS, as among the Iatmül), we can be fairly confident that we shall find in the sphere of institutions some explicit expression of a mode of descent (in these examples, patrilineal). But this can never be an absolute inference, as we have seen in sec. IV above, for there is no telling to what extent rights of other kinds may prove to be transmitted by different modes, and there is no *a priori* scale of evaluation by which it might be presumed that the mode exhibited in the terminology was the most important.

For that matter, it is conceivable, and may in one alleged

case be so in fact, that a terminology composed of matrilines should govern the affairs of a society that was preponderantly patrilineal. In any case, even if a rule of descent could be inferred from a terminology, nothing else could be. That is, one could not infer what groups were formed, how rights were ascribed, or what values were recognized.

3. Prescriptive terminologies can readily be identified, by the invariant relation that articulates relations between lines, and can thus be distinguished from non-prescriptive.

They fall into two main types: (*a*) symmetric, and (*b*) asymmetric. But this contrast, even when most clearly established, does not permit inferences about the ways in which alliances are actually contracted. A symmetric terminology does not entail symmetric (reciprocal) alliances but, on the contrary, may govern a strictly asymmetric transference of women. An asymmetric terminology, on the other hand, is indeed incompatible with symmetric alliance, but nothing more positive than this can be inferred. In systems with either symmetric or asymmetric terminologies, the exercise of preferences can lend a marked bias to the conduct of social relations, but a preference cannot necessarily be read off from a prescriptive terminology.

4. The employment of any type of terminology as a practical instrument of social classification can be considerably affected by innumerable factors which are not recognized in the terminology itself.

The most general factor of the kind is relative age. Individuals of the same age will belong naturally to different categories, and individuals of different ages will belong to the same category. Social relations may therefore be ordered, in principle, either by category or by relative age. If age is sometimes the dominant criterion in classification, then in such instances it is to some extent incorrect to regard the terms as denoting distinct classes of persons (Needham 1966a).

Other common factors are residence, which Kroeber indeed argued to be of fundamental importance (1938), genealogical degree, and collective sentiments. There are in addition innumerable further possible factors which affect the employment of terminologies but cannot be inferred from them. They can only be discerned, and their consequences gauged, by the empirical investigation of each particular case.

5. A limitation of a fundamental kind is placed on the interpretation of relationship terminologies by the fact that we cannot even infer anything about the degree of significance that a category may have.

This was so well recognized by Murdock, in *Social Structure*, that he went so far as to isolate what he called a criterion of 'immateriality'. By this he meant 'a negative similarity resulting from the functional unimportance of the relatives of two kin-types, whereby a sufficient basis for differentiating them is lacking' (1949: 136). Leach, similarly, in analysing the Jinghpaw system, stressed that 'On the one hand, individuals are classed together because, individually and as a group, they stand in a significant and important relationship to the speaker; but on the other hand they may be classed together precisely because they are unimportant and remote' (1961: 52).

The latter case is well exemplified in systems, as among the Kachin, of asymmetric prescriptive alliance. In these, the categories of lineal relatives are of the greatest jural importance, and it is in accordance with this importance that more terminological discriminations are made among these than among affines. The terms for affines, wife-givers and wife-takers, complete a universal classification of social relations. There are thus three major classes of persons and groups: wife-givers, lineal relatives, and wife-takers. Actual contact will be maintained with some people of all three classes, but how are those to be classified with whom there is no recognized relationship? The solution adopted by the Haka Chin of Burma and the Mamboru of Sumba is to classify them as agnates. So the terms for lineal relatives can apply both to the most important people in the social universe and to the least important. But there is no means of guessing this from a study of the terminology. In other words, we cannot even tell whether, or in what circumstances, a term will mean anything or not.

All of this looks pretty negative, I admit, but I should not wish it to be thought for a moment that I underrate the significance of relationship terminologies. What I am arguing against is, in the first place, the conventional typology which – by the very fact of assigning terminologies to substantive types – leads us to imagine that the form of a society's relationship terminology tells us more than it ever can. Secondly, I am arguing against the related assumption that societies with similar terminologies, in the conventional typology, are thereby sociologically similar also. But these objections do not at all mean that I am opposed to the analysis of terminologies or even to the construction of typologies. There are good and bad methods of analysis, after all, and good and bad typologies. Relationship terminologies are of prime and indispensable significance in the analysis and comparison of institutions and social action (Needham 1966b: 1967), especially once we realize what limitations we are under in our interpretation of them. The question is whether there is some method, or conceptual revision, by means of which we can escape the prejudices and confusions into which received anthropological ideas tend to lead us.

The means to an improvement in analysis has, I think, already been provided by Lowie, basing himself on Kroeber's brilliant paper on classificatory systems of relationship (Kroeber 1909). Instead of talking about a Hawaiian system, for example, and then being forced to decide whether a given case was or was not Hawaiian, he isolated a 'Hawaiian principle', i.e. a mode of classification which underlies non-lineal terminologies. Instead of adopting the Dakota system as a paradigm, he abstracted 'the Dakota principle', i.e. that which orders lineal terminologies. Then there were two 'variants' on the Dakota scheme: the Crow and Omaha principles of classification, i.e. matri- and patri-lineal identifications. Finally, he concentrated on the terminological correlates of special forms of marriage, including 'prescribed' marriage with the bilateral cross-cousin, a form which he saw as 'mirrored in the nomenclature' of certain Melanesian societies (Lowie 1917: 107, 119, 150, 151, 152, 172). Thus a terminology did not need to be labelled as a whole, and thence be assigned to one type or another, because of certain typological features that it happened to possess, but was regarded as 'molded by disparate principles'. This not only came closer to the facts of the matter, but it also provided a clearer view of the historical change of terminologies; e.g. instead of a clumsy succession of types, the Hawaiian principle could be seen as gradually taking over from the Dakota principle, producing a variety of terminologies of which none might wholly correspond to either the Dakota or the Hawaiian type.

Perhaps this will not sound like very much, but it was a great step to take and I do not think that essentially we can do much better. The central advantage of Lowie's method is that in any analysis it dispenses with a crude substantive class and concentrates instead on the operation of classification. Instead of relying upon a paradigm case, and a class of other cases bearing more or less attenuated resemblances to it, the method investigates the intricate combination of classificatory principles by which any particular terminology may in fact be constituted. The craving for generality is checked, and the quest for essential features is given up.

In the study of relationship terminologies as well, therefore, we find that analytical advance is blocked by the familiar conceptual habits which have so much hindered the study of descent systems. The remedy is not only urged by Wittgenstein but has actually been put into prior effect by Lowie. In this case too, however, there is the consequence that while analysis is made more exact, comparison is made more intricate and difficult. In fact, it is hard to see how a large-scale comparison can be carried out when each case is analysed rather than typed.

Nevertheless, it may be that this line of argument will be found far too simple, perhaps even obvious. Let me just quote, therefore, what an authority (Murdock 1955: 361) has not long ago concluded about the study of descent systems and relationship terminologies:

'In anthropology, the initial classificatory task has now been substantially accomplished in the field of social structure. . . . We now possess satisfactory criteria for differentiating types of family organization, kin and local groups, and kinship terminology and behavior patterns. . . . These features are combined with one another in particular ways to produce a finite number of types of social organization, which in their totality represent a systematic classification comparable to those of Linnaeus and Mendelyeev.'

Well, I do not wish to disparage Murdock's decades of industrious application to these matters, but I am bound to say that

I think these statements are mistaken in every particular. The notion of a finite and total classification is logically indefensible, and this methodological ambition has achieved no results which might give it a pragmatic justification.

Yet the ideal continues to guide research. A recent illustration is furnished by Romney's analysis of the Kalmuk Mongol terminology (1967). It is a long and painstaking piece of work, and I should not desire to call its analytical precision into question, but the formulation of its theoretical conclusions displays very clearly the typological concern which, especially since Radcliffe-Brown, has had such a deleterious effect on anthropological thought. It is simply that the Kalmuk terminology cannot be accommodated by Lounsbury's rules and hence that the differences 'warrant the recognition of an additional type of Omaha system' (Romney 1965: 141). Now this might be a positive result if only it meant that the Kalmuk Mongol system could be assimilated to a class of social phenomena about which there was a body of tested theoretical propositions. But merely to add a further type to the catalogue of 'Omaha' systems, when nothing enlightening or interesting has been said about this ill-founded class of systems, does not seem a very useful exercise.

VI

INCEST

Lastly, I want to make some remarks on the concept of 'incest'. This is a notion that is as prominent in social anthropology, and as persistent, as 'kinship' has been. The contributions to what is called incest theory have been very numerous, elaborate, and ambitious, culminating (as far as theoretical extremity is concerned) with Lévi-Strauss's dictum: 'The incest prohibition is . . . culture itself' (1969: 12).

The variety of explanations proposed has been remarkable: fear of menstrual blood, harmful genetic effects, instinctive repugnance (Radcliffe-Brown even declared that 'It is this emotional reaction that we have to explain if we are to have a theory of incest'), disruption of the solidarity of the family, disorganization of the status distinctions preserved by the prohibition, and so on. But two general assumptions are shared by the incest theorists, however much at odds they may otherwise be. (1) That we know what 'incest' really is, whatever form its regulation may take. Thus Radcliffe-Brown easily asserts, as though it were to be taken for granted, that 'incest is *properly speaking* the sin or crime of sexual intimacy between immediate relatives within the family' (1950: 69; italics supplied). (2) That the prohibition of incest, in spite of its highly varied patterning, is a universal. Thus according to Lévi-Strauss it is 'a rule, but a rule which, alone among all social rules, possesses at the same time a universal character' (1969: 8-9).

It is curious, therefore, that there is nevertheless nothing like any general agreement about the explanation of incest prohibitions. Yet the endless academic debate is carried on as if the variegated and often unrelated theories were (1) rival explanations of the same phenomenon, and hence (2) universally applicable. 'Disputes are multiplied, as if every thing was uncertain; and these disputes are managed with the greatest warmth, as if every thing was certain' (Hume, *Treatise*, Bk. I).

These circumstances give rise to the suspicion that here too something has gone radically wrong. The trouble may lie, namely, not in the comprehension of the facts or in the ingenuity of the explanations, but in the conception of that which is to be explained. It looks as though the classificatory concept of 'incest' may itself actually have conduced to the confusion, and to the negative results, which characterize the present theoretical situation.

Revel, in his irreverent critical comments on *Les Structures élémentaires de la parenté*, makes this excellent and revealing observation: 'If there is one thing that emerges from Lévi-Strauss's book, it is that it will not do to talk about the prohibition of incest in general, because the institutions falling under this concept are so diverse and sometimes contradictory' (1957: 154). It sounds a simple enough point, but I think it contains the key. Incest prohibitions do not in fact compose a definite class, and if this is so there cannot be a general theory that applies to all of them.

There are two prime considerations which support this view. The first is the wide and variable range of statuses to which the prohibitions apply. The scope of application is in each case an integral feature of the social system, and in some sense a

25

function of it; i.e. the complex of prohibitions in a society cannot be comprehended except by a systematic purview of the institutions with which they are implicated. By this account of the matter there are as many different kinds of incest prohibitions as there are discriminable social systems.

The second consideration is that incest prohibitions are in part moral injunctions; they are expressions of indigenous ethical doctrines and, whether or not they are touched with a peculiar emotional quality (something I doubt as a general concomitant), they have cultural meanings which no attempt at explanation can reasonably neglect.

Something of these latter connotations can be seen in the disparity of the words which ethnographers translate by the English word 'incest'. Let us begin with this word itself, taking it not as a quasi-technical term in social anthropology but philologically, as a particular testimony to a cultural tradition that remains implicit in its composition. It comes from the Latin *castum*, chaste, and belongs to a family of Romance words with the same root; e.g. French *inceste*, Italian *incesto*, Spanish *incesto*, etc. The idea ultimately underlying the English word seems therefore to be that incest is an offence against purity and moral decency. The Germanic family of languages, however, makes a significant contrast. In this we find related words such as German *Blutschande*, Dutch *bloedschande*, Norwegian *blødskande*, etc. These terms are all compounded of the word for 'blood' and the word for 'shame'. The implicit idea, then, is not apparently about the guilt of sullied purity but about the public disgrace of an offence against kinship, conceived (as we know from other evidence) as a community of blood. Next, to go far outside the European tradition, the Chinese term *luan lun* implies a more sociological view. It is composed of characters meaning respectively 'disorder' and 'social relationship' (also: kind, class, order, sequence). In classical Chinese political theory the stability of the state depended on the 'five relationships' (*wu lun*), viz. sovereign/ subject, father/son, elder brother/younger brother, husband/ wife, friend/friend. The offence in this case, then, is that of disrupting a jural and moral order, namely that of confusing statuses. Finally, as a further culturally distinct example, let us take the Indonesian word *sumbang*, a word that is found in

26

one or another form (e.g. *suvang*) in probably the majority of the islands of the archipelago. *Sumbang* is commonly rendered as 'incestuous', but it also means 'improper' or 'repugnant'. In social conduct it refers generally to what is offensive because it is out of place or unseemly, a subversion of propriety. Forbidden sexual congress is only one form of such unsuitable behaviour. For that matter, *sumbang* covers not only incest but simple adultery as well. And cheating at cards or some other game is also *sumbang*. Very prominently, moreover, the word has aesthetic meanings. A connexion between the sexually wrong and the aesthetically shocking is made revealingly by a phrase in horticulture: a tree which has been grafted so that it bears blossoms of two different kinds is a *pokok sumbang*. Perceptually, the word applies to what is deformed, disharmonious, or discordant. A person's voice can be *sumbang*, hard on the ear; and an everyday material object, such as a battered chess-board, can also be *sumbang*, unsightly. Incest, therefore, is indeed denoted by this word, but it would be a mistake for an ethnographer to translate *sumbang* simply by the English word 'incest'.

In these four linguistic areas, etymological indications or current usages thus exhibit a variety of meanings which cannot validly be classed together as the semantic component of the prohibition of incest.

In addition to all this, there are cultures in which there is no such explicit notion as that of 'incest'. In fifth-century Athens, not only was the verbal concept entirely lacking but there was no action at law which was or could be brought against those guilty of an offence of the kind (Harrison 1968: 22).

By the above criteria, therefore, it is evident that incest prohibitions do not compose a class of homogeneous social phenomena. The most that might be claimed is that they characteristically include certain minimal prohibitions, e.g. that on sexual intimacy between mother and son. This is in fact disputable as a universal proposition, but even to concede it would still not justify the conception that these supposedly common features are what essentially define the class which is the subject of incest theory. It is this presumption, however, which suggests the received idea that the differential patterns of prohibition are 'extensions' of certain basic interdictions.

Rodney Needham

Thus Murdock writes that 'incest taboos and exogamous restrictions of whatever sort seem clearly to be extensions of the sex taboos between parent and child and between brother and sister in the nuclear family' (1949: 284). This of course is neither logical inference nor established fact, but the very presumption indicates the diagnosis of the initial conceptual error about incest. In this case also the difficulties arise from the invalid constitution of a class and, especially clearly, the unbounded exercise of the craving for generality.

We obviously need to find a radically different solution to the problem of incest. A structural theory is unlikely to serve, since there are no systematic resemblances among all known sets of prohibitions. A formal approach via logical possibilities, as in the reinterpretation of the concept of descent, does not seem feasible either, for there are no self-evident or readily acceptable premisses. Nor, finally, should we commit ourselves to a reductionist type of theory, for this is precisely what most anthropological explanations of the prohibition of incest have been, and they have not worked. We have, it seems, to look for a quite different way of understanding the facts.

Before we do so, let us make a brief appreciation of the situation. Each set of cultural prohibitions forms a coherent but variable assemblage of rules; the contextual explication of these rules demands a recourse to history, language, moral concepts, and many other contingent particulars. The various sets of prohibitions thus do not compose a concrete class such as might be open to a unitary explanation; the functional or semantic explication of the rules of one society may not apply at all to those of another.

Here, then, is a possible line of argument about incest theory.

1. In each instance, we are dealing with explicit rules, i.e. with collective representations. These rules may perhaps have emotional concomitants, and for all we know may even be grounded ultimately in some common instinct or psychic character, but empirically we can deal with them only as social facts.

2. The rules, by definition, have to do with access to women.

3. Women are social valuables; for many peoples, and in the opinion of some anthropologists, they are the prime valuables.

28

4. Access to socially recognized valuables is always socially regulated; the regulation expresses the evaluation.

5. Rules define what is permitted and what is prohibited.

6. The regulation of access to women is in these respects just like any other kind of regulation: access to certain categories of women is permitted, and to certain others is prohibited. These rules, positive and negative, compose in any particular instance a coherent set and should be comprehended as such, i.e. correlatively. It is methodically defective to consider only prohibitions, apart from permissions and prescriptions, and it is yet more invalid to consider only isolated prohibitions as though these alone were definitive or essential.

7. What is at issue in the study of 'incest' prohibitions is simply the negative aspect of the regulation of access to women. All that is common to incest prohibitions is the feature of prohibition itself.

I conclude that 'incest' is a mistaken sociological concept and not a universal. There can hence be no general theory of incest.

VII

CONCLUSIONS

The intention behind these remarks has been to argue that anthropological research has been misguided, in even the supposedly basic topics of kinship and marriage, by certain conceptual failings. The most consequential of these is the uncritical attachment to an inappropriate conception of a 'class', namely that a class is a number of objects possessing certain attributes, or even perhaps only one attribute, in common. What is common, moreover, has been conceived as a specific or essential feature, and this feature has been represented in empirical terms. This mode of thought is the product, I have been contending, of a craving for generality. The craving is the resultant,

Wittgenstein maintains, of a number of tendencies, the first of which is:

> 'The tendency to look for something in common to all the entities which we commonly subsume under a general term. – We are inclined to think that there must be something in common to all games, say, and that this common property is the justification for applying the general term "game" to the various games; whereas games form a *family* the members of which have family likenesses. Some of them have the same nose, others the same eyebrows and others again the same way of walking; and these likenesses overlap' (1958:17).

The phenomena classed together under one term may be related to one another in many different ways; as we scrutinize instance after instance we find that what we had taken for characteristic features prove not to be such and that similarities crop up and disappear. 'We see a complicated network of similarities over-lapping and criss-crossing: sometimes overall similarities, sometimes similarities of detail' (Wittgenstein 1953, sec. 66).

There need not be, accordingly, any one thing that the phenomena of 'kinship' have in common, or that the phenomena of 'marriage', 'descent', 'relationship terminology', or 'incest' respectively have in common. Under each general term the instances may be classed together, instead, as in spinning a thread we twist fibre on fibre: 'And the strength of the thread does not reside in the fact that some one fibre runs through its whole length, but in the overlapping of many fibres' (Wittgenstein 1953, sec. 67). The trouble, however, is that we are inclined by our conceptual habits to assume that there must be something in common to all the phenomena that we class together as 'kinship' and the rest, and it is this unanalysed premiss that leads us into theoretical difficulty. Wittgenstein's response to this kind of confusion in other fields of inquiry is the injunction: 'Don't say there *must* be something common, or they would not be called [X] – but *look and see* whether there is anything common to all' (1953, sec. 66). The consequence of doing so in social anthropology is, I suggest, the realization that the phenomena classed as 'kinship', for instance, do not in all cases possess any specific features such as could justify the formulation of general propositions about them.

What is common to descent systems may be only that they variously exploit certain logical possibilities in a sexually defined transmission of rights from one generation to the next. What is common to the myriad forms of marriage may be only the contractual union of sexual statuses. What is common to relationship terminologies is the exploitation of certain formal possibilities in the classification of sexual statuses. What is common to incest prohibitions is merely the fact of prohibition. There may thus be something in common, under each general term, but not necessarily a definite set of characteristic, specific, or essential features. The common feature of prohibition, for example, does not entail that the incest regulations of different societies shall in any specific respect be at all comparable.

Another tendency which Wittgenstein argues is responsible for the craving for generality is our preoccupation with the method of science. 'I mean the method of reducing the explanation of natural phenomena to the smallest number of primitive natural laws . . .' (1958: 18). In social anthropology this preoccupation has most notoriously taken the form of a search for sociological laws, and although this particular ambition is now relatively out of favour, or less grandiosely declared, the outlook still flourishes in the attempts to find statistical correlations. Now these cannot be established without a precisely specified typology of phenomena, and it is necessary for the purpose that the phenomena classed under one type shall have in common certain specific features. But if it is conceded that the social facts in question do not necessarily compose a conventional class of this homogeneous kind, but may exhibit instead an immense array of serial and more complex resemblances, then the grounds for this method of comparison and explanation are removed.

This does not mean, though, that comparative studies are unfeasible or should be put at a discount. On the contrary, if we give up the reificatory typologies that are usual in social anthropology we shall actually be in a better position to compare, for we shall at least see the social facts in a less distorted way. More positively still, we can carry out comparisons by reference to logical features, and by the formulation of more suitable abstractions than have been customary. I have given some indications, here and elsewhere, of the formal approach.

31

That of improved abstraction may readily be illustrated by the study of prescriptive alliance. This type of organization is defined by the terminology, and the terminology is constituted by the regularity of a constant relation that articulates lines and categories. It is by reference to this relational abstraction – not to lineages, groups, offices, and other such institutions – that effective comparisons can be initiated.

For that matter, I think that there are not only logical features to which we can resort, but that there are psychic features as well which can be recognized through the screen of cultural differentiation and which make comparison possible. But that is another matter; at any rate, it does not seem directly relevant to the analysis of kinship and marriage. Yet it points in the same theoretical direction. If I may offer a more speculative observation, it may be that all social anthropology will be able to do – or perhaps what it may best be able to do – is to comprehend, in one case after another, the schemes in which cultures have variously taken advantage of logical and psychic facilities which are the elementary resources available to all mankind in the ordering of experience.

In this case, to adopt a phrase of Wittgenstein's (1953, sec. 90), 'our investigation ... is directed not towards *phenomena*, but, as one might say, towards the *"possibilities"* of phenomena'.

ACKNOWLEDGEMENTS

I am indebted to Dr Francis Korn for calculating the number of combinations of the six elementary modes of descent. Dr Ian Hamnett has kindly worked out other possibilities, on the basis of permutations instead of combinations, which show that according to the assumptions and methods adopted the total could be 325, 1,956, 3,125, or 46,656 types.

REFERENCES

EGGAN, FRED. 1937. Historical Changes in the Choctaw Kinship System. *American Anthropologist* **39**: 34-52.

FOX, ROBIN. 1967. *Kinship and Marriage: An Anthropological Perspective*. Harmondsworth, Middlesex: Penguin Books.

HAMMEL, E. A. (ed.). 1965. Formal Semantic Analysis. *American Anthropologist* (Special Publication) **67**. Menasha: American Anthropological Association.

Remarks on the Analysis of Kinship and Marriage

HARRISON, A. R. W. 1968. *The Law of Athens*. Oxford: Clarendon Press.

HOCART, A. M. 1952. *The Life-giving Myth*. Edited by Lord Raglan. (2nd impression, ed. with a foreword by Rodney Needham, 1970.) London: Methuen.

HUME, DAVID. 1739-40. *A Treatise of Human Understanding*. London.

KROEBER, A. L. 1909. Classificatory Systems of Relationship. *Journal of the Royal Anthropological Institute* **39**: 77-84.
—— 1938. Basic and Secondary Patterns of Social Structure. *Journal of the Royal Anthropological Institute* **68**: 299-309.

LEACH, E. R. 1961. *Rethinking Anthropology*. (London School of Economics Monographs on Social Anthropology, No. 22.) London: Athlone Press.

LÉVI-STRAUSS. 1969. *The Elementary Structures of Kinship*. Rev. ed. Edited by Rodney Needham, translated by J. H. Bell, J. R. von Sturmer, and R. Needham. Boston: Beacon Press; London: Eyre and Spottiswoode.

LEWIS, I. M. 1965. Problems in the Comparative Study of Unilineal Descent. In *The Relevance of Models for Social Anthropology* (ASA Monograph 1): 87-112. London: Tavistock Publications.

LOWIE, R. H. 1917. *Culture and Ethnology*. New York.

MURDOCK, GEORGE PETER. 1949. *Social Structure*. New York: Macmillan.
—— 1955. Changing Emphases in Social Structure. *Southwestern Journal of Anthropology* **11**: 361-70.

NEEDHAM, RODNEY. 1966a. Age, Category, and Descent. *Bijdragen tot de Taal-, Land- en Volkenkunde* **122**: 1-33.
—— 1966b. Terminology and Alliance, I: Garo, Manggarai. *Sociologus* **17**: 141-57.
—— 1967. Terminology and Alliance, II: Mapuche, Conclusions. *Sociologus* **18**: 39-53.
—— 1969. Gurage Social Classification: Formal Notes on an Unusual System. *Africa* **39**: 153-66.

ONVLEE, L. 1949. Naar Inleiding van de Stuwdam in Mangili. (Opmerkingen over de Sociale Structuur van Oost-Soemba.) *Bijdragen tot de Taal-, Land- en Volkenkunde* **105**: 445-59.

RADCLIFFE-BROWN, A. R. 1950. Introduction (pp. 1-85) to *African Systems of Kinship and Marriage*, ed. by A. R. Radcliffe-Brown and Daryll Forde. London: Oxford University Press for the International African Institute.

REVEL, JEAN-FRANÇOIS. 1957. *Pourquoi des philosophes*. Paris: Pauvert.

ROMNEY, A. KIMBALL. 1967. Kalmuk Mongol and the Classification of Lineal Kinship Terminologies. In Hammel (ed.) 1967: 127-41.

WITTGENSTEIN, LUDWIG. 1953. *Philosophical Investigations*. Translated by G. E. M. Anscombe. Oxford: Blackwell.

—— 1958. *The Blue and Brown Books*. Oxford: Blackwell.

2

Martin Southwold

Meanings of Kinship

I

INTRODUCTION

This paper is mainly concerned with the meaning of the word
«kinship»[1] in anthropological usage. I seek to show that the
word is notably imprecise and ambiguous, and therefore
obscures and confuses some important distinctions; and I go
on to suggest a terminology by means of which the distinctions
could be kept clear. In order to anchor this potentially abstruse
discussion in empirical reality, I begin by considering the
meanings of kinship terms among the Baganda. My difficulties
with kinship in fact began with my doubting whether some of
these terms really meant what they had to mean if they were
kinship terms; and these doubts became systematic after I
read Leach's paper on Trobriand terminology (Leach 1958).

I must make it plain that I am not interested, as a linguist
might be, in the kinship terminology as such, but rather in what
it indicates about the social institutions to which it refers. In
particular, if the meaning of the supposed kinship terms shows
them not to be kinship terms, then the roles and relationships
to which they refer should not be categorized as of kinship
either. Whether, or how far, kinship in Buganda is really kinship, is a problem which arises out of considering the meanings
of the supposed kinship terms, and which demands for its
resolution that we examine the meanings of our word «kinship».
At both levels, problems about kinship are inescapably also
problems about meaning.

Initially, of course, I was unaware of these ramifications.
As a simple-minded sociological anthropologist I wished to give
an adequate description and analysis of institutions in Ganda
society, in the course of which I should need to find English
translations for important role-terms (role-names). The accepted
translations of these terms (as kinship terms) seemed to me
plainly wrong: could I do better and, if so, how?

35

The easiest way to avoid the difficulty would be more or less completely to avoid translating the terms at all, as others have done (e.g. Leach 1961 [1945]; Beattie 1957, 1958; Lounsbury 1956, 1964; Goodenough 1956). I think this is defensible if one is writing a paper on the kinship terminology as such, or even more generally on the kinship system. I think it is impracticable when the centre of interest is elsewhere, in some other institutional area, or in the total social system. To ask a reader to carry in his head the significata of several dozen untranslated vernacular terms is to dispense with his company. Some sort of translation there must be. I do not expect to find very good translations; but that cannot excuse accepting very bad ones.

II

THE GANDA TERMINOLOGY

The table below is a modified version of one that appears in Mrs Fallers's Ethnographic Survey (Fallers, M. C. 1960: 60).

Kinship terms

Luganda	*English translation*
nnyina	mother
kitaawe	father
nnyina omuto	'little mother'
kitaawe omuto	'little father'
muganda	sibling of the same sex
mwannyina	sibling of the opposite sex
muganda omukulu	elder sibling of the same sex
mwannyina omukulu	elder sibling of the opposite sex
mutabani	son
muwala	daughter
ssenga	father's sister
jjajja	grandparent
mujjwa	child of female lineage member
mukoddomi	in-law
mukazi	wife
muzzukulu	grandchild
kizibwe	cross-cousin of the opposite sex
kojja	male of mother's lineage

The modifications I have made[2] do not affect the analysis, except that, in the original, the terms were keyed to a skeleton genealogical diagram (ibid.: 57), thus underlining the assumption that genealogy is relevant to their interpretation. The headings in the table, 'kinship terms' and 'English translation', are given in the original, without comment; Luganda is the language of the Baganda.

It may seem odd, not to say boorish, to excerpt an Ethnographic Survey for critical comment. I do so because Mrs Fallers's few pages on Ganda kinship are in fact the fullest published account specifically on this topic. The relative taciturnity of the many other writers on Buganda is, of course, highly significant. There is also a more positive consideration. An Ethnographic Surveyor is charged, I assume, to present a brief and straightforward description of the facts, without theoretical elaboration. As there are no facts without theory, this amounts to a prescription for swallowing conventional theory, hook, line, and sinker. Since my target is just that conventional theory, which is too readily assumed by most of us, an Ethnographic Survey is an excellent place to catch it *in puris naturalibus*.

If one examines the column of English translations in the table, one sees that they can be divided into four categories:

1 Straightforward English kinship terms, e.g. «mother», «grandchild».
2 Terms which, though they do not occur in normal English usage, are formed on similar principles to our regular kinship terms: e.g. «sibling of the same sex».
3 Terms which may be considered to combine English principles of formation with a qualification rather odd: «little mother», «little father».
4 Terms which are formed on principles quite alien to English social usage: «male of mother's lineage», «child of female lineage member».

Though it will be appropriate to comment later on the third category (pp. 52-3), it is the fourth I wish to take up at once.

It may be noted that the two terms in this category are

37

reciprocals. The translations offered are basically sound – except that, in a society where few people either can or care to trace ancestry more than two generations back, the term «clan» would be more apt than «lineage», so long as it is understood that Ganda clans are not even putative descent groups. I know of several clans the members of which have, by common consent, a plurality of unrelated founding ancestors. Moreover, it is openly and frequently asserted that it is easy to become a member of a clan other than that into which one is begotten, and that this has often been done. Clans, it might be said, recruit mainly by birth, but also by conversion. In this they differ little from, say, the Church of England or the Church of Rome; in which connexion it may be significant that Baganda regard the latter two institutions as having largely taken the place of clans in political alignments.

Thus amended, the English expressions offered as translations of these two terms make no reference to genealogical connexion: rather they categorize persons in terms of their membership of corporations linked by affinal alliance. Hence the English expressions cannot be treated as kinship terms; hence if they are (as they are) accurate translations of the Ganda terms, the latter cannot be kinship terms either. But then consistency would require us to interpret the other Ganda terms in a similar way: that is, as referring to membership of corporations rather than to genealogy: and hence to accept that these are not kinship terms either. But similar arguments applied to other societies – perhaps all other societies having unilineal descent groups – would suggest that their supposed kinship terms are not kinship terms either. And if the terms are not kinship terms, then the roles they label are not kinship roles; the relationships, the systems, the institutions are not those of kinship. . . . The whole grand edifice of kinship theory would seem to come tumbling about our ears.

A conclusion so apocalyptic would certainly not be accepted without more evidence than I have attempted to provide. I shall outline the evidence relevant to the Ganda system; but before this can usefully be done, a great deal of conceptual clarification is called for.

WHAT IS KINSHIP?

It seems merely perverse to doubt that kinship terms are kinship terms; but this is because the question is already begged when we refer to them as kinship terms. What then is our warrant? On what grounds does Mrs Fallers, for example, assume so profusely that the terms she discusses are kinship terms? This question is so rarely discussed that it is hard to know what people suppose. I suspect that we categorize them as kinship terms because we translate them by the English kinship terms, «father», «mother», etc. And we so translate them because they are kinship terms. . . . How do we get trapped in this charmed circle? Originally, I guess, because we suppose that the terms by which people refer to those we perceive as their fathers, mothers, etc., must *mean* 'father', 'mother', etc. – as if it were inconceivable that other people could categorize their close relatives in a way other than as English people do! Such a prejudice is developed into a systematic technique in those pages (79-84) of the 6th Edition of *Notes and Queries on Anthropology* which advise on the collection of kinship terminology. No account is taken of the fact that, although the term thus equated with, say, «father» is indeed applied to a person's father, it is much more often applied to persons who are *not* his father. Or rather, account is taken of this by use of the ingenious evasion of 'extension': the term which really means 'father' is extended to apply to all those other men.

But what, pray, is the evidence for that? We are agreed now that the order in which a child learns the application of such terms is nothing to the point (e.g. Fortes 1957: 175-6; Buchler & Selby 1968: 5-6). Is it then alleged that at some time in the past the word meant only 'father', and subsequently came to be extended? Where, then, is the evidence for this historical development? Where could it conceivably be found? Or is it that those native speakers who use the term in application to someone other than Father always introduce some qualification of phrase or of tone to indicate an extended signification? This is not stated by our authors: nor is it generally so. Or are we to suppose that they recommend it as a general rule for translation that one arbitrarily selects some minor part of the field of application of the word as giving its meaning, and accounts for the greater part of the field as mere extension? This would certainly facilitate the foisting of all manner of absurdities upon the public; I cannot however perceive it as a ready guide to truth.

I am not contending that the extensionist account is invariably wrong; on the contrary I believe it is often true. But where it is true it must be shown to be true, by citing relevant evidence: merely to rely on the reader's insular prejudice is not enough.

But the basic difficulty goes deeper: if anthropologists fail to present the evidence necessary to support assumptions that they are dealing with kinship terminology, and so forth, it is because they do not feel the force of the challenge. The question, 'Is this really kinship?' does not come into focus because the word «kinship» itself is grossly imprecise. Hence doubts are blunted, and dogma survives.

I have more than once had this produced as an explicit rebuttal of arguments such as those I offer here. My argument, I am assured, is invalid, since to deny that terms are kinship terms is without any meaning. Logically, however, if the denial of a statement is meaningless, so by equal measure is its assertion. This objection, therefore, disqualifies any use of the word «kinship» in statements: but in fact the objector is merely assaulting the denial in order the more complacently to go on making the assertion! Such illogic is not at all rare when people speak about kinship: I take it as evidence that the value of the term is much less cognitive than emotional and moral.

In a loose sense, I should agree that the term «kinship» is 'meaningless': and if we were all agreed about that enough to avoid ever using it, I should have accomplished half my purpose. But, to be literal about it, the trouble with the term is not lack of meaning, but surfeit. We apply the word «kinship» to a variety of things which we ought to distinguish, but rather, by this promiscuous application, confound. What the word lacks is any one single distinct and ascertainable meaning: and it is this which disqualifies it from use as a scientific term. It is even a counter-scientific term, since the author who uses it is likely to confuse himself as well as his readers; and in fact to create such a muddle that it becomes hard to see what is wrong, or even that anything is wrong.

It would seem therefore that what we need first is a definition,

an answer to some such question as 'What do we mean by
«kinship»?' But before tackling this we ought really to get
clear on the prior question, 'What do we mean by «mean by»?' –
which is of course another paper in itself. For the present, I
have space only to distinguish three among the numerous
senses in which the word «definition» is used.[3]

I use the term «lexical definition» in the sense of Robinson
(1954: 19); it corresponds to Scriven's (1958: 102) «dictionary
definition» and Hempel's (1966: 85-6) «descriptive definition».
Most of the definitions found in a normal dictionary are lexical
definitions: basically they are reports concerning the way the
defined expression is in fact used in a given language-community
at a given period. If I were to offer a lexical definition in the
present context of the word «kinship» I should seek to show the
various senses and nonsenses in which anthropologists do in
fact use the word. This would at least help to show that there is
need of reform.

Usually, however, when an anthropologist offers to define
his terms, he is not seeking to accept or display established
usage, but rather to change or reform it more or less radically.
He may be engaged on the task which I am about to essay,
which has usefully been labelled by Carnap, and following him,
Hempel and Quine, as «explication».[4] To explicate a word is to
propose a precise, unambiguous, scientifically acceptable concept to stand as the significatum of the word: such that this new
significatum expresses what is judged to be central or important
to the range of meanings that the word has in ordinary usage.
One seeks, that is, to preserve what is valuable in the meaning of
the unreformed word, while clearing away the weaknesses which
result from vagueness and ambiguity. Here, therefore, I shall try
to reduce to order the various vague and shifting significata
that the word «kinship» has in common usage among us.

A third operation, which is sometimes called «definition»,
consists of presenting a concept and, at the same time, proposing that the concept shall be labelled by some particular word.
Where, as is often the case, this word already has an established
usage, this operation is easily confused with lexical definition
and with explication. And this in turn leads people to suppose
that the meaning in established usage is relevant and normative
to the meaning of the label-word in its new use. Often it is not

41

so. An acquaintance with agriculture no matter how extensive is no help, but rather a hindrance, to understanding a definition of 'field' in mathematics. In all such cases the concept is defined apart from the label-word, which ought to be understood as meaning no more than what it has been employed to label. I shall now embark on some operations of this kind, which I would rather call «concept-building» than «definition».

IV

KINSHIP AND PARENTATION

When we speak of the 'mother–child relationship' we are usually referring to a rich pattern of interactive behaviours. If however we were to abstract away all this implied content, until we were left with the bare attribute of relatedness, we might call that the «mother–child relationship». Analysing that into a pair of unilateral relations, we should mean by the «mother relation» that relation which a person bears to another if and only if she is that person's mother. Let us label this «maternity», and define «paternity» in a similar manner. Let us define a relation «P» (short for «parentage») as the union of maternity and paternity – i.e. it holds wherever either maternity or paternity holds (cf. Tarski 1965: 91, where the union is labelled «parenthood»). We may now employ a simple concept from the logistic Theory of Relations and define the converse of P, written «P̆» (Tarski 1965: 93). The converse of a relation is that which necessarily holds in the reverse direction: therefore converse-P is approximately what we might call the «child relation» or «filiation».

We may now form *relative products* or *compositions* (Tarski 1965: 92) from P and P̆. P̆/P – converse-P of P – is, in more familiar language «child of parent of»; this can be recognized as a definition of siblinghood. Similarly, P/P̆ (parent of child of) may be seen as essentially the relation between spouses. These are 2-factor relative-products; obviously we can form meaningful relative-products with as many factors as we please. For example the relative-product:

$$P̆/P̆/P̆/P/P/P/P̆/P̆/P/P/P$$

would hold between oneself and one's MFBWMBDD. As this illustrates, we are all familiar with the use of relative-products

42

for specifying kinsmen: our normal convention, however, sets
out the factors in reverse order. We may now conceive of a
relation defined as the union of P, P̆, and all possible relative-
products thereof; I shall label this «parentation». More formally
I should define as «parentation to degree *n*» the union of P, P̆,
and all those relative-products thereof having not more than
n factors.[5]

Though my exposition may have obscured the fact, parenta-
tion is actually a very familiar relation to us: it is what Radcliffe-
Brown called «genealogical relations» (or « – relationships»)
(Radcliffe-Brown 1952: 52). It may be recalled how, in Radcliffe-
Brown's exposition, a network of these is created by the
interlocking of elementary families. And how he continued:

> 'In any given society a certain number of these relationships
> are recognised for social purposes, i.e. they have attached to
> them certain rights and duties, or certain distinctive modes
> of behaviour. It is the relations that are recognised in this
> way that constitute what I am calling a kinship system, or,
> in full, a system of kinship and affinity' (ibid.).

This brings out well enough the importance of genealogical, or
'parentate', relations to concepts of kinship. Indeed it brings
out more than the author intended. The word «recognised», in
this context, is revealing: it suggests that the genealogical
relationships are of primary importance and in some way have
rights and duties inherent in them, so that these need only be
perceived or recognized. This is no doubt the way a well-bred
Englishman is brought up to think of the matter: towards one's
relatives (parentates) one has categorical obligations. But it is
questionable whether people in all other societies see things in
just this light; and it is certainly a strange analytical approach
for a sociologist to adopt. I suggest that instead of 'certain
rights and duties, or certain distinctive modes of behaviour'
we might more sharply speak of 'social relationships'; and instead
of pretending that these are recognized in parentate relations,
we should say that they are attributed or allocated over (on the
basis of) parentate relations. As a first approach to a formal
definition (explication) I therefore suggest:

*Where an array of social relationships is mapped onto an array
of parentate relations, there we have kinship.*

F

It may be noted that this formula does not tell us what kinship is, but only where: it serves therefore to introduce a central equivocation. When we use the term «kinship» are we referring to:

(a) The mapped social relationships?
(b) The mapped-onto parentate relations?
(c) The product, i.e. both (a) and (b) together?

I have the impression that most of us would like to think that we mean the third, the product of (a) and (b) together. But in that case we do not take sufficient care to ensure that both do indeed go together.

In most societies social relationships of the kinship kind are sometimes attributed where there is no parentate base (of relevant degree); in some this happens rather frequently. However, it is not so much the frequency that matters as the relevance in the context of the society concerned. There is something, though perhaps not very much, to be said for categorizing together social relationships for the allocation of which parentation is a *necessary* condition; there is nothing to be said for so categorizing relationships that just happen most often to hold between parentates. For in most small-scale societies where people do not travel a great deal, most regular social relationships will be between neighbours (in a wide sense), and most neighbours will be connected by parentation. So, if by «kinship» we mean all cases where some kind of social relationship commonly holds between people who are also parentates, then in such societies all social relationships would be of kinship – which is not what we would wish to say, since it would render the term analytically vacuous. On the other hand, if we confine the term «kinship» only to those relationships which are explicitly allocated on the basis of parentation, then many so-called 'kinship' relationships would have to be reclassified. In Buganda, for example, the relationships called by 'kinship terms' are commonly allocated without reference to parentation: not only do people neither know nor care whether those concerned are parentates, they even consider reference to parentation in such contexts to be out of place. This is true also of Bunyoro (Beattie 1957: 322) and Gusii (Mayer 1965: 23, 29), and I guess it is likely to be true of a great many other societies. Once we take a clear decision concerning the connexion between kinship and parentation we find we must use the word «kinship» either more widely or else more narrowly than is customary. We hide this fact by the use of such equivocations as the definition of «kinship» in the 6th Edition of *Notes and Queries on Anthropology*: 'Kinship is relationship actually or putatively traced through parent-child or sibling relations, and recognized for social purposes' (p. 75).

The natural sense of this would imply that the tracing is done by the people under study. But the techniques enjoined (ibid.: 79-84) 'to elucidate the relationship system' presuppose tracing by the ethnographer, with no precautions taken to see whether the people themselves so trace. Applied in Buganda such techniques would produce the illusion of an orthodox kinship system, out of what is largely a notably different relational complex.

I am arguing, therefore, that bad definitions and muddled notions of this kind lead us sometimes to say what is not so, and regularly to say what is inexact, unclear, and confused. A major source of this confusion is our socialization in our own kinship system, which teaches us to regard parentation (to some degree) and social relationship as linked so inseparably we need hardly distinguish between them. We seem to find it hard to imagine that for other people there may be no such close connexion: that social relationships of a kinship kind could be allocated without reference to parentation, or that close parentates could be categorized in a manner which is not directly concerned with the parentation. It is all the harder when, irrelevantly, there is a high degree of overlap between kin-like social relationships and parentation.

Further confusion arises from difficulty we have in grasping clearly what parentation is. It is not named in our language. Nor do we have a convenient name for the kind of social relationships which are mapped onto it: we may refer to these as kinship in the wider sense, but more strictly they have to be referred to as relationships of kinship and affinity. Kinship in the strict sense, excluding affinity, has the simpler name, but is in some ways logically a less simple concept. To define it, we should first define a subclass of parentation, which I shall call «Q»:

The relation Q is the relation of parentation after all relative-products in which a P precedes a P̌ have been removed.

Martin Southwold

And we may stipulate

Where an array of social relationships is mapped onto an array of Q relations, there we have kinship in the strict sense.

Now Q closely resembles consanguinity – the two relations are isomorphic one to the other. But Q is not consanguinity, nor is it even a biological relation, since it is generated from parentage which includes mere social paternity. Unfortunately, long practice at distinguishing kinship from consanguinity has led us to assume that there is an exhaustive dichotomy between biological and social relations: thus in recognizing that Q is not a biological relation we are apt to imagine we have demonstrated that it is a social relation. In fact it is not, in any usual sense of the term «social relation» (or «– relationship»); though this is less obvious than it should be, because that term also is used imprecisely.

v

SOCIAL RELATIONSHIP

I now undertake to explicate the term «social relationship» in one of its major senses: which I believe is the normal sense in anthropological usage, and is surely the one most relevant here.

By «an interaction» I mean an act performed by one person and which has value for another: the persons may be labelled «interactor» and «interactee». By «reciprocal interaction» I mean an exchange of interactions between persons. The number of possible different sets, sequences, or clusters of reciprocal interactions is vast; in order to apprehend and regulate these we reduce their variety by classification. A social relationship, then, is a class- or type-concept for reciprocal interactions. But of course, as Nadel (1957) made very clear, the concepts are better explicated by way of some concept of *role*, partitioning the reciprocal interaction of social relationship between two linked roles.

By «a role» is meant a set, or cluster, of types of interaction performable by one interactor. Thus a role is by definition generic (cf. Nadel 1957: 21, 74) and therefore is itself a concept. (Every role is a concept – but of course this is quite different from the concept of role, which is a concept about concepts.) A role relates to actual interactive behaviour as a set of rules, a norm, a prescription – which reminds us of the derivation of

46

the word from «roll», i.e. an actor's script. A role entails obligations, however restricted and conditional these may be (cf.
Banton 1965: 2). To say that a person has a role is to say that
he is under an obligation to behave according to the prescription
if and when the appropriate situation arises; to say that he
performs or plays the role is to say that he also does so behave.
Where the behaviour is found without the obligation, the term
«role» should not be used. Where we find two roles such that the
prescribed behaviour for a role-bearer of either kind is interaction towards the role-bearer of the other, we may speak of
a «linked role-pair». This is an explication for the term «social
relationship» (cf. Banton 1965: 2).

Since a role entails obligation, it is necessary that, in addition
to the rules for behaviour of a role-bearer, there shall be further
rules to determine who does and who does not bear the role. I
shall call these «tenure-rules». We are familiar with rules for
entry upon a role, what we may term rules of recruitment or
allocation; we sometimes overlook that many roles have exit-
rules also. Tenure-rules cover both categories. They have the
effect of mapping roles onto attributes, or clusters of attributes,
which we may therefore speak of as «tenure-attributes». Often
the tenure-attributes include disposition to, and capacity for,
performing the role-behaviour, as evidenced by the actual
performance of similar behaviour.

Where a pair of roles are closely linked, it is useful, and
perhaps necessary, that the respective tenure-attributes should
also be linked: in other words, a social relationship, or linked
role-pair, should be mapped onto a relationship which is at
least part of the linked tenure-attributes. It is a great merit of
parentation that it provides a battery of such tenure-relations.
Moreover, parentation to any given degree provides a set of
such relations which are themselves interrelated in a determinate
structured manner: hence by employing it as a tenure-array
the roles are already arranged in role-sets.

VI

PARENTATION AND CONGENIACY

Parentation therefore is neither a biological nor a social relationship, but rather a class of tenure-relations onto which

social relationships may be mapped. Social relationships which have it as part of their tenure-rules that they are to be mapped onto parentate relations seem to have important common characteristics in whatever society they are found. But then we also find social relationships which share these characteristics but lack such a tenure-rule; should we class these with the others or not? Naturally, we may decide differently according to our immediate purpose. I would suggest, however, that for most sociological purposes it is more satisfactory to classify roles and social relationships with respect to the character of their behaviour-rules rather than to their tenure-rules. Consequently, I suggest that a proper sociological explication of «kinship» must concern itself with the nature of kinship norms, and must not make definitory reference to parentation or the like. It is important, but secondary, to ask why it is so often, but not always, found convenient to take parentation as a tenure-attribute for kinship roles.

Relationships governed by kinship-type norms are characteristically multiplex or involute – they arise with role-summation (Nadel 1957, ch. IV). It is perhaps worth remarking, however, that these idioms for describing the facts are somewhat tendentious, since they assume that people in primitive societies multiply or add together relationships or roles which are *really* distinct: whereas such distinction is real only as a feature of the organization of our own industrial society. For a more objective approach, let us imagine that we could count all the interactions in which a person engages (actively or passively) throughout his life, and could further weight each interaction according to its relative value to the person. We could then assign a measure for the total value to him of his lifetime's interactions. Those social relationships within which there occurred interactions contributing a higher proportion of this total value might be termed «richer» than those in which there occurred a lower proportion. Kinship-type norms are associated predominantly with 'rich' relationships in this sense.

Now the richer a particular instance of social relationship for one of its members, the more dependent he is on its maintenance. But it tends to be true, as a consequence of some kind of reciprocity or balance in social life, that a relationship which

48

is rich for one partner will be rich for the other also: there will be a degree of mutual dependence. And usually, though not always, such richness derives from a multitude of minor inter-actions accumulated over time in a variety of contexts. Typical relationships of this kind are not easy to conceptualize or regulate, since the variety of potentially relevant interactions is too vast. Rather than attempt to specify rules for conduct in every situation, it is more practicable to offer a model or para-digm for conduct. Behaviour in the elementary and expanded families provides a highly appropriate and well-known para-digm for the purpose. So appropriate is it that it was used very frequently by Jesus and the early Christians in their teachings about relations between man and God, and man and man. Many passages show that use of this idiom did not depend on notions about God's role in physical birth or parentation; e.g. John I:2, 'To all who did receive him . . . he gave the right to become children of God . . .'.

I propose to label as «congeniate» those social relationships in which appropriate behaviour is characteristically perceived as similar to that expected in familial relationships. I shall use the word «congeniate» as a noun to refer to persons related by such relationships. I shall use the word «congeniacy» to refer to the class of such relationships. This class may well have fuzzy margins, where there can be no certain decision whether or not a given relationship is congeniate; but I am here primarily interested in those many relationships where the familial allusion is plain. It is in fact such relationships which we are most ready to categorize as those of kinship; my neologisms are intended to convey this sense of the word «kinship» without any implication that the congeniates are necessarily parentates. Indeed, I have tried to divide the useful meanings of the word «kinship» between these two new words, «congeniacy» and «parentation». This seems essential if we are to talk clearly about those cases where congeniacy is found apart from parentation. It is also essential if we are to see that the very common association of congeniate social relationships with parentate tenure-attributes is not to be taken for granted, but is a contingent fact in need of explanation. The following is at least a sketch for such an explanation.

Because of the high degree of mutual dependence between

49

partners in rich relationships, severance of such a relationship tends to have painful consequences for them. And as a result of what Nadel (1957: 86-7) called the *«triadization»* or *«transitiveness»* of relationships, these consequences often extend to yet others. For these reasons it is commonly held that such relationships should be terminable only by death, if by that. There is, I suggest, a kind of balance in holding that they are most appropriately entered upon by birth. It is at any rate a fact that they usually are *ascribed*. But by birth people are inevitably placed in a network of parentate relations: hence it must happen, whether or not by conscious design, that to the extent that linked statuses are ascribed by birth, to that extent they must hold between parentates. However, I think the connexion is more comprehensible if one considers the intermediate variable of locality. If, for technological and economic reasons, the spatial range of most of a person's effective contacts is restricted, then people will interact a great deal with neighbours (in a wide sense), and relationships with neighbours will be characteristically rich, and probably congeniate. But if people do not travel very much, so that most tend to stay where they were born, and perhaps also marry close at hand, it will also happen that most who are neighbours are also parentates. But it will not necessarily follow, and should not casually be assumed, that the people themselves will regard parentation as a necessary condition for congeniate relationships.

In some ways Buganda is a valuable test case for these considerations, since we find congeniacy together with a marked tendency to travel far and often. Buganda is a country of settled agriculture where most villages are, ecologically, permanent settlements. But individuals and nuclear families move rather frequently between villages, often over considerable distances, and the custom of doing so is highly valued. Moreover men tend to prefer to take their wives from rather far afield. Hence the composition of any given village community is in constant flux, and the density of connexions of close parentation between members at any time is rather low. On the other hand, neighbours who are not actively quarrelling tend to apply congeniate ('kinship') terms to one another, if on no stronger warrant than the proverb which says that 'Neighbours are congeniates' (*'Ab'omuliraano ba Luganda'*). I found it exceedingly difficult to discover how, if at all, such persons were connected by parentation; and eventually it was explained to me that to spell out the parentate connexion to a congeniate would be *okuboola*. The verb *okuboola* is normally used to describe the behaviour of one who annuls a congeniate relationship by flouting its norms or even by explicitly repudiating it. Thus a person who absents himself from a funeral, or who hauls a congeniate to court, will be said to *okuboola*. The word was also applied to the expulsion from his clan of a persistent offender. Thus it may be loosely translated as «to repudiate congeniate relationship». In Buganda, in many though not all contexts, to trace parentation is considered to repudiate congeniacy. So much for 'kinship'!

The fact that in Buganda today congeniate terms tend to be applied towards those with whom one has, or would like to have, rich relationships, more or less independently of parentation, is obscured by another usage of the terms which was probably most functional under conditions now largely past.

I remarked earlier that the term «*kojja*» is translated by Mrs Fallers as «male of mother's lineage», rather than as «mother's brother», as one might have expected for a kinship term. Having worked in Buganda I can easily guess why she did so. The term «*kojja*» is applied not only to any brother of a person's mother, but also their sons, son's sons, and so forth. If one asks why, one gets the 'what a silly question' look and the answer 'Because they are all of one line/lineage (*lunyiriri*)'. In fact, any male of the mother's clan, unless old enough to be called «grandfather», will be called «*kojja*»: indeed the clan itself, or a relevant segment thereof, may be referred to as «*bakojja*» (the plural form), or as «*bukojja*» – the abstract noun which refers more specifically to the place belonging to the clan or clan-segment as a corporate group. So much is «*kojja*» a group-word that it cannot reliably be used to specify a real mother's brother. Indeed, when Kaggwa wanted to describe a custom giving rights specifically to a mother's brother, he avoided the word «*kojja*» and instead employed a roundabout expression:

'[When] a man and a woman are born of one father, and the woman goes and marries and bears children, boys and girls,

51

then the sibling-of-the-opposite-sex of that woman takes the children of his sibling as *endobolo* and they serve him in all kinds of work.'[6]

Now for every male one refers to as «*kojja*», his sister is referred to as «*nnyina*»: so it would seem logical to interpret this term as «female of mother's lineage» rather than as «mother». However, this would not cover the full application of the term «*nnyina*», which is applied also to any wife of a person called «*kitaawe*». Now «*kitaawe*» is applied to any male of one's own clan who in terms of genealogical reckoning if known, or else of age, is of the generation senior to one's own. Hence it might be more exact to interpret «*nnyina*» as 'female affine of senior clansman'. Similarly, it is possible to interpret each of the so-called 'kinship' terms as denoting the occupant of a status specified in a framework of corporate 'descent' groups.

Such an interpretation fits a large part, and almost certainly the greater part, of instances of use of these terms much better than does their more orthodox interpretation as kinship terms. If one holds that the application (i.e. Frege's *Bedeutung*)[7] of a word is the sole admissible guide to its signification, then I think one is stuck with that approach. Alternatively, one may allow that fully to understand, and hence to interpret, a word it may be necessary to grasp its sense, its intensional meaning (Frege's *Sinn*), which cannot always be inferred from analysis of observed applications. Although Frege's *Sinn* is not necessarily to be identified with *Sinn* in Weber's usage, I suggest that in order to see why in their clan-type application these terms do have a kin-sense, it is necessary to have some subjective understanding of what is conveyed by them.

Although these Ganda terms are frequently applied to relationships best described in a framework of descent-group organization, most of them also have properly kin-like usage. This is shown by the fact that when one wants to say definitely that a person is a close relative one may use a congeniate term with an intensive such as «*ddala ddala*». If one's own father for example, is called «especially *kitaawe*», this surely implies that the term applies to him primarily. So too does the fact that a father's brother is termed «*kitaawe omuto*» – approximately «lesser father». Here the qualifying adjective is sound

52

evidence that the application has been extended; and the same applies to the term «*nnyina omuto*». Unfortunately, no other congeniate terms are qualified in that way; nor indeed are «*kitaawe*» and «*nnyina*» when applied to persons more remote than parent's own siblings.

It is necessary to recognize, as Mayer did for the Gusii and Beattie did for the Nyoro,[8] that the congeniate terms have at least two different ranges of application in Buganda. They may be used to refer to and specify a small set of close relatives, in which case they are being used very much like English kinship terms. Or they may be used to refer to persons and categories of persons placed in terms of positions in descent groups. In this second usage there is no reference to, or reckoning of, parentation; an analysis which would explain this usage on the basis of the telescoping of parentate relations is misconceived. I am not sure that one should say that this usage is 'extended' from the first at all: rather, as I have suggested above, the connexion is that the first is posited as a moral paradigm for the second.

VII

CONCLUSIONS

In summary, then, I would argue that if it is to be useful to distinguish kinship terms, relationships, and so forth from others, it should be by reference to the character of the social relationships. I have proferred the new-minted word «congeniacy» to categorize relationships of a specific character. We might find it useful to make the following further distinctions:

1 «Congeniacy-german» shall be applied to congeniate relations with close relatives (parentates to degree 4 or 5?).
2 «Congeniacy-parentate» shall be applied to congeniate relations when these are specifically allocated on the basis of parentation of higher degree.
3 «Congeniacy-septal» shall be applied to congeniate relations allocated on the basis of position in descent-groups.

4 «Congeniacy-nominal»[9] shall be applied to congeniate relations allocated on the basis of the actual or intended character of achieved relationship.

I believe that congeniacy-parentate, commonly called 'classificatory kinship', does not exist in Buganda. I hope I have cleared the way for categorizing exactly what does exist.

NOTES

1. Where a word or phrase is printed between *guillemets* (« »), this is to be taken as indicating that I am referring to the word or phrase itself, and not, as would otherwise normally be the case, to that which it signifies or refers to. Among logicians the convention is current of using single quotes (' ') for this purpose; I have not followed them in this, since it would entail altering the usage of single and double quotes throughout the book. Hence my usage of single and double quotes can be understood in the normal way. In particular, if a word or phrase is printed between ordinary quotes (not *guillemets*), this may be understood as indicating that the word or phrase is quoted from someone in particular or from people in general; in the latter case it usually implies that I am critical of their usage. Thus in my text «kinship» is to be understood as referring to the word kinship, whereas 'kinship' is to be understood as referring to that which people call kinship.

2. Some of the terms take possessive suffixes, the correct application of which would add complications irrelevant to our present purpose. Unlike Mrs Fallers, I have presented the terms in the form they would have when referring to 'the – of So-and-so', so as to dispense with the possessive suffixes. Thus the prepositus is not Ego but So-and-so (i.e. a designated third party), which does not strictly fit some of the contexts in which I cite the terms in the text. I have written all terms in the Standard Orthography. And I have omitted the column of terms in Lusoga which Mrs Fallers has.

3. Robinson (1954) shows how many and various are the senses in which the word «definition» is used; and his inventory is far from complete.

4. Carnap (1956 [1947]: 7-8); Hempel (1952: 11-12); Quine (1960: 258-66).

5. The idea of forming a relation which is the union of all relative products of a relation and its converse is found in *Principia Mathematica* *97 (Whitehead and Russell 1910-13). Such a union-relation can be formed from any relation whatever in just the manner by which parentation has been formed from parentage. Had I first presented the purely abstract concept of such a union-relation derivable from any relation R, and then explained that by «parentation» I mean the instance of this which results when the particular relation *parentage* is subsituted for R, I should have made it clear that the structural features of parentation are in no way dependent on peculiarities of parentage. Naturally, such an exposition would have been more taxing for the reader. For a simpler account of what is presently relevant in PM *97, see Russell 1940: 228-9 (or 1962: 216-17).

6. Kaggwa (1952 [1905]: 101; my translation). The sentence seems clumsy to me in the original Luganda, which I have translated closely. The word *endobolo*

otherwise refers to booty in war; the verb *kulobola* from which it derives is *not* used of marriage-payments.

7. Frege (1952 [1892]).

8. Mayer (1965: 4-5); Beattie (1957: 319).

9. Cf. Mayer (1965: 21), where she refers to 'nominal, courtesy usages of the kind that has been noted for rural communities in South Africa or America'.

REFERENCES

(Where two dates are given, that in parentheses is the date of the first edition or publication)

BANTON, MICHAEL. 1965. *Roles*. London: Tavistock Publications; New York: Basic Books.

BEATTIE, J. H. M. 1957. Nyoro Kinship. *Africa* 27: 317-40.

—— 1958. Nyoro Marriage and Affinity. *Africa* 28: 1-22.

BUCHLER, IRA R. & SELBY, HENRY A. 1968. *Kinship and Social Organization*. New York: Macmillan.

CARNAP, RUDOLF. 1956 (1947). *Meaning and Necessity*. Chicago: University of Chicago Press.

FALLERS, M. C. 1960. *The Eastern Lacustrine Bantu*. (Ethnographic Survey of Africa, East Central Africa, Part XI). London: International African Institute.

FORTES, MEYER. 1957. Malinowski and the Study of Kinship. In Raymond Firth (ed.), *Man and Culture*. London: Routledge and Kegan Paul.

FREGE, G. 1952 (1892). Ueber Sinn und Bedeutung. Translated in P. Geach and M. Black, *Translations from the Philosophical Writings*. Oxford: Blackwell.

GOODENOUGH, W. H. 1956. Componential Analysis and the Study of Meaning. *Language* 32: 195-216.

HEMPEL, CARL G. 1952. *Fundamentals of Concept Formation in Empirical Science* (International Encyclopaedia of Unified Science, vol. II, no. 7). Chicago: University of Chicago Press.

—— 1966. *Philosophy of Natural Science* (Foundations of Philosophy Series). Englewood Cliffs: Prentice-Hall.

KAGGWA, APOLO. 1952 (1905). *Mpisa za Baganda* [The Customs of the Baganda]. Kampala: Uganda Bookshop; London: Macmillan.

LEACH, E. R. 1958. Concerning Trobriand Clans and the Kinship Category 'Tabu'. In J. R. Goody (ed.), *The Developmental Cycle in Domestic Groups*. Cambridge: Cambridge University Press.

LEACH, E. R. 1961 (1945). Jinghpaw Kinship Terminology. In E. R. Leach, *Rethinking Anthropology*. London: Athlone Press.

LOUNSBURY, F. G. 1956. A Semantic Analysis of the Pawnee Kinship Usage. *Language* **32**: 158-94.

—— 1964. A Formal Account of the Crow- and Omaha-Type Kinship Terminologies. In W. H. Goodenough (ed.), *Explorations in Cultural Anthropology*. New York: McGraw-Hill.

MAYER, IONA. 1965. *The Nature of Kinship Relations* (Rhodes-Livingstone Papers no. 37). Manchester: Manchester University Press.

NADEL, S. F. 1957. *The Theory of Social Structure*. London: Cohen and West.

(NOTES AND QUERIES). 1951. *Notes and Queries on Anthropology*, 6th edition. London: Routledge and Kegan Paul.

QUINE, W. V. O. 1960. *Word and Object*. Cambridge, Mass.: MIT Press.

RADCLIFFE-BROWN, A. R. 1952 (1941). The Study of Kinship Systems. In A. R. Radcliffe-Brown, *Structure and Function in Primitive Society*. London: Cohen and West.

ROBINSON, RICHARD. 1954. *Definition*. Oxford: Clarendon Press.

RUSSELL, BERTRAND. 1940. *An Inquiry into Meaning and Truth*. London: Allen and Unwin; Harmondsworth: Penguin Books, 1962.

SCRIVEN, MICHAEL. 1958. Definitions, Explanations and Theories. In H. Feigl, M. Scriven, and G. Maxwell (eds.), *Minnesota Studies in the Philosophy of Science*, vol. II. Minneapolis: University of Minnesota Press.

TARSKI, ALFRED. 1965 (1941). *Introduction to Logic*. New York: Oxford University Press.

WHITEHEAD, A. N. & RUSSELL, B. 1910-1913. *Principia Mathematica*. Cambridge: Cambridge University Press.

3

P. G. Rivière

Marriage: A Reassessment

INTRODUCTION

The category of marriage is itself the problem to be dealt with in this paper, and it is proposed that we must return to first principles if we are to get out of the difficulties in which, I think, we find ourselves. A restatement of first principles too often, if not always, sounds like a parade of the obvious, and I would be very surprised if anything contained in this paper is new to you.[1] However, unless I had thought that the only solution was a return to first principles there would have been no point in my preparing this paper. My decision to do so reflects my dissatisfaction with the current approaches to marriage, which are almost exclusively functionalist. I believe that few readers would accept such a purely functionalist approach to religion as that proposed by Professor Evans-Pritchard when he writes, 'For the social anthropologist, religion is what religion does' (1965: 120). If one does not accept this limitation with regard to religion, how much less can one accept it with regard to marriage? But having voiced my objections to functionalist explanations or definitions of marriage, and having proposed an examination and understanding of it through its basic constituents, I find myself in a quandary since, to all intents and purposes, I have analysed out of existence the object of my study. Indeed, I am left in the position of claiming that if we are not to condemn ourselves for ever to the tautologies of functionalist explanations we must come to realize that marriage as an isolable phenomenon of study is a misleading illusion.

FUNCTIONS

In fear of being misunderstood, I must state very clearly at the outset that I do not think there is anything wrong with functionalist approaches to marriage other than that they are in-adequate. At the best they provide part-descriptions, but these in no sense, because of their tautological character, can be regarded as explanations. Some functionalist explanations of marriage have been absurd; thus Bertrand Russell writes: 'The main purpose of marriage is to replenish the human population of the globe' (1958: 189). However, social anthro-pologists seem to have avoided making such patently naïve statements, and their attempts to define and to explain marriage have shown a far higher degree of sophistication, even if still cast in terms of what marriage does. Some of these approaches, such as Leach's open-ended formulation (1961: 107-8), have great practical and analytic value. For example, this aspect of Leach's typology has been recently, and well, demonstrated in an article by Crocker in which he shows that the two different forms of sexual relationship recognized by the Bororo can be distinguished by the type and number of rights involved (1969: 255-6). Even so, Crocker is simply expressing in Leach's terms the criteria which the Bororo themselves appear to employ in making a distinction between the two unions.[2]

My objection to functionalist approaches to marriage is grounded in my refusal to accept the Radcliffe-Brownian stand that function preserves the structure, which means that the latter is dependent on the former. I side with the view that function is a consequence of structure, although realizing that there is a complicated interplay between function and structure which is two-way. I will return to my position below, but first it is necessary to advance an argument against those who would give primacy to function. Firstly, because the recognition of structure depends, to a certain extent, on the observation of its functionings, there has been a tendency to place the emphasis on what can be seen and credit it with being the cause of what is not directly or so easily observable.

Secondly, the problem has been succinctly stated by Witt-genstein with reference to punishment when he writes:

'Compare the question: "Why do we punish criminals? Is it from a desire for revenge? Is it in order to prevent a repetition of the crime?" And so on. The truth is that there is no one reason. There is the institution of punishing

58

criminals. Different people support this for different reasons, and for different reasons in different cases and at different times' (1967a: 50).

I suspect that this is true of all social institutions, and one of the events which turned my attention to the topic of marriage was watching a television discussion about it in which the participants all held different views about the purpose of marriage. This resulted in deadlock, and, it would appear, for the following reason: if for any given society its members hold various views on the function of one of its institutions, then each view is a true explanation of the institution for the individual who holds it.

Thirdly, it is nearly three-quarters of a century since Durkheim drew to our attention the fact that functions and institutions are not necessarily linked, and that either can change without necessarily bringing about a change in the other. Accordingly it is not possible to provide an adequate explanation of one by reference to the other, which is just the approach adopted by functionalism. Take, as an example of this, that function of marriage which is the protection of the young. It is claimed that because of the nature, particularly the slow maturation rate, of the human young, there is, in order to survive, the need of some stable relationship. Furthermore, it is assumed that marriage is the only relationship which can provide this stability. Just how long this reason for marriage has existed as an idea it would be impossible to find out, but I say 'idea' on purpose. Regardless of whether 'pair-bonding' is essential for survival among primates, it is not universally regarded as so among the peoples of the world. Within our own culture it is undoubtedly true that the notion of the stability of the family as being vital for the children's physical well-being is or has been replaced by one which lays stress on the children's psychological well-being. It has been suggested to me that this adjustment in function of marriage can be related to the work of Bowlby (1951), in the sense that the importance of maternal care for the welfare of the child derived from him; he gave birth, so to speak, to one of our collective representations. It should be quite easy to demonstrate whether this has any foundation in truth, but it is not my intention to explore further this issue here. There are, however, some interesting additional points to which it is worth drawing attention. Hannah Gavron has shown that in a sample of middle-class and working-class wives the most frequently given reason for not working when they had children was that it would be wrong to leave them (1968: 115, 121), and one must assume that they meant harmful in a mental and not a physical sense. It is quite possible, even probable, that there are good practical reasons and difficulties which stop a mother going out to work, but the interesting thing is the way in which this is rationalized. It is an aspect of another very marked collective representation of western culture which lays greater emphasis on the young rather than on the old. Here marriage and its stability are defended on the grounds that it is important, even vital, for the young to grow up in a secure atmosphere. That marriage is for the benefit of the young is by no means a universally accepted notion; for example, the Trio Indians of Surinam regard marriage as bringing into existence a set of ordered rights and obligations which are mainly for the benefit of the aged.[3]

Finally, and this partly follows from above, all functionalist definitions and explanations of marriage belong to the conscious model, and because of this the functions of and the reasons for marriage become confused.[4] For example, the function of and reason for marriage may be closely bound together so that the same statement, depending on context, is either a definition or a reason. Thus Leach's Right A is 'To establish the legal father of a woman's children', which in his terms is a possible definition or part-definition of marriage. On the other hand, a frequently given reason for marriage is 'in order to have children', a statement which is clearly meaningless and untrue unless it is taken to mean 'have legitimate children'. This is simply another way of saying that marriage establishes the legal parents. This case illustrates well the tautological nature of the functionalist argument, and is, therefore, worth examining further.

Probably the favourite and most widespread reason for and definition of marriage (among both the populations and the anthropologists of the world) is the legitimation of children. In order to discuss this fully it is necessary to start by making certain remarks about the nature of social structure as part of the 'order of things'. I use this expression as a shorthand for the view of society, and the world in which it exists, as forming a symbolic system; a system which is inherent in and conveyed through the society's collective representations. The authority of this symbolic system lies in the fact that it is also a moral system; a moral order which reveals itself in the unexplainable phenomena of society which in an earlier age we would have described as 'God-given' and which all ethnographers (I imagine) have recorded in the form 'that is our custom' or 'that is the way it has always been done'. Every society has this sort of order (symbolic and moral) almost by definition since it is itself part of that order. This order is neither immutable nor unquestionable although the majority remains unaware of it and simply follows its dictates, allowing, of course, for the variations in idiosyncratic behaviour and attitudes. Change in the order of things may result from numerous causes: internal, such as demographic changes, or external influences, such as the introduction of a new technique for the exploitation of the environment.

Forms of social organization are, in part, constructs of the mind. They are not given in the nature of things (even if a society's members may view their social organization as if it were) although once they exist they take on a reality, have an empirical referent, and an independence in their own right. The social organization is an important part of the whole order, that part dealing with the classification of people, the divisions and distinctions to be made between the members of a given society. New individuals born into the society must be fitted into the existing order of things and this is really what we mean by legitimacy. Illegitimate births are untidy, random events which threaten the proper order of things. There are clearly a large number of ways in which legitimacy, taken in the sense of fitting newly arrived individuals into the social order, may be accomplished. There are certain logical possibilities which have never been recorded, such, for example, as allotting the newborn to groups in a strictly numerical and rotational manner regardless of parentage.[5] Allotting offspring to social groups other than that of the parent is a feature of Australian section systems, but here, as almost universally, the place in society of the parent (decisively, the mother) is the influencing factor. Perhaps the most obvious examples of the importance of the social status of the parent rather than any physical relationship exist in clan-based societies in which there is an accepted distinction between the role of *pater* and *genitor* with all the stress placed on the former in deciding the offspring's social status. However, societies with unilineal descent groups are not alone in this; sexual access to other men's wives is institutionalized among many peoples with bilateral kin groups (e.g. many Eskimo groups) without such behaviour questioning the social parentage of the offspring, which has already been assured by marriage.[6] In terms of Leach's definition, marriage in such situations is concerned with the legitimation of the children but has nothing to say about the monopoly in sexual rights. If one looks at our own culture, marriage alone is not sufficient to assure legitimacy, for, although it ideally grants the spouses a monopoly in each other's sexual services, in fact it is far more problematic to insist on the coincidence of *pater* and *genitor* in defining legitimacy than simply relying on the first of these.

One should note here that the whole notion of legitimacy rests on the assumption that an individual's status depends on what already exists and what has already happened. In other words, the newborn child automatically acquires through legitimacy an ascribed status, even if this amounts to nothing more than a set of relationships. Illegitimate children, by definition, lack part of this ascribed status.[7]

From what has been said, it should now be obvious that the marital institution and its function are being used to define each other. If the function of marriage is to legitimate the offspring, then it must be that the legitimacy of the offspring depends on marriage. There is no place for one without the other, and the argument is purely circular.[8] One is trapped in one's own argument and in the terminology employed in it, and the only escape from this sterile predicament seems to be to recognize both marriage and its function as expressions or statements about the order of things. In other words, my complaint against functional explanations is simply that they are the conscious rationalizations, the visible expressions and operations, of an underlying structure, and that it is to this last that we must turn in order to give, for any society, an adequate description of its marital institution. The first step in an adequate description involves an examination of the functions of marriage, and their relationship to other institutions in the society, but more than this marriages must be seen as expressions of social structure. A marriage may be a consequence of the social structure or it may have consequences for it. Thus the question 'would you let your daughter marry a Negro (dustman, or peer)?' is a statement about social structure, while each marriage which crosses a boundary has consequences for the social structure. This example, of course, is concerned with socially distinguishable groups, but it seems to me that it is only by emphasizing the relationships rather than the groups that progress can be made in understanding the organizational principles. Admittedly this type of approach has so far proved enlightening in only a very small number of cases, and although it concerns itself with a different level of abstraction from that under examination here, structural analysis does seem to offer some useful lessons. In particular, it draws attention to the fact that the important things are not simply the structural elements and the dyadic relationships between them, but the relationship between these relationships. It views society as an ongoing symbolic system. It seems to me quite startling that in our discussions on marriage we have never taken our eyes off what the institution does in order to look at its composition, its constituent elements, and the relationships between them.

III

CONSTITUENTS

The constituent units of marriage are men and women, and this seems to be marriage's single, universal feature. Thus the study of marriage must in the first place concentrate on the categories of male and female and the relationship between them. This may seem so obvious as to be not worth saying, but in writing on marriage we seem to have constantly overlooked this obvious fact.[9] We are fully aware of the importance of the distinction between the sexes. For example, Banton refers to sex as one of the criteria for defining basic roles but adds that as societies become more complex such roles become less important (1965: 33-4). This view is echoed by Mary Douglas when she writes, 'In primitive cultures, almost by definition, the distinction of the sexes is the primary social distinction. This means that some important institutions always rest on the difference of sex' (1966: 140). No one is going to deny that in more complex societies social distinctions are based on criteria other than that of gender, but it would be equally wrong to deny them all importance, especially in those areas of social life which we share with simpler cultures. Sex is still a structuring principle in our culture, and in spite of the enormous changes which have occurred during the last hundred years (including some remarkable attempts to eradicate sexual differences) a vast number of roles are still differentiated in terms of male and female. There is still behaviour appropriate for men, and behaviour appropriate for women, but if the distinction between these two categories were simply an expression of behavioural characteristics (perhaps biologically based) a problem would barely exist. However, the distinction is not simply behavioural; it is imbued with moral, attitudinal, and emotional attributes, and accordingly the categories of male and female and the relationship between them are part of the total symbolic system which is society. I would claim that in all societies there is a structuring principle based on the differences between the genders. The importance of this principle, i.e. the degree to which it operates in the organization of social institutions will vary with the complexity of the society, but it would seem that, almost by definition, it will manifest itself in marital institutions.

A feature of these differences between the genders is that they are invariably conceptualized as complementary. This complementarity may simply be an expression of the visible physical differences of the two sexes, but it normally receives expression at a more abstract or metaphysical level as well. Simple examples of this are the Tantrik distinction between *shukla* and *rakta*, male and female essence respectively, and nearer home the notions of honour and shame as an expression of the family as a moral universe, a universe founded on contrasting but complementary qualities.[10] Often tied in with such ideas is the notion that marital status is necessary for the full achievement of manhood or womanhood (perhaps further qualified by the need to have children), and is frequently and openly expressed by making marriage part of an initiation rite at puberty. In these terms, marriage becomes a symbolic statement about one of the proper relationships between adult members of the two sexes.

It should be fairly plain by now where the argument is leading. Anthropologists have limited themselves to examining the functions of marriage without stopping to consider the parts from which it is constructed. Once that is done, marriage must be seen as one of the possible forms of relationship between the sexes, or perhaps, more accurately, as the expression of one of the forms. The problem then posed is which of the forms of relationship between the sexes is, in any given society, to be regarded as the marital one. This, it seems to me, cannot be decided in advance, as so many definitions of marriage assume: a situation that is surprising in a discipline so fearful of ethnocentricity. The first step must be that which is recommended by Prince Peter, who suggests that marriage is 'The socially recognised assumption by man and wife of the kinship status of husband and wife' (1956: 48). I would agree with his critics (Fischer 1956: 87; Gough 1959) that this is no definition of marriage, but it must be the first step. It seems likely that anyone in any society will be able to tell the inquirer whether or not they are married (assuming that the linguistic and terminological difficulty can be overcome), and it seems curious that Fischer and Gough should imply otherwise. It seems more doubtful if there would be such universal ability to describe the particular society's reasons for and functions of marriage. However, at least a proportion of the population will be able to answer such a query, and, as has been suggested above, the variety of their answers will reflect different aspects of their conscious model. Thus the second step in the investigation of marriage is the application of Leach's typology which will provide the objective criteria of the relationship for the particular society. The third step, and the one I am advocating here, is the examination of marriage and its functions as an expression of an underlying structure. Without wishing to be too repetitive I believe that we have coped quite well with this in terms of prescriptive alliance, but not in terms of the union or relationship between men and women which we call marriage and which has some sort of counterpart in all known societies.

IV

RELATIONSHIPS

My proposal is that marriage must be studied as one of the possible relationships between men and women, and that this relationship is only meaningful in comparison with other relationships in the same structure. This idea owes almost everything to Leach and his suggestion that 'the essential key to understanding is to perceive that a particular relationship "p" is *the opposite of* another relationship "q" ' (1961: 28).[11] Thus the third step in this proposed approach to marriage is the study of the union as one of the socially approved and recognized relationships between the conceptual roles of male and female. This relationship will reflect an aspect of the particular society's conventional ideas about the two categories and it will be possible to define it by opposing it to other possible male/female relationships which exist in that society. The actual modes and number of ways in which the oppositions are expressed will vary and will be a matter for investigation in each case. This is neither a definition nor an explanation of marriage (indeed, I doubt whether either is possible), but it is an approach which, by retaining the relationship in its context (by recognizing it as one relationship among many), will allow a better understanding of it. My argument, and its debt to the method employed by Lévi-Strauss in his demolition of totemism must be very clear, is that in taking marriage as a category of study we have concentrated on a part-relationship rather than a whole one. What I am trying to do is to get marriage viewed as part of the total male/female relationship. I must now elaborate and defend certain aspects of this proposed approach.

Firstly, such a description will readily and needs must incorporate any functional definition. The inclusion of the functions of the relationship are important since they belong to the society's conscious model and they are thus used to distinguish marriage from other sorts of relationships between the sexes.

Secondly, the expected behaviour and activities of and the

attitudes towards men and women in any society are an expression of their ideal conceptualized nature, the moral and metaphysical attributes with which these two categories have been endowed. Furthermore, since these qualities are conveyed through the collective representations they are part of the order of things. However, it is equally clear that in all societies these categories are not homogeneous in any sense, even if the only distinction is that incorporated in an incest prohibition. In other words the category of male or female contains contradictory roles. This presents no obstacle since the marriage relationship is simply concerned with one of the aspects of the relationship, with certain qualities of the two categories which are not contradictory, or if they are the marriage itself may be regarded as providing some resolution to it – for example, the ideal representation of womanhood as portrayed in the notion of the virgin-mother, and where marriage licenses sexuality on condition that it aims at procreation.

Thirdly, it is possible to describe change in terms of this approach. The contents and meanings of the categories are not immutable although they may so appear to members of a given society at any one moment. The categories of male and female do not exist in isolation; they have empirical referents in the form of men and women, and the behaviour, activities, and relationships between men and women adapt themselves in accordance with other changes in the social and natural environment. Such changes bring about changes in the notions of the ideal male and female categories. It is not necessary to look very far to find an example of this; the changes in the status of women in this country during the last hundred years is a good one. The argument here is that factors which bring about changes at one level will bring about changes at another, and furthermore that changes in one category will bring about changes in a complementary category and influence the nature of the relationship between them. To understand the changing nature of the marriage relationship in our society it is necessary to examine the changing attitudes of the sexes towards each other. For example, the removal of the middle-class Victorian woman from her pedestal has had far-reaching results for our marital institution, but itself resulted from changes operating in society to which in turn it fed back the effects of its change.

This, of course, verges on perfectly orthodox functionalism of the interrelational sort which is and has been widely practised by social anthropologists who see social institutions as being functionally interlinked. Although it is frequently done, I suggest that we should concern ourselves first with the study of relationships within institutions before trying to relate them functionally. In other words one should not try to relate the institution of marriage to other institutions in the society without first examining and describing the relationship between its elements and their ordering principle. It seems likely that an interrelational approach to institutions has been easier in simple societies than in complex ones because in the former the same elements and ordering principles reappear in different institutions, and, perhaps, with greater symbolic consistency.

Next, it is necessary to consider some of the most obvious objections to this approach to marriage. To begin with there is the possible criticism that it rests on the claim that marriage is universally concerned with members of the opposite sex, and does not take account of such famous unions as the Nuer woman-marriage. My answer is that this form of union is called marriage because it shares much in common (appearance and function) with marriages between men and women. The Nuer woman who takes a wife is as far as she is physically capable playing a male role, and, of course, socially she is fully capable. The evidence for this exists in Evans-Pritchard's own ethnography, for in discussion on woman-marriages he states three times in two pages that such a woman is playing the part of a man (1951: 108-9). Thus the mistake which was made in the *Notes and Queries*' definition was in describing the marital union as being between man and woman rather than as being between the conceptual roles of male and female. It seems unnecessary to consider other examples of woman-marriage, but it is clear that one finds in numerous societies women acting out male roles, including that of taking a wife. The Lovedu are another good case (cf. Krige & Krige 1943) and the Banyoro another; among the latter princesses being regarded as socially masculine (cf. Needham 1967; Beattie 1968). In all these cases, and similarly in man–man marriage, all that seems to be happening is that when a person adopts the behaviour and cultural attributes of the opposite sex, he or she may be allowed further freedom in this direction.

Another problem concerns that of polygamous unions. There seems to be no difficulty in those cases where each union individually represents a monogamous union, but in situations where the roles of the spouses are differentiated there is an additional point to be made, and it is well illustrated by Gough's (1959) account of Nayar polyandry. Here there exists the ritual husband who is *pater* and the lovers who are the actual procreators, and together they play the roles which we bestow upon a single man. Or, to put it the other way round, the roles which we regard as appropriate for one man, the husband, to play, the Nayar divide among several men. One might suggest something similar in European areas where the female role is split between the wife (who is ideally a virgin-mother) and the whore who is concerned with the flesh and not with love and procreation.

A further apparent difficulty is the case where a single society appears to recognize more than one form of union. An extreme form is the thirteen types of Dahomean marriage of which one is woman-marriage. One cannot fail to be struck by the fact that Laura Bohannan (1949), in her analysis of Herskovits's material, starts by stating that only three criteria are involved in distinguishing between the thirteen types, and that one of these, the relationship between man and wife, is a constant. Indeed, the thirteen different forms are variations resulting from material concerns, such as dowries and inheritance, and not from different Dahomean ideas about the conceptual roles of men and women. It is interesting that in Britain the state of marriage technically involves a secular and/ or ritual consecration, but, in fact, the common-law wife is a wife in the eyes of the law if her behaviour has been for a long enough time such as for her to be thought of as the man's wife. In those countries, and this especially applies to many in Latin America, in which a very large proportion of the population remain unmarried by the national standards, there seems to be good evidence to suppose that the difference in marriage practices between different segments of the population is based on differing sets of socio-economic conditions, values, and expectations, and a corresponding difference in the conceptual roles of the two sexes. If this is so, then one must ignore the national and middle-class notions of marriage in these countries if one is to understand the 'marital relationship' among the lower classes.[12]

A final point which deserves some comment is the expectation of permanency in marriage, and although Margaret Mead has suggested that it is a feature of marriage in most societies (1949: 195), it is certainly not a necessary characteristic of the union. Indeed, there is a recent account of the Irigwe of Benue-Plateau State in Nigeria among whom the expectation is that a woman will move from husband to husband (Sangree 1969). Expectation of permanency, not statistical frequency of divorce and separation which is a different matter, may be a consequence of certain structural features of a society, but I would argue that one has to look beyond this to understand permanency, to, in fact, the very nature of the marriage relationship and what it is assumed to do. This is easily illustrated from Christian doctrine where marriage creates a genealogical link, a spouse's kin become one's kin.[13]

V

CONCLUSIONS

As you were warned at the outset of this paper, the result is almost purely negative. It is negative in the sense that I have tried to show that we mislead ourselves by describing with a single term relationships which in different societies have no single feature in common other than that they are concerned with the conceptual roles of male and female. Accordingly I would certainly agree with Leach that there is no single definition of marriage, but I would go further and say that the functions of marriage, as marriage itself, are simply an expression, a consequence, of some deeper underlying structure. I have suggested that the ordering principle of this deep structure, in so far as it relates to marriage, is the universal distinction between male and female, and that marriage is an aspect of the consequential relationship between the two categories. If this is so, marriage as an analytic category ceases to exist and it becomes merely one aspect of the total possible relationship between the male and female categories in any given society. I have convinced myself in the preparation of this paper that if we are to retain marriage as an analytic category we are condemned forever to examining marriage in terms of what it does. This does not mean that I think there is no such thing as marriage (as I have been accused), although I would say that part of our difficulties springs from its too obvious existence, the very concreteness of the relationship makes it appear to be a valid unitary object of study. I am arguing that this is not so, that marriage is not an isolable relationship, and, accordingly, it is not a useful analytic category. I do not pretend that I have offered a sound alternative means of approach – judgement on this must depend on its proved operational usefulness and the value of the insights it affords.

NOTES

1. 'Philosophy, unlike science, makes no discoveries, gives no new information, but simply reminds us of what we have always known' (Bambrough 1970: 121).

2. The interesting and valuable part of this paper is Crocker's demonstration of the fact that a different principle is in operation in each union. Symmetrical exchange in the case of the men's house associates, asymmetric relationships in the case of marriage.

3. It would seem to me that there is a built-in disharmony in a culture which places higher value on youth than old age. Indeed it seems to represent a parallel with Dumont's claim that a fundamental process of the human mind is the placing of things in hierarchies so that societies with egalitarian ideologies face an irreconcilable conflict. In the case of age the trouble seems to lie with the high valuation placed on youth, which must be lost for something which is held in low esteem.

4. This is not to say that all functionalist explanations belong to the conscious model, which would go against Merton's useful distinction between manifest and latent functions. However, I have found no definition or explanation of marriage which is not couched in terms of manifest functions. Although I have no intention of more than mentioning them here, there are certain problems one ought to face. Firstly, in any given society, functions which are latent to some people may be manifest to others. Secondly, and this is a rider to the first point, the revelation of a latent function by sociological analysis may make it manifest, as may have happened in the case of Bowlby's ideas about child welfare.

5. Another logical possibility is that proposed by Plato in *The Republic* (Book V) where certain lapses of time are to be used to define parentage.

6. One can refer here to Mary Douglas's extremely interesting interpretation of couvade, which she sees as a symbolic statement by a man about his relationship to either his wife or his child (1968). This is a valuable up-dating of the old evolutionary interpretation of couvade and one for which I can offer

some ethnographic support. For example, the Trio Indian whom I observed to obey the strictest couvade prohibitions was perfectly well aware, as was everyone else, that his wife's child was not his.

7. The removal of all social and legal handicaps from bastards would clearly seem to go hand-in-hand with the suppression of ascribed status and increased emphasis on achieved status, and a corresponding ideology of individualism. Love, probably the most common reason for marriage today in western cultures, is clearly a reflection of the same individualism. Historically, romantic love carried the connotation of illicit or impossible love, and elopement, the most romantic of events, only occurs when marriage fails to receive the approval of one or both of the partner's families. Love is the final expression of individual choice, and thus the logical ground for marriage in a society in which an ideology of individualism holds sway. The theologian Robert Grimm (1965) claims that marriage has a function in respect to love. He argues that time is the enemy of love, but that love is the enemy of society because it is non-conformist and hostile to regulation. Society socializes love through marriage, which then proves an ally of love against time.

8. The view of marriage as a device for ordering sexual relations suffers from the same faults as other functional explanations. It is by no means universal and if it were it would require an equation between marriage and sexual relations.

9. '. . . the difficulty . . .is not that of finding the solution but rather that of recognizing as the solution something that looks as if it were only a preliminary to it' (Wittgenstein 1967b: 58e).

10. Honour and shame are purely metaphysical concepts which refer to ideal standards against which the actual behaviour of men and women is assessed. While often symbolized by the basic physiological differences of male and female, the qualities are rarely regarded as belonging exclusively to one sex. For example, a man should share in male and female qualities but the former should predominate.

11. I am surprised that so few have attempted to apply this idea in the analysis of kinship organization. My own use of it proved fruitful, and revealed some important features of Trio social organization which had not previously been apparent, in particular that marriage provided the solution to a series of otherwise contradictory roles (1969: 193-5).

12. One of the most striking features of the communities which Oscar Lewis has described under the label of the culture of poverty is the flexibility of behaviour. Indeed, the socio-economic behaviour within the culture of poverty is curiously reminiscent of that associated with hunting and gathering peoples. There is a fluidity and redundancy of relationships which allow more chance in the exploitation of essential but scarce resources. An aspect of this, in the culture of poverty, includes an unwillingness to enter into rigid and permanent relationships of which formal (middle-class) marriage is one. Such a formal marriage may well prove a handicap in such an economic environment, and the ability to change one's partner or even to have several of them may offer a real safeguard against the pressures of the economy – especially if the women are earning.

Following the presentation of this paper at the Bristol conference, Dr James Woodburn informed me that he and Dr Alan Howard have been examining this very topic in the course of comparing the social organizations of the Hadza and the Hawaiian poor. I understand that seminar papers on this subject were

Marriage: A Reassessment

given at the London School of Economics in 1969 and that these may be developed for publication.

13. This leads one to the conclusion that marriage, in Christendom, creates a basically incestuous union.

Devlin also noted that marriage is both a contract and a status (1968: 63). Marriage is an achieved role but it results in an ascribed status, or, in other words, the contract of marriage provides one with a set of relationships which are theoretically as indissoluble as those obtained through the accident of birth.

REFERENCES

BAMBROUGH, RENFORD. 1970. Fragments of a System. *The Listener*, 22 January: 121-2.

BANTON, M. 1965. *Roles: An Introduction to the Study of Social Relations*. London: Tavistock Publications; New York: Basic Books.

BEATTIE, J. 1968. Aspects of Nyoro Symbolism. *Africa* **38**: 413-42.

BOHANNAN, L. 1949. Dahomean Marriage: A Revaluation. *Africa* **19**: 273-87.

BOWLBY, J. 1951. *Maternal Care and Mental Health*. Geneva: WHO.

CROCKER, C. 1969. Men's House Associates among the Eastern Bororo. *Southwestern Journal of Anthropology* **25**: 236-60.

DOUGLAS, M. 1966. *Purity and Danger*. London: Routledge & Kegan Paul.

—— 1968. The Relevance of Tribal Studies. *Journal of Psychosomatic Research* **12**: 21-28.

DEVLIN, P. 1968. *The Enforcement of Morals*. Oxford Paperbacks.

EVANS-PRITCHARD, E. E. 1951. *Kinship and Marriage among the Nuer*. Oxford: Clarendon Press.

—— 1965. *Theories of Primitive Religion*. Oxford: Clarendon Press.

FISCHER, H. TH. 1956. For a New Definition of Marriage. *Man* **56**: 87.

GAVRON, H. 1968. *The Captive Wife*. Harmondsworth, Middlesex: Penguin Books.

GOUGH, E. K. The Nayars and the Definition of Marriage. *Journal of the Royal Anthropological Institute* **89**: 23-34.

GRIMM, R. 1965. *Love and Sexuality*. London: Hodder and Stoughton.

KRIGE, E. J. & KRIGE, J. D. 1943. *The Realm of the Rain-Queen*. London: Oxford University Press.

LEACH, E. R. 1961. *Rethinking Anthropology*. London: Athlone Press.

MEAD, M. 1949. *Male and Female*. London: Victor Gollancz.

NEEDHAM, R. 1967. Right and Left in Nyoro Symbolic Classification. *Africa* **37**: 425-52.

PETER, PRINCE OF GREECE AND DENMARK. 1956. For a New Definition of Marriage. *Man* **56**: 48.

RIVIÈRE, P. G. 1969. *Marriage among the Trio.* Oxford: Clarendon Press.

RUSSELL, B. 1958. *Marriage and Morals.* London: Allen and Unwin.

SANGREE, W. H. 1969. Going Home to Mother: Traditional Marriage among the Irigwe of Benue-Plateau State, Nigeria. *American Anthropologist* **71**: 1046-57.

WITTGENSTEIN, L. 1967a. *Lectures and Conversations on Aesthetics, Psychology and Religious Belief.* Oxford: Blackwell.

—— 1967b. *Zettel.* Oxford: Blackwell.

4

Edmund Leach

More about 'Mama' and 'Papa'

I

INTRODUCTION

Ever since Morgan, the study of kinship terminologies by anthropologists has been principally concerned with principles of social classification. The ethnographer observes that a set of individuals, A1, A2, A3 . . . A*n* are all lumped together by speaker X as belonging to a single category A, and the argument then centres upon the principles of logic which could lead to this classification. The emphasis is almost entirely algebraic rather than linguistic. The words employed are usually reported but then quickly laid on one side. It is assumed (without any obvious justification) that the prime meanings of the terms in question are genealogical referents and that any supplementary 'meaning' which is not genealogically derived is a metaphorical extension of an 'original' kinship meaning. With rare exceptions, such as Radcliffe-Brown's famous observation that the Ba Thonga address their mother's brother as 'male mother' (Radcliffe-Brown 1923), there has been very little attempt by professional anthropologists to analyse the constituent elements of kinship language as such.

The current orthodoxy regarding the analyses of kin-term classifications is well represented by the austerely mathematical contributions of Hammel and Lounsbury in Hammel (1965). It is not my present purpose to offer any direct criticism of this orthodoxy, but my personal view is that these procedures are self-destructive. In their pursuit of elegance and formal rigour the more ingenious practitioners of the art of componential analysis habitually move so far away from the original ethnography that the whole exercise becomes worthless.

So I suggest that we should go right back to the beginning and think again about just what it is that we are talking about when we discuss 'a kinship terminology'. First and foremost we are discussing a list of words, so it might be well to consider what sort of words they are before we lose sight of the original evidence in a welter of algebra.

II

AFFECT AND PHONOLOGY

This is not the first time that I have joined battle on this issue. In several previous publications I have expressed scepticism about the usual anthropological assumption that the words employed in kinship terms in any natural language constitute a readily distinguishable closed set. In particular I have argued (Leach 1967) that we can learn at least as much by examining the relationship between kinship words and non-kinship words as by studying the content of classifications or the relationship of kinship words to one another. In that paper I also made the point that much of our discussion of the ethnography of kinship terms is distorted by the fact that, with rather rare exceptions, the argument centres upon the equivalents of formal dictionary terms such as *father, mother, sister*, rather than the colloquial equivalents such as *dad, mum, sis*.

So let us take off from there. It is a striking fact that, although ethnographers have often reported that the linguistic competence of a single individual is likely to include alternative kin-term labels for the same genealogical relative, they have provided very little information about the precise syntactic or social circumstances which might be likely to generate one form rather than another. This seems to me surprising. I know from introspection that, in speaking to my own child, there are circumstances which would lead me to replace the usual:

'Mummy says . . .'

by a more austere:

'Your mother says . . .'

and I suspect that this represents a linguistic phenomenon of wide generality, but I have very little evidence to support this belief.

All of which adds up to saying that, in my view, the utility of the study of kin-term systems as sets – which runs from Morgan to Rivers to Radcliffe-Brown to Goodenough to Lounsbury and, by a different route, to Lévi-Strauss and

Rodney Needham – is pretty well worked out. In saying that I do not wish to imply that analysis of the formal logic of kinterm sets is a wholly valueless activity but simply that, in our present state of knowledge, the marginal rewards which come from investigations of this kind are becoming very small. I believe it may be much more profitable, at this stage in the game, to concentrate our attention on the way that the linguistic performance of the individual (with respect to kinship terminology) varies as he moves from one social situation to another. This in turn will require us to pay more attention to the psychological as distinct from the sociological significance of particular words.

This paper is not, in any direct sense, a contribution to this relatively novel field of inquiry, but it contributes perhaps to the necessary prolegomena to such an investigation. The underlying general hypothesis is that when a speaker's competence includes two kinship words which are alternative referents for the same individual the words are differentiated in the speaker's mind by a complex of associations which we may call 'semantic colour'. The particular postulate of this paper is that this semantic colour has a phonological base which is, at least to some extent, of a cross-cultural nature. If this is really the case, how could we begin to investigate the facts? It is to this latter problem that I am now seeking to provide some sort of partial solution.

Murdock (1959) is immediately relevant. This paper reported the result of a statistical inquiry (undertaken at the suggestion of Roman Jakobson) into the phonemic constituents of kin terms rated in Murdock's World Ethnographic Sample as meaning 'father' and 'mother'. The sample contained 1,072 terms (531 of the class 'mother'; 541 of the class 'father'). Jakobson (1960) was a commentary on Murdock's data. Jakobson here drew attention to the fact that more than 76 per cent of all Murdock's terms included 'diffuse' consonants (mainly labial and dental sounds p, b, t, d, m, n) as against only 10 per cent which included 'compact' consonants (mainly the velar palatal, and post-alveolar sounds ($k, g, \eta, \int, \zeta$). The statistics also show a marked preference for simple stops (p, b, t, d, k, g) and nasals (m, n, η) as against more complicated sounds such as those represented by our letters f, v, s, z, etc. In short, the statistics confirmed the earlier observation by Lewis (1951)

77

that parent terms tend to be of the *mama, papa* type with the 'mother usually termed by the *m* form and the father by the *p, b, t, d* forms'. Let me emphasize immediately that there are *dozens* of particular exceptions to this general rule; however, the statistical tendency is there and invites some kind of explanation.

Jakobson suggested that these facts are to be explained by the circumstances of speech behaviour in very early infancy. In the first few months of life all human infants produce a very wide range of gurgling, babbling noises. At this stage, the noises produced by a Bushman child, an English child, and a Tikopian child are indistinguishable yet later, in adult life, these three individuals will make use of quite different inventories of phonemes; for example, Bushman speech includes a variety of click noises which the average adult Englishman finds very difficult to imitate at all (Jakobson 1968: 21f). The process by which the individual's phonemic inventory is differentiated and restricted is a progressive one. Apparently, at the very beginning, all children begin to attach meaning to noise elements in much the same way, partly because some kinds of gurgling, babbling noise are more easily brought under control than others and partly from the simple fact that meaning is most easily attributed to sound signals in which the contrast is maximized. This maximization occurs when a labial or dental consonant (*p, b, t, d*) is contrasted with a wide frontal vowel, e.g. in noises such as *pā, bā, tā, dā*. Actually (according to Jakobson 1960: 130) the very first controlled noises made by almost any infant are likely to consist mainly of a combination of the diffuse bilabial nasal *m* with a diffuse undifferentiated vowel sound *ə*, that is to say the first consistently recognizable speech-like noise generated by any small infant is a *məmə* kind of sound. Jakobson suggested that the values which become attached to such sounds may be related to the sensations of breast-feeding and the position of the lips assumed in the act of sucking. If this theory is valid it is easy to offer plausible extensions: if it is probable that close relationships of mutual dependence will be signalled by *m, n, p, t* sounds, which are 'easy' noises to control, then it should be equally probable that other relationships surrounded by awkwardness and taboo will tend to be signalled by 'difficult' sounds, e.g. the *k, g, ŋ, ʃ, ẓ*, which

78

Murdock recorded as occurring only infrequently at the parental level.

Jakobson himself has not pressed the argument quite so far, though he has made a number of comments along these lines. He agrees that after the initial *məmə papa*, the development of infant voice control becomes progressively more and more uncertain. Even so, he has stated quite categorically that 'the succession of phonological acquisitions in child language appears to be stable in its fundamental characteristics' and that 'it is apparently a universal fact that palatovelar sounds develop in child language only after dental sounds' (Jakobson 1968: 46-7). That being so, there are grounds for supposing that the discrimination of vowels and consonants will usually proceed in a sequence more or less similar to that indicated in *Table 1*.

TABLE 1

Developmental sequence of basic phoneme distinctions
Based on Jackobson and Halle (1956: 37-42). A much fuller account of the underlying theory is given in Jakobson (1968).

1. vocal tract closed	— vocal tract open
2. closed — part closed	— open
$\overline{\text{stop}}$ — $\overline{\text{nasal}}$	$\overline{\text{vowel}}$
p m	— ə
3. grave/acute	— $\dfrac{\text{compact } (ɑ)}{\text{diffuse } (ə)}$
p,m | t,n	
4. $\dfrac{\text{compact}}{\text{diffuse}} \dfrac{kŋ,}{p,m/t,n}$	— $\overline{\quad\text{wide}\quad}^{\;a}$ back narrow front grave / acute u i
5. (velar/palatal distinction)	— rounded / unrounded o:u :: e:i
6. unvoiced (tense)/voiced (lax)	— 'long' / 'short'
k/g p/b, t/d	vowels vowels

79

Jakobson (1960) applies this theory of voice-control development to Murdock's kin-term data in the following way. He argues that, in all societies, young children will develop denotative terms for their own parents at a very early phase of their vocabulary formation. That being so, the child's initial kinship language must everywhere consist of phonemically very simple words of the type *mama, papa, baba, tata, dada, nana,* etc. This infant terminology has provided the historical base for the adult terms reported by Murdock.

Most anthropologists are likely to approach such arguments with a certain amount of scepticism, but the thesis is not necessarily incompatible with other styles of anthropological discourse. Notice, for example, that Jakobson's theory is essentially 'extensionist' in much the same sense as the arguments of Malinowski and Lounsbury.

One obvious criticism is that children do not invent their kin terms *de novo*; they learn a language from their parents and there is no reason why the parents' kinship language should be phonemically simple. This comment is easily evaded. If it is really the case that the small child must learn to use kin-term categories for close kin at a very early stage in its linguistic development, then it will have to be taught words which are phonemically simple. The baby-language words need not be identical to the adult words for the same categories, but they are surely very likely to be closely related to them? This fits quite well with our English experience in which the child is first taught to use a baby language containing words like *mummy* and *daddy* which are later on reformulated as *mother* and *father*. I don't think we really know whether there are close parallels for this sort of thing in the sorts of tribal languages ordinarily used by anthropologists. There is, however, good evidence that baby languages may be very similar even in quite different cultural and linguistic contexts (see Ferguson 1964). If it is the case that the adult kin terms for parents as reported in ethnographers' listings are always reformulations of baby-language terms this would explain why the adult parental kin terms are from a statistical point of view so strikingly similar right across the map.

Perhaps you are not fully persuaded? To be quite frank neither am I. But Jakobson's thesis has got sufficient *prima facie* weight behind it to imply that we should look further. If the phonemic shape of *father* and *mother* terms is indirectly influenced by the phonemic limitations of small children what about the words for other close kin such as *brother* and *sister*, *grandparents*, *mother's brother*, *father's sister*? What about personal and possessive pronouns? It is fairly obvious that any attempt at a statistically quantifiable analysis of this extended problem would be enormously complex and laborious. In fact, I make no claim at all that any of the arguments which follow could stand up to a statistical check – if indeed a genuinely satisfactory check could even be devised. All that I am saying is that if we look at a limited range of kin-term systems – namely those mentioned in this paper – certain phonemic peculiarities can be recognized which seem to invite explanation. If you do not like the explanation which I myself offer, then what do you propose instead? Thorough sceptics need to consider Capell (1966).

It is an unstressed assumption of Jakobson's *mama/papa* argument that the child will 'naturally' tend to associate the parents together; consequently Jakobson's linguistic problem is to show how the child will distinguish between the paired individuals. Anthropologists will question the 'naturalness' of any such pairing, but they will probably be prepared to accept, without too much argument about why and wherefore, that the sociological pairing of certain categories is very common: *brother* and *sister*, *husband* and *wife*, *father* and *son*, and so on. In these particular English examples the phonological pattern of the words is in fact sharply contrasted, and a linguist from Mars, having no evidence at his disposal other than a tape-recording of English words recited in isolation, would have no grounds for supposing that the words in question should be paired in any particular way. On the other hand, if this same linguist from Mars were given the English words *mother* and *brother*, or the French words *mère, père, frère*, he would surely suspect that for each of these groups the referents have something in common? He might of course be wrong; words which 'rhyme' do not necessarily have any common element of meaning and the rhymes here are imperfect. Yet, the very fact that popular song, in such a wide variety of languages, makes extensive use of rhyme in order to establish meaningful associations shows that phonological similarity is *one* of the basic

81

ways by which the referents of words are put into categories. How far is this relevant for our anthropological understanding of kin-term systems?

Here let me say at once that I am very well aware of the pitfalls that beset the amateur phonetician. It is not possible to determine from first principles whether two sounds which are distinguishable on a sound spectrogram will be classed as similar or different by any individual listener, and the question of whether two words will be classed together because they contain similar sounds rather than (or as well as) because they have similar meanings cannot be determined except by empirical evidence. But this is an area where it is easy to become too sophisticated. The point I want to make is very simple. In anthropological discussions of kinship classifications it has always been assumed that what we are interested in is the classification of individuals according to their social roles. If the anthropologist gets around to investigating the details of actual kinship words he still tends to see the problem of lumping together word categories which have similar or related *meanings*. What I am saying, following Jakobson, is that when we do this we need to remember that words can be lumped together into classes simply on the ground that in some sense they are felt to 'sound alike'. And furthermore the psychological response which makes us say that two words 'sound alike' cannot be fully dissociated from the response which allows us to say that two words have similar meanings.

When anthropologists study kinship *behaviour* they take it for granted that roles will be distinguished in terms of emotional affect; consider, for example, the whole body of literature relating to 'avoidance' and 'joking' relationships. Surely such arguments presuppose that the terms by which such taboo-loaded behaviours are signalled will themselves be loaded with affect? Is it not probable rather than otherwise that such differences of affect will be, at least in part, a matter of phonology?

Obviously some languages lend themselves to this kind of discussion much more readily than do others. In what follows I shall concentrate on Kandyan Sinhalese partly because I know the context, partly because the literature is adequate, and partly because the argument in this case seems to me to work quite well. There may well be other cases where it does not work at all. My thesis is that phonemic patterning *may* have semantic significance, not that it must do so: it is a linguistic option. But if there are some languages which work that way then as anthropologists we need to be on the look out for such a possibility.

III

SINHALESE

We may start by recalling that scientific linguistics was an Indian invention and that the script employed in writing modern Sinhalese is derived from the Sanskrit syllabary devised on segmental phonemic lines some 2,500 years ago. Modern spoken Sinhalese does not always sound as it is written, but most of the phonetic distinctions recognized by the alphabet correspond to genuine phonemic distinctions in the spoken language. Furthermore, unlike English, there are few if any distinctions in the spoken language which are not reflected in the written transcript. This means that for our present purposes we can take the written spelling of Sinhalese words to be the equivalent of a phonetic transcription (cf. Robins 1967: Ch. 6).

I shall write all Sinhalese words in roman script using the transcription conventions recommended by Carter (1924), but to save the compositor tribulation I shall omit the actual Sinhalese letters. I shall also omit from the tabulation all Sinhalese letters which do not occur in the specimen words under discussion. With these limitations Carter's tabulation is shown in *Table 2*. The T class sounds are weakly retroflex as in 'top' and 'dumb'. The Th class dentals are closer to English

TABLE 2   *Selected Sinhalese consonants*
(Carter's romanization)

	(*Unvoiced*)	(*Voiced*)	*Nasal*
	Tense	Lax	
K class	k	g	ng (ŋ)
Ch class	ch	j	ny
T class	t	d	n
Th class	th	dh	n
P class	p	b	m
Semivowels	y r w		l
Sibilants	s h		

83

't' and 'd' than to English 'th' and 'dh'. The main distinctions which will concern us in this essay are those between the unvoiced unaspirated consonants in the left-hand column, the voiced unaspirated consonants in the middle column, and the nasal consonants in the right-hand column. For a full analysis of the script see Geiger (1938).

The following details have relevance for the discussion which follows:

(i) The letter 'h' is generally – not always – interchangeable with the letter 's'.

(ii) the letters 'y' and 'w' represent semi-vowels of ambivalent status. For example, *mawu* ('mummy') is practically a diphthong rhyming with the Mao of Mao Tse-Tung. The same diphthong appears in *pawulă* ('wife'). But *dhŭwă* ('daughter') is a word with two distinct syllables. Sometimes *ăyĭyā* ('elder brother') is spoken with a 'hang' on the first *y*, in which case it is a three-syllable word, the last two syllables rhyming with *pĭyā* ('father'); but the initial *ayi* can also be spoken so as to rhyme with English 'my', or the middle *i* can disappear altogether so that the word sounds as if it should be written *āyyā*. In an initial position as in *yēlĭ*, *y* is voiced.

(iii) Where *ā* appears as a final vowel it is unstressed and short.

Sinhalese contains a fairly complex inventory of vowel sounds and difference of stress may carry semantic implications. I shall follow the normal conventions and distinguish Roman and phonetic transcriptions, phonetic description, and approximate English sound (*Table 3*). I do not have sufficient linguistic knowledge to map all these various sounds – the consonants and the vowels of colloquial Sinhalese – onto a matrix of Distinctive Features in the manner of *Table 4*, but such a tabulation could be drawn up and it would almost certainly include basic components such as shown in *Table 5* (cf. *Table 1*). I am not aware that there has been any professional study of this matter.

Inadequate though it is, my table provides an indication of both the degree and the manner by which the sounds we are discussing may be contrasted one with another.

TABLE 3 *Sinhalese vowels*

Roman transcription as used here	Usual phonetic transcription	Phonetic description	Approximate English sound
ă (i)	ʌ	'mid-mixed – lowered – retracted'	m*u*mmy
ă (ii)	ə	'central unstressed'	m*o*ther
ā	a	'low-back-unrounded'	f*a*ther
ä (ɛ̆)	æ	'low-front-lax'	d*a*ddy
ā̈ (ɛ̄)	ɛə	'mid-front→central diphthong'	b*ai*rn
ĭ	ɪ	'high-front-lax'	s*i*ster
ī	i	'high-front-tense'	n*ie*ce
ŭ	ʊ	'high-back-lax-rounded'	f*oo*t
ū	u	'high-back-tense-rounded'	f*oo*d
ĕ	ɛ	'mid-front-lax'	fr*ie*nd
ē	e	'mid-front-tense'	f*a*te
ŏ	ǫ	'low-back-lax-rounded'	h*o*t
ō	o	'mid-back-tense-rounded'	l*oa*d

Let us then consider some of the category words of Sinhalese and try to make a guess as to what phonological characteristics distinguish one label from another.

As a start some pronouns:

$$\text{'I'} = mămă, mă\eta; \text{'me'} = mā$$
$$\text{'you'} = ŭmbă$$

This last term carries overtones of disrespect; the person spoken to is in some sense younger or junior or inferior to the speaker.

$$\text{'he' (lit- 'that person')} = ĕyā$$

This applies only to human beings. Animals are referred to as *ū* if masculine and *ɛ̄* if feminine. 'It' = *ēkă*

$$\text{'we'} = ăpĭ \qquad \text{'us'} = ăpă$$

Likewise notice: *ē* = 'that' and *mē* = 'this'

TABLE 4   *Distinctive features of American English**

| Compact | Grave | H | T | | W | | |
			P	F	N	J	V
0	0	h					
−	−		t d	s z	n	j	I
±	−						ε
+	−		ʃ ź	ʃ ʒ	ŋ		æ
+	±					r	ə
+	+		k g	θ ð	l		a
±	+						ɔ
−	+		p b	f v	m	w	ʋ

			P	F		N	J	V
Consonantal		−	+	+	+	+	−	−
Vocalic		−	−	−	−	+	+	+
Continuous		0	−	−	+	+	0	0	0
Tense		0	+	−	+	+	0	+	−

P = stop;   F = fricative;   N = sonorant;   J = semivowel;   V = vowel;
H = /h/; T = Turbulent; W = Nonturbulent.

* Source: L. G. Jones, 'English Consonantal Distribution', in *For Roman Jakobson*, p. 246 (Mouton, The Hague, 1956).

TABLE 5   *Partial distinctive feature analysis of Sinhalese consonants and vowels*

| Sinhalese phoneme | Distinctive feature | | | | |
	Compact	Grave	Consonantal	Vocalic	Tense
p	−	+	+	−	+
b	−	+	+	−	−
m	−	+	+	+	0
w	−	+	−	−	±
u	−	+	−	+	−
ʋ	−	+	−	+	−
t	−	−	+	−	+
d	−	−	+	−	−
n	−	−	+	+	0
y	−	−	−	−	±
i	−	−	−	+	+
I	−	−	−	+	−
k	+	+	+	−	+
g	+	+	+	−	−
ŋ	+	+	+	+	0
a	+	+	−	+	−

86

Particularly relevant in view of what follows is the contrast *mămă/ăpă* = I/us, and the fact that the only one of these basic pronouns which contains the /b/ phoneme implies juniority.

Next let me recall the most celebrated feature of Sinhalese kinship organization. The Sinhalese make a terminological distinction between virilocal marriage (*dhĭgă*) and uxorilocal marriage (*bĭnnă*) and give a very strong value preference to the former as against the latter. Among the peasantry *bĭnnă* marriages are not infrequent, but they are of low status.

And now the kinship terminology proper. Various lists of Sinhalese kinship terms have been published and still others can be extracted from diligent work in printed dictionaries. The fullest list is that given by Yalman (1967: 211), but this unfortunately pays no regard at all to the Sinhalese spelling and not very much even to the colloquial pronunciation. Pieris (1956: 212-15) gives a fairly informative list that is consistently spelled but uses a different romanization from that which I am using here. My own list of categories (*Table* 6) is restricted to key terms. Allowing for adjustments of spelling, it will be found that there is substantial agreement with both Yalman and Pieris. There are regional differences of pronunciation and some dialect variation both as between districts and as between caste groups, but such details need not concern us here.

In addition, as is explained in some detail by Yalman (1967: 211), nearly all the terms may be qualified by prefixes meaning 'big', 'little', 'medium', 'young', 'youngest', 'honoured', 'great', etc., so that, for example, 'big elder brother' *lŏkŭ ăyĭyā*, may be distinguished from 'small elder brother'. *pŭŋchĭ ăyĭyā*. The variables here are very numerous and to some extent idiosyncratic. I shall draw attention only to two aspects of the matter. When reduced to its skeletal Dravidian form, Sinhalese kinship terminology appears to be 'prescriptive'. Each individual falls into one definite slot definable by rule. In practice, the speaker has a considerable range of choice about how he will classify any particular kinsman and the choices are differentiated by 'affect' rather than by precise 'meaning'. The other detail I would mention is that one of the prefix terms mentioned above is *bālă* = 'young'. *Bālă ăppā* 'young father' is the normal term not only for actual younger brothers of the real father but for all males of rather indeterminate status of the father's generation.

87

TABLE 6 *Sinhalese kinship terms*

1 GENERATIONS ABOVE THAT OF GRANDPARENT
nāththā, pănāththā, kĭththā, kĭrikĭmŭththā, dōwĭkĭththā, mĭmŭththā, miāththā*

2 GRANDPARENTS' GENERATION

(i) *Males*	(ii) *Females*
sĭyā, mŭththā, āththā, āthā kĭrĭāththā, āthăppā	*āththā, āchchĭ, kĭrĭămmā*

3 PARENTS' GENERATION

(i) *Males*	(ii) *Females*
(a) 'Fathers' and 'father's brothers' *pĭyā, ăppā, thāththā, ăppŏchchĭ*	(a) 'Mothers' *ămmā, mawu, ămmăndĭ***
(b) 'Mother's brothers', 'fathers-in-law' *māmā, māmăndĭ*	(b) 'Father's sisters', 'mothers' brother's wives' *năndhā, năndhămmā*

4 OWN GENERATION

(i) *Males*	(ii) *Females*
(a) 'Elder brothers' *ăyĭyā (āyyā), ayiyăndĭ***	(a) 'Elder sisters' *ăkkā*
(b) 'Younger brothers' *măllĭ, mălăyā,*** *mălăyăndĭ***	(b) 'Younger sisters' *năŋgĭ*
(c) 'Male sibling' *săhōdhărăyā*	(c) 'Female sibling' *săhōdărĭ*
(d) 'Cross-cousin', 'brother-in-law' *măssĭnā, măchăŋ, hūrā*	(d) 'Cross-cousin', 'sister-in-law' *nĕnā*
(e) 'Husband' *mĭnĭhā*	(e) 'Wife' *gĕnĭ, pawulă*

5 SON'S GENERATION

(i) *Males*	(ii) *Females*
(a) 'Son' *pŭthā*	(a) 'Daughter' *dhŭwă*
(b) 'Son-in-law', 'sister's son' *bɛnā*	(b) 'Daughter-in-law', 'sister's daughter' *lēlĭ, yēlĭ*

6 GRANDCHILDREN'S GENERATION

(i) *Males* *mŭnŭbŭrā*	(ii) *Females* *mĭnĭbĭrĭ*

* For comments on these terms, see Leach (1960: 126) and Pieris (1956: 212 fn 74).

** These items appear in the dictionary but are not reported by recent ethnographers in Kandyan rural areas.

It does *not* however normally appear as *bālă ăppā* but in the
contracted form of *bāppā*. The use of the /b/ phoneme in this
way is strictly consistent with what we have already noted
about the pronoun *ŭmbă* and the marriage type *bĭnnă*. It is
relevant also to the category (5) (i) (b) *bɛnā* noted above.
From this I postulate that there is an affect distinction of the
following kind:

greater respect	less respect
unvoiced stops	voiced stops and nasals
p, t, k, ch, th, (y)	*b, d, g, dh; l, m, n, ŋ*

Since men are in general held in greater respect than women,
the 'unvoiced/voiced + nasal' distinction tends to correspond
to a male/female distinction: e.g. *pŭthā/dhŭwă* (son/daughter)
but this is far from being the sum of the matter.

The 'structure' of the kinship terminology is typically Dravidian in the sense that if male Ego and his male cross-cousin were
to exchange sisters and everyone consistently married his or
her first cross-cousin the categories would make logical sense.
I show in *Figure 1* a diagram derived from Yalman, which provides a schematic representation of this fact.

The following comments relate to particular terms listed in
Table 6:

(i) Terms listed under (1) are rarely used and will not be
considered any further.

(ii) *sīyā* in (2) and (3) *pĭya* are sometimes felt to be very
formal and are then not used in colloquial speech at all.

(iii) Pieris reports the variant (3) (ii) (a) *ămmăndĭ* as a
term 'of endearment'. But in fact all the special forms
ending in *-ăndĭ* carry implications of respect. The terms
marked ** appear in the dictionary but are not reported by recent ethnographers in Kandyan rural
areas.

(iv) The most relaxed of the grandfather terms under (2)
is usually *āththā*, and of the grandmother terms *āchchĭ*.
kĭrĭămmā – lit: 'milk mother' – could mean 'a wet
nurse', and its use to mean 'granny' is similar to the
English use of a grandmother term 'nana' to mean
'nanny' ('nurse').

Edmund Leach

(v) The most relaxed of the father terms (and the closest equivalent to English 'daddy') is usually *thāththā*.

(vi) In (4) (i) (d) *măchăŋ* (where current) is a less specific term than *măssĭnā*, which is often reserved for 'real' brothers-in-law and first cross-cousins.

(vii) Ref. (4) (i) (d) and (4) (i) (e): Note that the letters *h* and *s* are usually interchangeable. The plural of *mĭnĭhā* is *mĭnĭssu*; i.e. the two terms *măssĭnā* and *mĭnĭhā* are different combinations of a very similar group of sounds.

(viii) Comparably note that (4) (ii) (e) *gĕnĭ* ('wife', 'woman') is an abstraction of sounds shared on the one hand with *năŋgĭ* ('younger sister') and on the other with *nĕnā* ('female cross-cousin').

FIGURE 1 *Schematic arrangement of Sinhalese kin-term categories (after Yalman 1967: 220; Yalman's spelling)*

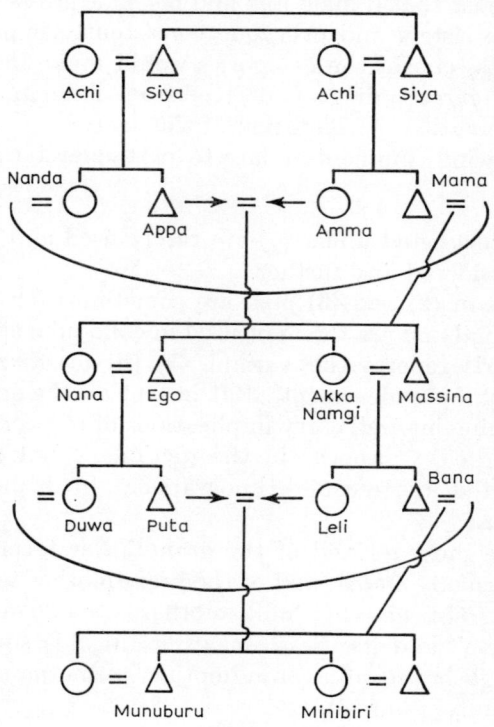

More about 'Mama' and 'Papa'

At this point the reader should consider how far the terms which I have now listed are or are not phonologically associated or contrasted in the same way as *mère* and *frère* or as *mama* and *papa*. The following 'pairs' and 'groups' seem to be fairly self-evident:

(i) *săhōdărăyā – săhōdărī*
(ii) *mŭnŭbŭrā – mĭnĭbĭrī*
(iii) *bēna – nēna*
(iv) *sĭyā – pĭyā – ăyĭyā*
(v) *āththā – ăkkā – āyyā – ăppā – ămmā*
(vi) *ămmā – māmā*
(vii) *thāththā – āththā*
(viii) *măssĭnā – mĭnĭhā*

But here I must sound several notes of caution. These suggested 'groupings' make use of a variety of different principles – e.g. in (iii), (iv), (vii) it is a matter of 'rhyme', in (vi), (viii) metathesis, in (v) form: VCCV. The fact that these characters are *apparent* does not mean that they *must* be significant. Moreover the various words could be classified according to phonological principles in various other ways. To be frank, I am 'cheating'; I am already making use of the fact that I know what the sociological category groups will turn out to be.

The reader will recall that Jakobson's original proposal was that the child, in learning to talk, first makes some sort of identification with the mother and then discriminates the father by maximizing the phonological contrast. In the Sinhalese case Jakobson's initial situation is represented by the words for (i) 'I' = *mămă* and (ii) 'mother' = *ămmā, mawu*, while the maximal contrast is represented in (iii) 'father' = *ăppā, thāththā*. The same contrast comes out in the pronoun distinction *mămă/ăpă* – 'I'/'us' already noticed. But the 'Jakobson principle' will take us much further than this.

In a *dhīgă* married household (p. 87) the members of Ego's home, at the point when Ego is learning to talk, will *all* ordinarily fall into one or other of the following categories:

'grandparents – *sīyā, āththā, āchchĭ*
'fathers' – *pĭyā, ăppŏchchĭ, ăppā, thāththā*
'elder sisters' – *ăkkā*
'elder brothers' – *ăyĭyā, (āyyā)*
'mothers' – *ămmā*

91

In these examples *all* the consonants, apart from those occurring in the 'mother' terms, belong to the unvoiced tense category in the left-hand column of *Table 2*; i.e. by Jakobson's argument *all* these non-mother relatives are contrasted in the strongest possible way with 'mother'. But the converse is true of the household members immediately junior to Ego, namely the 'younger brothers' and 'younger sisters', where the terms *mălli*, *năŋgĭ* are made up of nasalized and voiced consonants, implying that these categories are quite closely 'associated' with the primary 'mother' category *mawu* but contrasted with Ego's household kin other than the 'mothers'.

The general theory underlying this argument seems to be supported when we notice further that all the categories of relative who are known to Ego because they are members of the mother's brother's household share a nasalized phonology with the mother herself, but in this case a limited degree of contrast is established by using *m* as a signal for male sex and *n* for female.

The gist of this argument overall has been summarized in *Figure 2*.

It deserves note that most, though not quite all, of this process of sorting terms out into phonological boxes could be achieved by our imaginary Martian linguist from first principles without his having to know anything at all about the semantic or sociological background. It is true that this uninformed Martian linguist might make a variety of other guesses about possible associations and contrasts but the ones we have made so far stand out as 'rather obvious'.

But there remain some unexpected associations which call for sociological comment. The most striking of these is the phonological similarity of *nēnā* – female cross-cousin – and *bēnā* – son-in-law, sister's son (Boxes 3 & 7). The latter term suggests some association with *bĭnnă*, the term denoting a low-status uxorilocal marriage the characteristic of which is that the incoming husband is in an exceptionally dependent status *vis-à-vis* his father-in-law, his *māmā* (*māmăndĭ*).

The mother's brother/sister's son (father-in-law/son-in-law) relationship represented by the paired terms *māmā* – *bēnā* is a key element in Sinhalese social structure. Both parties have strong claims on the services of the other and the sister's son, *bēnā*, has a notional claim to demand his mother's brother's

FIGURE 2 *Sinhalese kin terms grouped according to phonological content and social space*

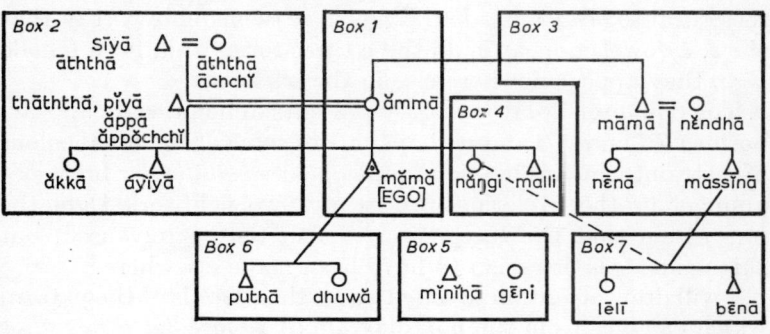

Box 2
'Grandparents', 'fathers', 'elder brothers', 'elder sisters'.
Maximal contrast with Box 1.
Unvoiced unaspirated consonants.
Vowels: 'a' and 'i' sounds only.

Box 1
Ego and 'mother'.
Minimal difference.
Diffuse nasal voiced bilabial consonant.
Low-mixed-lax vowel in *mămă*, low-back-unrounded vowel as terminal of *ămmā, unstressed.*

Box 3
'Mother's brother', 'mother's brother's wife', 'mother's brother's child' Only moderate contrast with Box 1. Males have initial '*m*', females initial '*n*'. All consonants voiced. Vowels as in Boxes 1 & 2 plus mid-front ε & $\bar{\varepsilon}$.

Box 4
'Younger brothers', 'younger sisters.'
Similar to Box 3 but vowels only as Boxes 1 & 2.

Box 6
'Son' and 'daughter'.
Terms share same vowel combination: high-back-rounded '*u*' followed by low-back-unrounded '*a*'; unvoiced consonants in *puthā*, voiced consonants in *dhuwă*.

Box 5
Husband, wife.
Modifications of terms for male cross-cousin and female cross-cousin (see p. 90, viii)

Box 7
'Son-in-law', 'daughter-in-law'
(see comment pp. 92-94).

daughter as a wife. Nevertheless *bēnā* is very definitely in a dependent position *vis-à-vis māmā. Nēnā* is *māmā*'s daughter; she is the girl over whom male Ego has potential claims and who may become his wife (*gēni*). If *nēna* marries someone other than Ego, Ego can demand a token payment from her husband for usurping his claims. Thus *bēnā* and *nēna* share the quality that in the case of a male Ego they are persons in dependent status.

The same argument scarcely seems to hold for a female Ego for in this case the *nɛ̆nā* term is self-reciprocal, while the reciprocal to *bɛ̆nā* is *nɛ̆ndhā*. Even so it seems noteworthy that the *ɛ*, *ɛ̄* vowels appear in all these three terms and, for a female Ego, they appear nowhere else in the whole set.

The daughter-in-law category presents difficulties. It appears both as *lēlĭ* and *yēlĭ* and perhaps carries some of the tonal colour of restraint which is implicit in the *ăyĭyā – mălli* (elder brother – younger brother) relationship. In my own fieldwork I got the impression that the category is in fact only rarely used, but this point does not seem to have been made elsewhere.

I will draw attention to only two further details of the pattern which emerges from the box diagram of *Figure 2*:

(i) The relation between *ămmā* ('mother') and *māmā* ('mother's brother') is that the second term is derived from the first by reversing the first syllable and strengthening the vowel. Social anthropologists are likely to be reminded of Radcliffe-Brown's thesis that in a variety of kin-term systems the term for mother's brother means 'male-mother'. Sinhalese do not regard their *māmā* in this way but the two terms (*ămmā, māmā*) are closely associated.

(ii) The terms in Box 2, although all contrasted with *ămmā* in a very similar way, are of differing degrees of sociological formality. The relatively friendly relaxed terms, equivalent to 'daddy' and 'granny', are *thāththā* and *āchchĭ*. *Sīyā* and *pĭyā* are usually considered very formal; there are marked elements of restraint embodied in *ăppŏchchĭ, ăppā, ăkkā, ăyĭyā* and the taboo associations of the /k/ phoneme in *ăkkā* are almost explicit. In Sinhalese *kā*- is a general prefix denoting dirt and evil; *kākā* is a 'carrion crow'.

Here it may be worth going back to Jakobson. It will be recalled that /k/ phonemes appear late in baby language. Jakobson (1968: 47 n) cites Jespersen as saying that 'children in all countries tend to substitute *t* for *k*'. On the other hand /k/ phonemes and glottal stops are prominent in words denoting 'dirt'. Jakobson in this connexion has remarked:

'the child's *a'a* (= 'excrements, defecation'), which is adopted to the sound structure of such languages as Russian or French as *kaka* and then, as part of the nursery language, is naturally reproduced as *tata* by children beginning to speak' (op. cit. 81).

If we apply considerations of this sort to the words we have just been considering, then the terms *thāththā, kākā, ăkkā* become related in a curious and ambiguous fashion. And that perhaps is a good point to stop. Just what should one make of this sort of thing? How can one verify that any particular phonological patterning has or has not got genuine semantic implications? Jakobson's 1960 article noted the infrequency of velar (and palatal) consonants in 'mother' and 'father' terms. I have ended my argument by drawing attention to the strong taboo associations in Sinhalese of velar /k/ which is also reflected in weaker form in the /g/ of *naygi* and *gēni*. It is a fact that, cross-culturally, the compact /k/ and /g/ sounds seem to occur with much more than random frequency in relationships marked by special attitudes of taboo and restraint. Is this accidental? I don't really know, but this paper at least suggests that there are other interesting ways of grouping kinship categories besides those which emerge from the tortuous pseudo-mathematics of the exponents of componential analysis.

IV
KACHIN

Nothing is 'proved' by citing a single case, and the evidence anyway is so tenuous that nothing very much would be demonstrated by piling on the data. Yet the value of this exercise (if any) is precisely that it provokes cross-cultural speculation. I will cite only one supplementary example and will put this forward only in very restricted form.

I have, in the past, published a good deal of information about Jinghpaw (Kachin) kinship terminology, notably in Leach (1961, Chapter 2) and in Leach (1967). Here I need recall only the following details. The adult Kachin term for 'excrement' is *hkyi*. *Mătsa* is to curse. Mother = *nu*. Father = *wa*. Wife (woman) = *num*. Husband (man) = *la*.

The basic structure of Kachin society is patrilineal. Women normally marry and show respect for men older than themselves. The marriage of a man with his matrilateral cross-cousin is prescribed; marriage with the patrilateral cross-cousin is prohibited. All unmarried members of Ego (male)'s own generation fall into one or other of the following four kinship categories:

(i) *nau* – 'younger sister' (ii) *nam* – 'marriageable cross-cousin'

(iii) *na* – 'elder sister' (iv) *hkri* –'unmarriageable cross-cousin' (joking-relation)

All unmarried members of the opposite sex of Ego ('female')'s own generation fall into one or other of the following four categories:

(i) *nau* – 'younger brother' (ii) *gu* – 'marriageable cross-cousin'

(iii) *hpu* – 'elder brother' (iv) *tsa* – 'unmarriageable cross-cousin' (joking-relation)

If we follow the principles which have been imprecisely formulated in the earlier part of this paper and distinguish these categories in terms of their phonological similarity, their distinctive feature contrasts, and so on, we are led to take note of the following details.

The vowels of *nu, wa, num, la, nau, na, gu, hpu, tsa* all lie in the high-back (*u*) – low-middle (*a*) range and are sharply contrasted with the high-front *i* of *hkri*. Most of the significant consonant distinctions may be inferred from Table 4 (p. 86). In terms of this pattern the complex sounds in the *hkr* of *hkri* and the *ts* of *tsa* are out of line. It thus emerges that not only in terms of sociology but also of distinctive feature analysis:

| FEMALES | nam | : | num | :: | na | : | nu |
| (ms) | MBD | : | W | :: | e.Z | : | M |

and also

| MALES | gu | : | la | :: | hpu | : | wa |
| (ws) | FZS | : | H | :: | e.B | : | F |

In each set of terms the 'unmarriageable cross-cousin', *hkri* for the man and *tsa* for the woman, is the odd term out. Perhaps all this is just accident, but somehow there seems to me to be more to it than that.

V

CONCLUSIONS

This brings us back more or less to where we started out. Anthropological studies of kinship terminologies have usually been concerned with the problem of how discriminations in the terminology distinguish social roles and the allocation of individuals to social groups. Most such analyses assume that the emotional loading of the different terms is neutral. It seems to me that this neutrality is not only open to doubt but rather improbable. Radcliffe-Brown's celebrated discussions of joking relationships were couched in a language which assumed that different kinship categories are likely to be loaded with widely different degrees of affect. Thus his argument refers not only to 'conjunction' and 'disjunction' but also to friendship, hostility, mutual respect, taboo avoidance, and so on. That being so, it would surely be logical to suppose that the terms which denote such differences should in themselves be capable of signalling different degrees of affect?

What I am proposing is that differing degrees of affect associated with particular relationship categories may, on occasion, be signalled by phonology; and further that, when this happens, the signals may be, at least to some extent, of a species-specific, cross-cultural, type. This would mean that the kind of explanation which Jakobson used to account for the frequent occurrence of *mama/papa*-type oppositions in the parental terms might have a much wider application.

REFERENCES

CAPELL, A. 1966. *Studies in Socio-linguistics*. The Hague: Mouton.

CARTER, S. 1924. *A Sinhalese-English Dictionary*. Colombo: Baptist Missionary Society.

FERGUSON, C. A. 1964. Baby Talk in Six Languages. In J. J. Gumperz and D. Hymes (eds.), *The Ethnography of Communication*. American Anthropologist Special Publication, December 1964.

GEIGER, W. 1938. *A Grammar of the Sinhalese Language*. Colombo: Royal Asiatic Society.

HAMMEL, E. A. (ed.). 1965. *Formal Semantic Analysis*. American Anthropologist Special Publication, October 1965.

Edmund Leach

JAKOBSON, R. 1960. Why 'Mama' and 'Papa'? In B. Kaplan and S. Wapner (eds.), *Perspectives in Psychological Theory*. New York: International Universities Press.

JAKOBSON, R. 1968. *Child Language, Aphasia, and Phonological Universals*. (Translation of *Kindersprache, Aphasie und Allgemeine Lautgesetze*, 1941). The Hague: Mouton.

JAKOBSON, R. & HALLE, M. 1957. *Fundamentals of Language*. The Hague: Mouton.

LEACH, E. R. 1960. The Sinhalese of the Dry Zone of Northern Ceylon. In G. P. Murdock (ed.), *Social Structure in Southeast Asia*. Chicago: Quadrangle.

—— 1961. *Rethinking Anthropology*. London: Athlone Press.

—— 1967. The Language of Kachin Kinship: Reflections on a Tikopia Model. In M. Freedman (ed.), *Social Organization*. London: Cass.

LEWIS, M. M. 1951. *Infant Speech*. London: Routledge

MURDOCK, G. P. 1959. Cross-language Parallels in Parental Kin Terms. *Anthropological Linguistics* **1** (9): 1-5.

PIERIS, R. 1956. *Sinhalese Social Organization*. Colombo: Ceylon University Press.

RADCLIFFE-BROWN, A. R. 1924. The Mother's Brother in South Africa. *South African Journal of Science* **21**: 542-55.

ROBINS, R. H. 1967. *A Short History of Linguistics*. London: Longmans.

YALMAN, N. O. 1967. *Under the Bo Tree*. Berkeley, California: University of California Press.

5

Francis Korn

A Question of Preferences
The Iatmul Case

I

INTRODUCTION

In the preface to the second French edition of *Les Structures élémentaires de la parenté*, Lévi-Strauss states that 'an elementary structure can be equally preferential or prescriptive':

> '. . . neither prescription nor preference is the test of an elementary structure. Its one and only criterion rests in the fact that, preferred or prescribed, the spouse is the spouse solely because she belongs to an alliance category or stands in a certain kinship relationship to Ego. In other words, the imperative or desirable relationship is a function of the social structure' (1967: xxi-xxii).[1]

According to this, it should be possible to categorize a system with preferential marriage into one or another type of elementary structure.

In relation to this problem we have chosen to analyse here the Iatmul system of alliances and the Iatmul relationship terminology because, according to Bateson, 'not only have they three positive marriage rules which conflict with one another . . . but the people do not adhere even to their negative rules' (Bateson 1936: 91).

The question whether this system should hence be classified, according to Lévi-Strauss's typology, as a 'complex structure' is ruled out, because for Lévi-Strauss 'complex structures' are those 'systems which limit themselves to defining the circle of relatives and leave the determination of the spouse to other mechanisms, economic or psychological' (1949: ix). On the other hand, since for Lévi-Strauss a preferential rule has the same analytical value as a prescription, and the Iatmul do have declared 'preferences', the system has to be considered in Lévi-Strauss's own scheme as an 'elementary structure'.

99

Francis Korn

The purposes of our analysis are twofold: (1) to classify the Iatmul relationship terminology and relate it to the actual system of alliances, and (2) to determine once more, but this time in the light of an empirical example, the consistency and applicability of Lévi-Strauss's definitions of 'prescription', 'preference',' 'elementary structure', and 'complex structure' (cf. Korn 1969b).[2]

II

IATMUL INSTITUTIONS

There are four reports of Iatmul society, in the form of three articles (Bateson 1932a; 1932b; 1935) and a monograph (Bateson 1936).[3]

The articles of 1932 were published by Bateson after his first contact, lasting six months, with Iatmul society. His admirable book *Naven* (1936) was published after he completed his field-work in the area with a second sojourn, extending to an additional fifteen months, among the Iatmul people: it consists mainly of the description and explanation of the *naven* ceremony among them.[4]

When Bateson refers to the Iatmul, he denotes a population living in a number of villages on the banks of the Sepik River in New Guinea. He calls Iatmul the part of the linguistic group (100 miles in length) that recognize themselves as a unit (1932a: 249). 'Iatmul' is, in fact, the name of a very small clan of one of the villages (Mindimbit), and the compound term Iatmul-iambonai[5] is used by the people of Mindimbit to denote the whole linguistic group.

Three divisions are distinguished: Eastern, Central, and Western Iatmul (1936: 142, 228 n.1, 239), which vary apparently in culture and in definiteness of organization. Bateson found the culture in this area sufficiently uniform for his purpose: 'there are, however, local variations of many kinds, not confined to superficial details, but definite modifications of kinship system, clan system, and the scheme of ceremonial life' (1932b: 450).

The Iatmul are characterized by Bateson as a 'fine, proud, head-hunting people' (1936: 4) who depend almost entirely on

100

the river and the fens for their food and life. Although they work sago for themselves, they also trade fish for sago produced by the 'bush people' (1936: 7, 234); trading-rights with bush villages are recognized and jealously guarded (1932a: 283). All communication with other Iatmul villages is done by canoe (except in the very dry season), which is also the way of travelling for any other purposes such as trading, fishing, or head-hunting.

There is no centralized organization and the separate villages are independent war-making groups, though a pair of villages may unite in a feud against another. They are independent units for ceremonial purposes also, though a great many natives go to see and to take part in dances in neighbouring villages. There is no hereditary rank or chieftainship.

There is not, in Bateson's works, any indication of the total population of Iatmul society. There is no indication either of the number of villages. Some of them are: Mindimbit, Palimbai, Tambunum, Malingei, Kankanamun (1932a; 1936). He states that the average population of each village amounts to from 200 to 1,000 individuals.

The villages are divided into two patrilineal totemic moieties and two patrilineal ceremonial moieties. The totemic moieties are subdivided into patrilineal clans (*ngaiva*): there are between fifty and a hundred clans of which 'between ten and twenty are represented in any one village' (1936: 307). The village of Mindimbit contained 'representatives' of eight clans (1932b: 402). The clans are paired and trace descent from a pair of brothers, one clan being called the 'elder brother' of the other. 'Larger groups of clans also occur' (1936: 310). There is also a grouping called *nggwoil-nggu*, composed of 'a close patrilineal group within the clan' (1936: 104 n. 2).

There is in some villages (Bateson describes Malingei as the most perfect of them) a complete correspondence between the division into patrilineal totemic moieties and patrilineal clans and the physical organization. Malingei is divided longitudinally by a big dancing-ground (*wonpunau*) on which the ceremonial houses stand. On one side of this area are the houses of one patrilineal moiety and on the other side the houses of the opposite moiety.

The names of the totemic moieties and their functional

Francis Korn

importance concerning initiation vary from the Eastern Iatmul (Mindimbit, etc.) to Central Iatmul (Kankanamun, etc). Among the latter, both the initiatory moieties and the totemic moieties are called 'Sun' and 'Mother', in spite of the fact that several clans which belong totemically to one moiety have gone across to the other moiety for initiatory purposes. But in Mindimbit the initiatory dual division is regarded as entirely distinct from the totemic moieties, and the initiatory moieties are not called 'Sun' and 'Mother' but Kiship and Miwot (1936: 228 n.).

A father has authority over his son, and elder brother over younger brother (1936: 98). Inheritance is patrilineal (1936: 211), and brothers are 'expected to quarrel over their patrimony' (1936: 212).

When Bateson worked among the Iatmul, the villages contained 'considerable numbers' of young men who had recently returned to their homes after spending from three to five years as indentured labourers on European plantations and in gold mines (1936: 167). During his stay in Mindimbit, where he did all his work on his first expedition, 'all the available young men had left the village to work for Europeans' (1932a: 275). His account makes a number of references to a marked degree of cultural change brought about both by these influences and by the British administration. A village constable and a government interpreter were permanentaly stationed in Mindimbit (1932a: 266, 282). Missionaries, too, worked to disintegrate Iatmul culture. At some villages they even lined up the women and got mission-trained men to perform on the sacred flutes in front of them – a gross and irreparable exposure of a 'mystery upon which the separation of the sexes is based' (1935: 163, 170). In Mindimbit the initiation system had broken down, the rising generations were in a 'lawless state', and the older men were 'fatalist before the decay of their culture' (1932a: 274-5). Bateson speaks indeed of a 'dying culture' (1932b: 440).

According to Bateson, 'neither of the systems of dual divisions controls marriage in a simple way', and there is a definite preference for clan exogamy (1932a: 257). Marriage is patrilocal (1936: 52), the wife going to live in the husband's *ngaiva*. This word has a definite local reference as well as meaning clan, and a clan can be referred to as 'part of the village' (1932b: 401).

102

A man has authority over his wife (1936: 98 n. 1); novices in initiation ceremonies, who are 'mercilessly bullied', are known as 'wives' (131). Wife-takers are inferior to wife-givers (1936: 79).

The totemic patrilineal clans are divided into *mbapma* (the literal translation of which is 'line') which contain members of the clan belonging to alternate generations. Thus, FF, Ego, and SS form a *mbapma*, while F and S form another *mbapma* of the same clan. The correspondence of generations in different clans, Bateson says (1932a: 269) can be traced by reference to the system of totemic names and by comparing the terms used by different persons in addressing the shamanic spirit. The Iatmul have a complicated system of personal names. Every individual bears names of totemic ancestors, viz. spirits, birds, stars, animals, pots, adzes, etc. An individual may have hundreds of these names which refer in their etymology to secret myths (1936: 127).

Regarding the *mbapma* system, Bateson adds that this system 'does not control marriage', and so the kinship terms used towards women are independent of *mbapma* (1932a: 269).

III

RELATIONSHIP TERMINOLOGY

The relationship terminology is as in *Table 1*.

The range of application of the terminology is not reported, but Bateson makes it clear that:

'By his genealogy at birth a man is provided with a series of relatives – not only real brothers and sisters, parents, uncles, etc., but also with a complete set of relatives-in-law and potential wives. According to this system of reckoning, a man's possible wives are the women of his father's mother's clan' (1932a: 263).

These women are termed Ego's *iai*. Their clan is referred to by Ego as *iai nampa*, father's mother people (*nampa*, people), or as *towa-naisagut*, a collective term for the members of the wife's clan (1932a: 263; 1936: 311).

Francis Korn

TABLE 1   *Iatmul relationship terminology**

1	*nggwail*	FF, FFZ, SS, SD†
2	*nyamun*	FF, eB, B (w.s.), eZ (w.s.)
3	*iai*	FM, FMBS, FMBD, FMSD; all women of the same clan as these
4	*tagwa*	FM, W (woman)
5	*mbuambo*	MF, MM, MBS, MBD, MBSW, FeB, MBSSS
6	*nyanggai*	FFZ, Z, SD
7	*tawontu*	FMB, WB, FMBS, FMBSW, FMBSS, FMBSSW, WBSS
8	*nyai'*	F, FB
9	*nyame*	M, MZ, MBD, SW (m.s.), MBSD, MBSSD
10	*iau*	FZ
11	*wau*	MB, MMZS, MBSS, SWB
12	*nondu*	FZH, DH, HZH
13	*mbora*	MBW, MBSSW, SWBW
14	*naisagut*	WF, WM, WMB, FMBW, WBW, FMBS, FMBSW, WBC
15	*laua*	ZHF, ZC, Z (widowed)
16	*tshuambo*	yB, HyB, SS (m.s.), yZ (w.s.)
17	*tshaishi*	eBW**
18	*lan*	H
19	*lando*	ZH, ZHB, ZSS, men who might marry Ego's sister
20	*nian*	S, D, BC, FZC (w.s.)
21	*kauggat*	BC (w.s.)
22	*na*	FZC, MMZS, DC
23	*ianan*	FZSS, ZSS, SS (w.s.)
24	*kaishe-ragwa*	ZSW
25	*nasa*	HZC

* From Bateson 1932a: 263-70; 1936: 16, 18, 50, 93, 243, 305-12. The terms displayed in Bateson's diagram (1936: 305) have been augmented by details taken from the text. For this and other reasons the numbering does not always accord that in his diagram.

† There is also a term, *warangka*, whose specification is FFF. The term also means 'patrilineal ancestors'.

** Bateson's diagram (1936: 305) incorrectly has *tshaishi*, Z; *nyamun*, ZH.

The terms for the other related clans — that are 'in constant use' (1932a: 268) – are *wau-nyame nampa*, mother's brother and mother people, *laua nyanggu*,[6] sister's child people, and *lanoa nampa*, husband people. Ego's own clan is referred as *nggwail warangka,* a collective term meaning 'patrilineal ancestors' (*nggwail,* FF; *warangka,* FFF). The clan where Ego's daughter marries is called *kaishe nampa.*

The use of the kinship terms, says Bateson, may be related by the Iatmul not to genealogy but to the system of patrilineal clans (*ngaiva*) (1932a: 268).

IV

RULES OF MARRIAGE

There are three explicit and conflicting rules of marriage:

1. Marriage with *iai* (FMBSD: in general, women of FM clan). This rule is expressed in statements such as 'a woman should climb the same ladder that her father's father's sister climbed' (1936: 88).[7] After marriage, this *iai* is called *tagwa* or *iairagwa* (woman, wife, FFW). Such a rule can be represented in a diagram as in *Figure 1.*

FIGURE 1   *Marriage with* iai (*FMBSD*)

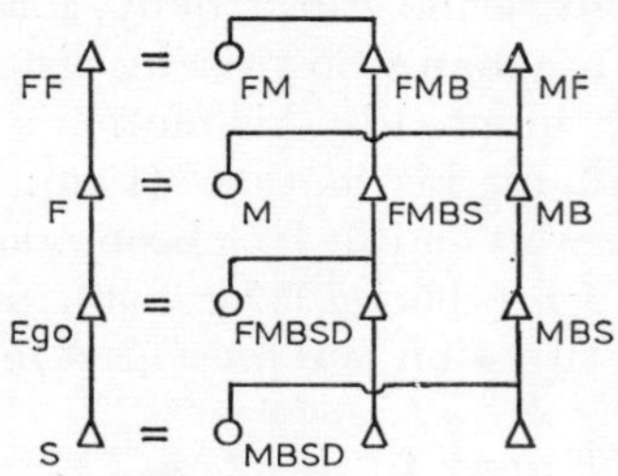

2. Marriage with *na* (FZD). This rule is expressed in sayings such as: 'the daughter goes in payment for the mother' (1936: 89). A rule of this kind is to be represented as a patrilateral asymmetric system as in *Figure 2.*

FIGURE 2   *Marriage with* na (*FZD*)

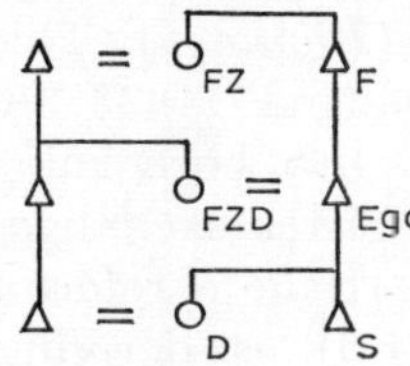

105

Francis Korn

Concerning rules (1) and (2), Bateson remarks that these two rules, although contradictory, are connected in a 'curious way' (1936: 89). He refers to the fact that in a system of FZD marriage the category that contains the specification FZD also contains the specification FMBSD. This situation he displays as in *Figure 3(a)*, which may more clearly be reconstructed as in *Figure 3(b)*.

FIGURE 3   *FMBSD marriage*

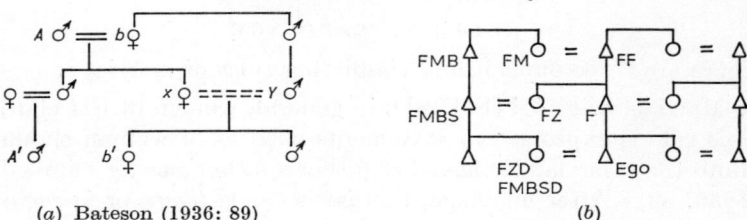

(a) Bateson (1936: 89)   (b)

A curiosity of another kind is that 'in certain cases, when the offspring of the marriage are male instead of female, one of the sons will be sent, while still a baby, for *adoption* into the family and clan of the man who gave his sister to the father for wife, i.e. the boy is adopted by his mother's brother, to whom he goes in payment for his mother' (1936: 89 n. 2). Bateson himself met a man who had in fact been adopted and brought up by his mother's brother (1932a: 266), perhaps under this arrangement. This situation is represented in *Figure 4*.

FIGURE 4   *Adoption of ZS*

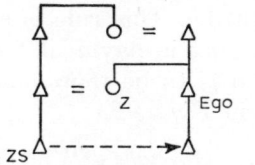

3. Exchange of sisters (*Figure 5*). This rule is expressed as 'women should be exchanged' (1936: 90). Bateson notes that although contradictory with both rule (1) and rule (2), this rule applies not only to sister exchange but to FZD marriage (rule 2). This type of marriage is referred to by Bateson in his first paper (1932a: 264-5) as deriving from the *tambinien*

106

relationship. *Tambinien* are partners from opposite moieties whose children ought to marry with brother-sister exchange.

FIGURE 5   *Sister exchange*

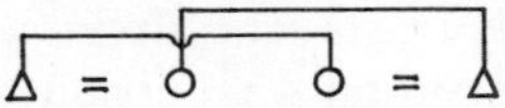

△ = ○⌐○ = △

Concerning these three rules (1, 2, and 3), Bateson says:

'It is quite likely that the marriage with father's sister's daughter has been evolved in the culture through interaction of the two systems, *iai* marriage and sister exchange. The whole kinship vocabulary would point to the *iai* system as the older, and the concept of exchange of women may well have been adopted from neighbouring peoples. In this connexion it is interesting that one of the young men whom I used as an informant had a strong impression that the correct term for father's sister's daughter was *iai*. But after we had discussed the matter in detail, he was uncertain and consulted one of the older men who stated definitely that *na* was the correct term for this relative' (1936: 90 n. 1).

In a note to p. 89 of *Naven*, Bateson refers in fact to a fourth 'cliché', as he calls it:

4. '*Laua*'s son will marry *wau*'s daughter.' Bateson says that this is another way of referring to *iai* marriage, but the *iai* specified as FMBD.[8]

The difference from rule (1), also referring to *iai* marriage, is that while the latter expresses a rule concerning people of the same genealogical level, this new one (FMBD marriage) relates people of two consecutive genealogical levels, as it is shown in *Figure 6*.

FIGURE 6   Wau'*s daughter*/laua'*s son marriage*

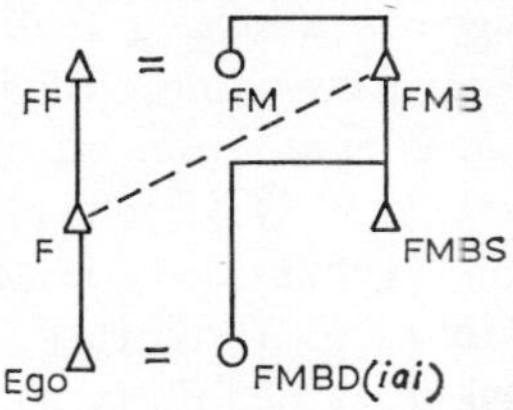

FF △ = ○ FM · · · ┐ FM3
F △ · · · · · △ FMBS
Ego △ = ○ FMBD(*iai*)

Note: - - - = *wau/laua* relationship

There is in addition a kind of 'extension of the affinal system'. This is the relationship between 'certain pairs of clans which regard each other reciprocally as *lanoa nampa* or *laua nyanggu* – both terms are used. . . . This relationship is reciprocal between clans and apparently rests not upon any particular past or present marriage, but upon a tradition that the women of the one clan often marry the men of the other and *vice versa*. . . . This clan relationship is practically without effect outside the ceremonial houses' (1936: 96 n. 2).

V

MARRIAGE PRACTICES

Iatmul men can have several wives. They may come from a number of clans, as many as eight or ten (1932a: 286-7). Among these, Bateson believes that the *iai* wife (*tagwa, iairagwa*) should be treated quite differently from the wives acquired in other ways (1932a: 280). The *iai* wife is not 'bought', whereas others may be (1932a: 280). A man's *iai* may enter his house and become his wife of her own volition, and he cannot refuse. He cannot divorce this wife, either, and there is a definite avoidance of her name. But although there is always among the wives of a man one who is more influential than the others (*nanwan tagwa*)[9] this one is not necessarily the *iai* wife (1932a: 286).

VI

BATESON'S INTERPRETATION

Regarding negative rules, Bateson says that they are 'very vague' (1936: 91). There is a strong feeling against marrying one's own sister, and he never knew of any case of this sort. The next strongest ban is that upon marriage with any of the relatives called *naisagut* (WM, WBD): 'A man must never marry his wife's brother's wife' (1932a: 288), i.e. a woman of the category *naisagut*. 'Such marriages are rare,' he says, 'but when we turn to the less stringent prohibitions, as of marriage with classificatory "sisters", women of own clan with whom genealogical connections can easily be traced, we find that such women are sometimes taken as wives' (1936: 91), though it is said to be wrong (1932a: 288). The Iatmul even rather approve of these endogamous marriages and say that from endogamy are produced long and widely ramifying lines of descendants (1936: 91). Moreover, marriages with classificatory 'mothers' are 'not uncommon' (92); and in fact the solitary marriage of which Bateson provides a genealogical illustration is precisely of a man with his MMZSD (1936: 103) – which may be reduced to MBD – i.e. his *nyame*, 'mother'.

Besides these rules and types of marriage, there are many marriages with outside groups, e.g. with women captured in war, or sent as peace offerings, women met in trading expeditions, etc. These women, however, occupy a segregated status, for they are 'foreigners' whose heads can be taken. One man met by Bateson even wore headhunter's insignia for the killing of his own wife, who had come from another village (1936: 139). It needs 'extraordinary courage' for a woman to go alone to a 'foreign village' (145).

To sum up the marriage system, Bateson says that, in practice, 'marriage occurs very nearly at random' (1936: 92). But this randomness does not seem to be an ideal for the Iatmul, nor do they seem to recognize it as a trait of their own behaviour. When talking about their neighbours they refer to them as 'dogs and pigs who mate at random' (1936: 91).[10]

VII

FORMAL ANALYSIS OF THE TERMINOLOGY

Before trying to assess what kind of 'elementary structure' the different Iatmul preferences fit, let us analyse the formal traits of the Iatmul relationship terminology.

Bateson's diagram of the Iatmul relationship terminology (1936: 305; my *Figure 7*), divides it into consanguineal and affinal terms. His diagram of affinal terms is not complete,[11] and this is probably due to the fact that in the Iatmul relationship terminology the majority of the terms have both consanguineal and affinal specifications, so that it is factitious to separate them into different diagrams.

109

Francis Korn

FIGURE 7 *Bateson's diagram of the Iatmul relationship terminology*
(1936: 280)

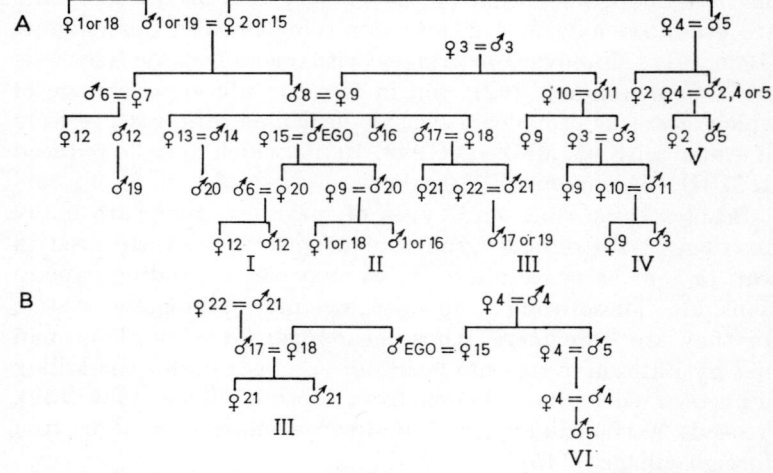

Note: The diagram incorrectly has *tshaishi* (13), Z; *nyamun* (14), ZH

KEY

A, Consanguineous terms (m.s.). B, Affinal terms (m.s.). ♂, male. ♀, female.
=, marriage. |, descent. ⌐——¬ siblingship. Arabic numbers refer to terms
for individuals. Roman numbers refer to terms for patrilineal groups seen
collectively.

1. *nggwail.*	7. *iau.*	13. *tshaishi.*	18. *nyanggai.*
2. *iai.*	8. *nyai'.*	14. *nyamun.*	19. *ianan.*
3. *mbuambo.*	9. *nyame.*	15. *tagwa.*	20. *nian.*
4. *naisagut.*	10. *mbora.*	16. *tshuambo.*	21. *laua.*
5. *tawonto.*	11. *wau.*	17. *lando.*	22. *kaishe-ragwa.*
6. *nondu.*	12. *na.*		

I. *kaishe-nampa.*
II. Own clan.
III. *lanoa-nampa* or *laua nyanggu.*

IV. *wau-nyame.* (Son's *iai nampa.*)
V. *iai-nampa.* (Become *towa-naisagut* if Ego marries one of their
women.)
VI. *towa-naisagut.*(Son's *wau-nyame.*)

Our own diagram of the Iatmul relationship terminology
(*Figure 8*), contains all the terms provided by the ethnography
(cf. *Table 1*), and is arranged according to the following traits:
1. *Linearity.* The equations and distinctions indicating linearity
are:

110

(i) F = FB
(ii) M = MZ
(iii) FB ≠ MB
(iv) FFB ≠ MFB
(v) FFZ ≠ MFZ
(vi) FM ≠ MM
(vii) FZC ≠ MZC
(viii) FBC ≠ MBC
(ix) ZC ≠ BC ≠ WBC

FIGURE 8　*The Iatmul relationship terminology (cf. Table 1)*

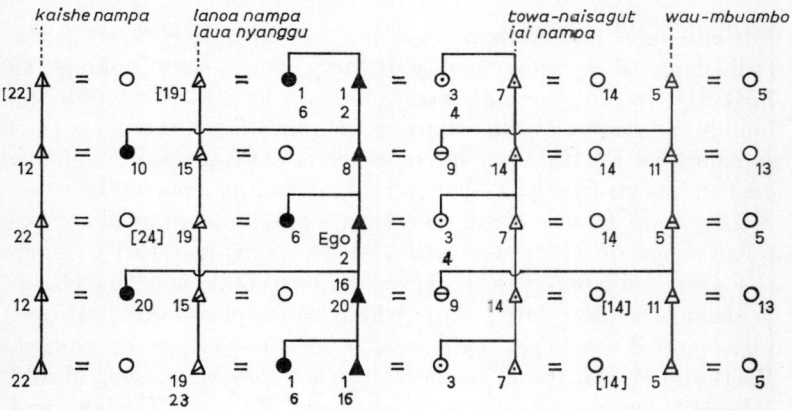

2. *Cycles.* There are two kind of cycles, exhibited in alternate genealogical levels:

(i) direct, connecting adjacent descent lines;
(ii) indirect, connecting alternate descent lines.

3. *Asymmetry.* The distinctions indicating asymmetry are:

(i) FFZ ≠ FMBW
(ii) FZ ≠ MBW
(iii) Z ≠ WBW

4. *Alternation of genealogical levels.* The equations indicating alternation are:

111

  (i) FF = SS; F = S
  (ii) FFZ = Z = SD
  (iii) FFW = W
  (iv) MF = MFSS; MB = MBSS
  (v) FMB = FMBSS; FMBS = FMBSSS
  (vi) ZH = ZSS; ZHF = ZS
  (vii) FZS = DS; FZH = DH
 (viii) MBW = MBSSW = SWBW
  (ix) MM = MBSW

VIII

LINES AND CATEGORIES

For all male and female positions in Ego's line there is the indication of a prescribed category consistently defined as FMBSD (*iai*) for the male positions, and FFZSS (*lando*) for the female positions. Thus, there is a prescribed category (*iai*) specified as FMBSD whenever there is ethnographic evidence on the line to which the category specified as 'spouse' belongs.

There are in the terminology five patrilines headed by the terms *nggwail* (FF), *tawontu* (FMB), *mbuambo* (MF), *lando* (FFZH), and *nondu* (FZH). The patrilines coincide with a classification of those related clans which have special designations, viz. *nggwail warangka*, own clan; *towa-naisagut* or *iai nampa*, FMB and W clan; *wau-nyame nampa* (or *wau-mbuambo*), M and MB clan; *lanoa nampa* or *laua nyanggu*, ZH and ZC clan; and *kaishe nampa*, DH clan.

In Bateson's account, the terms *lanoa nampa*, 'a collective term for the members of the patrilineal group into which the speaker's sister has married', and *laua nyanggu*, 'the patrilineal group which includes the speaker's classificatory *lauas*', are given as if they could refer to different patrilineal groups (1936: 309). From the composition of the relationship terminology it is clear that the categories by which the people of both patrilineal groups are addressed belong to the same patriline. They would belong to the same patrilineal group as well, if only *iai* marriages were contracted, the line being composed of *lando*, FZHF, ZH and DH, and *laua*, ZHF and ZS. But the existence of two designations for this set of categories probably derives from the fact that there are forms of marriage other than *iai*, so that one of the designations (*lanoa nampa*) is purely affinal for the group of relatives-in-law deriving from one of the sisters not married to a person categorized as *lando* (FFZSS).

The same probably applies to *iai nampa* and *towa-naisagut* (FMB and W clans). If a *iai* marriage is contracted by Ego, the categories *tawontu* (FMB, FMBSS, WB, and WBSS) and *naisagut* (WF, FMBS, and WBS) belong, together with *iai* (women of the FMB clan), to the same patrilineal group, just as they belong to the same patriline. But if Ego contracts marriages other than with the *iai*, the *towa-naisagut* (WF, WB) relatives he acquires are in a different patrilineal group from his *iai*.

Kaishe nampa is the patrilineal group into which Ego's daughter is supposed to marry. It coincides with the patriline composed by the terms *nondu* (FZH, DH) and *na* (ZC and DC) if Ego's daughter is actually married into the same patrilineal group where her FFZ was married. But here again there is an ambiguity, due probably to the same inconsistency in actual marriages. The designation for the whole group (*kaishe nampa*) derives from *kaishe-ragwa* (child's spouse's mother) which should be specified then only as FZSW, viz. *na*'s wife and *nondu*'s mother. But Bateson adds to these specifications of *kaishe-ragwa* that 'sister's son's wife may be called *kaishe-ragwa*' (1936: 309). This specification corresponds to the line into which Ego's sister is married, and not to the one where Ego's father's sister marries, and it could mean that both daughter's husband's mother and daughters' daughter's husband's mother are denoted by the same term, or that, again, marriages other than *iai* were contracted. In fact, the type of marriage that would coincide with the specification of *kaishe-ragwa* as ZSW would be the '*laua*'s son-*wau*'s daughter' marriage, already seen as rule (4).

IX

PRESCRIPTION AND ALTERNATION

Apart from *kaishe-ragwa*, there is no other inconsistency in the Iatmul relationship terminology. The terms can be consistently arranged in an asymmetric prescriptive terminology composed of five patrilines and with alternation by genealogical level (cf. *Figure 8*).

The ethnography provides data enough to arrange at least all positions in Ego's line according to this scheme. It does not provide, however, the necessary data for an understanding of the lines to which belong the categories specified as 'wives' of male positions of the other four lines not related affinally with Ego's line. This applies to *tawontu* and *naisagut* wives (FMBW, FMBSW, WBW), all designated as *naisagut*; *mbuambo* and *wau* wives (MM, MBW, MBSW, SWBW), designated as *mbuambo* (*mbuambo*'s wives) and *mbora* (*wau*'s wives); *laua*'s wives (ZHFW, ZSW), designated perhaps as *kaishe-ragwa*; and finally, *na*'s wives (FZSW, DSW), designated as *kaishe-ragwa*.

But still, even with this lack of information about some specifications, the connexions of Ego's line with the other four constitute an asymmetric prescriptive terminology, only one that is incomplete. It would be a case similar to that of an asymmetric prescriptive terminology composed of three lines in which the categories reported by the ethnographer were disposed as in *Figure 9*. The specifications do not (*ex hypothesi*) determine the line to which should be assigned the categories denoting the wives of the male positions of the line coinciding with the wife-givers of Ego's line. But there are specifications enough to determine which are the lines that would coincide with Ego's wife-givers and Ego's wife-takers.

FIGURE 9 *Hypothetical asymmetric ('matrilateral') system*

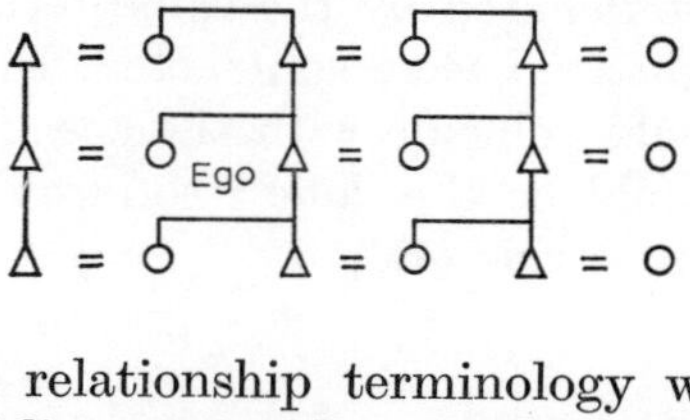

In the Iatmul relationship terminology we find the same determination of lines coinciding with Ego's wife-givers and Ego's wife-takers, and the same indetermination concerning the 'wife-giver' lines of Ego's 'wife-giver' lines, and the 'wife-taker' lines of Ego's 'wife-taker' lines.

The indications of prescription can be seen in the following equations derived from the Iatmul terminology:

(i)   W = FFW = FMBSD = WBSD (*tagwa; iai*)[12]
(ii) M = SW = MBSD (*nyame*)
(iii) ZH = ZSS (*lando*)
(iv) FZH = DH (*nondu*)
(v)   MB = MBSS = SWB (*wau*)
(vi) FZC = DC (*na*)

These equations indicate that each term has both consanguineal and affinal specifications following the principle of asymmetry and in alternating genealogical levels.

There is no specification of the genealogical level to which Ego's *iairagwa* (*iai* wife) belongs because *iai* is actually specified as 'all women of the same patrilineal clan' as FM (1936: 308). But the *iai* of Ego's genealogical level can be identified by the terms employed in addressing her father (*ncisagut*) or brother (*tawontu*). As the terms for the male positions alternate by genealogical level, the level of the woman can be defined by reference to these.

X

ALLIANCES

If actual alliances among the Iatmul were contracted in accordance with their relationship terminology,[13] it could be expected that marriages would occur with *iai* belonging to the same genealogical level or to the second descending genealogical level. This is a trait of other systems with alternation of genealogical levels such as, for instance, the Dieri (cf. Korn 1971). This feature is compatible with the type of terminology because the second descending level reproduces Ego's level, as Ego's level reproduces the second ascending level. But such marriages are not reported in the Iatmul ethnography.

Marriage with the *iai* specified as FMBSD is, as Bateson himself seems to suggest,[14] totally consistent with the relationship terminology. If constantly observed, this kind of marriage would lead, contrary to what Bateson thinks in this respect (1936: 249), to a closed system of alliances, as the diagram of the relationship terminology (*Figure 8*) shows. It would lead to

115

an asymmetric system defined by five patrilineal descent lines. The closed system implicit in the Iatmul terminology can be represented as in *Figure 10*.[15] There are five lines: A, B, C, D, and E, related in such a way that A takes wives from B and C, B from C and D, C from D and E, E from A and B, in alternate genealogical levels.[16] The prescribed category is specified by reference to the second ascending level by means of the specification FMBSD, because it is this level that is reproduced at Ego's level.

FIGURE 10   *Asymmetric prescriptive system with five lines and alternation by genealogical levels*

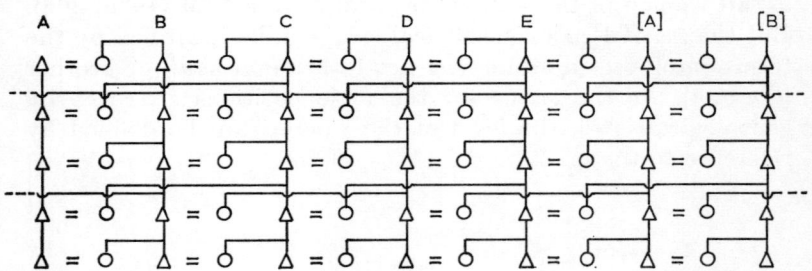

Note: lines A and B are duplicated in order to demonstrate more clearly the closure of the cycles

As in a four-line symmetric prescriptive terminology, Ego is related neither to the line to which the category specified as M belongs, nor to the line to which the category specified as F belongs. The alternation by genealogical levels probably derives, as in the Dieri terminology, from this fact.

The Iatmul relationship terminology can be represented in a diagram such as in *Figure 8*, which can be superposed on the ideal system shown in *Figure 10*. As we have seen, all the indications provided by the ethnography are consistent with such a representation. There are two types of unidirectional cycles of alliance relating the five lines in a consistently asymmetric way in alternate genealogical levels, One type of cycle links adjacent lines; the other links alternate lines. There is one prescribed category (*iai*), which is consistent with the disposition of all the terms in such a diagram.

EMPIRICAL CORRESPONDENCES

The Iatmul relationship terminology corresponds formally to some of the Iatmul actual institutions. The patrilineal clans coincide with the patrilines, and the *mbapma* with the alternation of terms in each patriline. Bateson states, as we have seen above, that the *mbapma* system does not control marriage (1932a: 269), but it is now clear that if marriages were contracted according to the prescribed category (*iai*), the *mbapma* system could be useful in categorizing people on the ground regarding these marriages. The people of one clan belonging to one *mbapma* should marry women from a different clan from the people belonging to the other *mbapma*. On the other hand, even though the terms used for feminine positions do not alternate, the women of alternate generations could easily be discriminated in relation to the *mbapma*, as well as by reference to *naisagut* and *tawontu*.

There is no indication in the terminology of any formal distinction coinciding with the totemic moieties. The difference in their relative importance for the different villages could indicate that they are not a decisive factor in Iatmul social classification regarding marriage. The relationship terminology, on the other hand, seems to be uniformly applied in the different villages.

The alternation of terms in the relationship terminology and the division of clans into *mbapma* are only two of the contexts in which Bateson sees the pattern of alternation applied. There are two other contexts: the alternation of initiatory grades and the alternation of siblings. There is also a further context in which he is 'tempted to see a development of the same type of pattern, namely . . . the structure of the flute music' (1936: 246).

The initiatory system is described by Bateson as constituted by two cross-cutting initiatory moieties (Ax, Ay, Bx, By). 'Each quadrant is divided into three named generation groups: 1, 3, 5, or 2, 4, 6; such that 1 are the fathers of 3, who are fathers of 5; while 2 are fathers of 4, who are fathers of 6' (1936: 245). The principle of alternation is indeed applied in the relationship between generation groups, but the whole

117

system of initiation, as described by Bateson, is difficult to grasp. The initiatory moieties are arranged in such a way that one moiety is always senior to the other (A senior to B, for instance), and that the members of Ax initiate the members of By, while the members of Ay initiate the members of Bx (1936: 245). But from his account, both in the 1932 article and in the 1936 book, it is impossible to gather what is the principle by which people of the A moiety, for instance, are divided into Ax and Ay, or who initiates the people belonging to Ax and Ay.

Regarding siblings, Bateson says that 'in large families in which there is a long series of brothers, the same sort of alternation is expected' (1936: 246). There are in Iatmul vocabulary five terms to designate the first, second, third, fourth, and fifth child. In their quarrels over the patrimony it is expected that the first and the third brothers will join forces against the second and the fourth (1936: 246).

Bateson's idea of explaining the structure of the flute music by the application of the principle of alternation is based on the fact that 'among the Iatmul the flute is always a duet instrument' (1935: 158). The flutes are always played in pairs and in each pair one flute is one tone higher than the other. 'The flute of lower pitch is spoken of as the "elder brother" of the other, though for totemic purposes the pair of flutes is taken as a unit' (1936: 246).

Bateson does not mention the system of personal names when describing the application of the principle of alternation. But it seems that the principle is followed in this sphere too, since 'most of an individual's names are passed to him from his father's father' (1932b: 403). The names are received from the father, who applies the names of his father to his sons, and the names of his father's sister to his daughters, But there is another series of names which are received from the mother's clan. 'Every clan has a certain number of names which it gives to its *laua nyanggu* (sister's children)' (1932b: 410). These names are also in pairs, 'elder brother' and 'younger brother', and are so distributed to the children.

The system of personal names shows the same traits as the relationship terms and gives another clue to an understanding of the alternation of terms by genealogical levels. A patrilineal and a matrilineal principle are involved in both cases. The system of names seems to reinforce the fact that an individual is linked with both his father and his mother clans and thus should marry in a third one. The alternation of terms in the patrilines and the alternation of personal names in one's own clan seem to indicate which is this third clan.

XII

PRESTATIONS

The system of prestations, on the other hand, supports the idea that the Iatmul system is not only ideally asymmetric but that it was so in practice also.

Needham writes that in prescriptive alliance systems there are some traits which although 'not diagnostic of this type of social organization, . . . taken in connexion with the defining character of the terminology of social classification . . . make up a complex of institutions that is significantly coherent'. In an asymmetric system these traits are: (1) arranged marriages, (2) corporate involvement of descent groups in marriage payments, (3) widow inheritance, (4) sororal polygyny, (5) absence of divorce (cf. Needham 1964: 232), and (6) 'masculine' and 'feminine' goods which are exchanged between descent groups at the contraction of marriage (Needham 1970: 257).

Among the Iatmul, not only are marriages arranged (cf. 1932a: 280) but the system of alliances also involves, as a consequence of the existence of two ideal cycles which relate five groups, groups other than the wife's and husband's clans. The most prominent context in which one finds this system of prestations, expressed in the exchange of two kinds of goods, is marriage, which necessitates prestations between a man and his wife's clan (exchange between *lando*, ZH, and *tawontu*, WB).

Wife-givers present *food* (coconut, fowl, pig) as well as women; wife-takers present *valuables* (shell ornaments, labour, support in war, etc.). This division of symbolic goods resembles the common South-east Asian classification into 'masculine' and 'feminine' prestations, the former being given to superiors and the latter to inferiors (cf. Needham 1960a: 93-5). The resemblance is strengthened by the fact that among the Iatmul the wife-givers, who receive the 'masculine' valuables, etc., are superior to their wife-takers who make the prestation. At the conclusion of a *naven* the shells are tied to a spear and are thus presented to the *wau* (1936: 14). In general, 'most' shells and ornaments are 'attached to weapons' (1932a: 279) when they are handed over – a fact which tends again to confirm (by comparative reference) their 'masculine' significance.

There are several instances in Bateson's account in which this kind of exchange is described. During the 'arrangement' of his marriage, a man 'made a big ceremonial present of shells and other valuables to the girl's parents'. The girl was 'very heavily ornamented from head to foot with valuables, while her companions carried large numbers of decorated useful objects – pots, fish traps, etc. – these being a reciprocal present to that which the husband had made to the girl's parents' (1932a: 281). The exchange of goods in the arrangement of a marriage is called *waingga*, which seems to mean literally 'purchase'.

> 'The wife's relatives have always the right to call on the husband for help in any task, like house building, for which a crowd of manual labourers is necessary. When the task is completed the wife's people will stand a small feast for the labourers or they will at least distribute coconuts to them' (1936: 79).

Another context in which this kind of exchange occurs is in the relationship between the *laua* (ZC) group and the *wau* (MB) group. 'A man will take steps to mark out his relationship to the *laua* group whose allegiance he specially desires' (1936: 95). The *wau* will give not only a name to the *laua*, but also a gift of a coconut (1936: 95), i.e. he will give his ZS a present of the kind that wife-givers give to wife-takers. The *wau-nyame nampa*, MB and M people, gives pig to the *lanoa nampa*, H people, or *laua nyanggu*, ZC people (1936: 19). The *laua* presents valuables to his *wau* (1936: 13). If a man imparts his clan secrets and spells to his sister's son, 'the esoterica *must be ceremonially paid for* with shell valuables' (1936: 37; cf. 60). There are also presentations of valuables to the shamanic spirits which are accompanied by the killing of a pig (1932b: 420). Bateson believes that this pig is eaten, as is usual among the Iatmul, by the *laua* of the clan to which the valuables were offered (cf. 1932b: 420 n. 57).

After the celebration of *naven*, a general presentation of food and valuables follows. On one of these occasions, 'eight pigs were killed and presented. Of these one was given by her *wau* to the little girl who had caught the fish. . . . Of the remaining pigs, three were given by *waus* to classificatory *lauas*', another one to the donor's sister's husband (also a *laua*, cf. *Table 1*), another was given by a woman to her husband's sister's child (i.e. *mbora* to *nasa*). In the case of the little girl, her father presented valuables to her *wau* (1936: 19).

In all of these *naven* presentations, the food is presented by the wife-giver clan (MB, WBW) to the wife-taker clan (ZS, ZD, HZC). This pattern of exchange between *wau* and *laua* is significantly reversed in a myth. In this narrative, *naven* is celebrated by a man's wife's brother and wife's father on the occasion of the birth of both his first and second children. These relatives present *valuables* to the husband, and he in return presents *food* to them. In reality, *naven* is not celebrated for the birth of the first child of a man, so that in the myth there is a complete reversal of the occasion for *naven* and of the kinds of goods normally presented by wife-givers to wife-takers and vice versa (1936: 48-9).

There are also presentations of valuables when offences are committed. In the case of homicide, the killer presents valuables to the victim's relatives (1936: 99), and 'homicidal ornaments are usually presented by his *lanoa nampa* (husband people) to the killer' as a symbol of 'the triumph of the maternal clan' (1936: 217). But in the case of a trespass there is also a presentation of food. The offender has to kill a fowl and present coconuts to the owners. The coconuts and the fowl will be eaten by the *laua* of the clan which owns the land. The offender has to present a basket of valuables and a *tambointsha* to the spirits of the ancestors (*angk-au*) of the offended clan. *Tambointsha* are tassels of feathers tied to string: 'they are symbols of successful homicide and worn on the lime stick as a tally of the owner's successful kills' (1936: 46 n. 1). The *angk-au* will take the 'soul' of the valuables and of the *tambointsha*, and after a few days the valuables will be returned to the trespasser (1936: 46).

Food seems to be the means by which a man is symbolically attached to his wife's clan and to his mother's clan. The counter-offering of valuables is apparently the way of counter-acting the

121

possible bad effects of such an attachment. If a man is affected by *nggambli* ('dangerous and infectious guilt'), this 'infection' will be passed on to his *lando*, ZH, only if the latter gives food to the former, but not if he presents valuables to him (1936: 54-8). So that there is an emphasis upon the one direction of the offerings of food (cf. 1936: 58 n. 1).

But there are some instances in which both food and valuables are presented at the same time to the same group. Apart from the case of trespass and the presentation to the shamanic spirits, already seen, Bateson refers to another situation in which this double offering of food and valuables occurs. Certain members of a clan had been killed. As a result of this, 'the names of those who were dead were "loose" ', and the remaining members of the clan were endangered. There was then a ceremony in which a pig was ritually killed and offered to the members of the clan, 'each of whom set his foot on it in turn', and they were offered *Turbo* shells and ornaments as well (1932b: 426).[17]

There is another instance in Bateson's account in which valuables were passed in the opposite direction, i.e. from wife-givers to wife-takers. He refers to a case in which a man, after his father's death, bought his name and his father's sister's name, offering a *Turbo* shell to the latter. Bateson says that 'this piece of ceremonial is the only context' that he knows in which 'valuables are ceremonially given to members of own clan' (1936: 50 n. 1). In fact, the valuables seem to have been passed in an unusual direction,[18] but the woman who received them (FZ) was probably not a member of 'own clan' but of one of the wife-taker clans.

In general, however, the 'masculine' goods are presented by the wife-takers, and the 'feminine' goods by the wife-givers. For instance, Bateson bought a pair of flutes which were presented to their owners by their 'sister's children' and were ornamented 'with shell work' (1935: 161). The prestations correlate with the fact that wife-givers are 'superior' to wife-takers and that the whole system tends to the arrangement of alliances between groups. 'A man should support his wife's people in all their quarrels, even against his own clan', says Bateson (1936: 80), and he adds that 'if all affinal linkages were observed no one would be able to quarrel with anyone else inside the community, and everybody would have to go everywhere and do everything with everybody else, since the genealogical links are actually ubiquitous' (1936: 93).

The absence of divorce, a trait that is present in other asymmetric systems of prescriptive alliance, such as the Kachin (Leach 1961: 15), is also found among the Iatmul. The *iai* wife has not only 'special rights', but cannot be divorced either (1932a: 280).

XIII

PREFERENCES

If we revert to the question of 'preferences' among the Iatmul, we can understand why it was so difficult for Bateson to grasp what sort of a system the Iatmul had.

Rule (1), covering marriage with *iai* (FMBSD), is perfectly consistent with the ideal system derived from the Iatmul relationship terminology. As we have already seen, if marriages of this kind were regularly contracted, there would be no inconsistency between the actual system and the 'ideal system' implicit in the terminology. The five related clans would coincide with the five lines in the terminology: *lanoa nampa* (ZH clan) would be the same group as *laua nyanggu* ('Ego's classificatory *laua*s' clan), and *iai nampa* (FM clan) the same as *towa-naisagut* (wife's clan). The system would then be a closed one, as shown in *Figure 10*.

If we consider rule (2), i.e. marriage with *na* (FZD), instead, the connexion between the alliances it implies and the relationship terminology is quite different. If a marriage of this sort is contracted, one of the consequences is that the *towa-naisagut* clan (wife's clan) coincides with *kaishe nampa* clan (daughter's husband clan). If subsequent marriages follow this one in the 'curious way' in which Bateson says this form of marriage is connected with the *iai* marriage (cf. *Figure 3*), in the second descending genealogical level with respect to this first marriage, not only would these two clans coincide, but also *iai nampa* (FMBSD clan) would be confused with them. On the other hand, in this second descending genealogical level, Ego's mother clan (*wau-mbuambo*), would be also superposed on his sister's husband clan, e.g. *lanoa nampa*. This superposition, and the superposition of relationship terms it implies, would be totally

123

inconsistent with the number and the specifications of the terms. On the other hand, a series of marriages following this rule leads to a patrilateral system with a constant reversal in the direction of the cycles of alliances that is not very likely to be maintained (cf. *Figure 2*; cf. Needham 1958; 1961).

If the third rule (exchange of sisters) is followed, the superposition of related clans that it implies is *towa-naisagut* (wife's clan) and *lanoa nampa* (ZH clan), as can be derived from *Figure 5*. If this type of marriage were consistently followed in subsequent genealogical levels and in accordance with *iai* marriage, the resulting system would imply a superposition of the following clans: *towa-naisagut* (W clan), *lanoa nampa* (ZH clan), *iai nampa* (FFW clan), *kaishe nampa* (FZH clan), and *wau mbuambo* (MB clan). In a system of this type, the Iatmul designations for related clans seem redundant, and so for that matter does the Iatmul relationship terminology.

If the fourth rule ('*laua*'s son will marry *wau*'s daughter') were followed, it could not be regularly repeated, and would never lead to the constitution of a system.

The rule relates two lines and two consecutive genealogical levels, but if it were repeated the gap between the levels would increase by one for each second descending level (cf. *Figure 11*). Thus Ego's son, in marrying his FMBD, would marry a woman belonging to Ego's level, and so on.

FIGURE 11   *Consequence of repeated FMBD marriage*

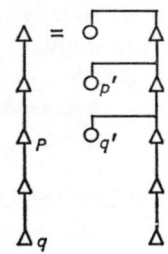

Note: p marries p'; q marries q'

The repetition of this type of marriage would also have the consequence that a single wife-giving line would supply women to Ego's line in consecutive genealogical levels, which is inconsistent with the alternation otherwise characteristic of the

Iatmul system. The same applies to the system derived from rule (3).

XIV

IDEAL AND VARIANTS

The Iatmul relationship terminology can be considered prescriptive and constituted by five lines with alternation of terms by genealogical levels (cf. *Figure 8*).

The first rule expressed by the Iatmul (marriage with *iai*, FMBSD) corresponds to this ideal system.

The second rule expressed (marriage with *na*, FZD) indicates a patrilateral asymmetric system constituted by three lines.

The third rule (exchange of sisters) implies a symmetric system with two lines.

The fourth rule (*'laua*'s son marries *wau*'s daughter') does not correspond to any system at all.

There are no records of actual marriages in the ethnography provided by Bateson. What he says, in fact, is that the Iatmul express certain rules of marriage and marry according to these rules or in any other way.

XV

PREFERENCE AND STRUCTURE IN LÉVI-STRAUSS

In Lévi-Strauss's work there is no operational definition of 'preference'.

Regarding actual marriages he claims that although 'the question of how far and in what proportion the members of a given society respect the norm is very interesting', this fact has nothing to do with the placing of this society in a typology (1967: xxi). So that, for the analysis of the 'elementary structure' under which the Iatmul system could be classified, the lack of records of actual marriages does not matter.

The four rules of the Iatmul, on the other hand, can be properly considered as the 'desirable relationships' that Lévi-Strauss talks about (1967: xxii), and should thus provide for the classification of the 'structure'. The 'desirable relationship',

125

he says, 'is a function of the social structure' and 'the spouse is the spouse solely because she belongs to an alliance category or stands in a certain kinship relationship to Ego' (1967: xxi-xxii). But which of the 'alliance categories' or 'kinship relationships' as expressed by the Iatmul (namely, *iai*, FMBSD; *na*, FZD; ZHZ; and *wau*'s daughter, FMBD) is a function of their social structure?

If, as Lévi-Strauss avers, there is no difference between 'prescription'and 'preference', then the four 'desirable relationships' should determine the classification of the structure.[19]

'A preferential system is prescriptive when envisaged at the model level', says Lévi-Strauss (1967: xxi). Consequently the Iatmul must, from this point of view, have three different systems at this level: (1) an asymmetric model with five lines and alternation by genealogical levels; (2) a patrilateral asymmetric model; and (3) a symmetric model. There is in addition a preference (4) that does not fit any systematic model.

If these different models, which may be derived from the various 'desirable relationships', are indeed a function of the Iatmul social structure, one is led to think either that the Iatmul possess four different social structures or that they possess an exceedingly complicated one which has apparently no analogues in the literature.

XVI

IATMUL SOCIETY AND ELEMENTARY STRUCTURES

So far, we have been applying the 'solutions' proposed by Lévi-Strauss in the preface to the second edition of *Les Structures élémentaires de la parenté* (1967). If instead we consider the preface to the first edition (1949), the 'solution' seems to be quite different. According to his statements in this place, Lévi-Strauss would probably consider the Iatmul case as one of those 'hybrid and ambiguous forms . . . where there are several preferential solutions' (1949: x). In this case, it might not be considered an 'elementary structure'. But in this same preface an 'elementary structure' is defined as one class of systems which, 'while defining all members of the society as relatives, divide them into two categories, viz., possible spouses and prohibited spouses' (1949: ix). Since among the Iatmul 'by his genealogy at birth a man is provided with a series of relatives . . . with a complete set of relatives-in-law and potential wives' (Bateson 1932a: 263), it is difficult to see why, if this aspect of Iatmul society fits so perfectly with the very definition of an 'elementary structure', it should not in the end be considered as such.

XVII

CLASSIFICATION

The difficulties in classifying the Iatmul system according to Lévi-Strauss's definitions do not arise from an inherent ambiguity in Iatmul society, but from the inconsistency between definitions and classificatory criteria in Lévi-Strauss's writings.[20]

Whereas he gives a formal, viz. terminological, criterion for the definition of an 'elementary structure', when he actually classifies a system he gives far more weight to explicit rules or preferences. The formal terminological criterion, moreover, seems to be completely forgotten by Lévi-Strauss when in 1967 he reconsiders the definition of an 'elementary structure'.

Following Kroeber and Hocart, Dumont and Needham, one can consider that the relationship terminology is a form of social classification implying an ideal mode of social organization. In the case of the Iatmul the form of classification and the principles involved are clear enough. Why these principles are not systematically followed in the actual behaviour is another matter. The fact that the Iatmul express certain marriage preferences which conflict with their form of classification does not disable the analyst in classifying the ideal system.

Of course, it would be better to be able to know why this ideal system is not applied in practice. But the ethnography does not provide enough data for such an explanation. The number and the size of the villages that Bateson includes under the label 'Iatmul society' could be one of the causes of the inconsistency. The asynchronous decay of Iatmul institutions (totemic moieties, ceremonial houses, division of clans, etc.) and the exchange of women between different villages has probably made it difficult to maintain the system. But the traces of prescriptive values among the Iatmul can still be

Francis Korn

found in Bateson's description. The special rights of the *iai* wife, as described above, seem to be one of them, and also the fact that the betrothal to *iai* takes place at a very early age Bateson 1932a: 263 n. 8). The system of prestations, and the absence of divorce as far as the *iai* wife is concerned, are some more indications. Finally, the fact that they explain their use of the relationship terms by reference to the *ngaiva*, patrilineal clan (1932a: 268), and that they do talk of 'wrong' marriage (1932a: 280) and 'wrong totemic group' (1932a: 285), suggests a prior state in which the actual institutions may have corresponded more closely with the terminology.

XVIII

METHOD

In the preface to the 1949 edition of *Les Structures élémentaires de la parenté*, Lévi-Strauss states that 'for the elucidation of any special problem that the reader has in mind, the definitions and distinctions used here should be applied, and the same method followed' (p. xi).

In the Dieri case, following his own method, Lévi-Strauss arrived at the conclusion that the Dieri were a case of 'transition' from 'generalized exchange' to 'restricted exchange', that their system was quite 'anomalous', that they exhibited the 'structure' of a moiety system and the rule of marriage of an 'Aranda' system, and that their relationship terminology was properly represented in a diagram composed of four patrilines (1949: 256-62). In an independent analysis of the system, however, we have found instead that they possessed a four-matriline symmetric prescriptive terminology, a set of matrilineal clans, and a rule of marriage totally consistent with these features (Korn 1971).

A similar discrepancy between the 'findings' of Lévi-Strauss and of other analysts working on the same societies can be found in, for instance, Needham's analysis of the Wikmunkan (cf. Lévi-Strauss 1949: 262-70; Needham 1962b),[21] in Needham's analysis of the Aimol (cf. Lévi-Strauss, 1949: 330-2; Needham 1960b), and in Leach's observations on the Chin/Kachin case (Lévi-Strauss 1949: 289-327; Leach 1969).

128

A Question of Preferences

In the case of the Iatmul system, we could not precisely follow Lévi-Strauss's particular method, because he did not analyse such a society; but we have seen what the conclusions would be if one tried to apply the 'definitions' and 'distinctions' that he alludes to. Our analysis has demonstrated that the Iatmul possess an asymmetric prescriptive terminology with five lines and alternation by genealogical levels. Following Lévi-Strauss's definitions we should probably have arrived at the conclusion either that they represented a 'hybrid' case or that they had four different social structures.

But if our intention were to correct or discuss some points in Lévi-Strauss's work on elementary structures, it would in his view be an impossible task, since, as he says: 'even if some aspect of the problem treated in [this work] were developed no new idea would need to be introduced' (Lévi-Strauss 1949: xi).

NOTES

1. Page references to Lévi-Strauss's monograph are to the original French edition of 1949, or to the second French edition of 1967 when referring to the preface to this edition. The passages cited may readily be located in the English edition (1969) by means of the page-concordance (Korn & Needham 1969).

2. This analysis is intended to form the basis of a chapter in a forthcoming monograph on the scientific status of Lévi-Strauss's theory of kinship.

I am obliged to Mr Bateson for a note of confirmation (July 1969) about the published sources on the Iatmul. At his suggestion, a request for literary and ethnographical guidance was sent to Dr Rhoda Métraux, who had recently returned from field research in the Iatmul village of Tambunum, but by the time of writing it had not been favoured with a reply.

I should like to thank Dr Rodney Needham for giving me the idea of analysing the Iatmul system in the first place, for helping me during the preparation of this paper with suggestions for formal and substantive changes, and for invaluable additions.

3. Hereafter, references to Bateson's ethnographic accounts of the Iatmul will be made by year and page only.

4. Bateson's book (1936) was reviewed by Nadel (1937), Elkin (1938), and Powdermaker (1940).

Murdock has analysed the Iatmul system in *Social Structure* (1949). He characterizes the system as patrilineal and patrilocal. He correctly records 'patri-moieties', but is mistaken in stating that these are exogamous, for Bateson expressly says that 'none of these groups [viz. moieties, phratries, clans] are strictly exogamous' (1936: 4). Murdock further states of the Iatmul that clans are 'unreported', whereas Bateson repeatedly refers to patrilineal clans (1932a: 257; 1936: 52, 310). The relationship terminology, finally, is typed as 'Omaha', i.e. as characterized by the features FZD = ZD and/or MBD = MZ (Murdock 1949: 224), whereas in fact, as will be set out below, although the

Iatmul terminology includes MBD = MZ, it definitely distinguishes FZD ≠ ZD.

5. *Iambon* is an adjective referring to the 'Upper River' and is applied equally to those who speak variants of the same language and to foreigners higher up the river (Bateson 1932a: 249 n. 2).

6. *Nampa* (people) and *nyanggu* (children) are used as synonyms (Bateson 1936: 310).

7. Bateson refers to this rule as being expressed as such in Kankanumun (1936: 89 n. 1).

8. This rule was collected in Mindimbit and Palimbai (1936: 89 n. 1).

9. The word *namwan* is not translated.

10. Bateson does not quote the Iatmul phrase or provide any gloss on the Iatmul equivalent of this statistical concept.

11. There are no affinal terms given for Ego's children or grandchildren positions.

12. *iai* = 'all women of the same patrilineal clan' such as FM, FMBSD, etc.; sister of MBSS, *tawontu* (1936: 308).

13. Bateson had 'no statistics' and made no 'random samples' of Iatmul behaviour (1936: 87 n. 1).

14. 'The whole kinship vocabulary would point to the *iai* system as the older, and the concept of exchange of women may well have been adopted from neighbouring peoples' (1936: 90 n. 1).

15. For a good representation of the system in *Figure 10*, Layard's technique of circular diagrams should be adopted. Oddly enough, it was Bateson who suggested to Layard this technique 'by which a sheet of paper is rolled so as to form a cylinder round something hard, such as a jam jar, so as to provide a surface for writing' (Layard 1942: 113). As Bateson thought that his own case (Iatmul) was different from the Australian systems because it was not *closed* (1936: 248-9), he did not try to represent it with his 'cylindrical' technique that seems so appropriate for the Iatmul.

16. The difference between this kind of system and an asymmetric system with five lines but without alternation, e.g. that of the Kachin (cf. Leach 1954), is that in the former system the five lines are formally necessary for the determination of Ego's 'wife-taker' and 'wife-giver' lines, whereas in the latter they are not.

17. Bateson does not say whether the pig was eaten or by whom it might be eaten.

18. Perhaps this is an instance of the symbolic reversal which often marks practices concerning death. See Needham (1967: 430-1).

19. For discussion of the definition of the terms 'prescription' and 'preference', see Needham (1962a), Lévi-Strauss (1967, preface), and Editor's Note to Lévi-Strauss (1969).

20. Further on Lévi-Strauss's method and definitions, see Korn (1969a), Korn (1969c), Korn & Needham (1970).

21. In the second edition of *Les Structures élémentaires de la parenté* (1967) Lévi-Strauss ignores Needham's analysis, which is quite discrepant with his

A Question of Preferences

own, of the Wikmunkan system; yet he responds to Needham's critical observations on his analysis of the Aimol system by leaving this out altogether.

REFERENCES

BATESON, G. 1932a. Social Structure of the Iatmul People of the Sepik River. *Oceania* **2** (3): 246-89.

—— 1932b. Social Structure of the Iatmul People of the Sepik River. *Oceania* **2** (4): 401-51.

B[ATESON], G. 1935. Music in New Guinea. *The Eagle*: A magazine supported by the members of St. John's College [Cambridge], (C.U.P.), **48**: 158-70.

BATESON, G. 1936. *Naven*. Cambridge: Cambridge University Press.

ELKIN, A. P. 1938. Review of Bateson 1936. *Oceania* **8** (3): 373-5.

KORN, F. 1969a. The Use of the Term 'Model' in Some of Lévi-Strauss's Works. *Bijdragen tot de Taal-, Land- en Volkenkunde* **125** (1): 1-11.

—— 1969b. The Logic of Some Concepts in Lévi-Strauss. *American Anthropologist* **71** (1): 70-1.

—— [1969c.]. Review of Boudon, R.: 'A quoi sert la notion de "Structure"?' *Critica* [México] **7**, in press.

—— 1971. Terminology and 'Structure': The Dieri Case. *Bijdragen tot de Taal-, Land- en Volkenkunde* **127**: 39-81.

KORN, F. & NEEDHAM, R. 1969. *Lévi-Strauss on The Elementary Structures of Kinship: A Concordance to Pagination*. London: Royal Anthropological Institute.

—— 1970. Permutation Models and Prescriptive Systems: The Tarau Case. *Man*, n.s., **5**: 393-420.

LAYARD, J. 1942. *Stone Men of Malekula*. London: Chatto & Windus.

LEACH, E. 1954. *Political Systems of Highland Burma*. London: Bell.

—— 1961. *Rethinking Anthropology*. London School of Economics Monographs on Social Anthropology, no. 22. London: Athlone Press.

—— 1969. 'Kachin' and 'Haka Chin': A Rejoinder to Lévi-Strauss. *Man* **4** (2): 277-85.

LÉVI-STRAUSS, C. 1949. *Les Structures élémentaires de la parenté*. Paris: Presses Universitaires de France (2nd edition, 1967, Paris: Mouton).

—— 1969. *The Elementary Structures of Kinship*. Translated from the French by J. H. Bell, J. R. von Sturmer, and R. Needham, edited by R. Needham. London: Eyre and Spottiswoode.

MURDOCK, G. P. 1949. *Social Structure*. New York: The Macmillan Company.

NADEL, S. F. 1937. Review of Bateson 1936. *Man* **38**: 44-6.

NEEDHAM, R. 1958. The Formal Analysis of Prescriptive Patrilateral Cross-Cousin Marriage. *Southwestern Journal of Anthropology* **14** (2): 199-219.

—— 1960a. Patrilateral Prescriptive Alliance and the Ungarinyin. *Southwestern Journal of Anthropology* **16**: 274-91.

—— 1960b. A Structural Analysis of Aimol Society. *Bijdragen tot de Taal-, Land- en Volkenkunde* **116** (1): 81-108.

—— 1961. Notes on the Analysis of Asymmetric Alliance. *Bijdragen tot de Taal-, Land- en Volkenkunde* **117** (1): 93-117.

—— 1962a. *Structure and Sentiment*. Chicago: The University of Chicago Press.

—— 1962b. Genealogy and Category in Wikmunkan Society. *Ethnology* **1** (2): 223-63.

—— 1964. A Synoptic Examination of Anāl Society. *Ethnos* **29**: 219-36.

—— 1967. Right and Left in Nyoro Symbolic Classification. *Africa* **37**: 425-51.

—— 1970. Endeh, II: Test and Confirmation. *Bijdragen tot de Taal-, Land- en Volkenkunde* **126**: 246-58.

POWDERMAKER, H. 1940. Review of Bateson 1936. *American Anthropologist* **42**: 162-4.

6

Anthony Forge

Marriage and Exchange in the Sepik

Comments on Francis Korn's Analysis of Iatmul Society

I

INTRODUCTION

I must first apologize for the nature of these rather disconnected comments. They were originally made immediately after Mrs Korn's paper, which I had been able to read the day before, and the deadline for the invitation to write them out for inclusion in this book allows me no time for extra analysis or much in the way of documentation. What follows is best taken then as a few ideas about the quite frequently reported statements about preferential marriage in New Guinea, and their relationship to some of the themes that seem common to most or all of New Guinea social and economic organization. At a more specific level I shall also be concerned with the Iatmul material and with comparing it with the Abelam evidence, a society with which I have much more familiarity.[1] The Iatmul and the Abelam are closely related members of the *Ndu* language group, and although their ecologies and the outward appearance of their culture are very different the social and symbolic structures are very similar (Forge 1966) and many of the kinship terms are identical.

I shall try to make two points: first that in New Guinea the exchanges established by marriage are considered to be inherently unequal, particularly as regards valuables and wealth items; and that this inequality has to be reconciled with the balanced exchange of the same or similar things between men of equal status which is the basis of most political systems and the emergence of leaders in New Guinea. One of the ways in which this can be done are the exchanges of women between groups, either by sister-exchange or, in the next generation, by patrilateral cross-cousin marriage. Second, that considering kinship

133

and marriage systems in isolation from fundamental ideas about the nature of men and women may be misleading, and more specifically that the Iatmul *iai* marriage preference, although it undoubtedly produced some marriages, is perhaps, looked at in the broader context, not so much a mechanism for producing a repetitive system, and thus ordering the relationship between groups, as one possible solution to the problems posed by the ambiguities in the concepts of men and women, and the reconciling of equal with unequal exchange, to which the Eastern Abelam material presents another, and in our terms different, solution.

Mrs Korn extracts from Bateson's material four different statements of preferred marriage and shows convincingly in a very elegant analysis that of these only the *iai* (FMBSD) marriage is compatible with the system of terminology. These four preferences can be conveniently grouped into two pairs:

Asymmetric

1	*Iai* marriage	FMBSD
4	'*Laua*'s son will marry *wau*'s daughter'	FMBD

Symmetric

2	*Na* marriage: 'The daughter goes in payment for the mother'	FZD
3	Sister-exchange	Z-exchange

Both (2) and (3) are compatible with the rule 'women should be exchanged'. Bateson himself describes preference (4) as another way of referring to *Iai* marriage and FMBD is called *iai*; the difference in generational level would indeed cause difficulties if a system were generated from such a preference. I have little to offer here except to repeat the point that struck Bateson when he first reported *iai* marriage: 'a man may marry a woman of any generation provided she be of the same clan as his father's mother' (Bateson 1932: 265), which would seem to suggest that the relationship between a man and all the women of a clan is what is important to the Iatmul concept of *iai*. Although Bateson collected this rule in Central and Eastern Iatmul villages whose kinship terminology Mrs Korn reproduces, in some Western (Nyaure) Iatmul villages I have visited the mother's brother and all males of succeeding generations of his

clan are called *wau*; in such a kinship terminology preferences
(1) and (4) are identical. A similar terminology is to be found
among the Sawos and among all the Abelam except the most
northerly villages.[2]

II

SYMMETRICAL EXCHANGE

It is a commonplace of anthropology that Melanesian societies,
and especially those of New Guinea, regardless of their form of
descent or principles of local organization, use ceremonial or
delayed exchange as a basic mechanism in political and economic organization. Symmetrical exchange of the same things in
this area takes place between equals in status, and is at the
same time the prime means of achieving prestige, each presentation being a challenge to demonstrate equality. These notions of
symmetry and equality are often taken to what seem to outsiders as extravagant lengths. Bateson documents among the
Iatmul the replication of misfortunes by a certain class of
exchange partner, for example falling down the steps of a
house (Bateson 1932: 271). Similar dedication to the principle
of equality and balance is to be found among the Abelam.
However, also throughout the area relationships set up by
marriage are, at least initially, characterized by asymmetric
exchange. Not only is the transfer of valuables, in the form of
brideprice, against the bride, an exchange of dissimilar things,
but throughout most of the area valuables continue to pass from
the wife-receivers to the wife-givers, usually in return for
food and ceremonial services, at least into the next generation,
that is between mother's brother and sister's son. These marital
exchanges are recognized as inherently unbalanced. From
the very nature of the items exchanged there is no possibility
of the exact accounting usually associated with symmetrical
exchange. Further, in that the supply of valuables is always
limited, while the supply of food can be increased by hard work
and ceremonial services (although some may involve getting
beaten or indulging in grotesque impersonations, for example
the mother's brother at initiation and *naven* ceremonies among
the Iatmul),[3] are easily performed, the wife-givers are usually

regarded as being in an advantageous position. The same principles apply even to Trobriand *urigubu*, in which wife-givers provide food in return for valuables, although in this case chiefly wife-receivers were undoubtedly the net gainers. Similar high prestige for the wife-receivers has recently been reported from the highlands of New Guinea. The Stratherns' recent study of Melpa marriage (Strathern, A. and M., 1969) ends by saying: 'To the Mbowamb, however, superiority is gained not by giving but by taking more wives from the other group. It is the group which has been "strong" and provided more bridewealth payments than the other which gains prestige.' Meggitt, in his introduction to the collection (Glasse and Meggitt 1969), adds: 'this attitude . . . may prove to be fairly common in the highlands'. In both these examples the imbalance of the relationship set up by marriage is explicitly recognized, and, although prestige may be gained by a great display of valuables, the valuables themselves are indubitably in the hands of the wife-givers.

Not only is marriage in New Guinea a means of forming relationships, and as such part of the political process, but also the exchanges associated with it are a major means of redistributing wealth within and between groups. Valuables themselves are usually vital to the maintenance of those relationships of balanced exchange that play the dominant role in prestige ranking and the political system. The two types of exchange are connected and every man is involved in both. The ideology of equality is very basic, especially in the non-Melanesian-speaking groups which compose the vast majority of the population of mainland New Guinea, and the imbalance inherent in the relationships set up by marriage presents something of a problem. It is no accident that in the Trobriands, the only society of the area with any considerable ascription of status for which we have adequate documentation, the basis of chiefly power is (1) an exaggerated version of the normal marital exchanges and (2) differential access to the balanced exchange between equals, the overseas *kula*.

The most obvious solution to the problem is of course sister-exchange, and the custom has been widely reported throughout the island. Of the ten Highlands societies discussed in Glasse and Meggitt (1969)[4] four practise sister-exchange: Manga,

Maring, Daribi, and Telefolmin; while two more, Chimbu and
Melpa, together with the Kuma and Siane not included in the
book, place an explicit emphasis on achieving balance in the
movement of women between groups. In the Sepik, the Iatmul
and the Northern Abelam among others have sister-exchange.
Another solution is the less frequently reported patrilateral
cross-cousin marriage (for instance, Siane, Iatmul, and Eastern
Abelam) in which the balance is achieved in the next generation.
I should make it clear that in New Guinea these are preferences
expressed principally in ideology; all available figures show the
incidence of both types of balancing marriage arrangements
to be low; even more rarely were true sisters exchanged.[5] There
are other methods of dealing with the problem: in some societies
the unbalanced affinal relationship may be gradually turned
into a balanced relationship of ceremonial exchange, as among
the Melpa (Strathern 1969), while in other societies the inherent
differences between the two forms of exchange may be preserved and even exaggerated. The Eastern Abelam, for instance, consider that each marriage sets up a relationship that
subsists for three generations between a man, his sons and
son's sons, and the sub-clan that provided his wife, the wife-
givers becoming mother's brother's sub-clan and father's
mother's brother's sub-clan to the two succeeding generations.
The details of very elaborate and numerous exchanges that
persist between the two groups for about a hundred years
cannot be given here, but they are unbalanced and dissimilar
at all stages and valuables flow only to, never from, the wife-
givers' sub-clan. The differences between the two types of
exchange are emphasized and are insisted upon even when the
same objects are exchanged; thus men give their ceremonial
exchange partners (equals) great quantities of displayed and
decorated yams and receive exactly the same in return; they
also give their mother's brother one or two lines of their displayed yams. These yams are whole and can be used either for
food or for seed. Mother's brothers never give their sister's
sons yams in this condition; they give them many more yams,
give them informally, and the yams are always either already
cut up or cooked, that is they can only be used for food. This
emphasis of imbalance and inequality between wife-receiver
and wife-giver is typical of all exchanges between them: either

the objects are different in nature or, as with the yams, difference is created by cultural means; no sort of accounting is possible.

Even when patrilateral cross-cousin marriage occurs, although the relationship between the sub-clans is to some extent balanced, the relationships of individuals, since the marriage must be between classificatory relatives, remains imbalanced, the actual descendants of the original wife continuing in a relationship of unequal exchange with the wife-giver's sub-clan.

Each married man thus has three sub-clans other than his own with whom he is in a relationship of unequal exchange: his wife's, his mother's brother's, and his father's mother's brother's. He also has a similar relationship in the reciprocal position, considered advantageous by the Abelam, with his sister's husband and later her son, and after his father's death with his father's sister's son and his father's father's sister's son's son. The equal exchange of similar things cannot take place between him and any of these sub-clans, that is, he cannot compete with any of their members for prestige, which can only be gained through success in the ceremonial exchange of long yams, ordinary yams, and pigs. Among a society as aggressively egalitarian as the Abelam, with all that means in constant rivalry and dispute, inescapable inequality provides a community of interest and no danger of betrayal, which goes some way to explaining the warm supportive and invariant nature of matri-lateral relationships, in a society where every other relation-ship, particularly that between close agnates, is full of rivalry and suspicion, leading frequently to rupture of relationship, and change of political position and even sub-clan membership.

The two stated Iatmul preferences for symmetrical marriage, then, fit well with general New Guinea emphases on balancing the inherent imbalance created by marriage, at least between sub-clans, although except in the case of the exchange of true sisters they cannot balance out the unequal exchange between individuals.

III

ASYMMETRIC MARRIAGE

Asymmetric preferential or even prescriptive marriage systems, especially matrilateral cross-cousin marriage, have occasionally been reported from New Guinea, but evidence has always been poor that any actually working systems of wife-giving and wife-receiving groups exist.[6] Indeed, given that marriage produces a substantially unequal relationship in terms of material items including valuables, any repetitive asymmetrical marriage relationships would perpetuate inequality and do violence to the ideology of balance and equality between groups and individuals. These considerations give me confidence in asserting that none of Lévi-Strauss's elementary asymmetric structures could exist in New Guinea as working systems and that they are unlikely even as ideology. The New Guinea situation contrasts with Australia, in that substantial transfers of material items are not associated with marriage in Australia and hence imbalance in material exchange and in consequent advantage does not occur; and with S.E. Asia, in that, although such transfers of valuables are typical, there is everywhere the concept of ascribed status and aristocracy and the associated inequality presents no problem.

What then of Iatmul *iai* marriage, which is essentially an option to repeat in the third generation a marriage contracted in the first? Encouraged by the first three papers in this volume (Needham, Southwold, and Rivière), I would like to indulge in some ethnographic comparison and to transcend to some extent our own ethnocentric categories of kinship and marriage. I have elsewhere commented on the similarities and differences between the Iatmul and the Abelam and have suggested that differences may on analysis reveal more fundamental similarities, the overt differences being related to such things as the environment and ecology (Forge 1966). For example, *wapi* among the Iatmul are long flutes, among the Abelam long yams, but both are the focus of male cults, phallic in imagery and closely associated with male prestige and power; as such they must both be protected from contact with women. This similarity is nicely emphasized by a Iatmul myth in which a hero invents the flute by blowing on a yam.

If one compares the terminology of the Iatmul and the Eastern Abelam, many of the terms are identical. In each a man is in relationship with the sub-clan of his mother's brother which he calls *wau* and with that of his father's mother's brother which he calls *iai/yai*.[7] It is at this point that the differences start,

Anthony Forge

FIGURE 1

Eastern Abelam terminology for relationships discussed in the text. The same terms, with slight modification, are used by all the rest of the Abelam (except the Northern), the Sawos, and the Western Iatmul

* If sub-clans are referred to, kinship term takes suffix *-nggu*:[8] *ka'singgu, waunggu,* and *yainggu*

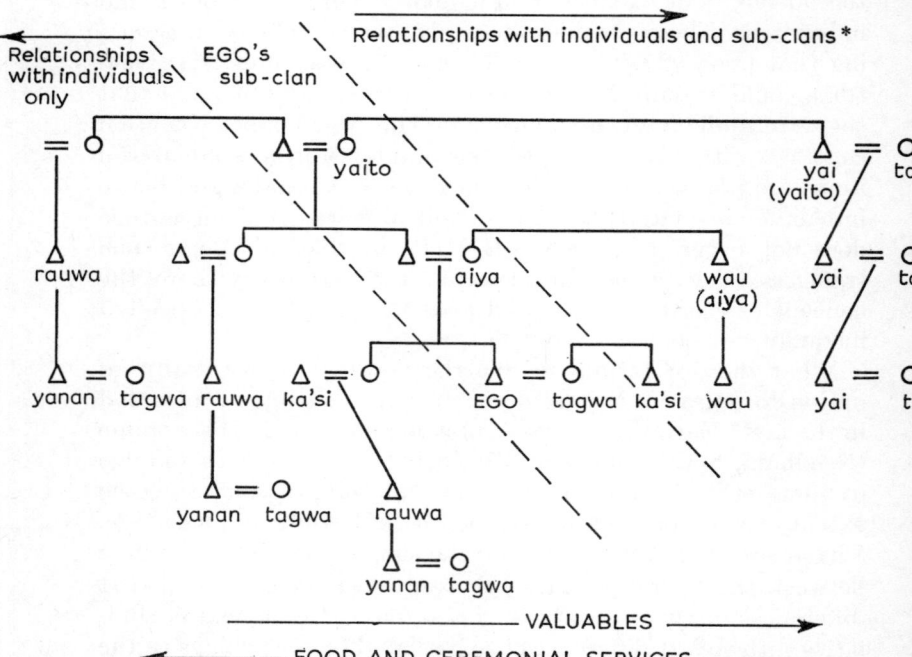

for although the terms for the sub-clans are the same, the use of *iai/yai* as a kinship term is contrasted: among the Iatmul all natal female members of the *iai* clan are called *iai* and are suitable spouses, although after marriage they are treated differently from other wives and Bateson 'observed a definite avoidance of her name' (1932: 281). Among the Abelam all the natal male members of the clan are called *yai*; their sisters (*yaito*) are forbidden as spouses, but their wives are called *tagwa* the Abelam (and Iatmul) term for wife. Further, the only kinship relationship with any element of avoidance among the Abelam is in the *yai – yanan* relationship and is expressed in

140

a form connected with marriage. If a *yanan* mentions his *yai*'s name in the presence of his (the *yanan*'s) wife she should at once leave him and go to the *yai*'s household and prepare him a meal and in general behave in a wifely manner (with the exception of any form of sexual relationship) for at least the rest of the day. At first sight these two practices have little in common in terms of anthropological analysis; among the Iatmul the FMBSD is a preferred spouse (to state it in terms of Mrs Korn's model, at the same genealogical level); in the Abelam case FMBSS calls Ego's wife by the term for wife and Ego reciprocates, while there is a one-sided avoidance of *yai*'s name in the marital relationship. Structurally in both cases the relationship between a man and his *iai/yai* sub-clan is the end of the relationships set up by marriage between the agnatic descendants of the original marriage and the sub-clan of the original woman; at the death of the *ianan/yanan* all relationship is broken. The difference is that among the Iatmul the relationship can be renewed by *iai* marriage; among the Abelam it may not. In both cases the crucial relationship is with an individual called *iai/yai*, although in one case it is a woman whose name must be avoided if the marriage takes place, in the other a man whose name must not be mentioned to one's own wife.

Perhaps too much should not be made of these terminological similarities but structural differences even among such closely related tribes as the Iatmul and the Abelam. Yet to me at least there is a problem, and to put the Iatmul case into a class of preferential marriage systems from which the Abelam are excluded is to evade facing it. I have no solution to offer and although I have a detailed analysis of relationships set up by marriage among the Eastern Abelam it is too lengthy to include here, whereas comparable Iatmul material is only available on certain aspects of the relationship. But certain points can be made. Both tribes are much concerned with maternal blood; for instance, both call the true mother's brother by the term for mother, and the Abelam extend this usage to true father's mother's brother who is called *yaito*, father's mother. Both think true creativity to be the perquisite of women, which men can only imitate with the aid of magic and elaborate ritual. Indeed, it is the difference between men and women that is the basic source of inequality. The fundamental ambiguity

141

is that women are treated as inferior by men, who nevertheless believe them to be basically superior. For example, among the Abelam, fire, all the crops, and both the exclusive male cults originated with women; while the older women at least are believed to attend, in invisible form, the cult ceremonies from which they are physically excluded. Abelam men in debate and ceremony constantly refer to themselves and their clans in terms of their bird totems, and indeed bird imagery in gesture and speech is important in all contexts, yet all birds are female and the whole order of birds (with the addition of bats) forms a model of Nature which is essentially parthenogenic and of the greatest symbolic importance.

Just as men refer to themselves as birds, that is as female, so they also arrogate to themselves and their sub-clans the female maternal role, not just in terminology as mentioned above, but also in behaviour in ceremonial contexts including transvestism, such as the Iatmul *naven*. Among both the Iatmul and the Abelam the unequal nature of relationships through women, and their ceremonial and symbolic importance, reach their highest intensity in the relationship between mother's brother and sister's son; in the next generation, the closeness and social and economic importance of the relationship have very much diminished prior either among the Abelam to a mandatory cessation or among the Iatmul to a possible renewal by a fresh marriage. Mrs Korn's analysis makes it quite clear that of the various marriage preferences recorded by Bateson only the *iai* is compatible with the system of terminology. Bateson repeatedly makes it clear that no such repetitive system operated to the extent of setting up permanent relationships between groups (Bateson 1936: 90, 92). Both systems focus attention in an ambiguous way on the nature of marriage; the Abelam by the reciprocal usage of the term for wife for a woman who is not and cannot in the future be a sexual partner, the Iatmul by a form of preferential marriage, the details of which are somewhat unusual, at that point in the third generation when relationships set up by marriage are about to be extinguished. [9]

IV

CONCLUSIONS

I am well aware that I have not provided an explanation for the phenomenon of *iai* marriage, but I offer these notes to set the diversity of Iatmul stated marriage preferences in the wider context of themes to be found more generally in New Guinea and in Iatmul society itself. The comparison with the Abelam material may help to explain why the Iatmul have a preferential marriage system, with matching kinship terminology, which they certainly do not operate as a system. I also hope it will suggest that it is in the area of cosmology, and concepts of the fundamental nature of men and women, together with the interrelationship between equal and unequal exchange, that factors relevant to the explanation of a phenomenon such as *iai* marriage are to be sought.

NOTES

1. I have spent about 27 months with the Abelam and have at one time or another visited most of the Iatmul villages, although unfortunately never spending more than a few days in any one. My two fieldtrips to New Guinea were made in 1958-9 and 1962-3, and I am grateful to the Emslie Horniman Scholarship Fund of the Royal Anthropological Institute and the Bollingen Foundation, New York, respectively, for the necessary finance.

2. Bateson reports this usage among the Sawos. He also states that one Palimbai informant told him MBS was called *wau* after the death of MB there, but others denied it (Bateson 1936: 39-40). This is of some interest, since Palimbai (Middle Iatmul) is one of the two villages in which he collected rule (4), the other being Mindimbit (Eastern Iatmul). For Northern Abelam terminology, see Kaberry 1941. I use Sawos here since, although Bateson's Tshuosh has the claim of priority, Sawos has been generally used since Laycock's survey of the *Ndu* languages (Laycock 1965).

3. As far as I could determine, no *naven* had been held since the war, although initiations still occur in most Iatmul villages. The reason invariably given for discontinuing the practice was the great expense involved, referring to the large quantities of valuables the performers had to receive from their sister's son and his father.

4. I have made no attempt to make any sort of survey of the vast literature available on New Guinea marriage. Virtually the only New Guinea societies for which there are published figures of incidence of various types of marriage are from the Highlands. To the ten in Glasse and Meggitt (1969), the Mae Enga, Siane, and Kuma can be added.

5. Although Louise Hogg (personal communication) reports that in the hinterland of Madang she was told that an increased survival rate of children and

143

larger families had enabled them nowadays to exchange actual sisters whereas previously they had to make do with classificatory sisters.

6. See for example the South Fore material discussed by Glasse (1969).

7. My orthography requires me to use *yai*, as did Kaberry's (1941); there is however no difference in the pronunciation of Iatmul *iai* and Abelam *yai*, and the same applies to the reciprocals *ianan* and *yanan*.

8. The suffix *-nggu* can be added to many Abelam kin terms to make a collective noun, its most frequent use is undoubtedly in *waunggu* and *yainggu*. It is also used by the Iatmul but apparently in a more restricted range of terms (Bateson 1936: 104 n. 2).

9. This option to repeat a marriage seems common among New Guinea societies. In the Sepik district G. A. Lewis (personal communication) reports that the Gnau of Lumi Sub-district have the option to repeat a marriage in the fourth generation, i.e. with FFMBSSD. Perhaps significantly in the light of this discussion the Gnau use either sibling or cross-cousin terms in the second generation, only sibling terms in the third generation, and either remarry or extinguish the relationship in the fourth generation.

REFERENCES

BATESON, G. 1932. Social Structure of the Iatmul People of the Sepik River. *Oceania* **2**: 246-89, 401-51.

—— 1936. *Naven*. Cambridge: Cambridge University Press.

FORGE, A. 1966. Art and Environment in the Sepik. *Proceedings of the Royal Anthropological Institute for 1965*: 23-32.

GLASSE, R. M. 1969. Marriage in South Fore. In: R. M. Glasse and M. J. Meggitt (eds.) 1969.

GLASSE, R. M. & MEGGITT, M. J. (eds.). 1969. *Pigs, Pearlshells and Women*. Englewood Cliffs, N.J.: Prentice-Hall.

KABERRY, P. M. 1941. The Abelam Tribe, Sepik District, New Guinea. *Oceania* **11**: 233-58, 345-67.

LAYCOCK, D. C. 1965. *The Ndu Language Family (Sepik District, New Guinea)*. Canberra: Linguistic Circle of Canberra.

STRATHERN, A. & M. 1969. Marriage in Melpa. In: R. M. Glasse and M. J. Meggitt (eds.) 1969.

7

David McKnight

Some Problems concerning the Wik-mungkan

INTRODUCTION

The Wik-mungkan are an Australian Aboriginal tribe who traditionally inhabited an area between the Watson and Edward Rivers on the west coast of Cape York Peninsula in Northern Queensland. They were studied independently, and at separate periods, by two anthropologists – Ursula McConnel and Donald Thomson. McConnel was in the field in 1927-8 and in 1934, while Thomson studied the Wik-mungkan in 1932-3. On the basis of their material, particularly McConnel's, the Wik-mungkan have been referred to or discussed at some length by a number of scholars, among them Radcliffe-Brown (1930: 245), Elkin (1940: 282-3), Lévi-Strauss (1969 *passim*; 1968: 33), Homans and Schneider (1955: 34; 1962), and lately the literature has been critically scrutinized by Needham in two articles (1962b, 1963a).

Since so many scholars have been concerned with this society perhaps a short biographical note explaining how I have become involved might be of interest. As is well known, we expect every budding anthropologist to spend at least a year or two in the field, and providing that he has not lost his notes, we tend to evaluate his account according to the length of time he has spent there. Let me therefore hasten to say that I visited the Wik-mungkan for only ten days. I was completing my third fieldtrip with another tribe in the Gulf area, the Lardil of Mornington Island. Before leaving Australia I was anxious to visit other Aboriginal societies, however short the visit would necessarily have to be, in order to help me place the Lardil in perspective. The superintendent at Mornington Island suggested that I visit Aurukun, which also was under the Presbyterian Board of Missions.

145

Fortunately I had read some of the Wik-mungkan ethnographic data so I was not completely unfamiliar with the society. Even so, I was desperately trying to recall what were the main problems and what I should investigate. I decided to concentrate on kinship and marriage, and especially patterns of kinship behaviour. Luckily the mission had copies of some of McConnel's articles. Much to my surprise the Wik-mungkan were out to meet me in force, for word had reached them about my work on Mornington Island. As some Lardil were related to some of the Wik-mungkan I too was related and in no time at all I moved into the village to live with a family. I extended my relationship to others according to their relationships with my adopted family. Many of the Wik-mungkan spoke good English so there was no language barrier. To make matters even easier for me, two members of the Summer Institute of Linguistics were there, and they had been studying Wik-mungkan for some time. Perhaps most important of all, since the founding of the mission, very extensive kinship and marriage records had been kept. These proved very useful, for the superintendent very kindly allowed me to use them and even to have a copy made.[1] So this paper is based on my reading of the Wik-mungkan material, the ethnographic data that I was able to collect during my short stay, and the mission records.[2]

The main questions that I shall deal with are: (1) How valid is McConnel's analysis and presentation of the Wik-mungkan system of kinship and marriage? (2) How many descent lines do they have? (3) What are the kinship terms? (4) What type of marriage system do they have? (5) Does the ethnography support Homans and Schneiders's interpretation and their theory of unilateral cross-cousin marriage? (6) Are the kinship attitudes in accordance with Lévi-Strauss's Law of the Atom of Kinship?

II

MCCONNEL'S ANALYSIS AND KINSHIP MODELS[3]

The basis of McConnel's interpretation and models of the Wik-mungkan kinship and marriage system seems to rest on

146

a weak foundation, viz. what a non-Wik-mungkan woman told her to be the case among the Wik-mungkan. Apparently she never verified what she was told at first hand. McConnel notes that marriage with a father's sister's daughter is taboo – as a rule of marriage – and also because she belongs to an older line (she never describes or defines what she means by 'line' although this is central to her exposition). Since men should not marry women who belong to older lines, a father's sister's daughter is therefore doubly taboo. This father's sister's daughter, according to McConnel's non-Wik-mungkan informant, is known as 'cousin–mother' (McConnel 1940: 444; 1950: 109).

McConnel considers that 'This "cousin–mother" and her husband are the crux of the situation'. But as I believe that from this stems much of the confusion of her kinship chart, descent lines, age spiral, and analysis of the marriage system, I think it worth while quoting her *in extenso*.' This taboo-cousin is called "cousin–mother" in pidgin English by Peninsular tribes, while her husband is called *pinya*, and regarded as "older father" thus placing them in the category of Ego's "parents" and their children of "older brothers and sisters". *This slipping down a generation in an older line that intermarries with Ego's taboo cross-cousin is what give Peninsular marriage systems their peculiar unilateral twist in a downward age-spiral'* (McConnel 1940: 444, my italics).

I have no quarrel with McConnel when she says that a father's sister's daughter is called 'cousin–mother', but as to her claim that her children are in the category 'older brother and sister', I was told that they are called *nengka*, i.e. 'son' and 'daughter'.[4] Naturally, kinship inquiries of this nature are subject to error – especially when one is in the field for a short period – so I could be wrong. Nevertheless, I think this is unlikely since I approached the problem in a number of different ways with different informants. Thus with one I asked what he called his father's sister's daughter's child, and with another I first asked what his father's sister's daughter's child called him. It seems to me that McConnel was misled into thinking that because the father's sister's daughter is called 'cousin–mother', then the logic of the situation must be that, just as one's own mother's children are called 'brother' and 'sister', so this must also be the case with the children of 'cousin–mother'.

There is little doubt that the Wik-mungkan, in calling an actual father's sister's daughter 'mother' or 'cousin–mother', are emphasizing that she should not be married. Just as one cannot marry one's own mother, or have sexual intercourse with her, or her classificatory sister (McConnel 1934: 339), so this taboo holds with a father's sister's daughter. The gist of what one of my younger informants had to say about this was: 'You cannot have your real *pinya*'s (FZ) daughter as your girl-friend as it is just too shameful to think about. If you were to do something with her she would get a beating from her mother, and then your *muka* (MoB) would bawl you out, and tell you that you should not make trouble for her, for she is your *kampan* (relative or member of the family).' One's own father's sister, and her daughter, are both regarded as *ngaintja taiyin* (*ngaintja*, 'tabu', *taiyin*, 'hard' or 'severe' – Thomson 1935: 483). They are also referred to as 'poison auntie' and 'poison cousin'. What one must realize is that calling a father's sister's daughter 'mother' is a restricted kinship term, or to put it another way, a genealogical restricted kinship term. It is restricted in use by Ego and his actual brothers (I am uncertain whether a man's actual sisters also use this term), to their actual father's sister's daughter. This being so, one must be careful of confusing gene-alogy and category, which is what McConnel does.

I would argue that in such instances of genealogical restricted kinship terms it is incorrect, and methodologically unsound, to trace the genealogical links through one person (for convenience, say, Ego), and then claim that because of the kinship term that Ego uses for those involved in the marriage, the rest of the society recognizes the kin relationship of the marriage partners as it is traced through Ego. But this is virtually how McConnel views the matter. This distorts the marriage system, for in this way it is analysed in terms of restricted genealogical kinship links, without taking categories into consideration. Because Ego calls an actual father's sister's daughter 'mother', it does not mean that an older classificatory brother is marrying a 'mother'. Quite the contrary – he is marrying a *kutth/moiya*, i.e. a cross-cousin, and this is the way the members of the society view the marriage. But if Ego were to marry the same woman, it would be as if he was marrying a mother, and this is the way that the Wik-mungkan would view such a marriage.

It might be argued that proof of my interpretation lies in my claim that although a man calls his actual father's sister's daughter 'mother', yet he calls her children, not 'older brother and sister', but *nengka*, i.e. 'son' and 'daughter'. For one could argue that by using the term *nengka* he views the marriage as one of an older classificatory brother with *his kutth/moiya*. There may be something in this. Nevertheless, McConnel could be right, and I could be wrong, about what an actual father's sister's daughter's child is called, yet I do not think that this would invalidate my argument. This is not a case of heads I win and tails McConnel loses. The Wik-mungkan could allow the individual to call his actual father's sister's daughter's child, 'older brother and sister', and so reinforce the fiction that a father's sister's daughter is a 'mother'. It is possible that they do a double-think in this matter caused by juggling the genealogical links and kinship categories. Thus on the one hand, an actual father's sister's daughter is, genealogically speaking, a 'mother', but in terms of categories, she is a *kutth/moiya* – hence her children are 'older brother and sister' when viewed genealogically, but 'son' and 'daughter' when viewed in terms of categories.

According to McConnel the marriage rule is unilateral, in that a man marries a mother's younger brother's daughter; as we have seen he may not marry an actual father's sister's daughter. *In order to show this separateness she constructs her kinship chart so that an actual father's sister is not married to an actual mother's brother.* Because of this, in the next descending generation, she is able to marry off Ego and his brothers to a woman who is a mother's younger brother's daughter, but not at the same time an actual father's sister's daughter. As we shall see, this has a profound influence on the final outcome of her chart, and the way that she interprets the Wik-mungkan kinship and marriage system.

In drawing up her kinship chart McConnel was grappling, without realizing it, it seems, with the problem of actual and classificatory relationships while trying to present both at the same time. This, and the fact she puts such emphasis on 'cousin– mother', separates father's sister's daughter and mother's brother's daughter, places men on the right and women on the left of her age/descent lines, has resulted in the peculiar

149

David McKnight

FIGURE 1   *Wik-mungkan system (McConnel, 1940)*

INTERMARRIAGE BETWEEN AGE LINES

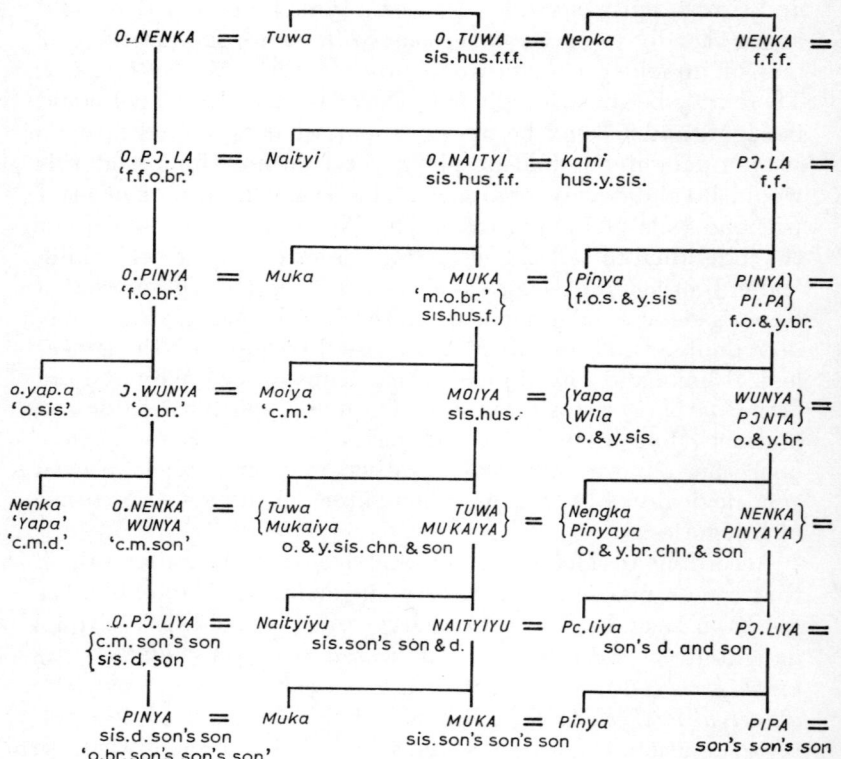

construction of her kinship chart. It is from her chart that she reasons what the Wik-mungkan kinship and marriage system is supposed to be like, viz. that men marry down, women marry up, that there is a marriage–age spiral and that there are six lines of descent.

To simplify an examination of her kinship chart let us start with *wunya* and *punta* (older brother and younger brother). She claims that the marriage rule is one of matrilateral cross-cousin marriage and that the Wik-mungkan have given this basic Aboriginal marriage rule a peculiar twist, namely, that a man should marry in a *younger* line, i.e. mother's *younger*

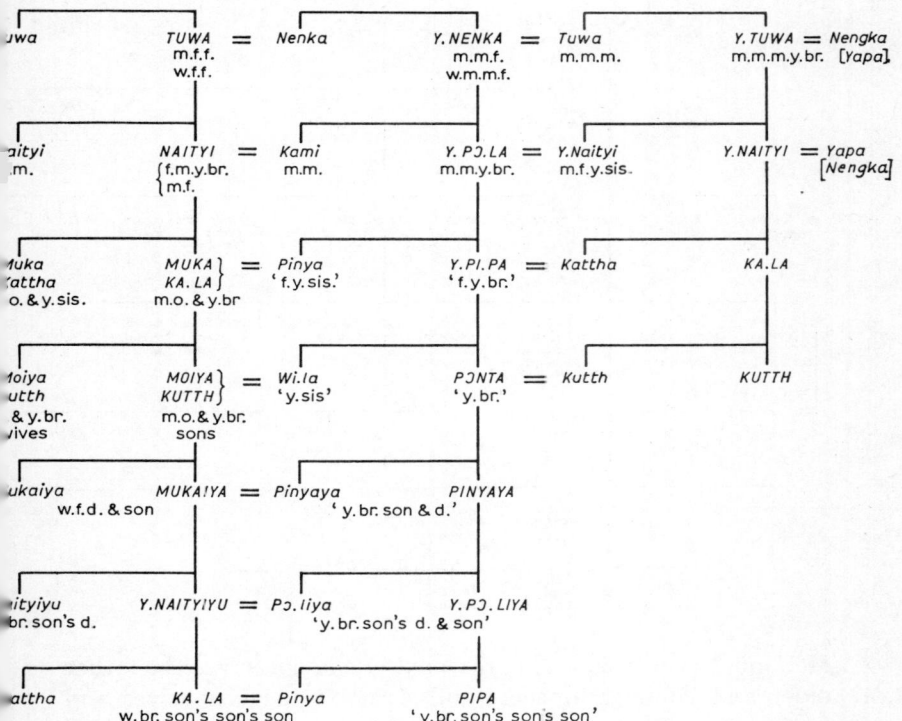

brother's daughter. In her chart the younger brother marries *kutth*, the daughter of *kala* (MyB), and the older brother marries *moiya*, the daughter of *muka* (MoB). There is at this initial point some confusion in what McConnel says in the text (McConnel 1939: 65) and her chart. For full brothers, older and younger, marry daughters of men that they call *kala* (MyB), but older classificatory brothers marry daughters of men that the full brothers call *muka* (MoB), and whom the older classificatory brothers call *kala* (MyB).

As I have already indicated, it is the diagrammatic placement of those in the parental generation that contributes to

David McKnight

FIGURE 2   Wik-mungkan system (McConnel, 1950)

1. JUNIOR MARRIAGE SYSTEMS OF CAPE YORK
PENINSULA. WIKMUNKAN: AGE SPIRAL

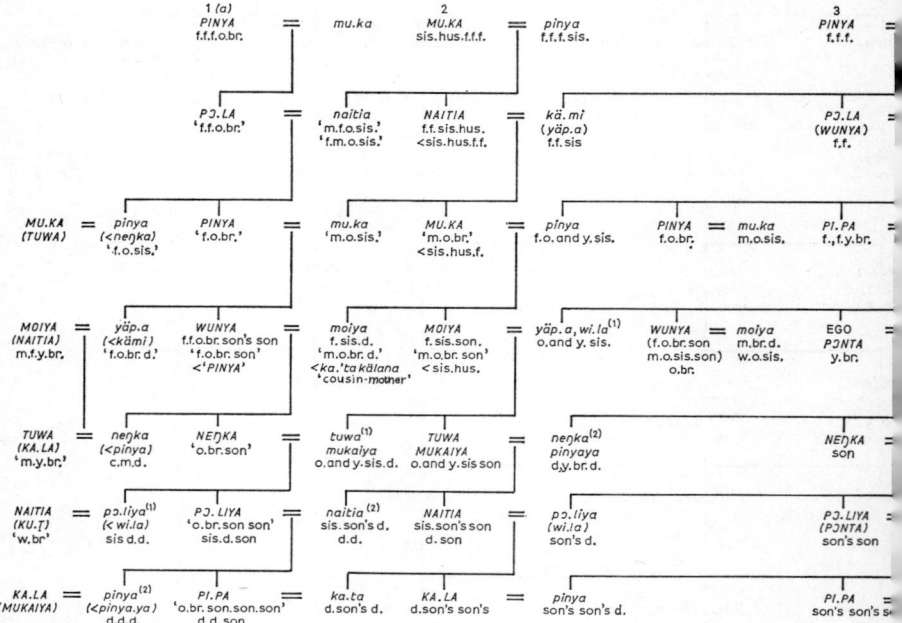

McConnel's confusion. She, reasonably enough, gives the father older and younger brothers and sisters, and gives wives and husbands to them. But she does not marry off the actual FoZ and FyZ to the actual MoB and MyB, for if she did this, then her chart would show *wunya* (yB) and *ponta* (oB) married to women who would be at the same time MBD and FZD. And this she obviously wishes to avoid, since marriage with a FZD is taboo. She could have married off the actual father's sisters to actual mother's brothers, and drawn the reader's attention to the fact that one should not be misled into concluding that an actual FZD is married. If she had done this her kinship chart would have consisted of just two lines instead of six. But instead she marries actual father's sisters to classificatory mother's younger brothers (*muka*). And in doing so puts *muka* on another descent/age line. On the other side, she has actual mother's

152

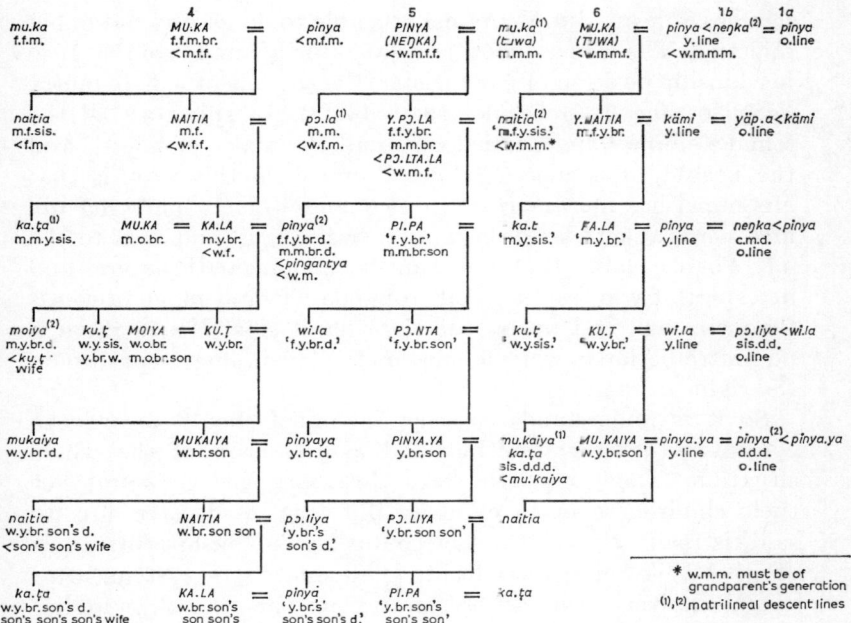

older and younger brothers married to classificatory father's younger sisters. She now has four descent/age lines, and the marriage system is so arranged that men marry to the right and women to the left, and men marry into younger lines while women marry into older lines. There is no need to go through all this step by step for each kinship position. For quite obviously McConnel marries the males of line 3 to the females of line 4, the males of line 4 to females of line 5, and in order to marry off the males of line 5 she creates line 6. Viewed in the opposite direction, she marries all the females of line 3 to men on their left in line 2, and the females of line 2 to males in line 1, so that finally she has a total of six lines.

McConnel has to deal with a very difficult problem of her chart, namely, that males have female relatives (and vice versa) – sisters to the left of them – who seek marriage partners in

153

the opposite direction. It would seem that this might go on and on, with the necessity of creating yet another line of males so that the females of the line before can be married. For each time that another 'male line' is created yet another batch of females appear. But McConnel was able to find a way out of her dilemma. The 'cousin–mother's daughter' ('c.m.d.') of line 1, in her kinship position of *yapa* (sister) fits the role of wife to marry *naityi* of line 6 (McConnel 1940: 444-8). In this way all the females of line 1 are married off to all the males of line 6. And the beauty of connecting lines 1 and 6, in this way, is that McConnel has men marrying down and women marrying up, and she is able to keep the women to the right and men to the left. For she claims that lines 1 and 6 are connected in a spiral, and in a spiral if you trace a point from the left and move upwards then you will end up on the right-hand side. Hence there is no contradiction in women being on the left in line 1 but also on the right of line 6.

So it is understandable why McConnel should regard the cousin–mother and her husband as the crux of the whole situation. They seem to start the marriage–age spiral yet their children seem to close it. But this, as I have already said, is really the crux of her confusion and misinterpretation of the Wik-mungkan kinship and marriage system. Her wrong analysis also partly stems from the fact that in her chart she does not have an actual mother's brother married to an actual father's sister, and that she mixes up actual and classificatory relationships. This last point is important, for in her chart she has two lines of actual kin (the centre lines 3 and 4) while the other lines are a mixture of actual and classificatory relationships. From all this emerges her contention that men marry in a younger line while women marry in an older line, men marry down while women marry up, men marry to the right while women marry to the left, that the marriage system is one of unilateral cross-cousin marriage, that there is a marriage–age spiral, with women of line 1 marrying men of line 6, and that there are six lines of descent. But, like Needham (1962b: 239 ff), I would argue that all this is not so, and I think I have shown the weaknesses of McConnel's analysis and kinship models, and where these weaknesses spring from.

III

DESCENT LINES

It would seem possible to draw up a simpler kinship chart than McConnel has done. Thus the Wik-mungkan kinship and marriage system might be better illustrated as in *Figure 3*. The reader will note that in this chart there are only two descent lines rather than the six claimed by McConnel. I take up this point below, but first I would like to make a few general remarks about kinship charts.

As I see it a kinship chart is a diagrammatic summary of what the kinship terms are and an illustration of which kinship categories are linked by marriage. Thus we collect kinship terms and we draw up a chart hoping to give a visual representation of how the system works. The convention is to start with Ego and give the terms that he uses for F, FZ, FF, etc. And in order to show what these relatives call Ego we also include two or more descending generations. At the same time these charts can give us some idea of the marriage and descent system of a society. However, there are a number of drawbacks to the conventional kinship chart.

One weakness of such charts is that they are male-dominated. We start with a male Ego and trace his links and what terms he uses for others. Hence it is often difficult, if not impossible, to place on the same chart some of the terms that are used by women. In this case we have to resort to footnotes and abbreviations such as w.s. (woman speaking), or else, as is usually the case, some of the terms that women use are left out. This is most noticeable when scanning a chart for the term that a woman uses for her children and her brother's children. This is often crucial for an understanding of the system, for a woman may or may not use the same term for her brother's children as for her own. Whether she does or not is a hint of the degree to which she and her children are incorporated into her husband's descent group. In addition, it is difficult to record on the chart the kinship terms that Ego uses for others in his own generation, and the term that they call him by. This weakness is often particularly noticeable with cross-cousins, as can be seen in my own chart. However, we have become conditioned to the genealogical kinship chart, and we think we know what

155

David McKnight

FIGURE 3   Wik-mungkan kinship chart

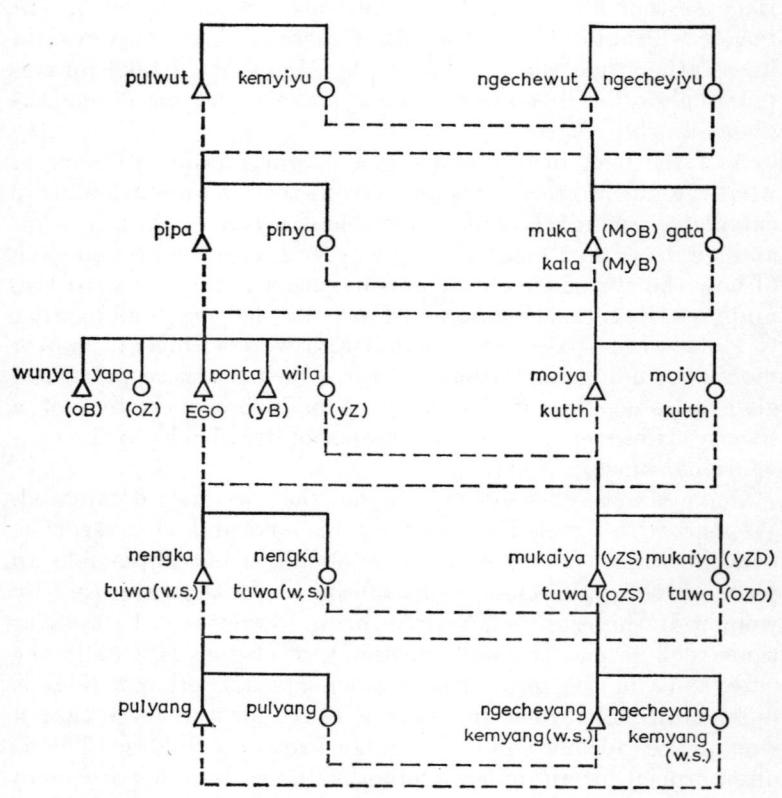

156

the ethnographer is trying to represent, even though he may not be able to do so.

As Needham has pointed out, there is a fundamental weakness in the conventional genealogical kinship chart, viz. its use of representing a quite different system, i.e. one of categories (Needham 1962b: 224-5, 259). When we use it for systems like that of the Wik-mungkan we are forcing our system into their system of categories, or more likely we are forcing their system of categories into our genealogical kinship system.

One of the most vexing problems to cope with in using the genealogical chart is to represent something that is three-dimensional, at least in concept, by a two-dimensional representation – to represent classificatory and actual relationships at the same time. I have tried to show how McConnel became confused over this, in her attempt to spread her kinship chart laterally in order to represent classificatory relationships.[5]

Needham has become so convinced of the shortcomings, misrepresentation, and distortions of the genealogical kinship chart that he seems to have eschewed it altogether, and has attempted to place the linguistic categories of kinship terms in 'boxes' (Needham 1962a: 76; 1962b: 244). Although the ghost of Ego still haunts his models, at least his method emphasizes to a greater degree that we are dealing with categories.

Returning to the problem of descent lines, Leach has argued that 'The number of basic descent lines . . . depends merely upon how many different kinds of relatives are recognized in the grandfather's generation' (Leach 1961: 57). Thus it would seem that if there is a different term for each of the following: FF, MF, FMB, MMB, then it might be argued that there are four lines of descent, and if there are only three terms for these kin, then there are three lines of descent. On this basis I think it is reasonable to argue that among the Wik-mungkan there are two lines of descent, and not six as claimed by McConnel, or three as is said to be the case by Lévi-Strauss (1969: 196). For there is one term for FF and MMB, i.e. *pulwut* and another term for MF and FMB, i.e. *ngechewut*.

I would however like to emphasize that only the surface of this problem has been touched upon. Without trying to evade the shortcomings of my own position, this problem really does require a more elaborate examination than I have space for.

I have tried to cut through it by using a quote from Leach. But this still leaves questions unanswered that I plan to follow up in another work. Such questions as: What is meant by different kinds of relatives being *recognized*? Why should it be in the grandparental generation, if this is the case, that the number of basic descent lines is determined? Is it not possible to have, say, four descent lines in one generation and three in another, in the same kinship system? Perhaps it is the kinship chart itself which determines the descent lines. I well recognize that my own kinship chart has all the weaknesses that I have discussed in this section. The main reason why I have drawn it is to show that with the conventional method it is possible to draw up a simpler one than McConnel has done. And that this can be accomplished with only two lines of descent.

IV

KINSHIP TERMS

McConnel's two kinship charts reveal some inconsistency as to what are the kinship terms. I have attempted to clear this matter up in my kinship chart. As I neglected to make a thorough check of the kinship terms for the third ascending and descending generations I have not included them in my kinship chart. A few explanatory remarks might help to clarify the issues. The suffix *yiyu* is usually added on to a kinship term to indicate seniority, older or oldest – this is a mark of respect – and it seems to me that this suffix is usually used, but not exclusively, for female relatives auch as *kemyiyu* and *ngecheyiyu* in the grandparental generation. For those in the grandchild generation there is no sex differentiation in the kinship terms and the suffix is invariably *yang* as with *pulyang, ngecheyang, kemyang*.

Needham has drawn attention to the fact that McConnel's data are contradictory as to what is the term for DS and DD. He writes:

'The term for daughter's son and daughter's daughter is variously given by McConnel as *naityiyu* (1940, pp. 442-3) and as *naitia* (1950, p. 121). To accept the latter raises an

158

analytical difficulty in trying to understand the categorical regulation of marriage (cf. McConnel 1934, p. 346; 1950, p. 121), and we are fortunate in having the reports of another ethnographer to aid in decision. Thomson (1935, p. 483; 1946, p. 160) clearly gives *ngatjiyang* (quite different from *ngatja*, which is equivalent to McConnel's *naitia/naitya*) for DS and DD; this is evidently equivalent to *naityiyu*, which I therefore adopt here' (Needham 1962b: 230).

But I think that Needham, from the contradictory information available to him, has made the wrong choice. In McConnel's orthography DS and DD should be *naitia* (Thomson's *ngatjiyang*) and MM should be *naityiyu*. I take up this point more fully below in discussing marriage.

V

MARRIAGE SYSTEM

I deal first with the problem of moieties. In one place McConnel claims that the Wik-mungkan recognize two exogamous patri-lineal moieties known as *Kuyan* and *Katpi* (McConnel 1934: 354). And although she says that the exogamous nature of the moieties is rigidly enforced, and plays almost a more important part in determining marriage than the kinship terms, yet later she admits that she has been unable to identify what moiety the clans belong to. And in still later publications – without an intervening period of fieldwork it seems – she claims that they have little or no use for the moieties although the upriver Wik-mungkan know of them from their contact with the *Kandyu*. Thomson claims that the Wik-mungkan have no moieties, yet in other places he mentions the different moiety membership of a woman and her child. It would seem that the point he wishes to make is that there are no named moieties (Thomson 1935: 463-4; 1936: 374; 1946: 158, 160).

From my inquiries it seems that the terms *Kuyan* and *Katpi* are inland (upriver) terms, possbly *Kandyu*. They are certainly not Wik-mungkan terms. I never heard them used in marriage discussions and indeed it took a while for my informants to understand what I was talking about (but that may have been

159

the result of my pronunciation). However, it is possible that they have unnamed patrilineal moieties. If so, I do not know how the clans are grouped. The only information that I have to offer on this matter is the fact that a number of the patricians are regarded as being patrilineally related. Whether this is extended to the formation of unnamed partilineal moieties I do not know.

There has been a number of different claims as to what type of marriage system the Wik-mungkan have. As I have already pointed out, McConnel argues *inter alia* that marriage is with a mother's younger brother's daughter. In contrast, at one point Thomson argues that marriage is with a 'second-cousin type' (Thomson 1955: 231). Needham claims something quite different, viz. that McConnel is mistaken in her unilateral claim and that the system is one of bilateral cross-cousin marriage with the genealogical qualification that an actual FZD may not be married (Needham 1962b: 259; 1963b: 44). Briefly, Lévi-Strauss claims that there are two forms of marriage in this society – one patrilateral and one matrilateral – and he further argues that there has been 'a gradual transition from generalized to restricted exchange' (Lévi-Strauss 1969: 209, 211).

Lévi-Strauss seems to rely rather heavily on McConnel's quote of one of her informants. I reproduce this in the same form as he has done, with his comments, so as to guard against misrepresenting his argument.

> ' "My mother's younger brother is my *KALA* . . . My *KALA*'s daughter, my *moiya*, I take for my wife . . . I may marry a woman from a distant ground given by a *"KALA"*. We two "change hands". I give my sister (*yapa* or *wila*) to my *Kutth* (*KALA*'s son). I exchange with him. Now I call my *KUTTH*, *MOIYA* (sister's husband) and my *KUTTH*, he calls my father KALA." '

Concerning this, Lévi-Strauss writes:

> 'Thus, in the Wik-mungkan system, which originally had a structure of generalized exchange, patrilateral marriage has been joined with the prior matrilateral marriage with two results. The first is a gradual transition from generalized to restricted exchange: "A man usually gives a *younger* half-sister from his own family or clan to the man who gives him

his sister for a wife" (McConnel 1940, p. 451). In the second place, the gradualness of this change is apparent in the fact that if a man marries his real unilateral cousin . . . and if the marriage is accompanied by exchange, at least one of the two cousins must be classificatory. This is what McConnel expresses, but in a way which does not seem to be fully in keeping with her description when she writes: "Exchange of wives takes place between distantly related clans". It seems quite clear in fact, that one of the two women might be a first cousin. In this case, a very important theoretical consequence must follow viz., that a twofold exchange of this type may in fact be a threefold exchange, i.e. I marry my cross-cousin, and I borrow from a parallel line a woman whom I give in exchange to my brother-in-law. Accordingly, for each woman there are two marriage possibilities: either a direct cycle of generalized exchange, or in an indirect cycle of restricted exchange' (Lévi-Strauss 1969: 211).

Unfortunately I blundered by not inquiring specifically whether wife-receivers could also be wife-givers to the same clan. While the marriage records might shed some light on this matter, yet they would seem to be inconclusive. For they indicate to which clans the marriage partners belong, and, of course, there may be quite a gap between the ideal and empirical reality. Of some importance to this problem is the fact that the Wik-mungkan speak of 'wife-givers' or 'woman-givers', i.e. *wanch a:than*. The wife-givers are in a superior position to wife-receivers. Thus a man is superior to his sister's husband. The wife's brother expects to receive things from the sister's husband. While the wife's brother may eat any fish caught by the sister's husband, it is *ngaintja taiyin*, i.e. taboo, for the sister's husband to eat fish caught by the wife's brother.

On the evidence that Lévi-Strauss uses, I see no reason for him to make a special claim of a transition from generalized to restricted exchange. Exchanging an actual sister for the brother-in-law's classificatory sister, or vice versa, must often occur in these types of societies. It would seem to me that whether we are dealing with generalized, or restricted, exchange would depend on what level we view the exchange, i.e. family, lineage, clan, etc. Thus a marriage may be an indirect exchange

161

at the family level but a direct exchange at the lineage, or an indirect exchange at the lineage level but a direct exchange at the clan level.[6] Perhaps our interpretation of the exchange should be based on how it is viewed in a particular society. Thus the Wik-mungkan appear to regard the patriclans as being the main units involved in marriage exchange.

As for Thomson's claim that the Wik-mungkan practise a second-cousin type of marriage with a FM'Z'DD, there is no doubt that Needham has shown that Thomson has misinterpreted the outcome of these genealogical links, and that marriage with a FM'Z'DD does not preclude marriage with a first cousin, i.e. a mother's brother's daughter (Needham 1963b: 44). But the fact that a FM'Z'D is the mother-in-law does eliminate marriage with an actual father's sister's daughter (Needham 1965: 22). I suspect that when Thomson writes of a second-cousin type of marriage he really means a classificatory cross-cousin and not, say, an Aranda type of second cousin.

This brings me to the final point of this section. McConnel has made what appear to be two self-contradictory statements, (1) a man's wife's mother's mother should always be of the grandparents' generation and (2) a man has the right to marry a 'daughter's daughter'. Concerning this, there is a very revealing passage, which illustrates McConnel's difficulties in understanding the Wik-mungkan kinship and marriage system, and their social structure. It also shows how her analysis is dominated by her chart. Thus she writes: 'Ego marries a woman of a younger generation in an older line who for this reason is taboo to Ego's son's son, since the latter may only marry a woman of a younger line in his own generation' (McConnel 1940: 436). But what she does not realize is that Ego's son's son is also Ego. And what the father's father can do in his generation the son's son can do in his own. So he is not restricted to only marrying 'a woman of a younger line in his own generation'.

Needham dismisses McConnel's claim that a woman of the genealogical position and generation level of daughter's daughter is married, on the grounds of McConnel's statement of wife's mother's mother having to be of the grandparents' generation (McConnel 1950: 124. See Needham 1962b: 232, 243). But from what I was told by my informants, the position is as follows. Although they claim that a cross-cousin should be married, nevertheless marriage with a classificatory daughter's daughter may also take place. By this is meant that marriage with the latter is a second-best type of marriage, and, of all the wrong marriages, it causes the least opposition. When I further inquired whether a classificatory son's daughter could be married my informants were most emphatic that such a marriage should not take place. They claimed that it would be like marrying a blood relative, since blood is passed on patrilineally.

With reference to McConnel's claim about marrying 'a woman of a younger generation in an older line', Lévi-Strauss argues that this eliminates competition for a woman between the grandfather and grandson. But surely his argument is wrong. In the first place a man may not marry his own daughter's daughter and it is precisely this woman who is his own son's son actual father's sister's daughter, i.e. the taboo patrilateral cross-cousin. So instead of only one of them being allowed to marry her, and the other not, thus eliminating competition, we find that neither of them can marry the woman, thus completely eliminating competition between them in a quite different manner from that alleged by Lévi-Strauss. Secondly, both, in a sense, will be in competition for women in these classificatory kinship positions. For although a man might marry a classificatory daughter's daughter, yet it must be realized that she will be a classificatory father's sister's daughter to his own son's son. And, as we have seen, his son's son has the right to marry his classificatory father's sister's daughter. They will be in competition, not only between themselves, but with all the other men in their generations who have either the right, or who attempt, to marry such women.

I turn now to a description of the behaviour patterns of some kin relationships.

VI

PATTERNS OF BEHAVIOUR AND ATTITUDES

In this section I describe the pattern of behaviour and expected attitudes between a number of kin relationships, viz. mother's brother and sister's son, brother and sister, father and son, and husband and wife.

There is no doubt that there is a considerable difference in the behaviour patterns and expected attitudes with a mother's older brother and mother's younger brother. This is so even though both are said to be *kampan*, i.e. a relative, one who is part of the family. I have drawn up a table summarizing some of the main differences. What we find is that with the mother's older brother, in contrast to the mother's younger brother, there is an easy, direct communication, with no fear of pollution, and that the mother's older brother has moral, jural, and ritual authority. With a classificatory mother's older brother, we find that the relationship is even easier and that it is a reciprocal joking relationship. With an actual mother's younger brother there is seldom any direct communication, and this is even more noticeable with a classificatory mother's younger brother with whom there is a typical affinal avoidance relationship.[7]

Owing to the subtlety of the behaviour pattern and conventional attitudes of some relationships it is at times difficult to discern them. But if one turns to the classificatory relationships, the behaviour patterns are more easily seen. For among the Wik-mungkan they are often the actual writ large. The essential characteristic or core of an actual kin relationship may be blown up or magnified in the classificatory relationship. Thus if the accent is on reserve and deference with an actual kin or relation, it is even more so in the classificatory relationship. If the actual relationship is one of warmth and friendliness, and allows humour, so to a greater extent is this the case with the classificatory relationship. While this may not always be so for all societies, yet I believe it to be frequent enough to warrant attention. I think that this magnification of the essential core is illustrated in the table. What also clearly stands out is the essential affinity of the mother's younger brother and the non-affinity or kinship of the mother's older brother.

During my short stay a number of marriage disputes and discussions took place. It was quite obvious that the maternal relatives, especially the mother and mother's older brother, dominated the discussions. This came out quite clearly in one discussion that took place just outside the house where I was staying. I think it worth while to describe this.

David wanted to marry Elsie's daughter, Jane. But Elsie

164

Behaviour patterns with mother's older brother and mother's younger brother

Mother's Older Brother	Mother's Younger Brother

ACTUAL

Mother's Older Brother	Mother's Younger Brother
1 Some restraint but an easy, friendly relationship. Expected to be indulgent.	Deference and respect. Not regarded as an indulgent figure.
2 Has moral, ritual, and jural authority. May comment to ZS about his behaviour.	Has authority but normally does not talk to ZS about his behaviour.
3 Has major say in marriage arrangement of ZS (& ZD)	Has a say but overshadowed by older brother.
4 May touch, scold, and drive ZS away from a fight.	Does not touch ZS.
5 Talk in a face-to-face manner. Little restriction in subject-matter.	Does not talk in a face-to-face manner. Restricted subject-matter and communication.
6 Can joke lightly.	Never make jokes.
7 Gives articles and food directly to ZS.	Gives articles, especially food, indirectly, either by placing on ground, or through third party.
8 ZS can take goods without asking.	Unusual to take goods without permission.
9 ZS allowed to call him by name (though not usual) or kinship term.	Taboo for ZS to call him by name or directly by kinship term. Refer to him by name of third party.
10 Said to be like mother.	Said to be a bit like father-in-law.
11 Eat at mortuary feast for ZS.	May not eat at mortuary feast.
12 May take anything that ZS steps over.	Does not take things that ZS steps over.

CLASSIFICATORY

Mother's Older Brother	Mother's Younger Brother
1 Can play, joke, and make sexual remarks of a very free nature.	Never make jokes or mention sex. Extreme deference and avoidance.
2 Speak in the vernacular.	Speak in the affinal language.
3 Food given and received freely.	ZS may not take food.
4 No fear of pollution.	Possible pollution.

165

was very much against the match, since she called David
'brother', and she thought it would be scandalous if the marriage
ever occurred. Apparently the romance had been going on for
some time and while Elsie's older brother, Harry, was out
working as a cattleman he had heard rumours that the marriage
had been arranged. He thought it most odd that this should be
done without consulting him and he was much put out about it.
Although he claimed that he had decided not to make a fuss
about it, nevertheless he took advantage of the meeting to air
his grievances, and to impress upon his sister that, if she had
agreed to the match, then she should stand by her word (by
this time I would say that he knew full well that she had not).
But she said that she never agreed to any such thing, and that
she certainly would not agree to any marriage concerning her
children without consulting her brothers.

Jane's father, practically throughout the whole discussion,
sat quietly in the background, as if the whole business was really
the concern of his wife and her brothers, as for the most part it
was. What I witnessed was in accordance with the ideal accounts
that I received from my informants. In marriage arrangements,
the mother's brothers, especially the mother's older brothers,
have a much greater say than the father. They claim that if a
man's wife's brothers should find a husband for his daughter
then he should accept their decision. On the other hand, the
Wik-mungkan realize that sometimes the father can be hard-
headed about the arrangements. The mother's brothers do not
roughly override the opinion of their sister's husband. Since
what is desired, in such a small community, is that everybody
should be in agreement, the mother's brothers sound out the
father to find out what he would like. In addition, the grandparents on both sides have a say. But of all the people involved,
the mother and mother's brothers have the main say.

Significantly enough, a couple of days after the meeting David
came to see Harry about marrying Harry's younger sister's
daughter. Harry, very softly, turned him down. He claimed
that he would like to agree, but he and David were too closely
related because they shared one grandparent (father's father, I
believe).

Turning to the father and son relationship, we find that it
differs from that of the mother's older brother and mother's

younger brother. On the one hand, it does not have the deference and distance as with a mother's younger brother, but
neither does it have the freedom, familiarity, and indulgence
characteristic of the mother's older brother and younger sister's
son relationship. While it is true that small children may play
up to their father and are treated with indulgence (Thomson
1935), nevertheless as they grow older they learn that a father
must be treated with respect. Children and older youths do
not make jokes of a sexual nature with a father, which, to some
extent, they may do with a mother's older brother.

While a father has moral authority over his children, and may
discipline them, from what I saw this did not go beyond a few
strong words. In the few quarrels that I witnessed it was quite
obvious that fathers backed up their sons. In one instance,
where I was present, after a quarrel a father took his son to one
side and explained to him what he had done wrong. He patiently
pointed out that his actions could cause trouble for others and
that he should behave himself. Children certainly are not in
fear or awe of their father. In contrast, I noticed that even very
small children were timid about visiting a mother's younger
brother.

There is an interesting pollution taboo separating a father
from his children. A man may not eat or consume anything
that his son or daughter has stepped over. Hence for this reason
children are often reminded that they should not step across,
in front of, their father but that they should go behind him.
Consequently if a man is eating, and he thinks that one of his
children might inadvertently step over his food, he will quickly
pick it up and turn slightly to one side. I noticed that even
when young men were visiting classificatory fathers, the latter
would put their food and tobacco out of the way and plead,
'Boy, you be careful. You don't want to step over my tobacco.'
If this should happen, the persons who may consume the goods
are primarily the mother's older brother and mother's father.

This seems to be an appropriate place to take up the oft-
made claim that a mother's brother is like a male mother in
societies with patrilineal systems of descent. Indeed, McConnel
says that among the Wik-mungkan the mother's brother 'is
something like a male mother' (McConnel 1934: 333). And it is
clear that she means the mother's younger brother, for she goes

on to say, 'In giving his daughters in marriage to them (ZS) he is providing for their future, as well as that of his daughters'. I inquired about this similarity, in a roundabout way, and I was told that just as a father's sister is like a father, so a mother's brother is like a mother. When I pressed my informants to be more specific about which mother's brother was meant, they said that both mother's brothers were loved, but that things were easier with a mother's older brother, for a mother's younger brother was a bit like a father-in-law. The fact that mother's older brother and younger brother and their sister are all referred to by the same term, i.e. *ami*, when their sister's child dies might indicate, as Thomson maintains, that both mother's brothers are regarded as being like a mother (Thomson 1946: 158). On the other hand, the fact that the mother's older brother but not the mother's younger brother, may eat at the mortuary feast indicates that the identification is not complete.

A number of problems converge here, viz. the corporateness of the sibling unit and its internal differentiation. For while there is a term for the sibling unit when a sister's child dies, there is also another term, *maki*, for this unit when a brother's child dies. This reflects the extent to which a woman and her children are regarded as members of her natal descent group and that of her husband. All this, coupled with the distinct difference in the pattern of behaviour with a mother's older and younger brother, has a bearing on the controversy of complementary filiation and affinity. Unfortunately for reasons of space I can do no more than draw attention to these engrossing points. But I hope to take them up at another time.

What clearly emerged from what my informants had to say was that as one should respect a father, so one should respect his sister. And even more so, for with an actual father's sister there is an element of avoidance. As I have already mentioned she is *ngaintja taiyin* and is referred to as 'poison auntie'. Yet she has every right to scold her brother's children. Thomson mentions that a father's older sister has the right to correct her brother's child should he swear (Thomson 1935: 470). Just as there are pollution and food taboos separating father and son, so we find similar taboos separating a woman and her brother's son. This applies particularly to those traditional foods which are regarded as being sexually suggestive, but apparently not to European food. Men do not converse much with their own father's sister, although there is no rule forbidding them to do so.

In contrast is the pattern of behaviour with the mother and mother's older brother. There is practically a special cooing voice that a woman uses for her children and any child with whom she stands in a mother relationship. While it is true that a woman may scold her children, it would be unusual for her to act harshly. Similarly, a mother's older brother has authority, and although he may give orders to his sister's son, such as telling him to stop fighting, it would be quite against the expected pattern of behaviour for him to act harshly. He is expected to be easy with his sister's son and to bend the rules in his favour.

The brother and sister relationship is also complicated by an age factor. While a man may talk directly, in a face-to-face manner, with his older sister, he may not do so with a younger sister. In the village I sometimes heard older sisters calling out their brother's name, and engaging him in an easy, friendly conversation. But a woman never does this with an older brother (in the marriage discussion that I described above, Elsie took care to sit sideways to her older brother, so as not to face him, and to talk away from him). While a younger brother and older sister may hand things to each other, in contrast an older brother and younger sister must give things to each other indirectly, usually through their children. An older sister, but not a younger one, might scold her brother. Notice the pattern of behaviour that emerges: I can converse and interact freely with my mother's older brother but not my mother's younger brother. My mother and my mother's older brother cannot interact directly, they usually do so through me and my siblings. In contrast, while I cannot interact directly with my mother's younger brother, my mother and mother's younger brother may interact quite freely.

This brings me to the final relationship that I wish to describe, that of husband and wife. Unfortunately I must end somewhat lamely but, as will be appreciated, such an intimate relationship as this is not readily understood in a short visit. It at least seemed to me not to be a relationship that was marred by much conflict. There was no hint of husbands being regarded as 'good' or wives as a source of evil. Nor did it seem that husbands were regarded as dominant and aggressive while wives were meek and submissive. I often saw husbands and wives sitting together, quietly talking to each other, or going out hunting with their children.

With the above information we are now in a better position to evaluate Homans and Schneider's theory of unilateral cross-cousin marriage, and Lévi-Strauss's Law of the Atom of Kinship.

VII

HOMANS AND SCHNEIDER'S THEORY

As is well known, Homans and Schneider have put forward a theory of cross-cousin marriage which can be summed up roughly as follows: given that a society has cross-cousin marriage, they maintain that they are able to predict which kind it will have, i.e. matrilateral or patrilateral, on the basis of the social structure and the locus of jural authority. Thus in societies with a patrilineal complex, with the father having jural authority, there is an easy relationship with the mother's brother and it will be sentimentally appropriate to marry his daughter. While in societies with a matrilineal complex, where there is avuncular jural authority, and the relationship with the father is the easy one, it will be sentimentally appropriate to marry the father's sister's daughter (Homans & Schneider 1955). Despite vigorous criticism by Rodney Needham, they have continued to adhere both to their theory and to the belief that Wik-mungkan ethnographic data support it (Homans & Schneider 1962).

There are a few points that I would like to make concerning whether or not the Wik-mungkan ethnography supports their theory and interpretation. First, it would seem that actual matrilateral cross-cousin marriage is very rare, and not favoured by the Wik-mungkan. They say that the children of actual cross-cousins will be sickly, and that it is better to marry more distant cousins. And not only for this reason, but because if you marry an actual cross-cousin, then in quarrels and fights close relatives become involved so it is better to marry far away (as is often the case among Australian Aboriginal societies, they express sociological distance in geographical terms,

170

although they well know that these terms do not always coincide). One actual matrilateral cross-cousin marriage was brought to my attention and this was mentioned in very scandalized and shocked tones. There may have been a couple of others. The only justification for marrying an actual cross-cousin seems to be that a more distant one is not available. To be fair to Homans and Schneider, there would have been little evidence for them to suspect that this is the picture, for McConnel repeatedly writes of actual matrilateral cross-cousin marriage – though in her genealogical material, as Needham has pointed out, there is only one such case. Nevertheless, if actual matrilateral cross-cousin marriage is rare, and not favoured, then this obviously weakens their case.

But suppose I am wrong, and that in the past, before European influence (I received the impression that the Wik-mungkan believe that Europeans frown on actual cousins marrying), actual matrilateral cross-cousin marriages were regarded as desirable and were frequent. Would this support Homans and Schneider's theory? I think not, because, as Needham has argued (Needham 1963a: 146-7), the marriage rule is that one should marry the daughter of a *kala* and not the daughter of a *muka*. Marriage is not with the daughter of an actual mother's older brother, with whom by and large there is an easy and friendly relationship, but with the daughter of a man in the category of mother's younger brother (*kala*). If marriage was allowed with the daughter of an actual *kala*, there would be nothing sentimentally appropriate about that, for there is nothing free and easy about the relationship with a mother's younger brother. It is one of distance and reserve. And with a classificatory mother's younger brother, this is even more the case, for it is an avoidance relationship. One must conclude, then, that not only are the Wik-mungkan not evidence for Homans and Schneider's theory, but that they would seem to constitute proof against it.

Homans and Schneider claim that the mother's brother (they do not distinguish between the two kinds of mother's brothers) among the Wik-mungkan does not have jural authority, and hence the Wik-mungkan are like the classic patrilineal complex (Homans & Schneider 1962: 531). But as I have indicated above, the mother's older brother undoubtedly does have jural authority. He may give orders, rather than just offer advice, but I think it would be rare for him to have to go to such lengths (see Homans & Schneider 1962: 529). I would also like to point out that although jural authority is exercised by the mother's older brother, this does not mean that the mother's younger brother is without jural authority. What happens follows quite logically from the fact that an older brother has authority over a younger brother. The older brother should be consulted in all family matters and normally he has the main say. This is what happens with matters concerning the sister's children, and all the more so since the mother's younger brother does not communicate directly with the older sister's son. Hence, as I have pointed out, the mother's younger brother is overshadowed by the mother's older brother.

VIII

LÉVI-STRAUSS'S LAW OF THE ATOM OF KINSHIP

This brings me to the final section of this paper. Lévi-Strauss, in his criticisms of Radcliffe-Brown's explanation of the mother's brother–sister's son pattern of behaviour, has formulated what might be called the Law of the Atom of Kinship. He claims that whether one is dealing with a society with a matrilineal, or a patrilineal, system of descent, there is 'a law which can be formulated as follows: In both groups, the relation between maternal uncle and nephew is to the relation between brother and sister as the relation between father and son is to that between husband and wife. Thus if we know one pair of relations, it is always possible to infer the other' (Lévi-Strauss 1968: 42).

Needham, in his criticism of Homans and Schneider's theory, has twice drawn attention to Lévi-Strauss's law, either with apparent approval, or with the indication that it should be seriously considered, when examining the conventional attitudes of these relationships. Thus in his last analysis of the Wik-mungkan material he writes:

'The result of a survey of Wik-mungkan conventional attitudes, then is:

$$MB/ZS : B/Z :: F/S : H/W$$
$$-\qquad -\qquad +\qquad +$$

This is in complete conformity with Lévi-Strauss' formula and with the confirmation it finds in other societies (cf. Needham 1962a, pp. 33-35), a fact which may be taken to indicate that the component attitudes have each been correctly determined' (Needham 1963a: 148).

But I would argue that there is no justification for believing that the component attitudes have, or have not, been correctly determined on the basis of whether or not they are in accordance with Lévi-Strauss's formula or law.

Let us for the sake of the argument accept that the relationships under discussion can be summarized by + and − signs (although personally at times I have found this difficult to do) according to whether the relationship is free and familiar (+), or one of hostility, antagonism, or reserve (−) (Lévi-Strauss 1968: 44).

As will be noticed, Needham summarizes the MB/ZS relationship with a minus sign. He is quite explicit that he is dealing with the actual mother's older brother. He seems to base his summary largely on Thomson's observation that the actual mother's older brother must be treated with some restraint, and some decorum, while one has a joking relationship with a classificatory mother's older brother. And so Needham concludes that 'it is precisely the mother's own brother who is singled out from the class of *muka* as demanding special respect' (Needham 1963a: 144). I readily enough agree with Thomson that some restraint and some decorum must be observed, for one cannot make jokes of such a crude nature as with a classificatory mother's older brother, or with a classificatory father's father. But one can make *some* jokes, and basically it is a friendly, easy, and indulgent relationship, which should more appropriately be summarized with a plus sign. Concerning this decorum and restraint, Needham seems to have failed to consider Thomson's observation that as a rule some restraint is required with actual or blood relations (Thomson 1935). On this point there is nothing singular in treating one's own mother's older brother with some respect. Nevertheless, if Needham were to persist in summarizing the mother's older brother and younger sister's son relationship with a minus, then I think that logically he would have to apply the same criteria to the actual father-son relationship, and sum that up with a minus sign too. But that undoubtedly would be a wrong summary. I doubt if anyone would quibble about giving the relationship of mother's younger brother and older sister's son a minus. Now in Wik-mungkan thought, in their conventional attitudes, and in the patterns of behaviour I have described, it is obvious that the two categories of mother's brothers are quite different. Yet if one were to accept Needham's summary of the mother's older brother and younger sister's son relationship, the result would be the same sign for two quite different relationships.

As for the father and son relationship, as I have already indicated, I would summarize this with a plus. Turning to the brother and sister relationship, we find once again that there are two categories to be taken into account. They both have different patterns of behaviour and conventional attitudes. It would seem reasonable to give the older sister and younger brother relationship a plus sign, but that of the younger sister and older brother a minus sign. As for the last relationship, i.e. husband and wife, I see no reason for quibbling with Needham's plus.

Taking all this into account, I would argue that the conventional attitudes might reasonably be summarized as follows:

$$1 \quad MOB/YZS \; : \; OB/YZ \; :: \; F/S \; : \; H/W$$
$$+ \qquad\quad - \qquad\quad + \qquad +$$

$$2 \quad MYB/OZS \; : \; OB/YZ \; :: \; F/S \; : \; H/W$$
$$- \qquad\quad - \qquad\quad + \qquad +$$

$$3 \quad MOB/YZS \; : \; YB/OZ \; :: \; F/S \; : \; H/W$$
$$+ \qquad\quad + \qquad\quad + \qquad +$$

$$4 \quad MYB/OZS \; : \; YB/OZ \; :: \; F/S \; : \; H/W$$
$$- \qquad\quad + \qquad\quad + \qquad +$$

Of these, only number 2 would agree with Needham's summary and would be in accordance with Lévi-Strauss's Law of the Atom of Kinship. It should be noted that of these four relationships only two have two categories, i.e. that of mother's brother–sister's son, and brother and sister. While the other two, i.e. father and son, husband and wife, have only one. For, following Lévi-Strauss, I deal only with actual relationships.

174

Thus if one were to ask what is the conventional attitude with mother's brother and sister's son, one would have to stipulate which mother's brother is being referred to. The same holds with the brother and sister relationship. But this does not occur with the relationships of father and son or husband and wife.

It might be argued that the reason why three out of the above four do not fit Lévi-Strauss's law is because of the peculiar system that the Wik-mungkan have, i.e. that his formula was never intended to fit such a system where an age distinction is made among the mother's brothers as well as other relatives. But the only qualification in applying the formula is that the society should have a patrilineal or matrilineal system of descent. Nevertheless, one out of the four fits Lévi-Strauss's formula, so to some extent it has proved applicable. And when all is said and done, we are dealing with an odd society, so if I am to make my point that Lévi-Strauss's formula does not always hold, I must turn to another society which is not so extraordinary. It seems to me that for another Australian society, the Walbiri of the Northern Territories, the relationships are all plus.

Concerning the mother's brother–sister's son relationship, Meggitt writes, 'ordinary daily intercourse between adult mother's brother and sister's son is informal, with no obvious display of respect by the junior men. Sexual joking is common although I never observed any physical horseplay' (Meggitt 1962: 138).

The brother and sister relationship seems also to be plus, for we are told that, 'Brothers and sisters generally remain on affectionate terms throughout their lives. They do not have to avoid each other in daily activities and their intercourse shows a relaxed familiarity' (Meggitt 1962: 139).

The father and son relationship is obviously another plus relationship, for according to Meggitt, 'The marked affective bond between father and son, which develops early in the boy's infancy and persists until death, is manifested in many situations. Until they are initiated, boys are indulged by their fathers to an extent rarely observed in our own society. Only on two occasions did I see a man strike a young son; and the mother who tries even mild and warranted castigation of the boy usually incurs her husband's displeasure' (Meggitt 1962: 116).

175

David McKnight

We are also told that there is an 'absence of formal etiquette' and that there is a 'relaxed relationship between men and their adult sons' and also 'Mild joking, including obscenities, is allowed, but it never develops into physical horseplay' (Meggitt 1962: 117).

The husband and wife relationship also seems to be plus, for despite some domestic bickering and quarrelling Meggitt emphasizes that there is a strong bond of affection between husband and wife (Meggitt 1962: 85 ff.). Clearly, this society disproves the universality of Lévi-Strauss's Law of the Atom of Kinship.

IX

CONCLUSIONS

In concluding, I sum up some of the main points of this paper. I maintain that in analysing any kinship and marriage system it is methodologically wrong to do so in terms of what I have described as Ego-restricted kinship terms, or genealogical restricted kinship terms. One cannot argue from the basis of the kinship terms that Ego and his actual siblings may use for particular marriage partners, that such a marriage is necessarily recognized, in the same terms, by the rest of society. McConnel attempts to do this, and so her analysis of the Wik-mungkan kinship and marriage system suffers. In addition, the fact that she elects to arrange her chart so that actual FoZ and FyZ do not marry actual MoB and MyB has serious implications for her analysis. It reinforces her erroneous claim that the Wik-mungkan marriage system is unilateral and contributes to the peculiar complexity of her kinship chart. In order to represent both actual and classificatory relatives, and deal with genealogical restricted kinship terms, she has drawn additional lines laterally and so has constructed a system with six lines of descent. I would argue that there are not six lines as she claims, or three as suggested by Lévi-Strauss, but only two. I think that the reader will agree that two lines give a reasonably clear diagrammatic illustration of the kinship system.

Such alleged characteristics as men marrying to the right and women marrying to the left, men marrying into younger lines while women marry into older lines, men marrying down while

176

women marry up, and that there is an age-spiral marriage system, are only features of McConnel's kinship charts. I think I have been able to prove this and how it arose. Since I in turn have drawn a kinship chart, I run the risk of being criticized for making the same mistakes as I have accused McConnel of making, and my chart could be faulted for having the weaknesses common to all Ego-orientated kinship charts. I well recognize the latter point and the only reason why I have drawn the chart is to illustrate that a much simpler one than McConnel's can be constructed. As for the former point, a careful reader will note that I have not attempted to analyse the kinship and marriage system, the conventional attitudes, and the various patterns of behaviour in terms of my chart.

I have attempted to set the record right as to what are the correct kinship terms, particularly for daughter's son and daughter's daughter. As for moieties, there is no doubt, as far as I am concerned, that the Wik-mungkan do not have named moieties but there is some indication that they have unnamed moieties.

Concerning the type of marriage exchange that the Wik-mungkan practise, i.e. generalized or restricted exchange, I have queried Lévi-Strauss's claim that there is a gradual transition from the former to the latter. His interpretation of the exchange of an actual sister for a classificatory sister of a brother-in-law would not make the Wik-mungkan unique in practising both types of exchange. How one interprets the exchange would depend on what units are involved in the exchange, i.e. family, lineage, clan, etc. In my view the largest descent groups (*vis-à-vis* categories) involved are the clans and it is at this level that marriage exchange should be viewed. The fact that the Wik-mungkan have a term for 'woman-givers' or 'wife-givers' (I do not know if they have a term for wife-receivers) does not seem to be conclusive proof that only restricted exchange between clans is practised.

I have drawn attention to the fact that marriage with a classificatory daughter's daughter may occur. And I argue that, contrary to Lévi-Strauss's claim, marriage with a woman in this category, i.e. 'of a younger generation in an older line', does not eliminate competition between the grandfather and grandson. At least not in the manner that he alleges.

Following Needham, I conclude that the Wik-mungkan ethnography does not support Homans and Schneider's theory of unilateral cross-cousin marriage. First, because actual matrilateral cross-cousin marriage seems to be rare and not favoured by the Wik-mungkan. Second, because marriage is with the daughter of a man in the category of *kala* (MyB) and not *muka* (MoB), which is the opposite of what would be expected if their theory is valid. I have also brought attention to the fact that, the mother's brothers, particularly the mother's older brother, have jural authority, so confirming Needham's contention that 'jural authority does not necessarily preclude or inhibit a warm and intimate relationship' (Needham 1963a: 149).[8]

In attempting to apply Lévi-Strauss's formula to the Wik-mungkan, I find myself in some disagreement with Needham's summary and also as to the validity of this formula (I think it only fair to add here that from personal communication I understand that Needham, since his 1963a article on the Wik-mungkan, has collected a great many examples which run contrary to Lévi-Strauss's Law and his views on this matter have changed). The matter is more complicated than he formerly realized, for in this society there seem to be four possible combinations. And of these, three do not fit Lévi-Strauss's formula. Further, relying solely on Meggitt's book, *Desert People*, it appears that among the Walbiri all the relationships are plus. So this at least is one society, not complicated by the factor of age, that is not in accordance with Lévi-Strauss's formula.

POSTSCRIPT

Since this paper was given I have been able to visit the Wik-mungkan for about ten weeks. I am indebted to the Social Science Research Council for a grant enabling me to do so. This subsequent field trip has encouraged me to believe that the main points of this paper will stand. I have therefore decided not to make any changes in the paper, although, naturally, there are additional points that I could have made. However, this was the case even before I revisited the Wik-mungkan, but for reasons of space I was unable to do so. I hope to deal with these points in another paper which I am now working on.

Some Problems concerning the Wik-mungkan

NOTES

1. I would like to take this opportunity to thank Rev. and Mrs John Gillanders as well as Mr and Mrs Neil McGarvie for their kind assistance.

2. I am indebted to the Australian Institute of Aboriginal Studies for a field-work grant which enabled me to visit Aurukun.

3. *Figures 1* and *2* are McConnel's 1940 and 1950 Wik-mungkan kinship charts. I might add here that in order not to complicate matters I have wherever feasible used McConnel's terms and spelling. Where this has not been possible I have turned to Thomson, and failing this I have had recourse to my own data.

4. There is some indication that McConnel might have been aware of the ambiguity of the classification of father's sister's daughter's son. For she has both *nengka* and *wunya* for cousin-mother's son in some of her charts. And in one chart, i.e. *Figure 2*, she has just *nengka*. Unfortunately what she writes, and what she puts in her charts and diagrams in different publications, are often at variance and self-contradictory.

5. It seems to me that much of the Murngin controversy is founded on this very confusion coupled with Ego-restricted kinship terms.

6. In another context Needham has drawn attention to this point (Needham 1957: 178).

7. The implications all this has on Radcliffe-Brown's famous hypothesis on the mother's brother–sister's son are, I feel, so obvious that I need not dwell on them here.

8. No doubt the reader has noticed the extent of my indebtedness to Rodney Needham. That I have not acknowledged this point by point is only due to the fact I have absorbed so much from his work that it would have been difficult to draw attention to every instance.

REFERENCES

ELKIN, A. P. 1940. *Kinship in South Australia.* Sydney: Angus & Robertson.

HOMANS, G. C. & SCHNEIDER, D. M. 1955. *Marriage Authority and Final Causes: A Study of Unilateral Cross-Cousin Marriage.* Glencoe.

—— 1962. Mother's Brother in Wikmunkan Society. *Ethnology* 1.

LEACH E. 1961. *Rethinking Anthropology.* London: Athlone Press.

LÉVI-STRAUSS, CLAUDE. 1968. *Structural Anthropology.* London: Weidenfeid & Nicolson. (1963. New York: Basic Books.)

—— 1969. *The Elementary Structures of Kinship.* London: Eyre & Spottiswoode.

MCCONNEL, U. H. 1934. The Wikmunkan and Allied Tribes of Cape York Peninsula. *Oceania* 4.

—— 1939. Social Organization of the Tribes of Cape York Peninsula. *Oceania* 10.

David McKnight

MCCONNEL, U. H. 1940. Social Organization of the Tribes of Cape York Peninsula. *Oceania* **10**.

—— 1950. Junior Marriage Systems: A Comparative Survey. *Oceania* **21**.

MEGGITT, M. J. 1962. *Desert People*. Sydney: Angus & Robertson.

NEEDHAM, R. 1957. Circulating Connubium in Eastern Sumba. *Bijdragen tot de Taal-, Land- en Volkenkunde* **113**.

—— 1962a. *Structure and Sentiment*. Chicago: University of Chicago Press.

—— 1962b. Genealogy and Category in Wikmunkan Society. *Ethnology* **1**.

—— 1963a. The Wikmunkan Mother's Brother: Inference and Evidence. *Journal of the Polynesian Society* **72**.

—— 1963b. A Note on Wikmunkan Marriage. *Man* **63**.

—— 1965. A Corrective Comment on Wikmunkan Marriage. *Man* **65**.

RADCLIFFE-BROWN A. R. 1930. The Social Organization of Australian Tribes, II. *Oceania* **1**.

THOMSON, D. F. 1935. The Joking Relationship and Organized Obscenity in North Queensland. *American Anthropologist* **37**.

—— 1936. Fatherhood in the Wik Monkan Tribe. *American Anthropologist* **38**.

—— 1946. Names and Naming in the Wik Mongkan Tribe. *Journal of the Royal Anthropological Institute* **76**.

—— 1955. Two Devices for the Avoidance of First-Cousin Marriage Among the Australian Aborigines. *Man* **55**.

8

T. O. Beidelman

Some Kaguru Notions about Incest and Other Sexual Prohibitions

I

INTRODUCTION

Since the beginning of anthropological interest in the study of kinship, it was recognized that the key issue was the incest prohibition. From Tylor to Lévi-Strauss, the sociological utility of such rules has been unhesitatingly affirmed, and, far before Freud, the psychological affect surrounding incest has been a topic for considerable speculation. But despite this long period of interest, we know relatively little regarding the attitudes towards incest in other societies. For that matter, our understanding of such behaviour in our own society is still far murkier than many would like.

It seems safe to assume that those factors which inhibit our own clear understanding of various aspects of our feelings toward incest resemble those which inhibit informants and researcher alike from discussing the topic clearly and frankly in the field. It is one thing to ask informants whom one may sleep with or marry, and quite another to persuade them to say how they 'really' feel about any acts which break these rules. Occasionally, a ribald song or lewd remark may hint at some libidinously pleasurable associations with these acts, but this hardly allows us to fill in much of a picture about these attitudes. It may be that one day subtler and more intensive psychological tests will be applied in the field. At present, while some such studies have been done, these have all, to varying extent, been directed in form. Either an interviewer (usually not the psychologist himself, who tends to be unfamiliar with a native language) guides – sometimes intentionally, sometimes unintentionally – an interview along certain channels, or visual cues will be used to suggest such behaviour. While these techniques are certainly a valid and useful path of analysis, another means does seem available for at least some societies.

This may provide a useful though modest complement to more direct research. I refer to the study of folklore.

By folklore, I do not refer to myths, those complex accounts explaining broad and profound aspects of man, nature, and society. Rather, I mean those stories, tales, sayings, and proverbs which colour everyday life and which people recount in their more relaxed and casual moments. If myths are re-counted at times of formality, stress, or perplexity, in guarded moments when men must dress and adorn experience into bearable and explicable garb, then folklore represents men at play in their shirt-sleeves and sloppy attire. Yet folklore is no less important than myth, for play too provides men with means for speculation and catharsis, perhaps even more radical and un-inhibited in nature than does myth, precisely because folklore's very status as play removes it from a stage of critical scrutiny which formal myth bears. Of course, it may be argued that folktales do not necessarily represent the typical attitudes or feelings of the members of a society. I would argue that in a society such as Kaguru, where there is little literacy and traditional folktales are known and told by most, this may be far more representative than any questionnaires. Its very spontaneity and removal from the stress of actual social situations may allow real feelings to be expressed more readily.

Unfortunately, not all societies seem to exhibit the same interest and taste for storytelling (or perhaps not all social anthropologists are keen on collecting folklore texts). But where such tales abound, they would seem a useful area for research into various attitudes and values. In the essay below I try to use such material gathered from one East African society in order better to understand that people's feelings about incest.

In the first part of this paper I present what is known ethnographically about Kaguru notions of incest and exogamy. In the next, I relate the few cases of such behaviour which I encountered during my fieldwork. In the following section I cite those folktales I recorded which seem to deal with incest and other prohibited sexual relations. In the conclusion I suggest what further insights folklore may provide regarding Kaguru feelings about such behaviour and make a few general-izations about Kaguru incest. It is hoped that even if the value

of these final sections is debatable, the initial sections will add
to the ethnographic record.[1]

II

PROHIBITIONS

The Kaguru are a group of cultivators inhabiting east-central
Tanzania, East Africa. They speak a Bantu-type language. In
terms of the problems raised in this paper, their most important
feature is that they are matrilineal, being divided into about
one hundred exogamous, matrilineal clans by which certain
important political and religious activities are determined and
by which marriage is regulated.

Kaguru dislike discussing incest. The most common term for
such acts is *uhai*, witchcraft (cf. Beidelman 1963b), it often
being said that such activity would be enjoyed only by witches,
that is, by profoundly antisocial persons. To talk about either
topic too much might suggest that one had first-hand knowledge.

The English term *incest* itself is not entirely appropriate for
Kaguru in the sense that it suggests a set of prohibitions comparable to those in European societies. In the sense that Kaguru
notions involve certain strict prohibitions against sexual relations and purported feelings of revulsion at the prospect of
such relations, such a comparison is valid. But matters are more
complex than this, especially in regard to the relation of these
ideas to the concepts of exogamy and endogamy. Perhaps the
best introduction to this complicated topic is to relate the
various prohibitions Kaguru hold regarding sexual relations
and marriage.

Marriage-wise, the most basic rule in Kaguru society is to
observe tribal endogamy. It is considered best if one Kaguru
marries another. If such a rule is broken, there is a sliding scale
for judging the badness of the lapse. Least of all, in terms of
badness, a Kaguru may marry a member of one of the matrilineal peoples neighbouring them. In such a case, a Kaguru
may even be marrying a person with a clan name similar to
that of a Kaguru group. This is considered nearly as good as

T. O. Beidelman

marrying a Kaguru since Kaguru legend derives all these matrilineal peoples from one stock. A union with a person from a non-matrilineal people is generally considered far less desirable. Such peoples, in turn, are further divided into those who circumcise and those who do not. The latter, such as the Nyamwezi, Hehe, and Sukuma, are sometimes spoken of as not properly human (cf. Beidelman 1964b: 40-1). Circumcision is seen by Kaguru as imprinting order and stability upon a man. For a Kaguru woman to cohabit with an uncircumcised man would be considered an act of pollution, but Kaguru are not opposed to Kaguru men marrying outsider women, provided that such women take up residence in Kaguruland. This may be related to certain features of Kaguru matriliny, for it is said that in the past many affluent men preferred to take a slave wife, that is, an outsider lacking any kin who might attempt to retrieve the woman and her offspring. In this way, an elder attempted to solve the 'matrilineal puzzle'.

The most stringent prohibition of incest is that against relations between members of the same matriclan. This is tantamount to witchcraft and is said to show that one does not recognize one of the basic criteria defining humanity. Kaguru say, 'One has many women [available], but few sisters', with the double meaning that others can be had so why be concerned with those few who are forbidden, and that because one's sisters are so few they should be treasured. However, Kaguru also speak of how a sister is the most appetizing (alluring) of foods. (Sexuality is often expressed in terms of cuisine.) Kaguru say that this prohibition extends to all persons whose clan has the same name. However, this is not as clear as it first appears. There are a few Kaguru clans with composite names, such as the Quarreller-Rat and Quarreller-Elephant clans, or the Cornborer-Wildcat, Cornborer-Anteater, Cornborer-Cow, and Cornborer-Mamboya (a specific mountain) clans. Kaguru say that these derived from a common clan but divided due to various legendary events. Kaguru are not agreed whether it is proper for such groups to intermarry, though most informants felt that it was wrong. Furthermore, certain other clans, without similar names, form phratries which are said to be exogamous. It appears that marriage between such groups only rarely occurs, but it may be that these links reflect a gradual fissioning process

184

accompanied by decreasing sanctions against such unions. It is thought that any sexual connexion between persons of the same or linked clans would endanger all of the members of these groups, whereas other kinds of prohibited sexual unions would only endanger the members of the lineages or households to which the offenders belonged. The punishment for such offences was harsh indeed. Sometimes the offenders' ears were cut off and they were driven from the neighbourhood or sold into slavery. It is said that the ears were cut off in order to mark them, even to strangers, as heinous criminals. Such persons were socially 'dead', and no bridewealth or bloodwealth could be collected for them. If they were slain, the clan's joking partners (*watani*) were given this polluting task.[2] The ritual joking partners also sacrificed a black sheep and then smeared its blood, entrails, and the entrails' contents upon themselves before eating it. This resembles the purificatory rites for other sexual offences, but in this case it is thought that the offence was so horrible that even these extreme efforts could not entirely purify the polluted clan. Only the death (actual or metaphorical) of the offenders would suffice, along with what appears to be a gradual waning through time of these malevolent forces.

Kaguru also prohibit sexual relations between persons whose fathers have the same matriclan. Such persons are said to be related by having the same *welekwa* (they were born; from *kuleka*, to bear). Sexual relations between persons of the same *welekwa* are called *matana* (abuse; from *kutana*, to abuse, insult) and are thought to cause sterility and illness among those closely related to the offenders, but not to the offenders themselves. Kaguru also say that were such persons to marry, it would place the two new fathers-in-law in a difficult position, for the fathers of a bride and groom are traditionally at odds with one another over bridewealth and the future control of the couple and their children, yet men of the same clan are supposed to exhibit solidarity. Nonetheless, some marriages of this sort take place. In the course of my fieldwork, I noted three such cases, although it was difficult to gain details about them. It is said that such unions would never involve close kin such as persons who could actually trace descent genealogically. Before such unions may take place, a payment must be made of a sheep, which is slain and eaten by the joking partners of the clan involved. The sheep is cut in half down its length; this is called *n'homa lukolo* (killing the clan).

However, most disputes and difficulties over infractions of sexual prohibitions do not involve clan incest or *welekwa* incest; these may well involve profound and powerful feelings among Kaguru, but actual offences seem to be uncommon. The commonest form of offence against sexual prohibitions, outside simple adultery, involves what Kaguru call *mahasa* (from *kuhasa*, to mix, confuse). Kaguru say that it is good that alliances be continued between clans which have intermarried, but they forbid more than one marriage at a time between persons of the same generation within two clans. The rule is phrased thus, that brothers of one clan should not marry or have sexual relations with sisters of another. However, Kaguru can hardly know or care about all such people when deciding proper sexual conduct. There are about one hundred matriclans for a Kaguru population which today exceeds one hundred thousand and the members of each clan are scattered over most of the country. Kaguru apply the rule in terms of their immediate kin, that is, those persons who can trace matrilineal relationship or even those of one clan who cannot trace descent but who live near one another. In short, it applies to all persons of the same clan who have meaningful social relations. It is said that this is to prevent women of the same clan from competing for sexual favours from the same man or brothers. Sexual competition and its associated affect is seen as opposed to authority and stability.

Such prohibited behaviour is thought to cause supernatural danger to the lineal kin of the offenders, especially to those of the woman or women involved. One of the most common patterns was for a man to seduce his wife's sister, though it would be equally bad for a woman to commit adultery with her husband's brother. However, this prohibition involves more than the idea of an adulterous union; a man who seduced two sisters, even though neither was married, would still have broken this rule. For Kaguru, all sexual relations outside marriage potentially involve the payment of a fine to those with jural rights in the woman. But *mahasa* involves more than this; for unlike an ordinary adultery no marriage could ever take place and the issue is not simply that of an infraction of jural rights but of serious mystical dangers to the kin of those involved. *Mahasa* is cleansed by the payment of *nhemera* (butchery, the removal of entrails from a carcass). The kin of the offenders provide a black sheep to their ritual joking partners. These along with the offenders go off into the bush, the area of wilderness and pollution. There the thighs of the offenders are rubbed with the head of the sacrificial sheep.[3] The joking partners then kill the sheep, rub its entrails and their contents on themselves, and then roast and eat it. It is said that this removes the most serious pollution which is thought to be especially dangerous for the women involved, whose roles as genetrices for a matrilineage are threatened with sterility and imperfect children. It is also said that sometimes additional payments of sheep or goats are made – *ndima* (guide) and *hangasa* (meaning unclear) – but I could not learn when or to whom these were made.

In general, one can say that Kaguru see *mahasa* as endangering the solidarity of matrilineal groups by setting women in competition against one another for the affection and loyalties of lovers and potential husbands. In any matrilineal system, sisters are already set in competition in the sense that each woman's children form a unit with reference to senior men (the women's brothers) from whom they seek resources and support. A woman's children are her route to security and power, and in her struggles, at least against her matrilineal kin, her husband is a potential ally. For this reason, Kaguru probably find it difficult for sisters to share the same man.[4] Kaguru are also especially concerned that sexual relations shall not jeopardize patterns of authority. Such acts are also *mahasa*. But in these cases, sexual congress forbidden during the life of an elder becomes possible, even obligatory, after his death. Here, the corporate aspects of a matrilineage present certain ambiguities, through time, with competition and self-interest. Thus, a Kaguru is forbidden sexual relations with his mother's brother's wife and any such adulterous relations require extensive purificatory ritual as well as adultery fines; but at the elder's death, the nephew may take the woman in widow-inheritance. Kaguru say that in the past, this was required. (Today it is illegal to enforce it.) Even if the woman were old or ill the men of the deceased's lineage were expected to marry her and care for

T. O. Beidelman

her. It also sometimes happens that a mother's brother may seduce a nephew's wife. This is also a serious case of *mahasa*, especially since such elders should never inherit the widows of their juniors. Similarly, young brothers and older maternal parallel cousins may inherit their 'brother's' wives, but not those of their juniors if they be closely related. It is thought that such inheritance would suggest that those in authority may have used their power against their juniors, much as David used his against Uriah in order to gain Bathsheba and legitimize her pregnancy. In the case of the Kaguru, such illegitimate use of the power in authority is seen as witchcraft. For Kaguru, all authority carries some ambiguous overtones of witchcraft, and this is especially so in their matrilineal relations (cf. Beidelman 1961a: 1963c). When Kaguru inherit widows who, while their husbands were alive, would have been forbidden to them sexually, the inheritance rites are always supervised by ritual joking partners who, half-jokingly, half-seriously, ask the candidate for inheritance whether indeed he is the witch who killed his kinsman to gain wealth or a wife.

This may further relate to another notion held by Kaguru – that to marry a woman always connotes some superiority over those who previously possessed jural authority over her. Thus I have heard affines of the same generation bickering, and sometimes the man who has secured the woman may allude to the fact that he is the husband while the other man, the wife's relative, is himself a kind of 'wife'. As I discuss later, Kaguru seem especially sensitive to the fact that 'outsiders' have secured their sisters, who sometimes even fall in love with these 'strangers', thereby weakening the affection they have towards their brothers.

Adultery with one's father's wife falls outside all of the prohibited categories of sexual relations mentioned so far. Yet it is considered a far more grievous offence than mere adultery. I could secure no first-hand accounts of such situations, but I was told that the wife would be sent home, her bridewealth returned, and the offending son disinherited and cursed. But both divorce and cursing are sanctions that apply to many other acts besides such adultery. No pollution adheres to those involved, though the woman would be thought shameless and the son, if cursed, would be ostracized by many of his kin.

188

Although I have discussed cursing elsewhere (1963c), a *résumé* is in order here since it throws some light on the notions associated with prohibited sexual relations between kin. The only persons who may curse (*kuligita*; *kuliga*, to abuse; *maligo*, foul language) are a person's biological parents. This is done by the parent confronting the child naked and making both physical and verbal references to sex. Since all references to sex in front of a parent are strictly forbidden, and vice versa, such a curse amounts to a kind of symbolic incest or witchcraft severing the bonds of kinship forever.

There is a further parallel between cursing and the supernatural sanctions punishing infractions against various sexual prohibitions. Both depend upon what Kaguru conceive of as biological bases. One cannot curse if one is not a true parent. Kaguru sometimes wryly remark that only a mother's curse is utterly certain, for one can never be absolutely sure who one's father is.[5] One Kaguru told me that it was important that one's children be biologically one's own for this reason. (Kaguru allow men jural control as fathers of children which are informally recognized as born from adultery.) Similarly, it is the biological ties of kin that generate the most serious supernatural dangers due to infractions of various sexual prohibitions. Thus, the ties of matriliny through blood (cf. Beidelman 1961b; 1963a) involve persons most seriously and deeply in such dangers: the most dangerous infraction jeopardizing the most persons is clan incest; and even in *mahasa*, which involves persons of several clans, it is the polluted women and their kinsmen who are most seriously endangered. Below I briefly indicate the nature of some of these processes as well as the etiquette related to the bodily expression of such prohibitions.

The offspring of prohibited unions are said always to be abnormal: malformed, feeble-minded, or short-lived. The blood of the offenders' kin is disturbed, turned hot, and this may cause them illness or sterility; it may even harm their livestock or crops, for even the land itself may be so heated and disturbed. If one breaks a minor rule of etiquette related to such prohibitions, such as stepping over the legs of such a person when he or she is seated with legs outstretched, one may suffer from *matulila* (*kutula*, to erupt, as in a rash), sores on one's body such as one often gets from infections in the tropics.

Significantly, prohibited sexual behaviour is actually enjoined on at least two occasions, in both cases to counteract malevolent disturbing forces which are thought to be cooled in this way: (1) if a field fails to yield, despite proper care, Kaguru may assemble and throw garbage and waste upon it, shout sexual abuse (*maligo*) at it and, some say, commit indecent sexual acts between persons prohibited from such behaviour; (2) if a newly circumcised youth seems in some danger of not recovering, it is said that sometimes his kin will assemble at night and dance, drink, and commit prohibited sexual acts – regardless, according to some Kaguru, of the rules of incest – in order to speed his recovery. In these two instances, one simply fights fire with fire and conquers disorder by greater disorder. It may even be that, from a broad and alienated perspective, the Kaguru witch is the strongest and most masterful of persons, the super-hero, in that he or she has gained powers to be used regardless of the moral limitations set by society. In this sense, perhaps the equation of witchcraft with incest represents, at least for Kaguru, the expression of their realization that sexual prohibitions (especially those involving one's sisters) are the central aspect of their social system.

Persons prohibited sexual relations should never eat together. In practice, Kaguru men and women usually eat separately in any case, but sometimes one may see spouses eating together. (The mark of a boy's maturity is his no longer being allowed to eat food in the back of the house with his mother and the other, younger, children.) Prohibited sexual partners should not sit on the same mat or ever discuss sex, except in the most circumspect terms. Nor should they ever walk hand-in-hand (something otherwise common among Kaguru of both opposite or the same sex). Nor should such persons ever sleep under the same roof, although with the introduction of larger, multi-roomed European-type houses this rule is now relaxed. Nor should such persons ever use the same bathing spot, even at different times. (In general, the two sexes should not bathe near one another, since women are polluting and therefore should bathe downstream from men.) Such persons may enter one another's houses, but they should never approach, much less touch, a bed. Thus, when I lived for some months in a European-type house of a Kaguru couple, I had some problem with the children playing with some of my things. I found, on the advice of the parents, that I could leave my camera and other fragile items safely by placing them on the parents' bed.

III

INFRACTIONS

During my stay in Kaguruland I encountered relatively few cases involving the infraction of sexual prohibitions, although I was told that *mahasa*, at least, was not uncommon. The cases I learned about appear below:

1. A young teacher's wife became ill and went to hospital and her sister was sent to keep house for the man, cooking and cleaning. He had sexual relations with her and she later told others about this. One of the relatives of the women was an influential official and forced the teacher to pay *nhemera* as well as other fines. The case was heard informally, not in a court, and the couple are still married. Since the young man had a well-paying job with the mission, all concerned were keen to keep the matter quiet. The main concern was removing pollution and sufficiently punishing the youth so that he would not commit a similar offence again. The entire issue was precipitated by illness in the girl's matrilineage, thought to be caused by this infraction.

2. It was rumoured, that a man had sexual relations with his daughter. She had produced a child out of wedlock and the father was unknown. Naturally, it was impossible for me to secure any information on this delicate issue, other than local gossip and rumour.

3. A very prominent Kaguru official married his sister's son's widow. This deeply upset people, who gossiped that this would never have been allowed in the past and that it showed he might be a witch who had killed his nephew in order to secure a young wife. Some said such a forbidden union (not forbidden by national law, however) would not have been possible were the offender not such a powerful official.

191

4. A couple with the same *welekwa* sought to marry. Both sets of kin refused to recognize the union or to pay or receive bride-wealth. The couple eloped to a nearby town. Three children were born, one dying prematurely, one retarded, and one normal. Kaguru dwell on the two unfortunate births, not the normal one. The couple later separated.

5. Musa was impotent. It is said that he built his house far from others so that he could keep track of his dissatisfied wife. Nonetheless, the woman seduced Musa's sister's son, a lad of fifteen. The affair is reputed to have continued for more than a year, until she became pregnant. Since the husband apparently could not father a child himself, perhaps it is not surprising that he was somewhat reluctant to press a case. However, some of his matrilineal kin insisted that a case be made and a cleansing ceremony performed. The youth confessed, arguing that he had been afraid of his aunt and therefore had complied, suggesting that perhaps she had used witchcraft to seduce him. The youth's kin paid *nhemera*. The offence was mitigated by the offender's youth. The wife was not divorced; the new child became legally that of the uncle. When the uncle died, soon after, his younger brother, who lacked a wife, inherited the wife.

IV

FOLKLORE

In this section I indicate what insights Kaguru folklore provides to our understanding of Kaguru sexual prohibitions. My conclusions are sketchy, at best, but the data do seem to express ideas and feelings more dramatically yet quite consistently with the preceding information.

In surveying the occurrence of incestuous themes in Kaguru folklore, it is difficult to determine what value to assign the frequency with which these themes appear. For one thing, at some times such acts are explicitly rendered while at others they are suggested only indirectly. Whether the motifs I list in this latter category always deal with prohibited sexual behaviour depends in part upon my own subjective understanding of Kaguru society. Furthermore, the tales I collected are not all equally well known. Some, such as those about Hare and Hyena and their mothers (1961a, 1963d) or about Mukejuwa (1963c) seem fairly widely told and popular. Others seem less well known and are perhaps the creations of individual story-tellers today. While it is true that all of these, regardless of popularity, are in some sense illustrative of Kaguru culture by the very fact that Kaguru have conceived and told them, some are doubtless more representative than others. However, even this point is more complex than first appears, for certain drama-tic and unusually extreme patterns are still grounded in the same set of social forces which usually fail to take such bold expression. For example, it is difficult for us to be sure to what extent classic Oedipal situations simply represent an extreme and dramatic expression of a far more general familial situation involving sexuality, affect, and authority in our society.

Since my data were not collected with such complex issues in mind, I lack the information to clarify these issues. I cannot even be sure how popular each of the texts collected is, since I worked in only three areas of Kaguruland and relied on only three or four informants for most of my folktales. I collected one hundred and seventy folktales as well as many riddles, a few proverbs and some legends of clan origins. Sixty-nine of the tales have been published or are in press and all of the riddles and some of the legends have been published. Below I provide a brief description of each tale in which a theme of prohibited sexual relations seems to appear. Where this seems somewhat questionable, I indicate in footnotes the reasons for my views. After all of these tales have been related, I try to make a few brief generalizations about this material.

1. A youth grossly mistreats his sister after their parents are dead, mainly by depriving her of food. Eventually she exposes him by magical powers (unpublished).[6]

2. A youth wants to marry a girl as beautiful as his sister. While searching for a wife, he comes upon a girl bathing whom he at first mistakes for his sister. She conceals her lower body in the water but promises to emerge if he first shoots his parents and sister. He does so but when he returns she taunts him and disappears into the water. Another youth with similar notions and aims comes upon the girl and pretends to shoot his parents and sisters for her. She taunts him and he shoots her; when he

examines her body she is found to have no lower half (unpublished).[7]

3. A chief repeatedly kills his daughters but spares his sons. One son conceals a sister when she is born. When his father dies, he fetches his sister and resides with her and their mother (unpublished).

4. A youth's grandmother cheats him over food, but this act indirectly provides him with the means of securing a wife (unpublished).[8]

5. A father kills his daughters and spares his son. The son saves one of his sisters and goes off with her. When she matures, the sister betrays her brother and has him killed in order to marry a stranger. The brother does not die but is transformed into a child which is found by the evil sister, who raises it. When he is again mature, the brother kills all of his affines and his sister and then returns home (unpublished).

6. A youth sees his maternal uncle's wife give birth and later marries that child, which soon dies (unpublished).[9]

7. Hare and his maternal uncle Hyena trick one another over food. Hyena is deceived into killing and eating his mother. Hare pretends to commit a similar act. Later Hare saves his mother from Hyena, who has discovered the ruse. Hare and Hyena travel about, with Hare repeatedly tricking Hyena as they struggle over food. During their travels Hyena deceives a woman into eating her daughter. In the end Hyena is killed by Hare (unpublished).[10]

8. A brother and sister are orphaned and live alone in the wilderness. The boy repeatedly deceives his sister over food. Later they move to a rich village where people lack anuses. They kill the inhabitants by wounding them to make anuses and then later kill a kinswoman of the villagers by means of witchcraft (unpublished).[11]

9. A man behaves in a witch-like manner which involves his child. His sister exposes him (unpublished).

10. Hare and his maternal uncle Hyena struggle over food. Hyena is tricked into killing his mother and eating her while Hare hides his. Eventually Hyena dies and Hare prospers (1961a).[12]

11. A man has two wives and the junior wife dies. The surviving senior wife persecutes the dead woman's daughter. In

the end the woman is exposed and is slain and the girl lives with her father (1963e: 302-9).

12. The same story is told although in this case the junior wife is slain by the elder (1963e: 309-11).

13. A diviner tells a childless couple that they will bear malevolent daughters who must be slain but that they may keep their sons. A man saves one of his sisters and goes off with her into the bush. The sister secretly marries a stranger who is really a snake endowed with supernatural powers. The girl bears the snake a son who is loyal to his maternal uncle rather than to his mother and snake-father. The sister plots with the snake to kill her brother through witchcraft. The boy prevents this and kills the snake. The boy goes off to snake-land while the brother kills the sister and returns home to his parents (1964a: 1-5).

14. A nearly identical tale is told 1970: 348-54

15. The son of a lion and son of a cow are brought up together. The lion-mother kills the cow-mother, but the two youths then kill the lion-mother. They then go off and marry after many adventures (1965a: 27-33).

16. A man sleeps with his wife's sisters and as a result loses all his good fortune (1965a: 37-9).

17. Two daughters are abandoned by their father owing to a trick of a wicked stepmother. The girls grow up in the wilderness. One day they meet their half-brothers who try to seduce them but who are repelled by the girls, who disclose their identity. The children inform their father and he kills the evil stepmother and then lives with his children (1965b).

18. A youth slays a monster which had been swallowing people. He frees the people and becomes chief. He then kills his mother's brother and takes up residence with his mother (1967a: 8-11).

19. A widower runs off into the wilderness with his daughter. The father brings up the daughter and mates with her, producing a daughter. The father sings that the girl's father is a Baraguyu tribesman, whereas the girl sings that the father produced the child incestuously. When they visit their homeland, each sings his song and the father beats the girl. She denounces him to the people and he is made a slave (1968b: 383-5).

20. A girl kills her elder sister's husband and then tricks her sister into eating his flesh. She is unpunished and merely returns to her parents (in press, a).

V

CONCLUSIONS

All Kaguru sexuality involves themes of aggression and food imagery. Withholding food among kin often seems associated with covert sexual-aggressive themes, especially between siblings. This is probably a thinly disguised expression of incestuous activities.

While a wide range of sexual connexions is prohibited by Kaguru — parent/child, clan members, certain affines, persons whose fathers share a common clan — the most prominent, in terms of its appearance in folklore and the frequency and intensity with which it occurs in Kaguru jokes and conversations, involves siblings. When discussing incest with Kaguru, I found them describing the mother/son form of incest as very wrong but most unlikely; father/daughter incest as reprehensible but understandable; but sibling incest not only as comprehensible but even somewhat seductive, despite its immorality. A famous Kaguru initiation riddle-song goes, 'The *mupululuji*-tree at the riverside! However good it may be, it is not good to cut it down for [building] a house!' This was said to be an imprecation against sibling incest. Sisters are compared to fine trees ideal for building a house [founding a household].

It may, of course, be argued that the factor of age alone should make a sister a more 'logical' sexual object than a parent, but this would suggest that sexual objects were defined with little response to culture, for such an interpretation may well simply be our view of the situation. In the case of the Kaguru, the problem of sibling incest is complexly related to the 'matrilineal puzzle' as Audrey Richards once described the dilemma of balancing exogamy against domesticity in a matrilineal system (1950: 246).[13]

Every Kaguru youth must give out his sisters to others as wives; yet he must depend upon these same girls to produce heirs and wealth, the latter from the bridewealth he receives from her daughters. Furthermore, he himself takes a wife from another clan, sometimes even taking up residence with these hostile affines. Some Kaguru folktales describe the deep fears and imagined dangers to men residing with such 'strangers', and such marriages are often strongly resented by youths. One solution to this dilemma would be to couple with one's own sister, an answer forbidden Kaguru.

In these tales where Kaguru siblings reside together in what appears to be a thinly disguised incestuous relation, the siblings invariably reside apart from their parents who are either dead or, at the least, very far away. One of the siblings exhibits unmistakably witchlike behaviour. Usually the bad sibling is punished and the virtuous one leaves the forbidden situation. The survivor returns to a situation in which authority is more clearly delineated, either in terms of parenthood or husband–wife relations. Brothers tend to return to parents, sisters to their husbands. In these cases the forbidden union has generated further unfavourable conditions and has had to be ended. From the tales themselves, however, one does not sense any explicit condemnation of the co-residence of brothers and sisters, although, of couse, this is never clearly presented as incestuous; rather, such co-residence and domestic interdependence are shown to be unworkable between siblings because of their inherent characteristics.

A girl plays off her domestic loyalties to her brother against those to her husband, whereas a boy's main source of social strength against his sister lies not with his own wife but with his parents, especially his mother, who will often exert influence to persuade the girl to defer to her brother's authority. At the risk of making too many hypotheses on the basis of little explicit ethnographic evidence, it seems likely that Kaguru men are more preoccupied with the problem of their sisters than women are over their brothers. This rests upon the assumption that the root of such concern relates to the factors of authority, age, affect, and sexuality. It is precisely a woman's sexuality (fertility) that makes her of value to her brother, but it is this same quality that often leads her to ignore her brother's demands and instead heed her husband's. For that matter, one of the most serious threats to lineage solidarity in any lineal system, whether patrilineal or matrilineal, is the particular focus of affect generated by domestic ties. The family is both the vehicle by which lineage members are recruited and the area in which interfamilial, lineage loyalties are often betrayed. It cannot be otherwise.

It seems that Kaguru speak of possible sibling incest far more than people do in many other societies – certainly far more than in our own. I doubt whether Kaguru commit more sibling incest than people do in other societies; and the frequent talk about this topic does not necessarily indicate any deep-seated desire, however repressed, to do so. Rather, it may well be that such frequent tales, jokes, gossip, and comment are simply a highly condensed way of describing the insoluble paradoxes or tensions centering upon the conflict between authority, age, and sexuality, and the refusal on the part of Kaguru to allow these free play in the same sector of social relations. The main factor common to all forms of sexual prohibition discussed above is that they are seen by Kaguru as confounding authority and age by the introduction of sexual affect. Parent/child incest is the least problematic for Kaguru because the appreciable gap between the ages of parent and child profoundly reinforces parental authority. But age is less a factor in sibling relations, at least in theory, for a brother should command a sister regardless of age. It may be that Kaguru belabour sibling incest, not because it is an imminent danger to their social stability but as a way of heightening consciousness of sexual differences in an area of kinship where age seems at time a weak and even contradictory key to making distinctions of authority. It may be that such sentiments are useful in creating tension and self-consciousness among the participants in these situations. This too would help explain why the forms of prohibited affinal sexual relations which also seem most to disturb Kaguru involve jeopardized relations between persons of the same generation rather than those already sharply defined by generation.

NOTES

1. A bibliography of publications on the Kaguru is available elsewhere (Beidelman 1967b: 1968a); a broader picture of Kaguru society and culture is available (Beidelman, 1971). I discuss Kaguru descent groups in detail in a forthcoming paper (in press, b).

Some Kaguru Notions about Incest

This essay was prepared for the ASA conference held at Bristol in April 1970. I was unable to attend owing to my university's failure to provide funds for my visit.

2. I discuss ritual joking partners (*watani*) in some detail elsewhere (1966).

3. The head is seen as the centre of spiritual activity, of the essence of a living creature. The heat of pollution is cooled (*kuhosa*) by the death of the sheep and dispersal of its internal organs and blood.

4. Of course, sororal polygyny is practised by some matrilineal peoples, such as the Navajo; these argue conversely from the Kaguru that sisters are such close persons already that they make happy co-wives.

Kaguru give a series of reasons for practising the sororate. The most convincing is that it allows them to continue an alliance. This is especially plausible in view of the fact that the substitute wife is never a uterine sister of her deceased predecessor. Kaguru sometimes rationalize the sororate by saying that if a woman with children died, her child would be better looked after if her successor were a kinswoman (the evil stepmother is a common theme among Kaguru). While such a kinswoman might be subject to more pressures not to mistreat such children, the stock wicked stepmother theme would still seem appropriate since the new woman's children would also be in competition with those of her predecessor.

Doubtless the Kaguru custom of mother-in-law avoidance is based on related grounds. Men avoid their wives' mothers until after their wives have borne several children. Kaguru say simply that this is out of respect and also shame: respect because she is of a parental generation and allowed you to secure her daughter, and shame because one has had sexual relations with her daughter and must not mention this to her because of her generational position. The implications of this would seem to be that notions of seniority (authority) and sexuality create a highly problematical situation.

5. It is said that in the past Kaguru possessed medicines to divine who was a child's biological father. Today these are no longer used (perhaps because the law does not recognize their results) and Kaguru sometimes rationalize any exceptions to their explanatory system of supernatural sanctions as due to lack of true biological paternity which now cannot be determined beyond a doubt.

6. A very large proportion of texts emphasize aggression between kin and neighbours and this most often takes the form of withholding food. This, in turn, is usually associated with witchcraft suspicions and accusations. Sexual relations and food are the major themes for expressing kinship and morality among Kaguru. Kin share food but not sexuality; non-kin share sexuality but need not share food; and witches, who are incestuous but who withhold food from kin, confound these distinctions. I maintain that such aggressive behaviour over food between kin automatically suggests witchcraft (and therefore incest) when, among Kaguru, it is directed against potential sexual objects. The situation of a brother and sister residing together alone always implies, as far as Kaguru are concerned, some kind of questionable sexual situation.

7. Kaguru often use the terms for hunting or shooting to refer to sexual relations. Indeed, such terms play a central part in Kaguru ritual and humour.

8. Kaguru equate grandparents with a loosely sexual relation. However, here, the grandmother manifests witchlike characteristics. It is questionable whether the morally inverted behaviour of a kinswoman who represents a category of sexually available yet somewhat illicit persons can be related to the legitimate sexuality between a husband and wife.

9. There is a double implication of prohibited sexuality here, for one should avoid any intimate access to one's maternal uncle's wife and one should have had no intimate access to one's wife's mother.

10. The witchlike aggression and cannibalism of Hyena seem likely to imply incest as well (cf. my discussion of a similar text, 1961a).

11. The implications here involve a brother and sister who live together and who give every indication of witchcraft behaviour. This tale is analysed and discussed in detail in a forthcoming paper (in press, c).

12. I have discussed these issues in reference to Text 7.

13. The problem of relative age within a kinship category has generally been neglected by social anthropologists, although Needham has nicely indicated the issues involved in a recent paper (1966). Unfortunately, I was not aware of these important factors when I collected my data on the Kaguru. I am ignorant of the subtleties of Kaguru views on these topics. It is clear, however, that in general Kaguru assign primacy to seniority and masculinity in social relations. However, neither of these is entirely sufficient and Kaguru themselves are aware of the inadequacy of both these criteria. Thus, a mother should be respected and followed by her son, and yet in many situations, such as bringing a case to court, conducting ritual, or assuming jural authority over her offspring, she should and usually does defer to her eldest son, at least formally and in public. The case is more complex with siblings. Brothers should be superior to sisters in authority, but where the first-born is a girl and her brother is considerably younger than she, Kaguru sometimes say that in some respects her views are treated like those of a man. It is said that sometimes in the past such a girl might conduct certain ritual propitiating ancestral ghosts, rites ordinarily reserved for men. Unfortunately I lack data to treat this important issue properly.

In any case, age by itself is obviously not a sufficient criterion for respect and distance, for members of a grandparental generation are treated with great familiarity, even disrespect, at least in certain situations.

REFERENCES

BEIDELMAN, T. O. 1961a. Hyena and Rabbit: a Kaguru Representation of Matrilineal Relations. *Africa* **31**: 61-74; reprinted in J. Middleton (ed.), *Myth and Cosmos*. American Musuem of Natural History, New York, 1967.

— 1961b. Right and Left Hand among the Kaguru: a Note on Symbolic Classification. *Africa* **31**: 250-7.

— 1963a. The Blood Covenant and the Concept of Blood in Ukaguru. *Africa* **33**: 321-42.

— 1963b. Witchcraft in Ukaguru. J. Middleton and E. Winter (eds.), in *Witchcraft and Sorcery in East Africa*, pp. 57-98. London: Routledge & Kegan Paul.

Some Kaguru Notions about Incest

BEIDELMAN, T. O. 1963c. Some Kaguru Riddles. *Man* **63**: 158-60.
—— 1963d. Further Adventures of Hyena and Rabbit: the Folktale as a Sociological Model. *Africa* **33**: 54-69.
—— 1963e. Mukejuwa: Two Versions of a Kaguru Tale. *Baessler-Archiv* **11**: 201-26.
—— 1964a. Ten Kaguru Texts: the Folklore of an East African People. *Journal of African Languages* **3**: 1-37.
—— 1964b. Intertribal Insult and Opprobrium in an East African Chiefdom (Ukaguru). *Anthropological Quarterly* **37**: 33-52.
—— 1965a. Six Kaguru Tales: the Traditional Folklore of an East African People. *Zeitschrift für Ethnologie* **90**: 17-41.
—— 1965b. A Kaguru Text. *Zeitschrift für Ethnologie* **90**: 42-8.
—— 1966. *Utani*: Some Kaguru Notions of Death, Sacrifice and Affinity. *Southwestern Journal of Anthropology* **22**: 354-80.
—— 1967a. Eleven Kaguru Texts. *African Studies* **26**: 3-36.
—— 1967b. *The Matrilineal Peoples of Eastern Tanzania.* London: International African Institute.
—— 1968a. Addenda to Bibliography of *The Matrilineal Peoples of Eastern Tanzania. Tanganyika Notes and Records* **69**: 71-2; *Africa* **39**: (1969) 186-8.
—— 1968b. Eight Kaguru Texts. *Anthropos* **62**: 369-93.
—— 1970. Some Kaguru Folktales. *Baessler-Archiv* **18**: 335-61.
—— 1971. *The Kaguru: A Matrilineal People.* New York: Holt, Rinehart & Winston.
—— in press, a. Nine Kaguru Tales. *Zeitschrift für Ethnologie.*
—— in press, b. Kaguru Descent Groups. *Anthropos.*
—— in press, c. The Filth of Incest. *Cahiers d'études Africaines.*
NEEDHAM, RODNEY. 1966. Age, Category, and Descent. *Bijdragen tot de Taal-, Land- en Volkenkunde* **122**: 1-35.
RICHARDS, A. 1950. Some Types of Family Structure amongst the Central Bantu. In A. R. Radcliffe-Brown and Daryll Forde (eds.), *African Systems of Kinship and Marriage* (pp. 207-51). London: International African Institute.

9

William Wilder

Purum Descent Groups
Some Vagaries of Method

I

INTRODUCTION

The Purum are now part of the established order, in the textbooks (Fox 1967; Harris 1968; Buehler & Selby 1968) and in theoretical works (White 1963; Livingstone 1969). The Purum tripartite social classification *pu/ta-nau/tu*, 'wife-givers', Ego's groups, 'wife-takers', and the marriage rules have already been elucidated in an exemplary, even definitive, manner (Needham 1958). It would seem that no further explanation is necessary; indeed, that the Purum are one of the most thoroughly analysed peoples in the literature.

Lévi-Strauss, on the other hand, has lodged certain objections (1966), and there are one or two lacunae that I think may usefully be filled in. Moreover, there are two types of theoretical argument now afoot that purport to use Purum facts. They are not new but they are farther from the Purum facts than even the earlier arguments were.

For these reasons I wish to present an interim discussion of Purum descent groups. My main question is specifically this: How many alliance groups do the Purum have? The question is not original; it appears in Rodney Needham's re-examination of Purum society (1958). But the question has been somewhat obscured since 1964, I feel, by certain methodologies to which Purum data have been exposed.

We know that the Purum marriage rules are bound up with Purum descent groups. Among the Purum 'The corporate group is the lineal descent group' and 'local groups of men . . . constitute the social and political segments of Purum society *between which women are transferred*' (Needham 1962: 83; my emphasis). Despite intensive analysis, however, the nature of the Purum groups, as distinct from Purum categories, is not perhaps as clear as it might be. Lack of specification has, I am quite certain, been further exacerbated by the methodological callosity of some later recensions of the Purum data. Or, more precisely, the matrix built up after them, for in two of the arguments exploiting Purum material (Harris 1968; Livingstone 1969) the 'Purum statistics' are derived from the cell-matrix constructed by Ackerman (1964).

II

THE ACKERMAN MATRIX

Those who know of the Purum may or may not be familiar with Ackerman's matrix. Its main feature, aside from a graphic simplicity and compactness, is the way the entries appear on its grid in the form of: (*a*) black-bordered cells and (*b*) numbers. The whole thing neatly summarizes a table assembled by Das from (*a*) statements of informants (Das's column a) and (*b*) village census and genealogical charts (Das's columns b-c) (Das 1945: 133-7).

The matrix, it should be noted, is similar to the earlier Purum alliance tables (Needham 1958; 1962) in which wife-givers and wife-takers are placed on either side of a list of the Purum lineages. On the face of it, the matrix tabulation is a more economical presentation[1] because two sorts of entries (*a*) and (*b*) above, can be distinguished and the numerical values of (*b*) retained (cf. Müller 1964: 1373).

The rationale for these various diagrammatic arrangements is the Purum marriage rule. Marriages among the Purum are not randomly exogamous but are defined by a rule of matrilateral cross-cousin marriage (equivalent to systematic asymmetric alliance or, in Lévi-Strauss's terms, generalized exchange). Genealogical information is deficient for the Purum (Das 1945: 141) but it is clear that in general all groups categorized by terms of reference as classificatory 'father's sister's husbands' ' side (*tu*) or as classificatory 'own' side (*tanau*) contain only prohibited women for purposes of marriage. All groups categorized by similar means as classificatory 'mother's brothers' ' side (*pu*) contain eligible women (own generation) for purposes of marriage (Needham 1958: esp. 80-1).

As an anthropological tool, Ackerman's matrix is treacherous.

It is behaviourist and oversimplified, and puts a decisive barrier between the reader and the ethnography. The later versions of this matrix and its statistics show how the built-in bias of prior assumptions and conceptual error is progressively magnified and the factual basis undermined as the discussions grow more distant from the original sources.

What will concern us here is the assumption that the exchanging groups are the 'lineages' or 'subsibs' – a direct transfer of the very notions in which the ethnographic data were originally cast (Das 1945).

What statistics can the matrix give us? Numbers or sums that spring first to the eye are: 13 (number of Purum lineages), 141 (number of recorded Purum marriages), 48 (sum of black-bordered entries, informants' statements), and 40 (sum of numerical entries, which becomes 39 with the exclusion of the single entry for clan incest). Not shown but readily marked off are the diagonally arranged areas voided by the rule of clan exogamy. For 13 lineages and 5 clans, this excludes 41 cells out of 169. With additional exclusion of half the number of remaining cells by the rule of asymmetric exchange a maximum of 64 $(128 \div 2)$ cells are available for lawful alliances.

The all-important discrepancy – in matrix terms – between the number of lineage alliances (cells) stated as permissible ('normative, ideal') by informants and actual recorded marriages is 15, equal to the number of numerical entries falling outside the informants' scheme of alliance. Twenty-five cells thus contain both entries, the 'black-eye' and numerical entries coinciding. Seventeen black-bordered entries are empty, 'thought-of' alliances not opted for in the three or four generations covered by Das's data.

Notice how easy it is to talk about the Purum marriage system as a construct of synthetic sums (cf. Geoghegan & Kay 1964: 1353; Cowgill 1964: 1360 f.; Müller 1964: 1373). It is this manipulation of numbers that pervades the two most recent discussions of the Purum. It is striking how, as before, the actual values of the numerical entries are never considered.

There are now two separate lines of argument on the Purum data. In one (Harris 1968, ch. 18) the Purum cycles of exchange are said to be badly broken up, hanging by the thread of 'ought', of mere consciousness. The cycles are ever shortening and the marriage system running down because of the weakness of the marriage rule. In the other (Livingstone 1969; cf. Buchler & Selby 1968) the Purum construct their cycles in norm and in reality albeit in a highly unstable demographic situation. Livingstone's puzzlement is about the means of maintaining 'equilibrium' and 'viability' in Purum society. He finds 5 clans too few to operate smoothly and, anyway, it turns out that 12 lineages is a much more mystifying arrangement than 5 clans.

Neither argument is new and they have in common a specific interest in locating failures in the Purum alliance machinery. Also, the use of Ackerman's matrix as a factual basis is for both a matter of course.

Thus, in Harris, we find the matrix yielding the astounding figure of 30 per cent direct exchange. We also find 15 out of 39 (above) numerical entries not following any 'rule' at all. Only '23' (sc. 25) numerical entries follow lawful rules of alliance (black-bordered cells or informants' statements) and the remaining black-bordered cells 'where women should have been exchanged' (Harris 1968: 508) are unoccupied by actual Purum marriages. And the old saw of prescribed *group* (mother's brother's sib) is repeated for good measure (see Note 5).

What is extraordinary is not the plausibility of these assertions; it is their bold tendentiousness and practised appeal to ethnographical ignorance. All the numbers derive from counting little boxes, not the individual Purum marriages. Because 12 cells out of 39 are *involved* in 'direct exchange' all 12 are counted as 'wrong' – whereas only half could possibly be 'wrong'. And so on.

Livingstone happily does not deal with the 'mother's brother' question but, by mere inclusion of the matrix scheme – he barely discusses it — effectively repeats the other assaults on the integrity of the Purum system. Here Ackerman's matrix is rearranged in two stacked tables (1969: 244). The black-bordered entries become 1 and 0 entries of matrix algebra and the numerical entries appear in a table below, with the contentious marriages (by reference to the superior ideal 'norms') given special markings.

With this as with the other cases of reliance on Ackerman's matrix, the mire of clerical and conceptual error thickens.[2] It is perhaps not surprising that while Buchler & Selby (1968) reproduce both clan alliances and lineage alliances of the Purum, they discuss only the former (Table 7-2 in Buchler & Selby [1968: 161] is just padding).

The numerological potentialities served up in Ackerman's matrix are a temptation some anthropologists have just not been able (or willing) to resist. The main subversion of the modern Purum analysis (Needham 1958) contained in these derivative arguments is the ossification of the wife-giver/wife-taker scheme *at the level of the named lineages*; in other words, the idea that among the Purum 'there are twelve alliance groups' (Livingstone 1969: 244). Now while we do not know nearly enough about Purum descent groups, it is my contention that we know more than we think we do. It is time to get back to the facts.

III

DIRECT EXCHANGE?

One of the remaining sources of confusion for almost anybody making a more than passing acquaintance with the Purum could well be the question of Purum descent groups. This I would regard as one possible reason for the persistence of the 'direct exchange' question, and the wilful confusions of 'group' and 'category' and of 'marriage' and 'alliance'.

Symmetrical exchange does not occur in the statements of informants (the 'normative' or 'ideal' black boxes). The informants' scheme is a perfect system of asymmetric alliance (Wilder 1964: 1370; Needham 1964: 1380) – that is, *from the point of view of the absence of direct exchange*. What I did not notice in my paper of 1964 and what nobody seems to have noticed since (in print, at any rate) is that the informants' scheme is incomplete: one lineage, by name Aihung (K_2), is not stated to give women at all and is allowed a small field (2 entries) for taking women. (Is this a bias of Khulen informants? See Note 6.)

Of itself this is something to arouse suspicion, but, even more, to raise an obvious but fundamental point: that the two classes of entry in the matrix, juxtaposed in Das's record (Das 1945: 133, col. *a*/col. *b-c*), simply do not tell us the same thing. They

207

are totally different kinds of information: (*a*) alliance, concerning groups; (*b*) marriage, essentially concerning individuals. By its facile ability to display the two sorts of information separately but simultaneously the matrix only shows visually what had been demonstrated by other means: that the same asymmetric principle operates in the two spheres of thought and behaviour and that, as it happens, this operation produces a very rough correlation of the two sorts of information at the lineage level.[3]

Informant's statements, as any beginning–anthropology student is or ought to be told, are bound to be 'wrong', or suspiciously 'right'. They are information to be sifted along with all else in the way of field data. This kind of datum needs to be put in its proper place.[4]

Purum analysis is bound to be chequered with omissions. Certainly we lack reasonably full and systematic data on residence, Purum village and descent-group composition, and adequate genealogies, but readers were forewarned of the possible technical deficiencies of the original report by Das himself (1945: 4-5; cf. Needham 1964: 1384, n. 5). What is more disappointing is the poor awareness of this contingency on the part of some latter-day commentators.

Crucial to the study of Purum descent groups is the analysis of 'direct exchange' (Needham 1958: 86-7; 1960; 1964: 1382; 1966: 174). The omission of this topic from *Structure and Sentiment* seems to have inspired would-be critics to speak of 'gross manipulation' of the Purum facts, whatever that may mean, or of 'disbelief' in Needham's presentation of them (see Harris 1968: 507). The question of direct exchange became a principled weapon of attack for those who would deny the Purum their marriage rule.

If only to show that this kind of thinking persists – to the effect that Purum 'actually' confused or forgot or were forced to defy the cardinal wife-giver/wife-taker distinction of their own society, at both category and lineage levels, and that we ought to accept *this* as an explanation of the disagreements in the matrix – it is necessary to examine Purum descent groups more closely, though our evidence is unavoidably circumstantial. (This paper can not aim to bring many new facts to light; only to restore certain omissions.) The many suggestions thrown out by Needham in the past on this matter and the comparative material cited indicate (at least to this observer) that a convincing solution to the category–group wrangle will only be forthcoming when the various aspects of direct exchange are fully examined, *including the groups involved*. These topics I shall now discuss.

IV

PURUM DESCENT GROUPS

In the debates over the Purum marriage rules, the terms 'alliance group', 'lineage' and 'wife-givers/wife-takers' have tended to be used synonymously. This vagueness has been further and needlessly perpetuated, as I have indicated, by the elevation to privileged status of the informants' 'norms' or 'ideals' and their consolidation with the system of named lineages.[5] Literal interpretations in terms of black boxes or matrix algebra have provided the biggest red herring in the whole affair or, to shift the figure, they are nothing less than attempts to add apples and oranges!

I would urge that we consider more carefully the 1958 Purum study, treat the Purum system as we do many other lineal descent systems, and, with due caution, call the named sub-clan groups 'maximal lineages'. The question of Purum marriage alliance would thus concern corporateness and processes of segmentation in the constituent descent groups of Purum society.

Let us bear in mind that 'Lineage ties may be recognized through more generations for some purposes than for others' (Mair 1963: 22). There may be corporate and functional levels in Purum descent groups other than those of clan or maximal lineage. Sadly, though, we do not have the right data. In Das's monograph the system is always phrased as one of five named clans and twelve or so named lineages. While Das does tell us that 'The subsib is either an expanded family or an embryonic sib' (1945: 119), he gives virtually no further data on descent-group composition and residence.

That the Purum are able to think about and verbalize their system for the anthropologist in terms of specific named lineages might have been expected (Wilder 1964: 1366; Müller

209

1964: 1374, 1376) and in a real sense this ability facilitates field-work, but it is as likely to be relevant to the interpretation of Purum social structure as is the ordinary man's estimation of the national balance of payments or the divorce rate.

It is much more desirable to know the categories in which the Purum think about their individual marriages (cf. Wilder 1970: 249-50). No amount of counting and closing the circles will give us a reasonable surmise on this question unless we know what we are counting (Lévi-Strauss 1966: 16-17). In my view, given the nature of the Purum data, Purum social space must be measured in a more radical way in order to provide at least some clues in the right direction.

Purum local and descent groups are as follows:

1. *Villages*
   Khulen: 40 houses, 42 married couples
   Tampak: 29 houses, 33 married couples
   Chumbang: 12 or 13 houses, 10 married couples
   Changninglong: 8 or 9 houses
   ?Aihang Machet (see below)

2. *Households* (Das: 'families')
   About 90 houses in 1936 as under 1

3. *Clans* (Das: 'sibs' or 'clans'; Purum *sagei*)
   Kheyang
   Makan
   Marrim
   Parpa
   Thao
   In places (Das 1945), Julhung (K_1) is listed as a clan; in 1934 Das considered that the Purum had 6 clans (Das 1935; see also Müller 1964: 1374).

4. *Maximal lineages* (Das: 'subsibs')
   See Table, column A.

5. *Local descent groups* (Das: 'distribution of the subsibs')
   See Table, columns C and E.

To make this classification stick I should have to show how these various levels of grouping are functionally distinguished. Some of the more significant discriminations (cf. Fortes 1945, ch. xii) seem to be these: The *village* is a politically independent unit; a hierarchy of offices is specific to it. *Households* ('families') are minimal economic units.

Clans are exogamous. What I call sub-clans or *maximal lineages* seem to be ritual units with a *pipa* 'who is regarded as head of the group' (Das 1945: 119).[e] The *alliance units* are certainly lineal descent groups but these may or may not be maximal lineages.

Concrete processes of segmentation are not readily ascertainable from the ethnography, which tends, as I have said, to stress the split-level arrangement of sib and subsib, which the Purum themselves have conveniently furnished with names.

The recurrent question concerns the number of Purum *alliance* groups. A precise answer to this question is only conceivable if the circumstances of every individual marriage among the Purum for some specified period are known – something like the psychoanalysis of every Purum. And such an answer would still be liable to the methodological failure already noted, namely the fallacy of artificial quantification.

What facts do we have? We know that there are named lineages, actual marriages recorded at the lineage level, and some

A	B	C	D	E
Julhung (K_1)	55	3	K_1 K_1 K_1 K_1 ... K_1 (Chumbang)	3 local segments
Kankung (Mk_1)	49	3	(1) (2) (3) ... M_{K_1} (2)	
(Parpa) (P)	47	3	P P (Khulen/Tampak/Chumbang)	
Aihung (K_2)	23	2	(3) (3) K_2 K_2 K_2	2 local segments
Thao-kung (T_1)	21	1	(Tampak/Chumbang)	
Thao-run (T_2)	21	1		
Rim-kung (M_2)	19	1		
Pilling (M_4)	16	2	M_4	
Rimphunchong (M_1)	12	1		
Rangshai (T_4)	8	1	T_4 (1)	1 local segment
Makan-te (Mk_2)	7	1	Mk_2 (Khulen)	
Rim-ke-lek (M_3)	4	1		

211

results of the 1936 village census – giving the external 'distribution' but not the internal composition of descent groups. These facts are assembled in the Table. [I hope this Table will facilitate the kind of inference Needham invited anthropologists to draw earlier (1958: 86-7).]

Column A is a serial listing of Purum maximal lineages with clan designations. Note that Parpa is a clan, it has no named lineages. Source: Das 1945: 118, *passim*; cf. Needham 1958.

Column B lists the total recorded marriages of each maximal lineage, the sum of women married in and married out. (Ackerman terms these 'marrying acts'.) Source: Ackerman 1964: 59, cf. 61; see Needham 1958: 87, Table 7; both from Das 1945: 133-7, cols (b) and (c). (Cf. Cowgill 1964: 1360; Müller 1964: 1375; and, on the different modes of calculation, Needham 1964: 1381.) The sums are arranged in order of decreasing magnitude.

Column C gives the number of villages in which the lineage is reported as represented, and which may be considered as local lineage segments. Certain reports on three villages only. Source: Das 1945: 118-19; Needham 1958; 1962: 75.

Column D specifies the irregular marriages.[7] Source: Das 1945: 133-7; also 122-3, *passim*; Needham 1958: 86-7. The arrows represent the apparently *improper* flow of women between maximal lineages. (Total number of women given in brackets.)

Column E summarizes lineage segmentation implied in C-D.

Column D shows that while all breaches at the maximal-lineage level involve *ipso facto* two non-local descent groups any pair of these non-local groups covers a total field of 4, 5 or 6 *local* segments. There are thus twenty (20) local descent-group segments among the Purum (largest villages).

For the sake of completeness it is worth noting the clan-composition of the fourth and smallest Purum village, Changninglong (Das 1945: Table XIII (38-39) 42, 175). All clans except Makan (Mk) are represented.

Kheyang: 5 houses (Wankhei, Kengba, Tomba, Ningthou, Shemchao)
Parpa: 1 house (Tumong)
Marrim: 1 house (Sanggoi)
Thao: 1 house (Amphot)

In addition, at least three wives in non-Thao houses in Chang-ninglong are Thao women born in Changninglong. The last representative of Teyu lineage (T_3) died in Changninglong (Das 1945: 119).

Another Purum village, Purum Aihang Machet, is reported too (Needham 1964: 1382). K_2 (Aihung) is not given for Khulen. Could a Khulen local branch of this lineage have removed at some time to Machet? We look to the full analysis of Purum for an assessment.

The existence of 5 Kheyang houses in Changninglong argues for the possibility of at least one more local descent group segment in the total. It seems unlikely that a single household, in the case of Parpa, Thao, or Marrim, could represent an independent corporate group.

The total of Purum village-localized lineage segments may thus be estimated as 20 for 3 villages and 21 or so for 4 villages. How many of these can be considered *corporate alliance groups*? This question brings us virtually to the outer limits of our evidence. It has already been noted that the irregular marriages involve, on one side at least, all the largest maximal lineages (as I have attempted to show visually in the Table) and that there is no reason why unnamed alliance groups may not be distinct in reality from named (maximal) lineages (Needham 1958: 87). Among the Purum 'there might well be no irregular marriages at all' (ibid.).

If we had the original village census records it might well be possible to decide whether local segmentation among the Purum appeared to lead to the formation of alliance groups, or whether local concentrations of the segments themselves split off for such a purpose. The tabulation of 'irregular' Purum marriages is probably the best index we have on present evidence. It certainly does seem that the distinctive correlation of lineage size, lineage dispersal, and irregular marriages, shown in the Table, is not a sign of entropy; it is evidence of the dynamic of

213

the Purum system. It all depends on how – or whether – you look at the overall structure.

V

CONCLUDING REMARKS

This brief survey may clarify the context, especially the local context, in which Purum behave (Needham 1964: 1382; cf. Needham 1960). May we hope that the discussion of the important issue of 'direct exchange' will be restored in the full Purum study?

The questions brought up here were raised in Rodney Needham's original Purum analysis. They seem to me worth reviving. Recent discussions of Purum have alternated between saying – or seeming to say – that the Purum do not have a rule of matrilateral cross-cousin marriage and saying – or seeming to say – that the Purum system is a topologically constructed one, though adaptively uncompleted. Now while 'it is wholly desirable that anthropologists, especially if they are of different theoretical persuasions, should examine the same evidence and see what different interpretations may be possible' (Needham 1964: 1377), some recent discussions which depend in common upon Ackerman's matrix for the 'evidence' are about as far removed from Purum facts as it is possible to get and still call the material 'Purum'.

Perhaps there has been little positive advantage in raising the Purum case; the recent discussions are *non sequiturs*. The present argument, I am afraid, will be lost on those so bemused by numbers and networks that they pertinaciously ignore the *relevant* issues and abandon the 'obvious facts' (Cowgill 1964: 1358). The Purum case in its recent history is another disconsolate reminder of the fits and starts of that kind of progress which, in opposition to the technological, we call truly scientific.[8]

NOTES

1. See its reproduction by Müller, with complicated overlays (1964: 1372); also Needham (1964: 1382).

2. Those who may be puzzled not only by the form in which Livingstone has adapted Ackerman's matrix but by its substantive entries may like to note

Purum Descent Groups

the following: In Livingstone's version only 12 lineages are used, thus giving only 42 ideal or 'normative' 1 (or 0) entries, those supplied by informants' statements. With an asymmetric rule, not 64 but a maximum of 55 cells are available as 'possible relations'. The 42 1 or 0 entries are curiously labelled by Livingstone as 'established relations' (1969: 244). (Presumably he would regard individual marriages as 'actual relations'.)

The underlining of certain numerical entries promised by Livingstone is mistakenly omitted. These *are* found in Buchler's rendition of Livingstone's table, but Buchler's total of 'ideal' entries is erroneously given as 39, not 42! There are further errors in dressing up the entries and it is manifestly not the printers who are responsible for this slapdash handling of data.

3. Defenders of Needham's general approach have pointed out that statistical tests on this correlation really only confirm what was known by 'common sense' (e.g. Cowgill 1964: 1358, 1359-60; Müller 1964: 1373-4). I feel that in this way they underestimate Rodney Needham's signal contributions in the analysis of Purum *categories* even though they decisively expose Ackerman's 'fiddling around' with numbers and formulas (Cowgill 1964: 1359). The pros and cons of statistics, while important, should not divert attention from the statistically insignificant but, in my view, crucial fact of direct exchange.

The recently published comments on models in the Purum case by Fortes, who does not defend Needham's position (Fortes 1970: 82, n. 35), seem to me very misleading on this subject. The Purum ethnographic and numerical data could be regarded as 'defective' *by modern standards*, but the Purum debate, as I have been attempting to show for some of the discussions, does not always make use of (or 'manipulate'?) 'Purum data' and really points the moral, which Fortes seems reluctant to allow, that Ackerman's correlation procedures 'satisfied' no model at all, but were simply destructive in intent, and invalid at that. The overall logic of Professor Fortes's comments therefore seems to be singularly shaky.

4. Cf. Jay (1969), in which a leading theme is the explicit evaluation of informants' statements in relation to topic and social context. That the interpretation of statements can still be, as in the Purum case, an uncertain business is I think illustrated in Jay's suggestion that the high rate of divorce in rural 'Modjokuto' may be rooted in a disillusioning shift from theory – ideal conceptions of marriage absorbed by Javanese in adolescence – to reality in married life (1969: 97). In my own work on Peninsular Malays I have dealt with informants' statements and, specifically, with this 'gap' between theory and practice in the broad field of socialization; I have argued, however, that while there may be 'conflict' there are also mechanisms of adjustment. The divorce rate question thus remains open (Wilder 1970: esp. 251 and 263, n. 49).

In the Purum case, the question of fit or discrepancy between (*a*) informants' statements and (*b*) actuality is simply a false issue, as I point out on p. 209 (see also Note 3). As for the place of informants' statements generally, this must depend partly on the nature of the fieldwork, but I heartily agree with Jay that the topic and social context of such statements must be made *as explicit as possible* in an anthropological study.

5. The conservatives thus hold what amounts to a notion of prescribed descent groups, a notion emerging in terms of cycles and genealogical grids; for example, asymmetric systems are claimed to be 'minimally defined by three points [!], clans or local groups' (Buchler & Selby 1968: 163) all of which is quite contrary to well-established theoretical maxims.

215

6. Das lists nine *pipa*, all resident in Khulen. It may be significant that no *pipa* is listed for two lineages:

M_3 (Rim-ke-lek), probably the smallest Purum lineage; and
K_2 (Aihung), a large lineage but one not represented in Khulen.

7. Including three cases of clan incest (far right in Column D). This is one of the more remarkable exceptions that proves the rule and deserves to be quoted in full for the capsule account it preserves of Purum social structure:

'Each of the five sibs of the Purums is an exogamous unit. There is only one instance in which this rule seems to have been broken. This is the case of Damshu and his two sons Lengmunnir and Phairel of Chumbang. Damshu married Jungai and they both belonged to the Kheyang sib but to different subsibs. Damshu was a Julhung and Jungai an Aihung. They had two sons and two daughters. The two daughters were married in the Makan sib while the two sons married in the subsib of their mother's brother, i.e. Aihung, the elder one having actually married his mother's brothers' daughter. These are the solitary instances of marriage within the same sib. The interesting point in this connection is that in spite of their non-observance of the exogamous rule in connection with the sib they were neither excommunicated nor punished in any other way for this social offence. They continued to remain members of Purum society and lived in a Purum village taking part in all socio-religious rites and ceremonies performed by the village community for the welfare of its constituent members. In short this was not regarded as an offence at all' (Das 1945: 122-3).

8. This paper was in press when two pertinent references came to my notice: first, Goodenough's curious little book about methods of kinship study (1970), which manages, in what seems a remarkable feat of parochialism, to omit all reference to the Purum or to Needham's work, and which takes only a few passing glances at the first edition of *Les Structures élémentaires de la parenté*, the book which can be said to have advanced our knowledge of the issues in kinship studies far more than has Murdock's oft-cited *Social Structure*, published in the same year (1949): and second, Korn and Needham (1970) who have dealt with White's book. Also I would add that the current devotion to the *trappings* of science, documented in my own argument, is neatly corroborated by the following (self-explanatory) bloomer in a new textbook: 'Lounsbury, F. G. 1964. *A Formal Account of the Crow- and Omaha-Type Kinship Technologies*. In W. Goodenough, ed. [etc.]'. (Keesing & Keesing 1971: 414.)

ACKNOWLEDGEMENT

I would like to thank the editor, Dr R. Needham, for welcome textual criticism. The content of the paper, however, is wholly my responsibility.

REFERENCES

ACKERMAN, CHARLES. 1964. Structure and Statistics: the Purum Case. *American Anthropologist* **66**: 53-65.

BUCHLER, IRA R. & SELBY, H. A. 1968. *Kinship and Social Organization: An Introduction to Theory and Method*. London: Collier-Macmillan.

COWGILL, GEORGE L. 1964. Statistics and Sense: More on the Purum Case. *American Anthropologist* **66**: 1358-65.

DAS, TARAK CHANDRA. 1935. Kinship and Social Organization of the Purum Kukis of Manipur. *Journal of the Department of Letters* **28**: 1-14. Calcutta: Calcutta University Press.

—— 1945. *The Purums: An Old Kuki Tribe of Manipur.* Calcutta: Calcutta University Press.

FORTES, MEYER. 1945. *The Dynamics of Clanship among the Tallensi, Being the First Part of an Analysis of the Social Structure of a Trans-Volta Tribe.* London: Oxford University Press.

—— 1970. *Kinship and the Social Order: The Legacy of Lewis Henry Morgan.* London: Routledge & Kegan Paul; Chicago: Aldine, 1969.

FOX, ROBIN. 1967. *Kinship and Marriage: An Anthropological Perspective.* Harmondsworth, Mddx.: Penguin Books.

GEOGHEGAN, WILLIAM H. & KAY, PAUL. 1964. More Structure and Statistics: A Critique of C. Ackerman's Analysis of the Purum. *American Anthropologist* **66**: 1351-8.

GOODENOUGH, WARD H. 1970. *Description and Comparison in Cultural Anthropology.* (The Lewis Henry Morgan Lectures 1968.) Chicago: Aldine.

HARRIS, MARVIN. 1968. *The Rise of Anthropological Theory: A History of Theories of Culture.* New York: Crowell; London: Routledge.

JAY, ROBERT R. 1969. *Javanese Villagers: Social Relations in Rural Modjokuto.* Cambridge, Mass., London: MIT Press.

KEESING, ROGER M. & KEESING, FELIX M. 1971. *New Perspectives in Cultural Anthropology.* New York & London: Holt, Rinehart & Winston.

KORN, FRANCIS & NEEDHAM, RODNEY. 1970. Permutation Models and Prescriptive Systems: The Tarau Case. *Man* **5** (3): 393-420.

LÉVI-STRAUSS, C. 1949. *Les Structures élémentaires de la parenté.* Paris: Presses Universitaires de France.

—— 1966. The Future of Kinship Studies (The Huxley Memorial Lecture 1965). *Proceedings of the Royal Anthropological Institute of Great Britain and Ireland for 1965*, pp. 13-22.

LIVINGSTONE, FRANK B. 1969. The Application of Structural Models to Marriage Systems in Anthropology. In I. R. Buchler and H. G. Nutini (eds.), *Game Theory in the Behavioral Sciences.* Pittsburgh: University of Pittsburgh Press.

217

William Wilder

MAIR, LUCY. 1963. Some Current Terms in Social Anthropology. *British Journal of Sociology* **14** (1): 20-9.

MÜLLER, ERNST W. 1964. Structure and Statistics: Some Remarks on the Purum Case. *American Anthropologist* **66**: 1371-6.

MURDOCK, G. P. 1949. *Social Structure*. New York: Macmillan.

NEEDHAM, RODNEY. 1958. A Structural Analysis of Purum Society. *American Anthropologist* **60**: 75-101.

—— 1960. Structure and Change in Asymmetric Alliance: Comments on Livingstone's Further Analysis of Purum Society. *American Anthropologist* **62**: 499-503.

—— 1962. *Structure and Sentiment: A Test Case in Social Anthropology*. Chicago: University of Chicago Press.

—— 1964. Explanatory Notes on Prescriptive Alliance and the Purum. *American Anthropologist* **66**: 1377-86.

—— 1966. Comments on the Analysis of Purum Society. *American Anthropologist* **68**: 171-7.

WHITE, HARRISON C. 1963. *An Anatomy of Kinship: Mathematical Models for Structures of Cumulated Roles*. Englewood Cliffs, N.J.: Prentice-Hall.

WILDER, WILLIAM D. 1964. Confusion Versus Classification in the Study of Purum Society. *American Anthropologist* **66**: 1365-71.

—— 1970. Socialization and Social Structure in a Malay Village. In *Socialization: The Approach from Social Anthropology*, ASA Monograph 8, pp. 215-68. London: Tavistock Publications.

10

James J. Fox

Sister's Child as Plant
Metaphors in an Idiom of Consanguinity[1]

'... meaning can and must be stated in terms of linguistic
discriminations and identifications, just as, on the other
hand, linguistic discriminations are always made with
regard to their semantic value.'

R. JAKOBSON[2]

I

INTRODUCTION

A persistent problem in the semantic analysis of relationship
terminologies is that posed by the occurrence, within these
terminologies, of elements that encode more than the analyst
wishes to define as 'kinship'. Despite their considerable comparative usefulness and their occasional revelation of unconsidered
relational properties, formal analyses remain inconclusive
at the ethnographic level to the degree that they fail to
exhaust the semantic 'value' of the elements they analyse.
This may be more fully expressed: elements that occur within
the procedurally defined boundaries of a 'kinship' terminology
may also occur in other 'non-kin' linguistic contexts. These
other occurrences are commonly referred to, in Bloomfieldian
terms, as 'transferred', or 'marginal' meanings or as 'metaphoric extensions'. The determination of these metaphoric
extensions has been described (Lounsbury 1964: 1087) as 'one
of the last, and sometimes one of the most interesting' steps
in semantic analysis. Yet this poses an immediate dilemma, since
the initial delimitation of a semantic field that purposely excludes what are judged to be metaphoric usages necessarily
precludes the possibility of an intended 'unitary' definition of
elements – the motivation, it is argued, of the analysis in the
first place. It follows from this procedure that what has been
excluded by definition can only be regained by 'metaphoric
extension'. This dilemma has been recognized by Lounsbury, in
a clearly important and deservedly reprinted paper on Seneca

219

consanguineal terminology (1964, reprinted 1968, 1969). The difficulty, however, remains. That extensionalist procedures can be applied to genealogically ordered data is certainly operationally possible (Lounsbury 1965; Tyler 1969); that, as is specifically indicated in this paper, genealogy serves as a crucial native means of locating individuals within categories is not disputed; but how, if at all, these extensions may be formally and systematically applied to metaphoric usages remains unclear.

If, on the other hand, one accepts as an ethnographic goal some attempt to represent the social classification of a people (as proposed by Needham 1960: 117; Leach 1961), it is precisely these metaphoric usages that appear to be indicators of significant forms of native semantic patterns. The possibility – indeed the probability – of complex semantic patterns in social classification cannot be ignored. Therefore, in questioning the basis and adequacy of a theory of 'metaphoric extensions', this paper considers the consequent complexity and involvement of a semantic analysis that favours more open, multi-contextual attention to linguistic use. It is an attempt to show, in a particular case, that metaphoric usages ought neither to be excluded by definition nor be postponed for some indefinite final step of analysis, but that, to the contrary, a serious consideration of the implication of these usages can lead to a productive ethnographic semantics.

II

A FORMULATION OF THE PROBLEM

A relational analysis of Rotinese terminology reveals that all relationships but one between proximate generations have the form: $X \leftrightarrow ANA$ where X is a member of the ascending generation (and may or may not be specified by other modifiers) and *ana* (gloss: «child») may be further distinguished by sex as either *ana manek* («male child») or *ana feök* («female child»). [The English glosses in parentheses or terms or phrases between *guillemets* (« ») are intended as tentative descriptive aids to facilitate an exposition; they ought not be taken as definitive or exhaustive translations of native terms.] Affinal relationships also approximate this form. Ascending generation affinal terms

220

are marked by a prefix *ali-*. In Rotinese, *ama* and *ina* are «father» and «mother»; *ali-ama* and *ali-ina* are «father-in-law» and «mother-in-law». *Mane-feuk* is «son-in-law» and *feto-feuk* is «daughter-in-law».[3] The address term for son- and daughter-in-law is *ana* and, after an appropriate adjustment period, *mane-feuk* and *feto-feuk* are dropped as reference terms in place of *ana* (*manek/feök*). Similarly, but after a longer period of time, *ali-ama* and *ali-ina* are usually replaced by *ama* and *ina*. The array of all but one of the relationships of proximate generation, with specific modifiers and genealogical specifications, may be displayed as a set of reciprocals in the following manner. In keeping with this analysis, however, it is important to note that these 'genealogical specifications' do not exhaust the semantic 'value' of the elements of this array: the unmodified reciprocals, *ina↔ana*, for example, are the chief means in Rotinese of distinguishing «large» and «small» for objects of a similar (or familiar) kind.

	X		*Ana*
1.	Ama (F, FB, MZH, FZH, WF, HF)	1.	Ana (C, BC, WZC, WBC, SW, DH)
1a.	Ama Kaäk (FeB)	1a.	Ana (yBC)
1b.	Ama Fadik (FyB)	1b.	Ana (eBC)
1c.	Ama Teök (FZH)	1c.	Ana (WBC)
1d.	Ali-Ama (WF, HF)	1d.	Ana (DH, SW)
2.	Ina (M, MZ, FBW, MBW, WM, HM)	2.	Ana (C, ZC-w.s., HBC, HZC, SW, DH)
2a.	Ina Kaäk (MeZ)	2a.	Ana (yZC-w.s.)
2b.	Ina Fadik (MyZ)	2b.	Ana (eZC-w.s.)
2c.	Ina Toök (MBW)	2c.	Ana (HZC)
2d.	Ali-Ina (WH, HM)	2d.	Ana (DH, SW)
3.	Teök (FZ)	3.	Ana (BC-w.s.)

There remains only one proximate-generation relationship which assumes a different form. This is *toök-selek* where *toök* «mother's brother» may be further specified by the suffixed modifier *-huk* and where *selek* («sister's child», m.s.) is not distinguished according to sex. Formally, this would suggest that the relationship, *toök-selek*, is significantly marked for the Rotinese. A further facet of this relationship is that *hu(k)*, «trunk, stem, cause, origin», when used as a suffix, serves as a numerical coefficient for counting «trunks» of trees (*Au hapu tua-huk esa*: 'I have one trunk of lontar palm') and *selek*

221

is formed from the verb *sele*, «to plant» (final -*k* being a noun or noun phrase formative). A longer, more formal referent term for the sister's child is *sele-dadik* and *dadik* is formed from the verb *dadi*, «to grow», «to become». A hypothetical, context-free statement: *Au selenga*: 'My *selek*' would leave it unclear whether the referent of *selek* was a plant or a person. Were this a peculiar feature of a single relationship, it might be possible to skirt this problem by recourse to some concept of homonym. But among the class of males of the second ascending generation (*baï*), there occurs the individuating referent, *baï-huk*: «stem grandfather» or «grandfather of origin»; in some dialect areas (Bilba) of east Roti, a similar individuating referent term, *solo-huk*, occurs among the class of males of the third ascending generation (*solok*); among cross-cousins, a terminological distinction can be made between «planting» and «growing» cousins; and, in the last labelled descending generation (the fourth descending generation in some areas, the fifth in others) there occurs the term *kaik*, which may be related to the common (generic) word for «tree», *kai/ai*. In this view, the succession of generations represented by the terminology seems modelled on the development of a tree, from root to stem (*huk*) to whole tree (*kaik*). Moreover, the fact is that both Rotinese ritual and ordinary speech are suffused, if not overloaded, with highly involved botanic metaphors. Individuals, lineages, and clans are said «to plant» other individuals, lineages, and clans and virtually the whole of Rotinese ritual life is concerned with caring for and making these «plants» grow.

My object in this paper is to examine an aspect of this botanic idiom. My problem is one of focus and selection, since the whole of this idiom requires lengthy monographic treatment. Sociologically, I concentrate on the relationship of mother's brother to sister's child and refer to this as a relation of maternal affiliation; linguistically, I concentrate on the language of this relationship and refer to it as the idiom of planting. After outlining certain relevant features of Rotinese political and social life, I discuss first the social application of the category *toök*, «mother's brother», and then the determination procedures for establishing an individual mother's brother, *toö-huk*, «the stem mother's brother, the mother's brother of origin». Contrary to what might be expected, determining a class of mother's brothers is a relatively easy matter when compared to the processes for determining who is to act as the individual mother's brother. This is often a subject of contention and frequently requires the intervention of native court officials. The question itself is, in several senses, a first question in an ethnography of the Rotinese. Who was to be my mother's brother was the first question posed of me on my arrival on Roti, and before I could take up residence in a Rotinese domain the question had to be answered by the Lord of that domain.[4] Given the determination of the mother's brother of origin, I consider the set of minimally required performances necessary to the maintenance of the mother's brother–sister's child relationship, focusing on the language of these performances. Much of my evidence on this relationship is, however, drawn from other areas of Rotinese life: individual statements, agricultural practices, marriage negotiations, and particularly the decisions as well as the aphorisms, labels, and longer verbal formulations of customary law cited when judgements are given at the native courts.

III

THE ROTINESE OF EASTERN INDONESIA

The Rotinese, who number over 100,000, occupy both the island of Roti and the south-western corner of the island of Timor to which they have migrated in large numbers during the past 150 years. In this area, they are economically remarkable for their reliance upon a mixed range of agricultural staples (rice, maize, millet, sorghum, a variety of tubers, peas, grains, beans, peanuts, squash, sesame, onions, garlic, and cucumber); for their continuing shift from dry-field agriculture to a combination of irrigated orchards, semi-permanent house gardens, and collective rice cultivation; and, most importantly, for their indispensable dependence on lontar-tapping for their major subsistence requirements. This palm (*Borassus flabellifer L.*) yields a sugar juice that is cooked to a syrup, stored and consumed daily; fermented to a beer, and distilled to a gin, 'the water of words'—the catalyst at all articulate social gatherings. In addition, the Rotinese herd horses, water buffalo, goats, sheep; tend pigs and keep chicken. In an area notorious for its denuded and eroded soil, irregular rains, and increasingly arid landscape, this mixed economy is capable of supporting a population density of on the average of 58 per sq km and, in some states, in excess of 130 per sq km.

The island of Roti is divided into 18 native states, or domains (*nusak*), each ruled by its own Lord whose court is the centre of political life. The separate existence of the majority of these states can be traced, in archival records, to the mid-seventeenth century when they and their Lords were first recognized by treaties of trade with the Dutch East India Company (Fox 1971a). To the present, these states are afforded administrative existence within the bureaucratic structure of the Republic of Indonesia, their Lords are acknowledged as administrative officials, and their courts retain jurisdiction over most civil disputes. Appeal rests, however, with a government court on the island, itself staffed largely by Rotinese and invariably presided over by a Rotinese judge of lordly lineage. Disputes and litigation, as occasions for verbal display, are an overriding preoccupation in Rotinese life.

Each domain is comprised of a noble and commoner class. The Lord (*manek*) heads the highest noble clan, while his executant lord (*fetor*) heads a lesser noble clan. These two lords and their respective clans are to each other as *mane-feto*, a «male» and «female» pair («brother» and «sister»). The remaining clans of a state are commoner clans. The clans (*leo*) are the political units of the domain; each is named and is confined to one domain; each has a right, in theory, to be represented at court by its own clan lord (*manesio*); and each is uniquely defined by its own constellation of ceremonial and legal privileges. Clans are divided in turn, into named «lineages» (-*teik*: «stomach, belly, abdomen») and can be further verbally distinguished according to «birth groups» (*bobongik*) and «households» (*uma*). The term, *leo*, however, which alone specifies the highest level of social segmentation, can also be used to refer to all subsidiary levels of segmentation. In ordinary social discourse this permits a high degree of fluidity in reference as well as, when necessary, a precision of specification.

Clans are essentially political in nature and their recognition

and existence are dependent upon the Lord and his court. Consequently, although segmentary processes occur within clans;
clan formation requires court permission. The result of this
court control of the clans has produced an irregular arrangement of clans that varies from domain to domain. Detailed
Dutch reports, from as early as 1838, provide a record of clan
development in each domain. In the domain of Termanu (on
which this paper is principally based), no new clan has been
permitted to form since the middle of the last century. The
Lord's clan has thus grown large and has segmented, for status
reasons, into numerous ranked lineages. A commoner clan,
closely allied with the Lord's clan, has also grown large; but
because status is of far less concern, it retains what are regarded
as its founding lineages, several of which have a larger membership than many court-recognized clans. Certain clans have
diminished in numbers to the point where they constitute, in
effect, small lineages. Two clans formerly allied by marriage
exchange have declined to the point where, with the permission
of the court, they have established themselves as a single
marriage unit. Exogamy and endogamy cannot, therefore, be
specified in terms of the clans. Some clans, particularly the
Lord's clan, are highly endogamous; other clans are rigorously
exogamous. No native structural principle nor any single
mythological theme serves to account for the heterogeneity,
social discrepancies, and unique privileges that exist among the
clans and lineages of a state. Recourse is therefore made to a
complex of native histories that centre on the Lord and his
court and serve, as charters, to explain obvious social difference
and privilege. On the island of Roti, from the state level at
which each domain cultivates its distinctive variation of dress,
speech, and customary law to the level of clan and lineage, the
Rotinese identify themselves with, and pride themselves on, their
differentiating peculiarities rather than on their overall similarities.

All of this has immediate consequences for any discussion of
a terminology of relations. Individuals may inhabit remarkably
different positions within a universe of social groups, and whereas it is linguistically possible – as is done in ordinary native discourse – to map a terminology onto various social groups, the
terminology is distinct from these social groups, for there need

be no coincidence of mapping. The assumption of some form of isomorphism or correlation between terminology and social group would be essentially misleading. Furthermore, a terminology is a subtle mode of classification. A single set of specific genealogically gathered referents does not exhaust its use since there may exist multiple means of reckoning relations among individuals. Intention is as important as context. It is not, for example, unusual for an individual in an endogamous clan to subsume, as common clansmen within a set of «agnatic» categories (*ama-kaä-fadi*: «father-elder-younger brother»), both his mother's brother and all his affines and, then in another context, to distinguish all three as radically separate. This is of great importance in determining who is a mother's brother.

IV

DETERMINATION OF THE MOTHER'S BROTHER (*Toök*)

The concern here is twofold: (1) to sketch briefly the boundaries of application of the category term, *toök* («mother's brother»); and (2) to discuss, in somewhat more detail, the means of determining the individual, of the class *toök*, who is to serve as the *toö-huk* «mother's brother of origin»). The first question is to whom the term *toök* may be applied to create and define a social situation and beyond what bounds its application is considered inappropriate or inconsistent. But the appropriateness of application of the category has, within it, a range of possibilities. Although various strategic boundaries within this range may be reasonably established, it is necessary to point out that not every individual in a domain possesses precisely the same set of possibilities. In contrast to the relatively loose texture of the category *toök* is the uniquely restricted category *toö-huk*, which defines a single individual and for which a number of procedural rules can be invoked to determine unequivocal specification. Furthermore, in cases of dispute, the full powers of the native court are called upon to adjudicate on its exact referent. Thus within a class of men known as *toök*, there can exist one and only one living *toö-huk*.

Initially, it is possible to state that a person's mother's

226

brothers (*toök*) are those men whom that person's mother (*ina*) considers her «brothers» (*nak*): (*a*) within the recognized bounds of her birth group, *bobongik* (men specified as *na bongik*: «sibling brothers»), (*b*) within the bounds of her lineage, -*teik* (men specified as *na daek*: «male parallel cousins»), as well as (*c*) within the bounds of her clan, *leo*. The term *toök*, however, may override other specifiable relationships. In its widest social application, it may include all men of the mother's birth group, lineage, and clan *regardless* of age, exact genealogical connexions through the mother, or specific terminological designations that a person might in other contexts apply to persons within these groups.

There are, however, a number of further constraints on use of the term *toök*. In those common cases of marriage within the same clan, the widest application of the term *toök* carries to the recognized bounds of the mother's lineage, but not beyond it, since its further application to all members of the same clan would be tantamount to the inclusion of oneself and close agnates (*ama-kaä-fadi*) in the category of mother's brother (*toök*). While it may be socially and linguistically acceptable to subsume all members of one's clan, including all *toök*, within the agnatic categories (*ama-kaä-fadi*) the converse is contradictory and unacceptable. There is also a further social constraint on the use of the term *toök*, based on the distinction between noble and commoner. A commoner whose mother comes from one of the ranked lineages of a noble clan would be hesitant to apply *toök* to all members of that clan, for the simple reason that its application, while highly respectful, might be taken as pretentious effrontery. This hesitancy would be directly related to the rank and status of his mother's lineage within the clan. A commoner whose mother came from the royal lineage would not be particularly reluctant to claim as *toök* all male members of the noble clan. The point to be made is that in ordinary speech there exist, depending on context and intention, both a degree of specificity and a range of flexibility in the application of the term *toök*. *Toök* may include from two to two thousand or more individuals. Whereas it would be an arduous task to enumerate genealogically the individuals classed as *toök* in different contexts, for different purposes, by just a few persons in a small domain, it is possible, with relative simplicity, to indicate, as

227

follows, the limits of the term's application for persons native to a domain:[5]

Mother as Linking Element	Toök; Limits of Application
I Mother from another clan →	All male members of mother's clan
Ia Mother from noble clan →	All male members of lineages of approximately the same rank as, or lower rank than, mother's lineage
II Mother from same clan →	All male members of mother's lineage

V

DETERMINATION OF THE MOTHER'S BROTHER OF ORIGIN
(*Toö-huk*)

Generally, from within the class of individuals definable as *toök*, it is essential, for social and ritual reasons, to designate a single individual as the *toö-huk*. Inherent in the role designated by this category are rights and obligations which terminate, or rather are transformed, only on the death of the sister's child. Consequently, given a generational difference in age between mother's brother and sister's child, the role of *toö-huk* is regularly inherited. The suffixed element *-huk* restricts a member of the class, *toök*, in the same fashion as the coefficient *-huk* designates a single tree-trunk. The root *hu-*, in its varied usages, has a cluster of related meanings indicating: «trunk, root, stem, origin, beginning, cause, and reason» (cf. Jonker 1908: 193-5). In response to my request for a gloss to the term *toö-huk*, one Rotinese offered the Indonesian phrase, *akar besar*, 'great root', as an appropriate translation.

There exist certain native precepts or injunctions (though not what might be called strictly formulated rules) for determining the *toö-huk*. They are, in part, genealogical in application and invariably favour the eldest of a set of male siblings. The first, readily offered native precept is that a woman's eldest brother is *toö-huk* and he, in turn, transmits this to his eldest son [♀eB → ♀eBeS]. Several factors mitigate the strict application of this precept. The first and most obvious of these is that a woman may lack a brother within her «birth group». In this case, the role of *toö-huk* is opened to a number of potential candidates within her lineage. The second factor is that the role of *toö-huk* is something of a titled right and may – within limits and with recognition from the native court – be disposed of personally by its holder. The third factor is one of active role fulfilment. At any time, if a *toö-huk* fails to carry out the performances required of him, another potential candidate may come forward and, by performing the role, assume legitimate title to it. A final factor is the existence of defined exchange procedures which publicly affirm a relationship that may be in doubt or in dispute. These same procedures are also available to establish the relationship of mother's brother–sister's child for clients who have immigrated to a new domain.

In discussing the precepts for determining the *toö-huk*, I list a set of native rubrics in order of their potential application.[6] The first of these are: (1) *Na bongik*, (2) *Na daek*, and (3) *Feo poik*. They concern the initial establishment of *toö-huk*. The second set of these, which parallels the first, are: (4) *Ana bongik*, (5) *Ana tolanok*, and (6) *Feo poik*. These concern the transference of the title. For the sake of summary, I do not quote the native sayings adduced to confirm these rubrics since they are often complexly linked to other legal usages and therefore require considerable exegesis, nor do I do more than footnote a few of the illustrative cases that also confirm them. The discussion is intentionally succinct.

1. *Na bongik*. In ideal circumstances, a woman's eldest brother has exclusive rights to the role of *toö-huk*. In Rotinese, *na bongik* defines (for a woman) a class of male siblings. Within this class, since elder/younger distinctions (*kaäk*: «elder»; *fadik*: «younger») are used only among members of the same sex, the brother whom all other brothers refer to as *kaäk* has the right of *toö-huk*. A *kaäk* is *toö-huk* for all children of all his sisters (*feto bongik*).

2. *Na daek*. In the case of a woman who has no sibling brother (*na bongik*), one among her close parallel cousins (*na daek*) must assume this role. The *na daek* constitute a broad social field. Elder/younger distinctions precisely order a «birth group» (*bobongik*); occasionally they may be used among close parallel cousins and may, more rarely, be applied in reference to an entire lineage, but his application beyond the *bobongik* is not concernedly systematic and lacks the rigour necessary to distinguish either elder/younger lines or a consistent elder/younger cline throughout a lineage or clan. In consequence there is no

specific rule for the exact determination of the *toö-huk*. An individual is designated (generally during the marriage negotiations) by the woman's family and preference may be given to the eldest son of her father's eldest brother. This is the *na daek* who, as the child (*ana*) of the woman's father's eldest brother (*ama kaäk*), is *kaäk* to all his male siblings. What is significantly different in this case is that, in contrast to an eldest brother, whose rights extend to all the children of *all* his sisters, a different male parallel cousin may theoretically be designated as *toö-huk* for each female parallel cousin of a household. Furthermore, there exists enough latitude for a request for or an active assumption of this role by an individual to suffice to permit its establishment. In cases of dispute, what is necessary is the social recognition of a gift initiating this relationship.

3. *Feo poik*. This is the Rotinese expression for a gift from the mother's brother to the sister's child. Literally, it means «to wrap the top»; exegetically, it is described as 'the placing of a cloth on the head and shoulders' to imply a relationship of protection. The gifts that constitute *feo poik* are formally categorized as (a) *tua boboik*: «a coconut shell of lontar syrup», (b) *kakau pingak*: «a plate of cooked rice», (c) *pela lalamek*: «a tied bundle of ears of maize». These categories are frames that may cover anything from an extravagant noble prestation of a stand of lontar palm, rice fields, and dry fields, to a simpler unobtrusive gift of a pot of lontar syrup, a basket of rice, and an actual bundle of maize. The repayment for these gifts is called *kedi nduna ise*, «to cut the cord of the rice basket», and may be postponed until the death of the (last) sister's child. Repayment is a *kapa ina esa* (*kap'in'esa*), «a mature female water buffalo», another standard frame whose specific, material content is subject to the negotiation of the parties concerned. But a characteristic, continuing feature of this exchange relationship is that the choice of gifts must accord with a series of opposed categories: cloth, cooked food, and harvestable plant produce (from the mother's brother); gold, silver, or other valuables, livestock, and raw meat (from the sister's child).

Feo poik is an optional prestation; it validates a relation that might otherwise be disputed. To avoid dispute, it may even be given as an accompaniment for a bride «to nourish» her future children. The gift may also inaugurate a relationship and, as such, the request for *feo poik* is the conventional procedure by which clients, immigrants from other islands or other states on Roti, seek to gain mother's brothers for themselves, since the lack of a *toö-huk* is a more grievous social deprivation than the lack of agnates or affines.

The rules for the transference or disposal of *toö-huk*, in effect, repeat those for the establishment of *toö-huk*.

4. *Ana Bongik*. Given his right of disposal,[7] a man may, if he has several sisters for whose children he is *toö-huk*, allocate the children of each sister to each of several sons. (This is not an allocation of separate children but an allocation of all the children of one woman.) Although this is not a common procedure,[8] it is nonetheless an acceptable court-sanctioned one in the state of Termanu.

The common rule is for the eldest male of a set of children (*ana bongik*) to inherit this role on the death of his father. In fact, if the father has not previously designated another *toö-huk*, this is the only rule of inheritance that the native court will recognize.

5. *Ana Tolanok*. If a man has no sons, his role of *toö-huk* passes to one of the children (*ana tolanok*) of his brother or parallel cousins. This is, again, a limbo area where there is no rule to define precisely who is to be *toö-huk*. Preference may be given to the eldest son of the next oldest brother but assumption of this role by one among a number of *ana tolanok* is usually sufficient. To act and be recognized as *toö-huk* at a ceremonial occasion requiring the performance of this role is enough to validate the assumption of the role without any payment of *feo poik*. The conventional mechanism, in case of dispute, is *feo poik*.

6. *Feo Poik*. Given a certain passage of time, when the role of *toö-huk* is to be inherited, it may no longer be possible to give a single gift *via* a woman to all the children of her household. Some or all of these children may be established in their own households and, after this point in time, a gift, if it is necessary, has inevitably to be given by a *toö-huk* to each of his individual *selek*. It is at this stage, in deciding to accept or reject a particular gift, that a *selek* may choose his mother's brother of origin. In the end, children of the same sister may have different mother's brothers.

Furthermore, *feo poik* cannot be viewed as the ultimate conventional mechanism for establishing the role of *toö-huk*. A person locally recognized as the rightful *toö-huk* may have emigrated to another domain or, as is more often the case, to the island of Timor. The gift of *feo poik* cannot in this case override a legitimate claim unless it can be shown that this previous relation has indeed lapsed. A lapse can only be shown to occur at the moment when a *toö-huk* fails to appear at a ceremony for which his presence is required.[9]

What seems initially to be a straightforward matter of the application of a few simple precepts often becomes a complex issue that hinges on the interpretation of specific, detailed information. The issue invariably comes to a head at the funeral ceremony, the last performance for the sister's child. These large gatherings are rarely attended by fewer than 200 persons, who are all well fed, in an almost festive mood, and are intent on enjoying their chief pastime: verbal dispute and litigation. The older the sister's child, the longer the role of *toö-huk* has been transmitted, the more liable it is to contention.

The Lord of a domain is traditionally among the first to be notified of a death and to be invited to the funeral ceremony. If he or his delegate and several lords of the court attend the funeral, an *ad hoc* court session is convened. (In Termanu, I attended no funeral at which a court session was not convened.) Before proceeding to other cases, the court hears evidence – if necessary – to determine the rightful *toö-huk*. This evidence may initially involve a genealogical link through the mother, but thereafter it concerns the relative birth order of a set of male siblings, possible disposal of the role of *toö-huk*, its inheritance among another set of siblings, possible lapses of the role, and payments of *feo poik*. When the *toö-huk* has been determined, the court must still decide what gifts were given and which gifts must still be reciprocated.

The *toö-huk–selek* relationship is transformed at the death of the *selek* and continues to be reckoned, through female *selek*, for at least another generation. A *toö-huk* becomes the *baï-huk*, «grandfather of origin», for his sister's daughter's children. (In Rotinese, there is no terminologically marked sub-category to distinguish these persons within the general class of *upuk*, «grandchildren».) The role of *baï-huk* is subject to the same vicissitudes of transmission as is the role of *toö-huk* (though *feo poik* is never given to confirm it), but it is rarely the subject of contention since the role's requirements are limited and its rewards minimal. At a funeral, and only at the funeral, is the *baï-huk*'s presence and performance necessary. Nonetheless, native social identification of individuals is made first by reference to an individual's lineage or clan and then by reference to his *toö-huk* and to his *baï-huk*. The first reference locates an individual in terms of an «agnatic» relation; the second reference distinguishes the same individual, more specifically, in terms of a line of maternal affiliation. For the Rotinese, a person is the intersection of these two relations, and what follows is an attempt to examine the semantics of the relation of maternal affiliation.

VI

MOTHER'S BROTHER AND SISTER'S CHILD:
PERFORMANCE AND IDIOM

The relation of mother's brother and sister's child is one of close personal intimacy; yet the performances entailed in this relationship consist of a proliferation of conventional, highly stylized procedures, an entire canon of verbal forms. In these performances, as in nearly all situations of formal social interaction, the Rotinese utilize a ritual language. As a special speech form, this ritual language is distinguished by its own formal binate semantics and formulaic syntax. (For a lengthy discussion of ritual language and its relation to ordinary language, see Fox 1971b.) Idioms anchored in ordinary language are elaborated in ritual language. In this discussion, I consider the same idiom, the idiom of planting, in both language forms.

Selek, the term that specifies the sister's child as «plant», does not specify which plant is to represent the sister's child. In the idiom of planting, any of the cultigens which the Rotinese summarily label as the *pule sio*, «the nine sprouts», may denote the sister's child. To every ritual performance, there corresponds at least one (two, in ritual language) named plants or trees. These material icons form part of a complex semiological system. But unlike some ritual systems (Turner 1967) which emphasize the physical use and manipulation of material icons, Rotinese rituals – with their insistence on verbal manipulation – often minimize the physical use of named icons. Saying that something is so is usually a sufficient condition for a ritual performance.

The semiology of plants and trees parallels the whole of the Rotinese botanic idiom. In this discussion, a crucial distinction is that made between soft, humanly planted cultigens and large, hardwood trees, since this distinction carries the opposition between relations of maternal affiliation and relations of agnatic connexion. In this sign system, certain plants are «female»; others are «male». In the paired sets of ritual language, «coconut//areca nut» (*no//pua*) and «rice//millet» (*hade//betek*) are generally feminine, while «banana//sugar-cane» (*huni//tefu*) and «taro//tuber» (*tale//fia*)[10] are masculine. But in the paired set «areca nut//piper betel fruit» (*pua//malu*), the areca nut is feminine and the piper betel fruit masculine. The mother's brother's performances, whose intention is to make the sister's child «grow», form the rituals of the life-cycle. In the semiology of these performances, there is a progression from «seed» to «sprout/shoot» and from this to the mature plant. The timing of most performances is made to coincide with the waxing of the moon which governs this growth. Even when they are not used as material objects in the rituals, the naming of certain plants, at different stages of their development, carries a specific semantic load.

Performance 1: Sasaok (*Marriage*)

This begins with the search for a marriageable girl and is described, in Termanu, as *leo nggen*: «to go/search for seed grain». Overtures are made formally through intermediaries who carry to the girl's house a number of whole areca nuts in a small round basket called *bulak*, «moon». If these are accepted, bridewealth negotiations may begin. In Thie, a domain of southern Roti, the marriage suit is equally explicit. In seeking a girl, the formal request is for «the nine sprouts», the *mbule sio* [*mb = p*]. Formerly, as part of the agricultural rituals now rarely performed, the plants selected to represent the *pule sio* were the first harvested; they were swaddled in cloth like a child, and carried from the field to the inner section of the house. This «inner section of the house» (*uma dalek*) where the *pule sio* are kept is a woman's exclusive domain. It is used for cooking, for storing food, for giving birth, and as the sleeping-place for the daughters of a household. Men may enter this section only with permission and may regularly resort to sleeping there only in time of illness.

The bridewealth (*belis*) necessary for marriage is divided into three portions, each with its formal ritual name. In ordinary discourse, these portions are: (1) *Toök*, «mother's brother», (2) *Amak*, «father», and (3) *Nak*, «brother». Each is negotiated separately and in the sequence *Amak-Nak-Toök*, since by convention these portions are proportionally 3 : 2 : 1 units of value (water buffalo or their equivalent). If divorce occurs, all or part of the portions *Amak* and *Nak* may have to be returned depending on the reasons for the divorce and the circumstances of the marriage. The payment of *toök* to the *toö-huk* is under no circumstances returned, and it is paid only once at a woman's first marriage.[11] The *toö-huk* has the right to escort the bride to her husband's house; his wife has the right to decorate her for the marriage ceremony. The abduction of a girl is an offence against the *toö-huk* and entails the payment of a fine to him.

The marriage ceremonies of Thie are performed over a coconut, which is referred to as «the coconut of the sun and moon». The bride remains in the inner section of her house until just before the ceremony in the outer section. In elaborate rituals, the coconut is carefully husked and its fibres eventually buried beside an areca nut palm. The coconut is then split or is said to be split (the groom's party must, in either case, supply the machete for this performance) and the whole coconut or its germinating half is given to the bride to carry to her husband's house. Among several variants of the ritual formulas used at the marriage ceremony, the following (cf. Wetering 1925: 640-1) is one of the most explicit:

No ia tadak lima	This coconut has five layers
Mbunu holu soën	The husk embraces the shell
Soën holu isin	The shell embraces the flesh
Isin holu oen	The flesh embraces the water
Ma oen holu mbolon.	And the water embraces the germ.
De ela leo be-na	So let it be

Ana touk no ana inak ia	For this young man and woman
Ela esa holu esa	Let one embrace the other
Ma esa lili esa	And one cling to the other
Fo ela numbu non, ana dadi	So that the shoot of the coconut may grow
Ma sadu pua, ana mori	And the germ of the areca nut may sprout
Fo ela bonggi sio lai sio	So that she may give birth to nine times nine children
Ma rae falu lai falu.	And she may bring forth eight times eight children.

Performance 2: Kekela teik (*Opening the Abdomen*)

Areca nut is as important a botanic icon as is the coconut. In ritual language, they form a single dyadic set. As early as 1843, the missionary ethnographer Heijmering observed that commoner girls all had their teeth filed as a sign of their eligibility for marriage but that noble girls had their teeth filed as part of the marriage ceremony (pp. 531-49); he further noted that a girl's teeth-filing (*fola nisi*) had to be directed by her 'eldest uncle' [?] (p. 533) and that to staunch the blood and lessen the swelling after the operation the girl was obliged to bite on a piece of roasted coconut flesh (p. 541).

Teeth-filing for both classes is now performed casually and without ceremony, but its significance has not altered. Teeth-filing is the prelude to the chewing of betel and areca nut and a girl's first public chew, after the operation, is a recognized sign of her readiness to marry. Areca nut is an icon of her sexuality just as the finger-long catkin or fruit of the piper betel is an icon of male sexuality. Thus formal marriage requests require the offer of areca nut; after the consummation of a noble marriage, whole areca nuts are returned to the bride's family as a sign of her former virginity (*mata tema*: «the eye of wholeness/integrity»), broken areca nuts are returned as an insult; similarly, any clandestine offer of betel-areca nut by a man to a woman is an explicit invitation to sexual intercourse: if a woman is married, such an offer may be fined at court; its acceptance is regarded as evidence of *hohonge*, «adultery».

In Termanu, the formal name for the brother's portion, *nak*, of bridewealth is *huka bafa*, the payment «to open the mouth». The name reflects the kind of noble marriage ceremony that Heijmering described. But it is still explained by reference to the fact that a brother's permission is required for his sister's teeth-filing. Both literally and figuratively, a brother, particularly the brother who is to serve as *toö-huk* for her children, guards access to his sister. He, not the father, is concerned to preserve her «virginity»; he is said «to open her mouth» to permit her teeth to be filed before marriage; and most vitally, he is obliged to perform a ceremony that, in about the seventh month of her first pregnancy, is intended symbolically to *kekela teik*, «to slice open the abdomen».

This ceremony, as the Rotinese explain, is performed 'to keep the child from harm', to 'facilitate the birth', and 'to make the child whole'. One of the essential features of the mother's brother–sister's child relationship is that it begins with the child in the womb and it is the mother's brother's responsibility to see that the child comes forth from the womb. For this reason, it is crucial that the ceremony of *kekela teik* be performed in phase with the waxing moon: just before the full moon, so that the child may become whole (*tema*) as the moon becomes full (*tema*). In ritual language, the first child is called *mbule ulak do boa sosak*: «the eldest sprout or the first fruit». An ordinary-language expression for the first child is *manatola ndunuk*: «the one who bursts the womb». In word-play, the Rotinese recognize the word *ndunak*, «a woman's betel-areca nut basket» as a substitute for the word *ndunuk*, «womb», so that the first child may be described as «the one who bursts [his mother's] betel-areca nut basket» (cf. Jonker 1908: 427).

Performance 3: Nggeu Langak (*Head-shearing*)

The next obligatory ritual performance requiring the mother's brother is *nggeu langak*, the head-shearing ceremony. For Christians, this is combined with baptism, at which time, in addition to cutting the child's hair, the mother's brother serves as godfather, his wife as godmother. In *Eaä*, hair-cutting is combined with name-giving and an excerpt from the principal prayer of the mother's brother at this ceremony is in the same insistent botanic idiom: 'may he [the child] be like a plant, that he may be capable of growing, that he may become tall and have flowers and fruits; his trunk, may it send forth roots and his leaves, may they broaden so that he may grow to serve the

237

needs and the wants of us all and [especially] his mother and father for all their time'.

Besides these ceremonies, there are two other optional ceremonies that may occur in early childhood. The first of these is *lange* which amounts to a ritual sale of the child to the mother's brother in return for a special protective necklace (*lange*). This is performed if there have been a succession of children's deaths in a family or when it is believed, as in the case of some lineages, that the line is cursed. (To engender a curse by killing someone is described as *sele ai teas*: «to plant a hard wood»; this is a reverse statement – see below – of the normal function of the mother's brother.) The purchase of a child is symbolic, an aspect of the mother's brother's role as protector, and it does not affect the status of the child who remains within his own home as a member of his father's lineage, though he may be nicknamed teknonymously as child of his mother's brother. The second ritual, *safe dak*, «to cleanse the blood», is less a ceremony than a silent exchange of prestations, when a child is ill, cries continuously, or has been caught eating his own excrement. A male intermediary takes a white ram and tethers it beneath the mother's brother's house; three days later a female intermediary brings to the house of the sister's child cooked rice, cooked meat, and a piece of red cloth, *lesu safe dak*: «the cloth that cleanses the blood». This cloth is hung in the house to protect the child.

Performance 4: Fe Dak *and* Nafuli Dak (*To Give the Blood and To Drive Away the Blood*)

Fe dak and *nafuli dak* are the most important, frequent, and revealing ritual performances of the mother's brother–sister's child relationship. *Fe dak* is «to give [a payment for] the blood»; *nafuli dak* is «to drive away the blood». They are predicated on a simple principle: *No man on Roti has rights over his physical person, his flesh and blood; these rights belong exclusively to his mother's brother*. Any physical injury to one's physical person requires payment of compensation to one's mother's brother.

This principle is one that is consistently observed in Rotinese social life and is, moreover, firmly upheld at court. Any accidental, self-inflicted injury requires the payment of «blood damage» (*dak*) to the mother's brother: a father pays for the injuries of his children; a man for his own injuries and those of his wife. (This inevitably leads to not infrequent attempts to conceal minor wounds, since payment need only be made on demand.) Similarly all instances of battery are actionable, even when blood has not been spilt. The mother's brother will intervene, demand «blood damage», and carry his claim to court where mutually acceptable terms of compensation are determined. For most injuries the real value of these payments is relatively trivial: none that I witnessed was more than the price of a chicken, yet nobles boast of the considerable costs attendant on the spilling of their blood. The most common occasion for «giving blood damage» is when a man strikes his wife. The blow itself is grounds for divorce and to mend a potential breach a man is usually willing to pay damages. The court of Termanu ruled, in one case, that a blow of this kind to a pregnant wife necessitated the payment of «blood damage» both to the woman's mother's brother and to the mother's brother of the child in the womb. The husband immediately paid the damages and the court recognized the reconciliation.

When blood is spilt, especially if it has been spilt in a field under cultivation, the mother's brother is required to *nafuli dak*: «to drive away the blood». Such blood is potently dangerous and is described as *da kalauk, da manamatungak*, «the foul blood, the blood that follows after». The curses that haunt certain lineages are attributed to such blood shed in homicide; this blood is like 'fine red ants that pass from generation to generation'. The exorcism of the blood is a simple service. The mother's brother sprinkles the milk (in Rotinese terms, «the water») of a red coconut at the spot where the blood was spilt and then takes a red cock and some cooked rice to a tree. The choice of tree is dependent on the practitioner: at least four species of large hardwood tree are used for this ritual by different practitioners. (The trees chosen as appropriate icons are characterized either – as in the case of the *bubuni sela* (*Cassia Fistula Linn.*) – by the differential colouring of the wood of their inner core and outer trunk, or – as in the case of the *nitas* (*Sterculia foetida Linn.*) – by the differential hardness of inner core and outer wood.) The tree is told simply 'to receive the blood, do not give it back again'; the cock is then sacrificed, a meal is eaten, and the remains of the meal and the ingredients

239

for a betel-areca nut chew are hung in a coconut shell from a branch of the tree. The service has all the proper elements of a prestation from the mother's brother.

This prestation, the request that a tree «receive blood», is a further aspect of the idiom of planting. The term *dak*, which I have glossed as «blood», refers, in Rotinese, not only to blood but to all inner plant saps (cf. Jonker 1908: 66). *Dak* is the vital component of both man and plant. The giving of «blood damage» is also the giving of «sap damage».

Dak is not, however, the only component that man and plant share together and although it is not feasible to present here, in a systematic fashion (as, for example, in Friedrich 1969), the discriminations and identifications that characterize the classes of man, plant, and animal, these classes, in their representation as bounded substance-producing bodies (Douglas 1966), share a sufficient number of similar semantic labels to permit the creation, within native speculative exegesis, of complex correspondences. Many of these labels, it should be noted, are composite terms and appear to be formed by compounding two recognizable, simpler elements. Man, plant, and animal share *louk*, «skin or bark», and *dok*, «leaf»: human hair is *langa dok*, though birds and animals have *buluk*: lips are *difa dok*; ears are *dii dok*. In the Rotinese agricultural rituals, a coconut was regularly substituted for a human head: both coconut shell and human skull are labelled as *soëk*. Teats are *pule*: «sprouts» or «buds». Most liquids exuded or contained externally by plants and animals are labelled *oe*, «water», and distinguished according to their source: *suü oe* is milk, «breast water»; *no oe* is coconut milk, «coconut water», lontar juice is *tua oe*, etc. (Urine is, however, *moe*, tears are *lu*, and snot or mucus is *pinu*: plants do not exude these liquids.) *Kaik/aik* is the most general term for plant or tree; it also occurs at lower contrastive levels and in numerous specific plant names. A man's rib-case is *kai usuk*; the navel cord is the *use-aik*: in the case of a boy, this cord along with the first hair cut from his head, if it is not sunk at sea, must be hung at the top of a lontar palm. The afterbirth must, in all cases and for both sexes, be hung in the fertile, sanguine-fruited boughs of the *kai-nunak*, Rumphius' *Arbor glutinosa* (*Cordia obliqua Willd.*).

Although this list of similarly labelled body components could

240

be extended, it is sufficient to indicate a further basis of the Rotinese botanic idiom and to suggest the further appropriateness of botanic icons. The same idiom used to categorize the parts of the human person is also involved in Rotinese descriptions of their cosmos as an immense, branching waringin tree; in their genealogical tales about ancestral «planting» contests that established the sovereignty of certain domains or the possession of special ritual privileges; and in their discussion of clan segments as flowerstalks of the male lontar palm or as the branches of hard-cored, enduring trees. The power of this idiom lies, it seems, in the analogy of man, plant, and cosmos. What is still needed is a lengthy linguistic specimen that fully develops this analogy.

Performance 5: Feta Mamates (*Feast of the Dead*)

The mother's brother is the central ritual participant at the funeral ceremonies, *feta mamates*, of his sister's child. In a certain sense, it is his physical person that has died and he has the chief responsibility to see that it is properly conveyed to the grave. A mother's brother is immediately notified of the death of his sister's child. He must bring gifts: rice, some animal as food for the feast, and (in most domains) a shroud to wrap the corpse. His first task is to direct the washing of the corpse; his next task is to pay for the cutting of a tree and the preparation of a coffin. A named position of the outer section of the house, near the corpse, is reserved for his presence and he must eat first to initiate the feasting that occurs the night before the burial. On the day of the burial, an *ad hoc* court session may occur if there are any disputes as to the legitimate mother's brother of origin (*toö-huk*) and the various payments to him. The first of these obligatory death payments is *pa-buik*, «the hind leg» of a water buffalo. This must be carried away on the day of the burial.[12] The second obligatory payment is *lilo-mangok*, literally, «gold (or silver) and a plate». This, like other named prestations, is a ritual formula subject to negotiation. The highest noble interpretation I witnessed was a string of braided gold and a wet-rice field (i.e. a bowl of rice); the simplest commoner interpretation was a small quantity of paper money and a cheap china plate.

It is at these funeral ceremonies that the *baï-huk*, «the maternal mother's brother», must perform his ritual role. His principal task is to direct the digging of the grave. He is seated at a position in the house opposite the *toö-huk* but further from the corpse. He receives, as death payment, the front leg of a water buffalo and *te-dope*, «spear and sword» – some small gift that will accord with this ritual label. In most domains of Roti, the relation of maternal affiliation is reckoned only as far as the *baï-huk*.

The day after burial the mother's brother's role is indispensable, since he alone can free the family of the deceased from the «pollution» (*salak*) of death. This is given various interpretations in different domains. In Dengka, the mother's brother must bring small amounts of three basic Rotinese foods, rice, meat, and lontar syrup, to break the fast of the deceased's family who should theoretically (though they rarely do in fact) fast from the moment of death. In Termanu, although he brings no food to break this fast, the mother's brother must bring several coconuts whose «water» is used to wash the heads of the deceased's close agnatic kin.[13] This is called *nangapeē nok*, «the rubbing with coconut». In return for this final ritual service, the mother's brother receives [back] a coconut tree to compensate for the loss of his sister's child. There is a symmetry in the ceremonies from marriage to death.

To provide some idea of how elaborate and explicit is the analogy of man and plant, I quote here the funeral chant for a young child who dies suddenly.[14] In characteristic Rotinese fashion, it develops its analogy, not singly but rather in terms of four distinct botanic icons, each a different cultivated plant (*selek*).

Lae:	They say:
Amang mame nakaboin	My father's well-cared-for wet garden
Ma toöng osi nasamaon-na	And my mother's brother's well-kept dry garden
Ala sele huni lai dalek	They plant bananas within it
Ma tane tefu lai dalek.	And they sow sugar-cane within it.
Boe-te tale make tuak	The taro as sweet as lontar sugar
Ma fia malada hadek	And tuber as tasty as rice
Sele lai ndia boe	They plant there too
Ma tane lai na boe.	And they sow there too.
Boe-ma ala toli oe fafain	They pour water in the morning
Ma ala fuä dae leodaen	And they turn the earth in the evening
De hun-na laifata	The roots thrive

Ma don-na eloaka.	And the leaves flourish.
Boe-te huni lalapa lusi	Banana trees have blossoms of copper
Ma tefu langgona lilo	And sugar-cane have sheaths of gold
Ma tale lamaloa do	And taro grow broad leaves
Ma fia lamatua hu.	And tubers grow long roots.
De tao neu namahenak	This creates hope
Ma tao neu nakabanik.	And offers promise.
De malole-la so	Things were good
Ma mandak-kala so	and things were right
Nai fai makabuin	In time past
———	[line missing]
Te-hu sanga tao leo ndia	But at that place
Ma noi tao leo na	And at that spot
De faik esa manunin	On a certain day
Ma ledo esa mateben	And at a particular time
Boe-te sangu mai heheli	A storm comes striking
Ma luli mai dedele.	And a cyclone comes pounding.
De ana heheli	Thus it strikes
Amang mamen nakaboin	My father's well-cared-for wet garden
Ma ana dedele	And it pounds
Toöng osi nasamaon.	My mother's brother's well-kept dry garden.
Boe-te hau feon-na ngga	The surrounding stones come loose
Ma lutu ndulen-na kono.	And the encircling rocks fall.
Boe-te huni malapa lusik-kala	The banana tree with copper blossoms
Kono lapa nai saön	Drops its blossoms in its shadows
Ma tefu manggona lilok-kala	And the sugar-cane with golden sheaths
Olu leu hun.	Sheds its sheaths about its trunk.
Boe-te tale make tuak-kala	The taro as sweet as lontar sugar
Lona oka	Lets droop its tendrils
Ma fia malada hadek-kala	And the tuber as tasty as rice
Male polo boe.	Lets wither its shoots.
De ala toli oe lahelen	They pour water steadfastly
Ma fuä dae lanepen	And they turn the earth constantly
Te-hu toli oe tunga seli	They pour water on a side
Na kono lapa tunga seli	Yet it drops its blossoms to the side
Ma olu nggona tunga seli.	And sheds its sheaths to the side.
Boe-ma fuä dae tunga seli	They turn the earth on a side
Na lona oka nai seli	Yet it lets droop its tendrils on a side
Ma male polo nai seli.	And lets wither its shoots on a side.
Boe-ma sangu nala amang mamen	The storm has taken my father's wet garden
Ma luli nale toöng osin.	And the cyclone has taken my mother's brother's dry garden.
De huni malapa lusik	The banana with copper blossoms
Ma tefu manggona lilok	And the sugar-cane with golden sheaths
Boe-te tale make tuak [-kala]	The taro as sweet as lontar sugar
Ma fia malada hadek-kala	And the tuber as tasty as rice
Ta dadi namahenak	They do not grow as hoped
Ma ta dadi nakabanik.	And do not grow as promised.
Boe-te lu lamasasi mata	Tears run from the eyes

Ma pinu lamatuda idu	And mucus falls from the nose
De leo faik ia boe	As on this day too
Ma deta ledok ia boe.	And as at this time too.

VII

COMMENTS AND CONCLUSIONS

The general argument of the foregoing discussion may hardly be considered surprising. Since Frazer, some notion of an analogy between man and plant has lingered on in social anthropology. A similar analogy underlies certain Western notions of family reckoning and social imagery. Bosch (1960) and Viennot (1954) have provided convincingly copious linguistic and iconographic evidences of the elaboration of this analogy for Indonesia and India. Leenhardt (1947) made this analogy central to his study of myth and person in Melanesia. Nor is this argument peculiar in the literature on the kinship of the Indonesian peoples. In his discussion of 'Metaphors for Kinship' on Tikopia (1936: 230-4), Firth notes the use of botanic metaphors similar to those of the Rotinese, and Conklin, in a paper on 'Ethnogenealogical Method' (1964), resorts repeatedly to native Hanunoo icons of flowering branchlets and potato-like plants. It is also possible to cite other instances of the 'kinship' use of this analogy in eastern Indonesia. Among the Savunese, on the nearest island to the west of Roti, *hubi*, «flowerstalk», is the native designation for matrimoiety (Fox 1971c); in Kodi of western Sumba, male and female descent groups are expressly described as «fruit» and «flower» (Needham, personal communication), while among the Sikanese of Flores (Fox 1971d), the term *pu*, cognate with Rotinese *hu*-and with essentially the same meaning of «stem, trunk, root, origin», is prefixed to the term for mother's brother, *mame*, to form *pulame*, another reported term for mother's brother. The mother's brother, in turn, refers to his sister's children as *pu*, which, according to the ethnographer Arndt (1933: 58), expresses their derivation from him.

The Rotinese interpretation of this botanic analogy is, in Leach's phrase, 'a pattern of organizational ideas' (1961: 9). The idiom of planting which describes relations of maternal

244

affiliation is one aspect of this pattern. From another view-point, the idiom of planting is an idiom of consanguinity, since the mother's brother's claim over his sister's child is expressed as a right over blood-sap. It may also be recognized as a parti-cular elaboration of a common Asian conception of social pro-creation: that a person is composed of flesh and bone; that the soft flesh is derived from maternal blood and that the hard bone is derived from paternal semen. What is needed – as Hocart (1954: 97-105), Lévi-Strauss (1949: 486-502), and Leach (1961: 13-14) have suggested – is a comparative study of the varying social expressions of this widespread doctrine.

On Roti, a person's blood, flesh, and hair are derived through the mother and remain, until interment, the property of the mother's brother, the maternal trunk (*toö-huk*); a person's bone and, more importantly, his enduring social person as embodied in his genealogical name, his *nade balakaik*, «the hard-tree name», these are established by his father. (Bridewealth pay-ment is as necessary to their establishment as is procreation.) Thus, whereas a physical injury to an individual will demand the intercession of maternal blood relatives, the hint of a slur on the name of an individual or his clan will provoke an immediate clamour for retribution and indemnification by a group of agnates.

A feature of the idiom of planting is its selection of botanic icons from among those cultivated plants and trees that are regarded as dependent upon human plantation. The distinction is awkward to phrase but essential to the native ideology, since there exist tended, food-yielding plants whose seeds or seedlings the Rotinese would never themselves consider planting. The distinction therefore approximates that of domestication, and the occurrence of wild specimens of supposedly humanly planted cultigens does not contradict this, since these are attributed to spirit plantation. The lontar palm is the chief source of Rotinese subsistence: it is tended and tapped, but not planted. For this and other reasons, it is a focal icon for the Rotinese. It is a large, dioecious fan palm, whose wood grows hard with time. The female palm, marked by its clusters of large fruit, is unmistakably distinguishable from the male palm, whose flower-stalks end in metre-long, ithyphallic, secondary branch seg-ments. These branch segments (*nggi*) are subjected to what the

245

Rotinese describe as a circumcision, a pincer operation that is technically required to break the fibrovascular tissue of the stalk to initiate its flow of juice. This juice is then caught in a leaf-bucket (*haik*) hung directly below the stalks. Like branching, unplanted, enduring hardwood trees, the lontar palm is also used as an icon for agnatic relations. In Rotinese, male and female palms are sexually distinguished as a brother and sister pair. A common phrase for agnatic relations is *nggi leo nggona haik*. It is based on the image of lontar tapping. Translated, it is «the lineage segments whose birth caul is the same leaf bucket».

There exists a complementarity of relations on Roti, a principle that Leiden-trained anthropologists have long insisted on. But this complementarity requires neither a prescriptive marriage system nor a moiety system (though parts of Roti do have moieties); nor is its expression best described as a bilineal or double unilineal descent system. Differentiating aspects of this complementarity are essential to its description. There may exist differential rights over the same social persons: on Roti, these rights are vested in two men; a woman is the link by means of which they establish them and, once established, divorce does not alter them. Native physiology, sociology, and iconology make these crucial distinctions.

There is a temptation to take the idiom of planting too literally and reduce its verbal expression to a naïve native belief in a quasi-genetic transmission of physical substance. This, I would argue, is contradicted by the evidence of the procedures for determining the mother's brother of origin. Clearly, the idiom of planting encodes a social knowledge, a basic premise – in the Rotinese case, a cosmological premise – about the nature of procreation. But the Rotinese are not concerned with establishing, by degrees, some physiological actuality of substance in the *toö-huk–selek* relationship. Their criteria for the relationship are cultural. As *toö-huk*, the eldest brother and his eldest son are favoured over his younger siblings and their children; one parallel cousin of the woman may be chosen from among numerous candidates as part of bridewealth negotiations or in the case of any lapse in a relationship, a number of individuals may vie for the role; the role may also be established, by payment, for a client with no attachments.

Ritual performances are equally effective if performed by an elder brother, a distant parallel cousin, or a person who has given *feo poik*.

There is also the temptation to regard the idiom of planting as a static mould, a fixed form that girds maternal relations. This, too, does not seem to be the case. In the 1920s and 1930s, there was a concerted campaign on the part of certain European missionaries to do away with all bridewealth payments and also the death payments to the mother's brother. This was contested by Rotinese native ministers on whom most preaching was dependent. The issue was settled in favour of native law. Since that period Christians, who are now in overwhelming majority, as well as pagans pay both bridewealth and death payments. The relationship of mother's brother–sister's child has continued to develop, Christians insisting that the mother's brother serve as godfather to his sister's children, and the formal Indonesian of the Malay Bible, itself rich in botanic metaphors, is intermixed with Rotinese at some rituals. It therefore seems likely that the idiom will continue to develop with the relationship itself. An old Christian minister from the domain of Bilba, who was proud of his part in defending the traditional payments, quoted to me a two-line saying as explanation of the need to pay the mother's brother:

| Moli au memengok | I wax like the *memengok* |
| Dadi au boa lelak. | I grow like the fruit of the *lelak*. |

The *memengok* and *lelak*[15] are both climbing plants that entwine themselves about large trees. According to the Rotinese, they have no proper trunk root (*huk*). Like the *memengok* and *lelak*, the minister explained, a person who did not recognize his *toö-huk* would be rootless in Rotinese society.

A final comment needs to be made on the concepts of idiom and metaphor. What this paper has tried to suggest is that kinship and plant taxonomies may not necessarily be the discrete, ordered, and recognizably bounded semantic domains that recent analyses have tended to portray. The implication is that these semantic appearances are the product of procedural restrictions, either definitional exclusion or confined elicitation and that lurking just out of analytic reach are a host of problems that seem central to the study of language. Yet when one

attempts to examine the concept of metaphor, from Stutterheim's massive study (1941) to Meier's more recent survey
(1963), or contrasts linguistic definitions of metaphor (Henle
1958, ch. 7; Chafe 1965), or reads fresh, innovative studies on
the use of metaphor (R. Rosaldo 1968; M. Rosaldo 1970), the
impression is that this concept merely locates an area of interest,
a complex of processes that characterize the use of language. In
this regard, Roman Jakobson (Jakobson & Halle 1956) has proposed his own definition of metaphor that develops Saussure's
notion of association. The definition has already been utilized to
advantage by social anthropologists (Lévi-Strauss 1962; Tambiah
1969). But Jakobson has also provided specific indications on
how, within the oral traditions of the world (1956: 76-82; 1966),
this concept of metaphor may lead to a systematic formal study
of native correspondences. Rotinese oral tradition has developed, to an elaborate degree, the parallel correspondences
whose study Jakobson has urged, and some indications (Fox
1971b) are that a study of this kind need not rely on Bloomfield
form classes or their derivatives. This is one way to mine the
rich field designated by the concept of metaphor, and to this
end the present paper is but a prelude.

NOTES

1. The research on which this paper is based was supported by a Public
Health Service fellowship (MH-23, 148) and grant (MH-10, 161), from the
National Institute of Mental Health and was conducted, in Indonesia (1965-6),
under the auspices of what has now become the Lembaga Ilmu Pengatahuan
Indonesia. I am particularly indebted to Dr Rodney Needham for his direction
of this research. In preparing this paper, I have benefited from discussions
with Drs Roberto Da Matta, Gary Gossen, Michelle and Renato Rosaldo and
Professor David Maybury-Lewis. I regret being unable to attend the ASA
conference at which a version of this paper was to have been delivered.

2. This quotation, also quoted in Lounsbury (1964: 1087), is taken from Roman
Jakobson's 'Boas' View of Grammatical Meaning' (1959: 143). In following
Jakobson's affirmation that 'the elicitation of meanings through the meta-
linguistic operations of native speakers is a more reliable and objective device
than the appeal to these natives for an evaluation of sentences in regard to
their acceptability' (p. 143), I have not utilized standard linguistic display
procedures. My attempt has been to elucidate aspects of the same Rotinese
idiom in two recognizably different speech forms. This paper is a preliminary
to a further semantic analysis.

3. Native etymological speculation recognizes the relation of *feto* and *feö*,
«female, sister, daughter» and the relation of *feuk* and *beuk*, «new, recent».

Son- and daughter-in-law are sometimes described as the «new male» and the «new female».

4. At the time, this Lord's decision struck me as a peculiar, if not evasive, form of verbal artifice. The Rotinese, since the Dutch period, have conventionally referred to all forms of government (*paleta*: «rule, order»; from the Malay word *perintah*, government) above the level of their local domain as *ina-ama*, «mother–father». Although I was sponsored by a research department of the Indonesian government, I was clearly not an Indonesian citizen. Therefore the Lord argued that the Government could not be my «mother–father»; it had to be my *toök*, «mother's brother». In retrospect, I realize that having the entire Indonesian government as one's mother's brother was, in Rotinese terms, a formidable form of protection. As an official representative of the Government, the Lord was, in effect, offering himself as my *toö-huk*. I was to be his *selek* and when I had concluded my research in his domain, he saw to it that I moved to the domain of his own mother's brother of origin, an elder Lord of the neighbouring domain who thereby became my *baï-huk*.

5. These rules would hold for Termanu and most of the other domains of Roti but alone would not be sufficient for Thie and Loleh, domains which have moieties. In Thie, one moiety is internally subdivided. I have not done sufficient fieldwork in either of these domains, to be certain of the range of application of the category *toök*. Furthermore, these rules would not cover certain élite speech usages in which royal Rotinese relate whole domains to one another on the basis of past royal marriages.

6. These rubrics are native terms; their arrangement is my own and has not been suggested, as such rubrics often are, by native informants. The gifts listed under *feo poik* are, however, a traditional threefold list.

7. The right of *toö-huk*, which will persist to the death of the last *selek*, may within certain limits, be freely disposed of by its holder. A case in point, from Termanu, was that of a mother's brother whose sister's child was so frequently involved in serious litigation before the native court (for which the mother's brother is obliged to defend his sister's child) that he chose to surrender his rights as *toö-huk* to the lord of his clan, one of the most influential men at court. Provided the relationship never lapses, a sister's child has no right to decide who is to be his or her *toö-huk*. The right to determine this rests with the native court.

8. I encountered one clear case of this in Termanu where a nobleman allocated to his five sons his right of *toö-huk* over the children of his five sisters. Although I discovered no other case of this kind of allocation, I was assured by informants that such an allocation is acceptable, given the insistence of a father, the willingness of an eldest son, and the permission of the court.

9. A case illustrative of this kind of situation occurred at the funeral of an elderly noble woman in Termanu. Her recognized *toö-huk* had migrated, years before, to the neighbouring state of Talae. The main topic of speculation on the day of her funeral was whether this *toö-huk* would arrive to claim his rights over those of the individual who, from the previous evening, had been performing the role of *toö-huk*. There was a kind of gleeful anticipation of the dispute that would arise on his arrival. Unfortunately, the man did not appear.

10. Ritual language poses problems for the taxonomic identification of some plants. Plant designations, in ritual language, are generic rather than specific; that is, for some plants there may be a dozen or more sub-categories recognized

in ordinary language. In addition, terms for certain plants occur only in ritual language and differ radically from plant terms in ordinary language. Piper betel, for example, is *dae-dok* in ordinary language; *malu* in ritual language. For *tale//fia*, native exegesis provided the glosses «taro» and «tuber». Until I have done more fieldwork, I consider these probable, yet tentative, glosses.

11. Although the bridewealth payment is made only once to the *toŏ-huk* of the girl, he or his successor will nonetheless function as the *baï-huk* for the children of all the girl's marriages.

12. In the domain of Korbaffo, *pa-buik* may be used as a crude slang substitute for the term *selek*; a mother's brother may jokingly refer to his sister's child as his «hind leg of meat».

13. There are no precise bounds drawn to determine who these are; beyond the resident family, purification seems largely a function of the number of coconuts available.

14. This ritual chant was given to me by Stephanus Adulanu of clan Meno, Termanu, who was my tireless tutor in ritual language.

15. *Lelak* is the Ash Pumpkin (*Benincasa hispida* COGN); *Memengok*, also known as *Tali Putri* in Kupangese Malay, remains unidentified.

REFERENCES

ARNDT, P. P. *Gesellschaftliche Verhältnisse im Sikagebiet*. Ende, Flores: Arnoldus-Druckerei.

BOSCH, F. D. K. 1960. *The Golden Germ*. The Hague: Mouton.

CHAFE, W. L. 1965. Meaning in Language. In E. A. Hammel, *Formal Semantic Analysis. American Anthropologist* **67**, 5 (Part 2): 23-36.

CONKLIN, H. 1964. Ethnogenealogical Method. In W. Goodenough (ed.), *Explorations in Cultural Anthropology*: 25-55. New York: McGraw-Hill.

DOUGLAS, M. 1966. *Purity and Danger*. London: Routledge and Kegan Paul.

FIRTH, R. 1936. *We, The Tikopia*. London: Allen and Unwin.

FOX, J. J. 1971a. A Rotinese Dynastic Genealogy: Structure and Event. In T. Beidelman (ed.), *The Translation of Culture: Festschrift for Evans-Pritchard*: 37-77. London: Tavistock Publications.

—— 1971b. Semantic Parallelism in Rotinese Ritual Language. *Bijdragen tot de Taal-, Land- en Volkenkunde* **127**: 215-55.

—— 1971c. The Savunese. In F. LeBar (ed.), *Ethnographic Survey of Island Southeast Asia* [in press].

—— 1971d. The Sikanese. In F. LeBar (ed.), *Ethnographic Survey of Island Southeast Asia* [in press].

HEIJMERING, G. 1842-43. Zeden en gewoonten op het eiland Rottie. *Tijdschrift voor Nederlandsch- Indië* V, ii: 531-49; 623-39; VI, i: 81-98; 353-67.

HENLE, F. 1958. *Language, Thought and Culture*. Ann Arbor: University of Michigan Press.

HOCART, A. M. 1954. *Social Origins*. London: Watts.

JAKOBSON, R. 1959. Boas' View of Grammatical Meaning. In W. Goldschmidt (ed.), *The Anthropology of Franz Boas. American Anthropologist* Memoir 89, **61**, 5 (Part 2): 139-45.

—— 1966. Grammatical Parallelism and its Russian Facet. *Language* **42**: 398-429.

JAKOBSON, R. & HALLE, M. 1956. *Fundamentals of Language*. The Hague: Mouton.

JONKER, J. C. G. 1908. *Rottineesch-Hollandsch Woordenboek*. Leiden: E. J. Brill.

LEACH, E. 1961. Rethinking Anthropology. In *Rethinking Anthropology*: 1-27. London: The Athlone Press.

LEENHARDT, M. 1947. *Do Kamo*. Paris: Gallimard.

LÉVI-STRAUSS, C. 1949. *Les Structures élémentaires de la parenté*. Paris: Presses Universitaires de France.

—— 1962. *La Pensée sauvage*. Paris: Plon.

LOUNSBURY, F. G. 1964. The Structural Analysis of Kinship Semantics. In *Proceedings of the Ninth International Congress of Linguists*: 1073-90. The Hague: Mouton.

—— 1965. Another View of the Trobriand Kinship Categories. In E. A. Hammel (ed.), *Formal Semantic Analysis. American Anthropologist* **67**, 5 (Part 2): 142-85.

MEIER, H. 1963. *Die Metapher*. Winterthur: P. G. Keller.

NEEDHAM, R. 1960. Alliance and Classification among the Lamet. *Sociologus* **10**: 97-118.

ROSALDO, M. Z. 1970. What's in a Name: The Classification of Plants in Illongot Magic. [Unpublished Specials Paper, Harvard University].

ROSALDO, R. I. 1968. Metaphors of Hierarchy in a Mayan Ritual. *American Anthropologist* **70**: 3: 524-36.

STUTTERHEIM, C. F. P. 1941. *Het Begrip Metaphoor*. Amsterdam: H. J. Paris.

TAMBIAH, S. J. 1969. Animals are Good to Think and Good to Prohibit. *Ethnology* VIII, 4: 423-59.

James J. Fox

TURNER, V. 1967. *The Forest of Symbols*. Ithaca: Cornell University Press.

TYLER, S. A. 1969. The Myth of P: Epistemology and Formal Analysis. *American Anthropologist* **71**, 1: 71-9.

VIENNOT, O. 1954. *Le Culte de l'arbre dans l'Inde ancienne*. Paris: Presses Universitaires de France.

WETERING, F. H. VAN DE. 1925. Het huwelijk op Rote. *Tijdschrift voor Indische Taal-, Land- en Volkenkunde* LXV: 1-36; 589-667.

NOTES ON CONTRIBUTORS

BEIDELMAN, THOMAS O. Born 1931, USA; educated at University of Illinois, B.A., M.A.; University of California at Berkeley; University of Michigan; University of Oxford, D.Phil.

Assistant Professor of Social Anthropology, Harvard University, 1963-5; Fellow, Center for Advanced Study in the Behavioral Sciences, Stanford, California, 1965-6; Associate Professor of Anthropology, Duke University, 1966-8; Associate Professor of Anthropology, New York University, 1968-   .

Author of *A Comparative Analysis of the Jajmani System*, 1959; *The Matrilineal Peoples of Eastern Tanzania*, 1967; *The Kaguru; A Matrilineal People*, 1971; and numerous papers on the ethnography of Africa, symbolism, folklore, etc.

Editor of *The Translation of Culture*, 1971.

FORGE, ANTHONY. Born 1929, United Kingdom: studied at Cambridge, M.A.; London School of Economics.

Horniman Scholarship, 1957-60; Part-time Research Officer, London School of Economics, 1960-1; Assistant Lecturer in Social Anthropology, London School of Economics, 1961-4; Fellow of the Bollingen Foundation, New York, 1962-3; Lecturer in Social Anthropology, London School of Economics, 1964-70; Senior Lecturer in Social Anthropology, 1970-   .

Co-author (with Raymond Firth and Jane Hubert) of *Families and their Relatives*, 1970.

FOX, JAMES J. Born 1940, USA; educated at Harvard University, A.B. (1962); University College. Oxford (Rhodes Scholar), Diploma in Social Anthropology (1963), B.Litt. (1965), D.Phil. (1968).

Visiting Assistant Professor of Anthropology, Duke University, 1968-9; Assistant Professor of Social Anthropology, Harvard University, 1969-   .

Notes on Contributors

Author of: 'On Bad Death and the Left Hand', *Right and Left: Essays on Dual Symbolic Classification*, forthcoming; 'Semantic Parallelism in Rotinese Ritual Language', *Bijdragen tot de Taal-, Land- en Volkenkunde*, 1971; 'A Rotinese Dynastic Genealogy: Structure and Event', *The Translation of Culture*, ed. T. O. Beidelman, 1971.

KORN, FRANCIS. Born 1935, Argentina; educated at University of Buenos Aires, Licenciada en Sociología 1963; and at Oxford University, D.Phil. 1970.

Researcher at the Institute of Sociology, University of Buenos Aires, 1958-64; Associate Professor in the Methodology of Social Research, Department of Sociology, University of Buenos Aires, 1965-6. St Anne's College, Oxford, 1966-70. Professor of Social Anthropology, University of Buenos Aires, 1970- .

Editor of *Conceptos y Variables en la Investigación Social*, Buenos Aires: Nueva Visión, 1969; author of *Elementary Structures Reconsidered* (forthcoming); and a number of papers including 'Asimilación de inmigrantes en Buenos Aires', *América Latina*, 1965; 'The Use of the Term Model in Some of Lévi-Strauss's Works', *Bijdragen tot de Taal-, Land- en Volkenkunde*, 1969; 'Terminology and Structure: the Dieri Case', *Bijdragen tot de Taal-, Land- en Volkenkunde*, 1971; 'Permutation Models and Prescriptive Systems' (in collaboration with Rodney Needham), *Man*, 1970.

LEACH, EDMUND RONALD. Born 1910, England; educated at Cambridge University, B.A. (Maths., Mechanical Sciences); London University, Ph.D.

Research Officer, Sarawak, 1947; Assistant Lecturer in Anthropology, London School of Economics, 1948; Lecturer, 1949; Reader, 1950; Lecturer in Anthropology, Cambridge University, 1953; Reader, 1958. Fellow of King's College, 1960; Provost, 1966.

Author of *Social and Economic Organization of the Rowanduz Kurds*, 1940; *Social Science Research in Sarawak*, 1950; *Political Systems of Highland Burma*, 1954; *Pul Eliya: A Village in Ceylon*, 1961; *Rethinking Anthropology*, 1961; *A*

Runaway World?, 1968; *Genesis as Myth and Other Essays*, 1970; *Lévi-Strauss*, 1970.

Editor of *Aspects of Caste in South India, Ceylon, and North-West Pakistan*, 1960; *The Structural Study of Myth and Totemism*, 1967; *Dialectic in Practical Religion*, 1968; (with S. N. Mukherjee) *Elites in South Asia*, 1970.

MCKNIGHT, JOHN DAVID. Born 1935, Canada; studied at Bishop's University, Lennoxville, Quebec, B.A.; University College, London, B.A. (Hons.), 1960-3, M.A. 1963-5.

Research Fellow, University of Queensland, 1965-8. Lecturer, University of Edinburgh, 1968-70. Lecturer, London School of Economics, 1971- .

Author of 'Extra-descent Group Ancestor Cults in African Societies', *Africa*, 1967.

NEEDHAM, RODNEY. Born 1923, England; educated at the universities of London (S.O.A.S.), Leiden, and Oxford; Diploma in Anthropology, B.Litt., M.A., D.Phil., D.Litt. (Oxon.).

University Lecturer in Social Anthropology, Oxford, 1956- . Fellow, Center for Advanced Study in the Behavioral Sciences, Stanford, California, 1961-2; National Science Foundation Senior Foreign Scientist Fellow, University of California at Riverside, 1970-1.

Author of *Structure and Sentiment*, 1962; *Belief, Language, and Experience* (forthcoming); numerous papers on the ethnography of Indonesia, social organization, symbolism, and classification.

Editor, translator: *Death and the Right Hand* by Robert Hertz, 1960; *Primitive Classification* by E. Durkheim and M. Mauss, 1963; *Totemism* by C. Lévi-Strauss, 1963; *Ngaju Religion* by H. Schärer, 1963; *Yoga and Yantra* by P. H. Pott, 1966; *The Semi-Scholars* by A. van Gennep, 1967; *The Development of Marriage and Kinship* by C. S. Wake, 1967; *Types of Social Structure in Eastern Indonesia* by F. A. E. van Wouden, 1968; *The Elementary Structures of Kinship* by C. Lévi-Strauss, 1969; *The Life-Giving Myth* by A. M. Hocart, 1970; *Kings and Councillors* by A. M. Hocart, 1970; *Imagination and Proof* by A. M. Hocart (forthcoming).

Notes on Contributors

RIVIÈRE, PETER GERARD. Born 1934, London; educated at Cambridge University, M.A.; Oxford University, B.Litt., M.A., D.Phil.

Tutor and supervisor, Institute of Social Anthropology, Oxford University, 1965-71; Senior Research Fellow, Institute of Latin American Studies, London University, 1966-8; Visiting Professor of Anthropology, Harvard University, 1968-9; Assistant Lecturer, Faculty of Archaeology and Anthropology, Cambridge University, 1970-1; University Lecturer in Social Anthropology, Oxford, 1971- ; Fellow of Linacre College, Oxford.

Author of *Marriage among the Trio* (1969), 'Factions and Exclusions' (*ASA 9*, 1970), and papers on structural analysis, myth, and Latin American topics.

Editor of J. F. McLennan's *Primitive Marriage*, 1970.

SOUTHWOLD, MARTIN. Born 1929, England; studied at Cambridge University, B.A., M.A., Ph.D.

Bursarship EAISR, Makerere College, Kampala, Uganda, 1954-6; Research Assistant in Social Anthropology, Manchester University, 1957-9; Assistant Lecturer in Social Anthropology, Cambridge University, 1960-2; Lecturer in Social Anthropology, Manchester University, 1962- .

Author of *Bureaucracy and Chiefship in Buganda*, 1960; and various articles on Buganda.

WILDER, WILLIAM DEAN. Born 1939, USA; educated at Harvard College, A.B., and London School of Economics, M.A. Lecturer in Anthropology, University of Durham, 1966- .

Author of 'Socialization and Social Structure in a Malay Village' (*ASA 8*) and papers in *American Anthropologist, Man*, and *Modern Asian Studies*.

Name Index

Compiled by James Urry

257

Name Index

Name Index

Name Index

Subject Index
Compiled by James Urry

Subject Index

Australia
  Cape York Peninsula, li, 145, 152,
    see also Wikmunkan
  kinship and marriage systems in,
    xxviii, xl, lx, lxi, lxxx, lxxxiv,
    lxxxv, 61, 130n, 139, *see also*
    section systems and Wik-
    munkan, marriage
  see also aborigines, Australian
avoidance, 164, 199n

'baby talk', *see* children, speech of
Bali, 19
Bambuti, xlviii
Baraguyu, 195
Batak (Sumatra), 9
  Dairi, lxiv
  prescriptive alliance in, lxii, lxix
  Toba, lxiv
Ba Thonga, kinship terminology, 75
betrothal, xlvi, 127
Bible
  Book of John, 49
  David, Uriah, and Bathsheba in, 188
  Malay, 247
bilateral kin groups
  Eskimo, 62
blood
  menstrual and incest, 24
  payments (Rotinese), 238-241
Borneo, lvii
Bororo
  marriage, 58, 71n
  men's houses, 71n
  sexual relationships among, 58
botanical metaphors *see* plants
Brazil, xvix, 16
bride price, *see* marriage, payments
Britain, marriage in, 69, *see also*
  England
Buganda, *see* Ganda
Bunyoro, *see* Nyoro
Burma, alliances in, lxxiii, 21, *see*
  also Chin and Kachin
Bushman, child language, 78

Carib, lxxx
case studies, *see* Dieri, Murngin, and
  Purum
ceremonial, *see* ritual
Chawte, cii
  kinship terminology, ci
Cherokee, kinship terminology. 15

Chickasaw, kinship terminology, 15
children
  development of
    marriage and, 59-60, *see also*
      socialization
  speech of, 78-82
    Bushman, 78
    English, 78
    Tikopian, 78
Chimbu, marriage among, 137
Chin, *see* Haka Chin and Kuki-Chin
China, lxxx
  incest terms in, 26
Choctaw
  kinship, 15-16
    historical changes in, 15, 16
    terminology, 15-16
Christianity
  doctrines of, 70, 73n
  early, 49
    teachings of, 49
  Iatmul and, 102
  Rotinese and, 247
Church
  of England, 38
  of Rome, 38
circumcision, Kaguru and, 184, 196
clans
  Abelam, 137, 140
  Ganda, 38, 51
  Iatmul, 100, 101, 102, 103, 104,
    108, 117, 118-119, 120, 122,
    123, 124, 128, 129n, 130n
  Kaguru matrilineal, 183, 184, 185,
    186, 196
  Purum, 205, 206, 210, 211, 212
  Rotinese, 222, 224-225, 227, 229,
    250n
    political nature of, 224-225
    segmentation of, 224, 225
  Wikmunkan, xliv, xlv, 159, 160,
    161, 177
class, social
  marriage and, 60, 69-70, 72n
classification, social, 61, 75, 220
  Gurage, xxxvii, 17
  Kachin, xxxviii
    of prestations, 119, 122-123
  Rotinese, 221-222, 226, 240
    dualism in, 234
    human body and, 240-241, *see*
      also plants
  sexual, 64-65

262

Subject Index

English
  incest terms, 26, 27, 183
  marriage terms, 6, 7
  terminology, kinship, 35, 37, 39,
    45, 53, 81
    child language and, 78, 80
    translation problems and, 37-38,
      39, 45, 53, 76, 81
Eskimo, bilateral kin groups among,
    62
'Eskimo'-type terminologies, 16
exchange, xlv, lxx, lxxii
  balance in, 137-138, 139
  cycles of, 205-206
  direct, 207-209, 214
  generalized, xlv, xlvi, lxii, lxvi,
    128, 160, 161, 177, 204
  the *kula* as, 136
  in New Guinea, 133, 135-138
  restricted, xlv-xlvi, 128, 160, 161,
    177
  sister in marriage, 89, 106-107, 124,
    134, 136-137, 144n, 161
  status and, 136
  Wikmunkan food, 165, 168
  see also gifts and prestations
exogamy, xcii, 28
  Kaguru, 182, 184, 196
  Purum, 211, 216n
  Rotinese, 225

family, the, 26, 28
feud, Iatmul, 101
Fiji, xxxviii
  marriage in, xlv
folklore
  Kaguru, lvii, 182
    animal motives in, 195
    Hare and Hyena, 193, 194
    incest and, 182, 192-198
    Mukejuwa, 193
    sexual prohibitions and, 182,
      192-198
    themes of, 192-198
    myth compared to, 182
food
  as sexual symbol, 184, 190, 193,
    194, 195, 196, 199n
  exchange of
    Penan, lvii
    Wikmunkan, 165, 168
formal analysis of kinship, xxi-xxxiv,
  xxxv, 10, 75, 219, 220

French, 94
  incest terms in, 26
  marriage terms, 6
  terminology, kinship, 81
functionalism, xvii, lvii, 8, 57, 68, 71n
  marriage and, 57-63, 65, 66, 68, 70,
    71n
  Merton's concepts of, 71n
  religion and, 57
funeral(s), 165, 168
  Rotinese, 241-244, 249n, 250n
    MB/ZS and, 232-233, 241-244,
      249

Ganda, xxi, 50-51
  clans, 38, 51
  genealogies, 37, 38, 52
  kinship
    problems of, 39
  marriage, 50
    payments, 55n
  neighbours as congeniates, 50-51,
    53
  politics, 38
  terminology, kinship, xcviii, 35,
    36-38, 44, 51-53, 54n
    problems of, 51-53
  villages, 50
genealogical levels, 126
  Dieri, 115, 116
  Iatmul, 115, 116, 118-119, 123, 124,
    141
genealogies, 43, 220
  Ganda, 37, 38, 52
  problems in charts of, 155, 157,
    158, 176-177
generations, see age categories
German
  incest terms, 26
  marriage terms, 6
gifts, Rotinese, 230-232, 249n, see also
  exchange and prestations
Gilyak (of Siberia), lxiii, lxv
Gnau, marriage among, 144n
Gogo, xlviii
gossip, in Kaguru, 191, 198
Greece, cv
  Classical, lviii, 6, 26
Gurage
  social classification, xxxvii, 17
  terminology, kinship, xxxvii, 14,
    17-18, 19
Gusii, kinship terminology, 44, 53

264